D0555622

Bird of Paradise

Bird of Paradise

Marilyn Anne Hughes

and

Emily Hughes Johnson

• WRITE WAY •
PUBLISHING COMPANY
RALEIGH, NORTH CAROLINA
www.writewaypublishingcompany.com

Bird of Paradise
Copyright © 2021 by Emily Hughes Johnson

This is a work of fiction. Names, characters, places, and incidents either are products of the author's imagination or are used fictitiously. All rights reserved. No part of this publication may be reproduced, distributed, or transmitted in any form or by any means, including photocopying, recording, or other electronic or mechanical methods, without the prior written permission of the publisher, except in the case of brief quotations embodied in critical reviews and certain other noncommercial uses permitted by copyright law. Permission requests should be sent to info@writewaypublishingcompany.com.

Printed in the United States of America
ISBN 978-1-946425-86-7

Book Design by CSinclaire Write-Design
Cover Art by James Hislope

• WRITE WAY •
PUBLISHING COMPANY
RALEIGH, NORTH CAROLINA
www.writewaypublishingcompany.com

For my daughter, Emily—

May you find Paradise, that place where you know who you are and you like what you know, where dreams go beyond your wildest imaginings, where life is celebrated, not merely lived, and where love is only the beginning.

May you always be my little dreamer. Dreams are desires you hope to fulfill. Passions are dreams you fight for. There are no passions without first having dreams. A life without passion is only a life half-lived. Continue to dream, never settle, and never let your passion fade into the background.

May you find Sanctuary. Your life will be filled with your visions grown from the seeds that your father and I worked so hard to plant but are very much your own. As you grow and experience life, you will find your own voice. You will find your Sanctuary. Not a place in the world, but a place in your heart. A place that, when opened, you will see your own visions and you will speak with your own voice, and that voice shall shout to the world *I AM HERE!*

I know now that this is where my story ends, so I hope you will begin where I left off. I will watch over you through the good times and the bad. I will be there with you to share the joys of becoming a mom, and I will be there watching as you and Matt grow old together. And each night I will be there to whisper sweet dreams. I love you.

Forever and Beyond,
Mom

For my mom, Marilyn—

Thank you for entrusting me with Ari's story. You have given me the gift of a lifetime, and it has been an honor to finish your story for you. I miss you each and every day, but I know you're looking down on me from above. Sweet dreams, Mom. I love you.

Forever and Beyond,
Emily

Acknowledgments

I would like to thank my mom for leaving this incredible gift for me. Even though she is no longer with us, her voice will forever be captured in the words of her characters. Adding my voice to them has been the greatest honor of my life.

To my dad, thank you for being the first to read this manuscript and catching my extra commas and mistakes. I should also thank you for editing all my college papers as well. Clearly, I've learned nothing when it comes to grammar. Seriously, your suggestions helped to make Bird of Paradise what it is today, and I will always be grateful for your support. I love you, Dad!

Thank you, Lee Heinrich, Charlotte Sinclaire, and all the team at Write Way Publishing, for all your help and guidance and for putting up with my 5,000 emails along the way. It goes without saying that without you this book would not have been possible.

Thank you, Judy Davenport, for beta reading all 500+ pages . . . very quickly I might add! If it wasn't for you, I'm not sure I would have had the courage to move forward with sharing Ari's story.

Thank you, James Hislope, for your amazing cover design. You captured Ari's Island beautifully, and I know my mom would be thrilled to see her Island come to life.

To my two My Peak Challenge girls, Jasmine and Carolyn, thank you for your friendship and encouragement along the way. I'm grateful to have you both in my life.

And finally, a big thank you to my husband for supporting me and believing in me and to my son for telling all his friends that his mom is going to be famous. Love you both.

Prologue

SHE SAT ON the Sunset Bench, as she had so many times before, looking down past the craggy cliffs graying in the twilight; past coconut palms and wild impatiens; past viridian ferns that nestled in the shadows and viney bougainvillea that danced on the winds and crystalline waters that plunged and splashed and cascaded their way back home to the sea. There, as always, she paused to gaze at the tranquil lagoon that so long ago had taught her to swim and to listen to the laughter of the new water babies that floated up from the beach on the warm, sweet air. It was not the carefully conceived laughter of adults. It was the full-bellied laughter of the very young who know nothing of social graces or care. "Innocence," she whispered and wished she could remember what that felt like.

From the western edge of the lagoon, she heard the faint murmurings of friends and family coming together again at the end of another day. The voices emanated from the old wooden dock where Islanders gathered to await the return of the evening launch from the Mainland. She watched as the last of them trickled out of the palm grove in two's and three's, strolled down the beach past neat rows of dugout canoes and headed out over the water between the brightly painted little fishing boats that bobbed up and down in perfect 4/4 time. The Islanders looked almost indistinguishable from their ancestors as they milled about in their bare feet and richly patterned sarongs, but the illusion would end with the arrival of the launch and the impeccably tailored suits that nightly filed down her gangplank.

She had been coming to the bench for many years now, climbing the steep cliff side path with flashlight in hand for

1

the safe return home after sunset. Tonight though she carried a bottle of Grandfather's wine and Mama's favorite goblet, the cobalt blue one she said took its color from the night sky over the Island. She held the goblet at arm's length and spun it gently by the stem until she was mesmerized by the kaleidoscopic patterns of light and shadow that danced on her arm. *This goblet should have been Mama's.*

She put the goblet to her lips and sipped long and slow, letting the wine wash over her tongue before swallowing. By the time it had cooled her throat all the way down, she had turned her thoughts to a happier time—the day she first came to the bench on that glorious spring when the family returned to the Island from Papa's posting in San Francisco. She remembered that day clearly, how she left the cool, jade-blue waters of the lagoon behind and followed after Grandfather and Mem and Mama and Papa as they snaked in and out of view on their daily ascent to the bench. She remembered the arduous climb and how hot and breathless she felt, and how, when she finally reached the shade of the plateau, the cool damp of the jungle floor on her bare feet renewed her. She could almost hear the bits of laughter and easy conversation that had reached her ears long before she was in sight of the bench and how, when she arrived there, she found the couples already lounging comfortably, sharing a bottle of Grandfather's chilled Island wine, red-cheeked and smiling and, as always, demonstrably affectionate.

She could hear them speaking, even now, about that day and many before it in no particular order, just a random collection of remembrances, which together fashioned a collage of their family history or at least a small part of one. They were recalling some of the special places to which Papa's work had taken the family—the funny little attic bedroom in London, the marble floors in the Paris apartment where she and Emma played Ice Capades in their stocking feet, and the big house that perched on the peak over Hong Kong where she held little James up to the telescope on the veranda so he could watch the ships come into port.

When Mama looked up and saw her approaching, she didn't seem surprised. She just smiled and said, "I've been waiting for you," and without further comment, handed her a half-filled goblet of wine, her first, which had been well diluted to a pale pink color by the numerous ice cubes that clinked against the glass.

She remembered exactly how everyone looked that day. Grandfather sitting at one end of the bench, his arms wrapped around Mem except when he was expounding with animated gestures on the great mysteries of life; Mem, whose gentle expression on her still beautiful face belied the depth of her wisdom—a wisdom that came from just living life, not over-thinking it; Mama, whose extraordinary elegance was evident even in bare feet and a sarong and hair still wet from her after-noon swim to the reef. And Papa, sprawling lazily next to Mama, smiling and relaxed, a million miles from the corporate world that loomed just offshore. His sandy brown hair and blue eyes were so incongruous next to the black hair and green almond eyes that filled the rest of the bench.

That was the day she began imagining the man with whom she would share her own sunsets, peering up at Mem and that expression she wore when she looked at Grandfather, as if she were seeing him for the very first time, and finding that same expression reinvented on Mama's face, like a fashion trend that was repeating itself with a slightly different twist. And as young women often do, she began molding the image of him in her mind, and it acquired detail and depth until one day, she imag-ined him into reality. The sunsets they shared were everything she knew they would be—wet, warm bodies and cool Island breezes, lusty red wine, and Van Gogh skies. But even her wild-est imaginings couldn't prepare her for the sunrises and how she would feel each time she awoke beside him, listening for the changes in the pattern of his breathing, and watching the slight shifts of his body as he dreamed, waiting for that moment just before waking when he would stretch and roll and reach out for her. "Arianna," he would whisper and nothing more.

The sun was in its descending arc over the western head-land now. It was an artist's sun, all big and orange, spreading its sepia light over the Island, transforming it from brilliant con-trasts to silhouetted images against a vibrant sky. There was a light trail that extended across the lagoon and out to the open sea, a *golden touch* she had called it when she was very young. But first she needed to cry the tears she had been suppressing all that day. It wasn't a moment of weakness. She just needed to leave the tears behind. And when the last one had descended her cheek and dissolved into the fabric of her linen shirt, she knew she was ready. So she resettled herself on the sleek wooden bench that Grandfather had lovingly crafted out of a single koa log all those years ago and into which he and Mem had carved their names, and then Mama and Papa had done the same after them. She followed the light trail as far as she could see and searched the horizon until she found what she was looking for— the ferry that was sailing away with everything she loved most in this world. She stared at it for a very long time, watching it grow smaller and smaller. Then she closed her eyes and tried to remember what her life had been like before Michael.

Part One

San Francisco

1

10 Years Earlier

ARI ENTERED THE house and the scents of Mama's dinner greeted her as usual. She could smell the dinner rolls baking and the curry and fresh ginger from her favorite peanut chicken. And of course, there was Mama's jasmine, always her jasmine. Ari heard James's tiny voice, laughing over a shared joke with Mama, probably a joke only a five-year-old would think funny, but Mama was laughing too. This was their special time together, when James awoke from his nap and Mama put her writing away, and for a few hours each day, he was the sole object of her affections.

James always knew when it was time for Ari to come home from school. He couldn't actually tell time, but she had taught him to count the chimes on the old grandfather clock in the front foyer—three chimes for her return, six chimes for Papa's and seven chimes plus two sets of church bells for his favorite television show—*Walt Disney's Wonderful World of Color*. Today he had counted the three chimes and was waiting for Ari to call out to him. *"I'm home, big guy."* That was his signal to climb down from his bright yellow aluminum step stool and go speeding through the dining room and down the hall to Ari's waiting arms.

It always made Ari smile to see James hurtling toward her, his arms flailing and his hair flying off in a million different directions from his nap and his insistence that hair didn't need to be brushed more than once a day, if at all. But not even her affectionate baby brother could make her smile now—not

7

after the worst day any girl ever spent in high school. She knew she should call out to him, but she was so tired, she just leaned her hundred fifteen pounds against the heavy timbered door until she heard the iron latch clank behind her. Then, after what seemed like her first real breath of the day, she shuffled quietly into the foyer.

There was a tall mahogany hallstand just to the right of the front door. It had at its center a small beveled mirror surrounded by ornate carvings and two large filigreed candle holders, a remnant from an age when houses were gas lit and furniture was handcrafted. Ari usually stopped there to look at her reflection—a kind of ritualistic closure to the school day rather than a simple vanity—but she didn't even glance at the mirror today.

Instead, she moved along the row of brass hooks that ran down the wall leading toward the living room entrance, removed her navy woolen pea coat and hung it in its appointed place, right next to the tiny camel hair John-John coat that James wore on *"going out good days."*

At the center of the foyer was a round pedestal table on which a simple floral arrangement of money tree and white orchids attempted to balance the ostentations of the old Tudor house. The day's mail was piled there as usual, and Ari stopped briefly to shuffle through it for any foreign-stamped letters addressed to her. There was only one envelope of any promise, a bright yellow parchment one, made thick by a multi-page letter inside, with postal stamps from Bombay. But the handwriting was Madu's, Mama's friend, and not her daughter, Gita's. As was his custom, Papa had laid the daily newspaper next to the mail for anyone who wanted to read it after he finished. It wasn't uncommon for Ari to glace over the headlines, but today she had her own problems to deal with, and she didn't have room to be concerned with what President Johnson did or didn't do that day.

It was from the kitchen that Mama listened for the sounds of her daughters returning home each day, and she always felt a little frisson of relief when her chicks were safely back in the nest after a day in the big world. She knew the sounds of their return by heart and could always tell who entered the house first. Today it was Emma with her soft footsteps and graceful, rhythmic moves as she unburdened herself of her hat and coat and binder, stopped by the kitchen for a quick greeting, and then floated upstairs to wait for *him* to call. Arianna's return was always faster paced, more energetic. She would burst through the door, dump her things on the floor next to the hall stand, call out to James, and come bouncing into the kitchen with her baby brother securely fastened around her neck.

So, the moment Ari entered the house Mama knew that something had gone wrong. Her movements were slow and her sounds were those of someone who had been exhausted by her day, not exhilarated by it. There was no customary greeting for her or James. Mama waited for Ari's appearance at the kitchen door but heard her daughter climbing the stairs instead. Perhaps this was a time for sisters, not a mother. So she returned her attention to James's story about his best friend's brand new puppy, smiling at the increasing frequency of new puppy stories that filled the warm air of the big country kitchen each afternoon.

Upstairs Ari dove onto her bed and pulled her big over-stuffed comforter around her until only her black hair and emerald eyes were visible. She could hear music coming through the wall from Emma's bedroom—"Misty," as usual. After months of play on the little portable hi-fi, the song rasped and skipped and faded in and out, and the sound grated on Ari a little, but Emma didn't seem to mind. Ari didn't know if Emma had ever listened to any of the other songs on the album. She thought it kind of silly to buy a whole album for just one song. But forty-fives were out, and albums were in, and "Misty" was Emma and Roger's song. It was clearly destined to be played over and over again until either the grooves wore out or Emma and Roger broke up.

A tear perched itself at the corner of Ari's eye and finally spilled over onto her cheek, down her chin, and onto the floral duvet cover, where it disappeared into a crimson rose. For some time after, Ari didn't know how long, she just lay staring at the wet spot made by the tear until a sound at the door brought her out of her deep thoughts. "Come in," she whispered to her sister's familiar knock.

Ari and Emma had always been there for each other, able to read each other's thoughts and feel each other's feelings, almost as if they were identical twins, not sisters separated by twenty-one months. They were anything but identical, on the outside anyway. Ari had inherited Mama's dark, exotic looks and Emma Papa's All-American athleticism. Mama called her girls *"opposite ends of the same circle."* Ari didn't know what that meant when she was younger, but she did now, and she was glad to have her soulmate so close at hand. Not that Emma's being there would change anything, not really, but she could help her get through the long night of dreading tomorrow.

"Are you all right?" Emma asked. Ari wasn't one to go to tears easily.

"I don't know," she answered honestly.

Emma took a seat at the end of the big four poster, stretched her long legs out straight in front of her, and leaned back against the footboard, squirming and twitching in search of a comfortable place to rest her back. "Here, you better take this," Ari said, throwing her a plump green toile pillow. "This could be a long story."

"Thanks," she smiled back and waited while Ari marshaled the energy to revisit the day's events.

"I could just kill Brittany!" Ari suddenly blurted out.

Emma didn't have to ask who Brittany was. She had become a household name. She was one of those girls who could be found on every high school campus, a female bully who isolated other girls and then got everyone else to gang up on them without seeming to have been remotely involved herself. "Tell me what happened," she said gently.

It had all begun innocently enough at Susannah's slumber party last Saturday night. Ari and a dozen other girls were circled around big bowls of popcorn and M&M's with only their heads and arms protruding out of their sleeping bags, as they alternately stuffed their mouths with food and spewed out gossip with the reliable rhythm of ocean waves. At eleven o'clock they played Truth or Dare. Ari learned that there weren't quite as many virgins at her high school as she thought. At twelve o'clock they froze Mary Lupinski's underwear, the price she paid for falling asleep too early. Shortly after midnight about half the high school football team pulled a panty raid, hoping to catch the girls in scanty nighties, but they were met instead by Susannah's father, a retired naval officer from Treasure Island, and by a symphony of giggles from the girls. After that everyone settled down to sharing secrets about boyfriends, boys they wished were boyfriends, and boys they met last summer at the beach that their boyfriends would never know about. By early morning, the conversation grew more high-spirited and less careful. That's when Ari blurted it out.

"I really didn't tell them all that much about the Island," Ari insisted. "I just told them about our holidays on the Island and what it was like there and what the people were like and . . ." she couldn't bring herself to say what she was sure her sister already knew.

"Oh, Ari, you didn't," Emma gently chided.

Ari lowered her eyes and aimlessly twirled a lock of her long, thick hair around her forefinger until no more would fit. "Well, Brittany was going on and on about all the places she had been last summer and all the things she had done, and I guess I just got tired of her one-upping everybody. So . . . so I told them about Celebration Night," Ari finally admitted.

"What exactly did you tell them, Ari?"

"Well, I told them how every year there's a special celebration on the Island with a big feast made by all the families, kind of like a luau. And how there's drums and music and how all the women dance for the men they love, but that the celebration is really for the women who are dancing for the very first time. And I kind of told them about how the couples go off together when the dancing is over to . . . well, you know. And how when you and I were younger, we used to hide behind the banyan tree and watch the dancing part." She stopped there, not sure what else to say.

"Is that all?" Emma asked.

"I tried to explain that it wasn't some kind of wild orgy or anything." Her voice trailed off as she shrugged her shoulders and looked sheepishly at her sister.

"Oh, Ari!" Emma exclaimed, exploding into laughter.

"I thought they understood. I really thought they did." Ari pulled her outstretched legs toward her and leaned her head on her knees.

Emma reached out to place a comforting hand on her sister's shoulder. A wayward curl from the bangs she was growing out fell over her face and covered her nose. With some slight irritation she pulled it back and tucked it behind her ear with her other curls. She said, "I don't know what Brittany did to you today, but it should blow over pretty quickly. Girls like her already have their next victim lined up before they've even finished with the current one."

"You wouldn't say that if you'd been at school with me today," she said despondently. "I'll never tell anyone about the Island again!"

Ari had gone to her locker before first period class to retrieve her physics book and found a larger than usual gathering of oxford cloth, lamb's wool and pinwale corduroy in the hallway. She didn't think anything of it at first, but then conversations faded to whispers when her classmates saw her coming and then to silence as they exchanged those knowing glances that told her they all shared a secret. Many of the girls from the slumber party were there, standing in groups of threes and fours, in perfect *clique* formation, and a number of the boys who had pulled the panty raid milled around the fringes. But Ari knew there was trouble for sure when she saw Brittany, who had positioned herself to one side of the crowd, like an innocent bystander, flanked by the girl guard that followed her on command. She was standing there, rhythmically stroking her perfect blond flip and wearing her too-tight royal blue sweater that was intended to bring out her eyes but only accentuated the padding in her bra. She flashed Ari a smile, not a congenial one, more like a warning shot across her bow. Ari had seen that look before, and all she could do was return the smile and steel herself against whatever awaited her.

She dialed the combination on her lock. With each turn of the wheel, she heard muffled snickers behind her. Obviously, Brittany's nasty little joke was waiting for her behind her locker door. How had she gotten the combination? A horrible thought flitted through her mind. Only her best friend, Meghan, had her combination. Surely she wouldn't. No, that was too horrible to think. Probably just some spy of Brittany's looked over her shoulder one day. She considered not opening the locker and just going to class, but she needed her physics book and wasn't about to let Brittany cost her valuable grade points by showing up to class without it.

She had only three turns of the wheel to think of the perfect comeback—the one you usually think of a day late. Nothing was coming to her. When the last number clicked into place on the tumbler, she opened her locker and the snickers erupted into riotous laughter. Ari stared silently at the object of their amusement taped inside her locker door. It was a picture of a naked woman on a beach, obviously a centerfold from Playboy, with long black hair and green eyes drawn on with permanent marker. Across the belly it said, "Will you be my date for the dance?" and it was signed, "The Football Team." Ari froze in place, knowing that everyone was staring at her, just waiting for her to fall apart, especially Brittany. As she turned toward them, willing her face to remain expressionless, she was still desperately trying to think of something clever to say, but all she could think was, *if only Emma were here, like in the good old days.*

Ari and Emma had learned to depend upon each other in ways siblings do when they live in faraway places. Being independent and outspoken as a youngster, Ari had gotten herself into a few playground scrapes over the years, and Emma had always stood with her, daring anyone to take them both on in that subtle way she had of standing her ground without being confrontational. Emma was so like Papa. Ari, however, was not as conciliatory. One day the school bully decided to ridicule Emma in front of everyone for wearing her family sarong to school on *Family Tree Day*. Ari was not about to let that injustice go unpunished. She marched right up to that bully, made a fist, cocked her elbow as far behind her head as she could, and fired one startling blow to the bully's mouth. The day ended with the bully at the dentist, Ari in the Headmaster's office with Mama, and a lot of children knowing that they would never tease the Heywood girls again. That night Ari got a stern lecture from her parents in Papa's study, but as she was leaving, she was sure that she heard laughter from beyond the doors that had closed behind her.

Ari had the sudden impulse to send Brittany to the dentist, and this caused her to smile, which perplexed her onlookers and irritated Brittany, who was hoping for a far more flamboyant response. Recognizing her momentary advantage, Ari swallowed her anger and calmly retrieved her Physics book from her locker. Then she looked directly at Brittany, rolled her eyes and shook her head to convey boredom with her childishness, took the picture down from her locker, crumpled it up, dropped it in the nearest garbage can, and exited the building without looking back.

It felt like every pair of eyes followed her as she made her way across the quad and into the math and science building on the other side. When she entered the building, she was sure that the hallway had grown at least a hundred yards longer since yesterday. But finally she reached what she hoped would be the sanctuary of her classroom and the temporary protection of the teacher who, for fifty minutes at least, would give her a chance to regroup. What greeted her instead was a sea of staring faces whose expressions left no doubt that they too were in on Brittany's little joke. Ari began to wonder if there had been some kind of announcement on the P. A. system before she arrived at school. *There will be an all-school assembly in the gymnasium today to celebrate National Make Fun of Arianna Heywood Day!*

Ari maneuvered down the narrow aisle toward her desk at the front of the room, and a wave of whispers behind her replaced the silent stares in front. When she reached her destination, she stopped abruptly and just stared. Stuck to her desk was a half-naked plastic hula dancer, the kind that bobs up and down in the rear window of old cars. She loudly exhaled her contempt. Then she moved calmly but swiftly to her seat and, without emotion, pulled the doll off of her desk and dropped it in her purse. The loud pop from the suction cup at its base evoked snickers all around, but Ari just kept her eyes focused straight ahead and wondered how she would get through what was sure to be the longest day of her life.

At lunchtime, she looked for her best friend, Meghan O'Leary, who usually met her outside U.S. Government class, but apparently even Meghan didn't want to be seen with her today. No matter. She wasn't really hungry anyway. She headed for the back corridors, making a wide arc around the quad where she knew most of the kids would be congregating, and retreated to the solitude of the art room. She was still staring at her feet when she entered the door and barely noticed Jonathan Mallory, a pale-faced, overweight boy sitting in the far corner of the room as he did every day at lunch. She looked at him without speaking, trying to tell from the expression on his face if he too was in on her humiliation. But he looked the same as always—blank to the point of being almost invisible.

Ari had never been mean to him like some of the other kids had. It simply wasn't in her nature to do that, but as she looked at him now, hiding behind his easel in the remotest corner of the room, she understood for the very first time how even she had contributed to his loneliness. "Jonathan, do you mind if I sit at the easel next to yours? The light's much better over there."

"Sure, if you want to," he said nervously, his paintbrush flying out of his hand and landing in a big gooey vermillion splotch on his blue smock. She laughed and he smiled. It was the first really nice exchange she had had with anyone all morning.

That afternoon, Brittany left school in her fancy yellow Thunderbird feeling triumphant. As she drove by a group who had gathered on the sidewalk, she waved and shared a last laugh with them at what she was sure was Ari's expense. It wasn't until she arrived home that she discovered the half-naked hula dancer bobbing up and down in her car's signature porthole. The doll wasn't suctioned there. It had been permanently cemented on.

"Oh, Ari, you didn't!" Emma exclaimed, unable to control the laughter that followed.

"You keep saying that, Emma." She slumped back on her pillow with dramatic flair and added, "Mama's going to know something happened today. She always knows, and I bet I know what she's going to say. "*Arianna, you must see your enemy as an opportunity to practice patience and tolerance. These are virtues that bring happiness.*" Ari loved Mama, and she loved her Island ways, but sometimes those ways seemed better suited to the Island than to San Francisco.

"She's right you know, Ari," Emma said. "If you were on the Island, you'd know it was true."

"Maybe. But right now the truth doesn't help me very much."

2

ARI LAY MOTIONLESS on her bed for some time after Emma left, staring up at the ceiling, tracing the random patterns in the cream-colored plaster that filled the spaces between the heavy blackened timbers. When she tired of that game and could think of no others to replace it, she scooted off the end of the bed and walked over to the full-length mirror. It stood in the corner near the bathroom door, just to the right of one of the two window seats that flanked the porcelain-tiled fireplace.

Ari usually liked the image that stared back at her from the glass, but today she wasn't so sure. She surveyed herself from every angle, trying to assure herself that she didn't look fat in her black and white watch-plaid skirt and her favorite green cardigan, which only that morning she was sure had accentuated her slim figure. She had to admit, she liked the way the outfit brought out her eyes, large, almost almond eyes that Mrs. O' Leary said looked like a Keene painting, but Tommy Lloyd once told her reminded him of his favorite green purie marble. She glanced over at her dresser and at the translucent green marble that sat there among her treasures, and she remembered fondly the day she found it inside a large red construction paper envelope, accompanied by a handmade valentine of pink paper and doilies and a fistful of pastel candy hearts that said *Be My Valentine*. Life was so much simpler when she was only eight.

She studied her hair, piling it up on top of her head movie star style and then releasing it, letting it fall in thick, straight sheets. It was Mama's hair, blue-black and smooth and shiny. Papa had always said it looked like Egyptian black onyx. She had

Mama's sculpted cheekbones too, and her full lips and tall slender body that curved in and out right where it was supposed to.

Ari turned from the mirror and aimlessly looked around her bedroom. She liked this room a lot, not as much as her own bedroom in the Great House on the Island, but still the fabrics and the furniture and the English country atmosphere were very cozy. The furniture was all British—dark polished hardwoods and heavy-doored, intricately carved and dentil molded. And the fabrics were chintz and pinstripes and toiles perfectly put together on fringed drapes and dressing table skirts, which matched bed linens and throw pillows, in layer upon layer. It was all terribly grand. In fact, Ari thought the whole house was rather grand, but she guessed that was only befitting Papa's position in the company.

The house was a half-timbered English Tudor that stood on a quiet, tree-lined street in St. Francis Woods. It was reminiscent of lawn tennis and gin and tonics and crocks of Christmas puddings hanging from rough-hewn rafters. There was a little pointed roof over the entrance to keep off the rain and a large, round leaded glass window in the door affording visitors their first blurry glimpse into the house's interior. Beyond the door was the two-story foyer with rich amber walls that looked like leather and a small crystal chandelier overhead that made shadows dance every time the door opened. To the left of the foyer was a pretty little powder room with a big cast iron clawfooted tub that sat under a frosted window and a skirted sink and matching paisley wall paper that reminded Ari of the silk waistcoats the male secretaries used to wear in Papa's Singapore office. Ari couldn't imagine how the tub had come to be there. After all, who would want to walk through the front foyer of the house to take a bath? But Mama explained that long ago the bath had probably been accessed from the other side where a series of tiny storage rooms off the kitchen had once been occupied by household staff.

To the right of the foyer was a long living room with a huge carved oak fireplace on one side, made almost black with age. The walls were wainscoted in the same dark oak over which silk wallpaper hung in an ancient shade of celadon green. On the far wall were two pairs of heavy paneled oak doors that faced toward the front of the house and beveled glass French doors that faced the English garden. The oak doors led to Papa's study and the glass doors to Mama's writing room. Taken all together it was the perfect room for an English country house Christmas. Except that it was even better because the house was centrally heated, the furniture was soft and comfortable, and the fog that lay as a gentle blanket over the rooftops was fresh-breezed and ocean sent and not one of those dank, coal-fed *pea-soupers that* frightened instead of refreshed.

"If only it really was Christmas," Ari mused aloud. "Grandfather and Mem would be here, and I'd have two whole weeks off from school."

Her thoughts were suddenly interrupted by the Westminster chimes of the old grandfather clock sounding the six o'clock hour. Papa would be home soon, and she hadn't even changed out of her school clothes yet, except to kick off her knee-high leather boots. She picked up the boots where they still lay in the middle of the floor and returned them to the closet, slipping out of her skirt and hanging it up before closing the door. Then she carefully folded her sweater and returned it to the bottom drawer of the mahogany wardrobe, before retrieving a comfortable pair of denim bell bottom hip-huggers and a purple t-shirt from the drawer above. Miss Higgins, the head counselor for the girls, wouldn't allow girls to wear pants to school, much less the hippie clothes so popular at Berkeley right across the Bay. Mini-skirts and the mod look completely undid her. It wasn't fair, Ari thought, because straight skirts and scratchy sweaters and blouses with little peter pan collars were not very comfortable. For a moment Ari considered fomenting a sit-in like the one the Free Speechers put on at Berkeley a few years earlier but decided that perhaps this wasn't the time to be drawing any more attention to herself, so she quickly dismissed the idea and headed for the stairs.

It was an impressive staircase, perfectly designed for the slow, graceful descent of elegant ladies in exquisite ball gowns. She had often stood at the top landing imagining her Senior Prom night when her date would stand in the foyer and wait breathlessly for his first glimpse of her. She would finally appear at the top landing, wearing Grace Kelly's gold lamé ball gown from *To Catch a Thief.* His gaze would draw her down the oriental stair runner to the landing below, where she would slowly turn and descend toward him in full view. Of course, there wasn't much chance she'd have a date for the prom this year. What a waste of a great staircase, she thought, and bounded down the stairs like a clumsy colt.

Before joining the others in the kitchen, she entered the living room and headed for Mem's rosewood-framed painting of the Island that hung over the cavernous old fireplace. She stood squarely before it on the claret Turkish carpet and stared as if she were looking at it for the very first time. She did this whenever she was feeling troubled or homesick or was particularly missing Grandfather and Mem. Nothing bad ever happened to her on the Island.

The longer she stared, the deeper her eyes penetrated beyond the peaceful waters and palm-fringed beaches, beyond the cozy bungalows and ornate pavilions, sinking into the terraced valleys and jungled mountainsides and to the confusion of brushstrokes that transformed tubes of gooey paints into the one place she loved most on this earth. For a moment or maybe longer, the birds sang, the air filled with seductive fragrances, the gentle breezes blew in off the waters, and Arianna was home again.

She floated there for a while in the sea of tropical colors— cadmium yellow deep and alizarin crimson, manganese violet and cobalt teal, ultramarine turquoise and phthalo green and earthy shades of sienna. These were Mem's colors, and over the years they had found their way, in large part or small, to all her canvases. Ari could almost see her now, standing next to Grandfather, dressed in their native sarongs and crisp cotton shirts, bronzed and vigorous, looking altogether too young and vibrant to be grandparents. They were the first Islanders ever to attend a university, and after graduation, Grandfather traveled the world until he knew it well, and Mem returned home and came to know every tree, every flower, every creature, every drop of water and grain of soil and every Islander who had ever walked among them. By the time they came together again, Grandfather was a very learned man and Mem had cultivated a wisdom rarely found in one so young. So, no one was surprised when the Elders selected them to be the Teachers, charged with guiding the next generation toward a harmony of old ways and new. It was even less surprising when Mem announced that she intended to dance for Grandfather at the next Celebration.

"Papa, you're home!" James shouted from the kitchen, jolting Ari back to San Francisco. She didn't go to the kitchen right away; instead, she stood in the shadows, unseen by Mama and Papa and her siblings, watching the portrait of her family unfold. She often did this, mentally filing away images of her family to be used as sources for future paintings. Ari's art teacher, Mr. Davis, said that her paintings showed real promise. Mama said that she had inherited Mem's special gift.

It was a warm and welcoming kitchen, one that invited family and friends to gather. A large butcher block table occupied the center of the room. Its contours waved up and down from years of knife blows, and it was stained several shades of brown to black by the foods that had been prepared there. The stove was a six-burner stainless steel Thermidor with two huge ovens. They could hold the biggest turkeys at holiday time, and there were warming drawers so that the dinner rolls were always the perfect temperature when the rest of the meal was ready. Big copper pots hung from a rack on the ceiling and large porcelain spice jars stood on open shelves on the wall. Above the brick floors, hand-built hickory cabinets reached to the ceiling, the tops of which were fitted with glass doors showing off the various sets of china, cups all hanging from shiny brass hooks in neat rows that Papa had meticulously measured out according to Mama's instructions. There was a big walk-in pantry that James sometimes used as his *downstairs fort*. As with the rest of the house, plenty of paned, double-hung windows showered the room with natural light and brought indoors the manicured lawns and wild English gardens.

Papa stood at the garage entrance, hanging up his coat

and tie on the heavy brass coat rack that stood by the door and unbuttoning his shirt collar and the buttons of his double-breasted vest. He turned just in time to receive James, who had climbed down off his stool, and was running to Papa's welcoming arms as fast as his little legs could carry him. Papa bent down until he was at eye level with James who stood on his tiptoes with his arms outstretched, waiting to be lifted. They looked just like a Norman Rockwell painting, Ari thought. One of those simple moments in life that ultimately are more fondly remembered than the most extravagant events.

Papa negotiated the length of the kitchen in just a few strides with James riding on his shoulders, squealing and ducking down every time Papa called "*low bridge*" to avoid bonking his head on one of the rough-hewn rafters that traversed the kitchen ceiling at regular intervals. He stopped to give Emma an affectionate kiss on the cheek and tell her how pleasantly surprised he was to see her as she usually spent Monday nights at the sorority, and then continued on to the other end of the butcher block where he lowered James onto his stool and then wrapped his arms around Mama, who was busy scooping orange sherbet into iced chillers. She stopped to return the affection, and they held each other just a bit longer than most couples of nearly twenty-two years might have.

"Well, this is how I like to find my family at day's end." Papa's voice resounded, as he took the seat at James's right hand. "Preparing a hearty meal for the Master!"

"Oh, we've made dinner for you too, darling," Mama retorted playfully, and just managed to grab a lock of her long, loosely held hair before it fell into the sherbet container.

It was James's job to stick a large wafer cookie into each of the chillers, but for each cookie that went into the sherbet, one went into his mouth. "James, no more cookies," Mama admonished, as he munched yet another. "If you get a tummy ache, it will spoil our plans for Golden Gate Park tomorrow."

James stood up on the top step of the stepstool, pulled up his Micky Mouse t-shirt with both hands, and stuck out his belly as far as he could. "See, Mama. I have a really big tummy. I can fit a lot more cookies inside!"

"James, you better do what your Mama says," Papa warned, winking at Emma across the butcher block. "You're getting so heavy I almost couldn't lift you onto your stool!"

"Really, Papa?" He looked down at his tummy and tried to hold it in his hands, but some of his baby flesh had disappeared with his perpetual motion and, being at the age of more is always better, looked a little disappointed at his diminishing girth.

"Don't worry, James," Emma smiled. "You don't want to be fat like Santa. You want to be tall and handsome like Papa."

"Yeah, like Papa!" he grinned and stood as tall as he could on his tiptoes. He would have toppled to the floor if it weren't for Papa's quick hands.

It was true. Papa really was handsome. Everybody thought so. Last summer at the company picnic in Sigmund Stern Grove, Ari overheard some of the wives talking. They were watching Mama and Papa playing tennis with Mr. and Mrs. Ramsey, the company president and his wife. Papa was wearing his white tennis shorts and navy pullover, and Mama her little pleated tennis skirt that accentuated her long, slender legs. They were both laughing and shouting out orders and rushing the net like teenagers. *"Ethan Heywood certainly is a handsome man,"* she heard one woman say. *"Ruggedly handsome,"* another added. *"And Mary . . . I wish I could look that good with no make-up on. How do they stay looking so young?"* People were always saying things like that about her parents.

"Ari!" James squealed, when he spied her standing at the door. "Mama said I couldn't go up and get you. I been waiting and waiting forever!"

"I know, big guy, but I'm here now," she said, crossing the room to give him a big hug. She smiled hello at Mama and then continued round the table, kissed Papa hello, and sat next to Emma who was busily working on a green goddess salad. Papa reached across the table and stuck his forefinger in the dressing and quickly whisked it back to his mouth, hurriedly licking the drips of sour cream and mayonnaise, anchovies, and garlic and chives, before they reached the rolled-up cuff of his shirt.

"Oh, Ethan!" Mama laughed. "Is that any way to set an example for your children?"

"Yes," Emma and Ari answered in unison, and stuck their fingers in the dressing as well. The kitchen erupted into laughter and spurred the onset of the congenial conversation that filled the warm country kitchen of the Heywood house every evening at this time. And soon Arianna assumed her place in the family portrait and was a million miles from the day that, just an hour ago, she was sure was the end of her life.

When the dinner was out of the oven and the chillers returned to the freezer, the family congregated as usual in the little family dining room off the kitchen to enjoy the evening meal and share the happenings of their day. Ari knew that this was a different experience from most of her friends, who sat behind collapsible TV tables watching *Gunsmoke* or *Jackie Gleason* or *The Wild, Wild West*, barely speaking while they munched away on a replica of roasted turkey from a shiny aluminum TV dinner tray. Perhaps it was because her family had lived in so many houses that didn't have televisions, or perhaps it was just good—no essential—to maintain some sort of family ritual inside the house when the countries outside the house kept changing. Or maybe it was because the whole family knew that one day they could be scattered to the four corners of the earth and they needed to make use of this time together. Ari took no end of ribbing from her friends who couldn't understand her apparent lack of typical teenage rebellion. She tried to tell them that she'd already gone through a whopper of a rebellious stage when living in Hong Kong, but they didn't really believe her. So, she just started nodding silently when the others complained about how their parents *"just didn't get it."*

The little family dining room was one of the most casual rooms in the house, second only, perhaps, to the adjacent TV den. It overlooked the gardens and a fountain that spewed water from the top of a stone umbrella perched over the heads of two small stone children. The walls were covered in warm sienna plaster, and there was a cottage-style china hutch with open shelves filled with Spode plates in the Blue Tower pattern. Encircling the room on a high plate rail was a collection of majolica platters whose hand painted country characters seemed to be eavesdropping on the family conversation at the dinner table each night. Most of the conversation tonight centered on the growing anti-war unrest at Berkeley, the absurdity of the Twiggy look, the excitement over the first heart transplant to be performed in December by Barnard, De Bakey, and Kantrowitz, Mama's new tie-dye t-shirt that confirmed Papa's suspicions that indeed his free-spirited wife had been born a hippie, and, of course, the brand new puppy that James wanted now that his "*bestest*" friend Georgie had gotten one. There was no talk of Ari's day.

After dinner Papa went upstairs to change his clothes and then went to his study to organize his papers for his morning meeting with the British and Dutch businessmen whose companies also had dealings in the Far East. James disappeared into the pantry to play Batman and Robin, Emma went upstairs to do her homework, and Ari joined Mama at the kitchen sink where she loaded the dishwasher and then grabbed a towel to start drying the pots as Mama finished scrubbing them.

Mama emptied the dirty water from the sink and refilled it with fresh water and a new supply of frothy bubbles. She gathered the serving utensils and put them in the water to soak. "Have you decided what you're going to do about Brittany?" she asked casually, handing Ari a spoon to dry. Mama's intuition when it came to her daughters always amazed Ari. It wasn't always a good thing though. Mama seemed to see all and know all, which made it very difficult for Ari and Emma to get away with anything. As long as it was a mistake that they could take back, Mama let the girls make them and learn from them, and she was always there to support and comfort them when those mistakes reared their ugly heads.

"I don't really know what to do," Ari replied, "short of praying that she moves to another state by morning."

Mama turned to look at her daughter, but her hands kept moving under the water, cleaning a small sauce pot by feel. "Oh, Arianna, if Brittany suddenly moved away tomorrow, someone else would take her place in twenty-four hours. The world is full of Brittanies."

"There's a gruesome thought."

"Perhaps."

"You weren't there, Mama. You don't understand."

"I understand better than you think." She took the dish towel from Ari's hand and led her over to the butcher block island where they sat facing each other. "Ari," she continued, "all teenagers want to fit in. People like Brittany count on that. It's only natural to hate what's happening to you. Just don't start doubting yourself in the process. As horrible as today was, it will all blow over eventually."

Ari knew by the way Mama was looking at her that she wished she could make all of troubles disappear. But Ari knew that wasn't possible. Only she could do that.

"Let me ask you something," Mama said at last, "and you must be completely honest with me."

Uh oh, Ari thought. "Sure, Mama. What is it?"

"Are you ashamed of me?"

"What!"

"Are you ashamed of me?" Mama repeated. "Are you ashamed of our Island and our people? Are you ashamed to be my daughter?" Her tone wasn't accusatory. She already knew the answer to her questions, but in her own way, she was trying to drive home a point to Ari.

"No, Mama! How could you even think that?" Ari protested. "I love the Island and everything about it, and I love you, Mama! How could you even ask me something like that?" Ari was hurt by the fact that Mama even doubted her feelings for a second.

Mama grabbed both of Ari's hands in hers, squeezing them tight. "Then that's what you want to remember when you walk into school tomorrow, Arianna. Brittany wants you to feel ashamed of who you are, of who I am. You're never going to change her, but you can choose how you respond to her."

"That's a lot easier said than done, Mama. Any suggestions on how I do that?"

"I'm not really sure," Mama admitted. "Only you can figure that out. But promise me one thing. Please make sure it doesn't involve a dentist." Mama smiled and Ari laughed. Mama always knew how to make her smile at even the hardest of times. It was a special gift she had, and Ari was ever so thankful for it.

They returned to the sink and finished cleaning in silence

until all the pots and utensils were neatly returned to either the pot rack or proper drawer, the food was put away, and only a small pile of wafers remained on the butcher block to be properly stored.

When Mama was satisfied that all was in perfect order, she thanked Ari for the help, grabbed up James from the pantry, and turned to go, but Ari stopped her before she reached the door. "May I ask you something, Mama?" she ventured.

"Of course," she replied.

"How do you know so much about people like Brittany?"

Mama answered without hesitation. "Jennifer Taylor Winthrop! She was my first Brittany," she said and left the room without explanation.

Ari stood at the base of the staircase, watching Mama climb the stairs with James in hand, on their way to their nightly ritual of face scrubbing, teeth brushing, and pajama selecting. James made a big production out of choosing his pajamas, as he was sure that they were somehow connected to the dreams he would have that night. And Mama, who was a dreamer herself, indulged her son's idiosyncrasy. Each night Mama went to James's pajama drawer, pulled out all of his neatly folded pajamas and laid them out on the bed. James marched down the length of his bed, stopping before each pair in silent consideration, looking much like a judge at a dog show. Mama always maintained a serious demeanor, never showing her amusement, as she assisted James in choosing between cowboys, outer space, Batman, dinosaurs, San Francisco Giants' uniform, sea creatures, or plain pajamas, which Mama said were a blank page on which he could write his own adventures.

Ari had finished all her homework in study hall, having spent no time in whispered conversations or note passing, so she didn't know how she was going to pass the time tonight. She wandered aimlessly into the living room, stopping first at the pedestal table between the burgundy duck club chairs to look at a silver-framed photograph of Mama and Papa lazing in a gondola in Venice. Mama was wearing a long, flowing silk dress, delicately embroidered and beaded in eggshell over minty green, and Papa was wrapped around her, the arms of his white dinner jacket looking like an evening shawl. They were obviously returning home from a party; the smiles on their faces were too broad for sobriety. Or perhaps it was anticipation that made them smile. With Mama and Papa, you could never be sure.

Italy was Papa's first posting, and with just one glass of wine on spaghetti night these days, Mama and Papa would spew forth a litany of memories. "Remember our picnics in the Chianti Ruffino, Ethan?"

"I certainly do," Papa's voice would lower an octave or two. and his eyes would drift to some far-off memory. Ari guessed that their picnics had included more than just eating and drinking wine, but it was not something she wanted to think of her parents doing. It was sweet though the way they were still in love with one another after all this time. She wondered if she would share that kind of love someday.

"Mmm . . . warm Tuscan bread and hearty red wine and those purple and orange sunsets over Venice,"

Mama would continue to reminisce.

"And more hearty red wine," Papa would always repeat before draining his wine glass.

They spoke of hot summer days on Venetian canals and cool summer nights at lakeside villas and cobble street strolls through ancient pastel hill towns that rambled down to the Ligurian Sea. Ari never tired of hearing about their romantic adventures in Italy. Or about Signora Grumaldi, the once-famous opera singer who opened her house by the sea to special friends each weekend and in whose gardens they breakfasted on dark coffee and speck and breads baked fresh by Guillermo, the affable Peruvian houseboy. "How romantic," Ari sighed, and was suddenly acutely aware of the absence of romance in her life right now.

It had been several months since she and Mark Bingham had broken up. For a while she enjoyed the single life, or at least that's what she told herself. Mark was the first boy who ever broke up with her. He said he still wanted to be friends, but that he was going away to college and she was going to be on the Island all summer, and they needed to get used to seeing other people. Later she found out from Micki Taylor that Mark had been *getting used to seeing other people* long before they broke up—namely Laura Pederson, one of Brittany's best friends. Mark didn't want to go to college a virgin, and everyone knew that Laura Pederson hadn't been one for a really long time. Ari was devastated for about a week or two, especially because she had lost her date to the Spring Semi-Formal. That seemed so long ago now; it was hard to remember why she felt so upset over Mark.

On the wall behind the club chairs there were three portraits in oil. Mem had done them from memory of her grandchildren and had given them to Mama and Papa for Christmas last year. Mama cried when she unwrapped them saying that they not only captured the look of her children but their spirits as well. Ari often found her parents looking at them, always with the same odd expressions on their faces, both sentimental and amused.

Mama said that Emma would always be proof of Papa's existence. She had his wavy brown hair, which lay to the middle of her back in layered cascades—a perfect backdrop to her beauty. She possessed a slender build, less curvy than Ari's, and the graceful elegance that could only belong to a classically trained dancer, yet she had the hardiness to strap a full pack on her back and survive a week in the wilderness. She was kind and gentle and vigorous and steadfast and always seemed to know exactly the right thing to say. She could do that, Mama said, from the time she was very little, probably because she knew how to listen and was genuinely interested in what others had to say, just like Papa.

Arianna was Mama's proof of life. Her beauty was both wild and serene, a creature of mountaintops and valley floors, of blue lagoons and steamy jungles, yet equally at home in the marble hall museums of the world's largest cities and at Formica tables in cafés of the quaintest small towns. Both sisters were beautiful, both standouts in a crowded room.

James was Mama and Papa's most intriguing concoction, from his unruly mop of hair that couldn't decide if it wanted to be black or brown or curly or straight to his big round eyes that were not quite blue but not really green to the liberal sprinkling of freckles that came from nowhere and sat between devilish little dimples. James was guileless and pure, able to cut straight to the core of adult pretensions, still possessing the innocence of youth that so charmed his elders. Ari thought that he would always possess such innocence.

A drawer slammed from somewhere upstairs, and Ari guessed that James had settled on tonight's pajamas. It wouldn't be long before she'd hear his bare feet scuffling down the stairs. She continued moving through the room, a bit more rapidly now, examining the mementoes of the family's travels scattered about the numerous occasional tables and curio cabinets. Finally, she came to her favorite treasures, Mama's collection of glass bottles that stood in order of purchase across the mantle. All together the bottles created a chronological history of the Heywood family, each having been purchased during the first week of Papa's new postings. Mama would set off on forays into the local marketplaces to ferret out the perfect bottle, taking the children just as soon they were old enough to accompany her. Together they would trek down thoroughfares and back alleys, through department stores and cellar hideaways, stopping along the way to enjoy the local delicacies and immerse themselves in the language and the culture.

There were bottles of all shapes and colors, most with some distinctive markings identifying the country of origin. There was the emerald green Venetian glass bottle bought at the Murano factory where glass blowers demonstrated their craft before taking customers to the showrooms upstairs. Then there was the saffron bottle from India that Mama found in the street market and the cranberry bottle with gilt edging that they discovered in a naval salvage shop in Annapolis, Maryland. And there was the aquamarine bottle from Singapore that the little boy with no shoes was selling and the little fluted bottle with an etched crystal stopper from Coco Channel's in Paris, which had once held an ounce of No. 5. Next came the cobalt blue bottle with the royal seal that they found in one of the antique stalls on Portobello Road in London. The hawker claimed it had once held mango chutney and had graced the side table of the Queen Mother. They didn't believe him, of course, but they so loved the enthusiasm with which he delivered his story in his delightful cockney accent that they bought the bottle anyway. Then there was the amber glass bottle from Hong Kong with the hand-painted Chinese lettering, which they found in a back alley cellar belonging to a Chinese herbalist who dispensed ginseng in the front of his shop and opium in the back. Finally, there was the San Francisco bottle, which wasn't a bottle at all, but a big kitchen salt shaker made to look like Coit Tower.

There were nine bottles in all, eight representing all the places Papa's business had taken his family since he and Mama were married, and one very special bottle that stood first in line on the mantle. It was a clear glass pear-shaped bottle, larger than the others, which Mem had given to Mama when she first left the Island for college. The bottle was filled with alternating layers of black earth from the terraced mountainsides and golden sand from the beaches and varieties of dried leaves and preserved orchids and other tropical flowers. The only ornamentation on the bottle was a single Bird of Paradise, which Mem had painted with a miniature brush and a delicate hand. It was Ari's favorite. Mem said that all of Mama's memories of the Island were held in that bottle, and that as long as she had it with her, she would never be very far from home.

Ari took Mem's bottle down from the mantle, opened the stopper, and breathed deeply the air held inside. The fragrances of the contents had long since dissipated, but they were so firmly engrained in her memory that she smelled them anyway. A smile crept across her face—the same one that always found its way there whenever she thought of the Island. It didn't matter how badly her day had gone or how black her mood. the smile always made its way to the surface.

She continued meandering around the room, running her fingertips over picture frames and figurines, not really taking notice of much, until she reached Papa's study. The big oak doors stood ajar revealing the masculine atmosphere of a fine old English men's club inside. Ari could just see bits and pieces of the oversized red Persian carpet that filled most of the room, the big square partner's desk covered in files and memos, and the dark green leather furniture that was arranged around a stone fireplace whose hearth was just begging for an old hunting dog.

A tall glass curio cabinet stood to the left of the fireplace. It was filled with Royal Doulton Toby Jugs—another of their collections that held memories of places visited.

She slipped quietly into the room where she found Papa relaxing before the fire in his favorite wingback, wearing some loose khakis and his lemon yellow lamb's wool crewneck. A cloud of smoke from his Meerschaum pipe perched over his head and swirled about whenever he exhaled. He was obviously deep in thought, but from the distant expression on his face, Ari guessed that it wasn't business that occupied his mind. A minute or two passed before he looked up and smiled her into the leather chair that sat opposite his. It was the only surface not covered with files. She lowered herself into the chair, fitting herself squarely into the soft impression made by all the other backsides that had rested there before her, and waited for Papa to speak.

Papa was leaning back with his feet planted comfortably on the hassock, his head resting on his left hand while he rhythmically puffed on his pipe. "I hear you had a tough day at school," he said at last. "Is there anything I can do to help?"

"Nothing I can think of, Papa. I got myself into this, and I guess I'll have to get myself out."

"Well, you have every right to be angry, Arianna. I have little control myself when it comes to bigotry. And Brittany wasn't just attacking you today. She was attacking Mama," he added, unable to keep the contempt out of his voice. "But perhaps you could find a slightly less flamboyant response next time. You know, Elmer's glue instead of contact cement!" Papa said this in a teasing voice, but Ari got the message.

"If we have to pay for damage to Brittany's car, I'll pay you back, Papa. I promise."

"We can settle all that if the need arises. In the meantime, I want you to come to me if you need anything, even if you have to wake me."

They sat silently for some time, Papa perusing his papers and Ari staring at the fire, whose warmth was therapeutic. Periodically, she glanced around the room at Papa's mementoes, pausing at the King's Arms Pub sign for a quick remembrance and at the maroon and black Pallio banner from Sienna and the photographs of the family in high mountain valleys and quaint coastline villages. Eventually she came to the giant world globe that waited patiently in the corner for Papa to retrieve it for another game of *guess where we're moving to next*.

Every couple of years the family gathered around the globe with bowls of popcorn and mugs of hot cider and listened to Papa's geographic and cultural clues to systematically narrow their guesses from hemispheres to continents to countries to exact locales. Especially memorable was the night in the London House when Papa pulled out the globe, and Ari had declared that she wasn't going anywhere because Mama was way too pregnant.

But since Mama hadn't seemed bothered by the move, Ari forgot her anxiety and was soon caught up in the game.

"We're going to the continent with the most populated country in the world," Papa had said, and Mama wrote it down. "That's China, Mama, so we're moving to Asia," Emma had shouted, and Mama wrote it down too. "We can rule out cities west of Istanbul," Ari had added. And so-on and so-on and so-on. Later that night, after they had gone to bed, the sisters wondered what their new rooms would be like in the Hong Kong house and what their school would be like and their friends. When they awoke the next morning, they were ready to take on another change in their lives, but they were wholly unprepared for the change that had already taken place. Their brother, James, had been born at sunrise.

"Arianna, a penny for your thoughts," Papa said, bringing her back to the present.

"It will cost you more than that, Papa," she replied.

"Really, Ari, would you like to talk? I can do this work later."

Before she could answer, James came bounding through the door wearing his monkey pajamas and clutching his Curious George book in his pudgy little hands. "Read to me, Papa, please. You promised! You promised!"

Papa put his files aside, pulled James up onto his lap and wrapped his big, strong arms around him. With a quick wink at Ari, he began, "This is George. He was a good little monkey and always very curious."

James squirmed himself into position, rested his head in the crook of Papa's arm, and alternately looked down at the page and admiringly up at Papa's rugged jaw and serious demeanor. Papa always kept his promises, and James adored him for that.

3

THE NEXT MORNING Ari was late coming down to breakfast. She had changed her clothes repeatedly before deciding on her coral pink crew neck, straight black skirt, which just passed dress code at an inch above her knees, and her soft leather Cappezios that showed off her long legs better than her boots. Papa and Emma were already seated at the table when she arrived in the little dining room and were watching Mama retrieve another waffle from the stainless steel waffle maker. It was now a well-worn appliance, all batter-dripped and scorched from extensive use by the waffle lovers who salivated like Pavlov's dogs the minute the top popped open and the aromatic steam escaped.

"Oh, Ari, you're just in time for a waffle," Mama said, disengaging it from the iron with a fork and plopping it on a plate.

"No thanks, Mama. Why don't you have it?"

"Are you sure? I made them just the way you like them with plenty of drippy butter and Log Cabin syrup," she replied, pointing to the red, cabin-shaped tin."

"I'm sure, Mama. Thanks anyway."

"Well, eat something, Arianna. I don't want you going to school without breakfast."

Ari didn't reply. She just grabbed the box of Cheerios that sat on the table and poured a small amount into her bowl. She covered the cereal with a layer of sliced bananas, splashed milk on them to make them wet, and then poured enough sugar on the bananas to transform her breakfast into dessert. She took a big mouthful and munched on it, a single drip of milk escaping her mouth and reaching her chin before she caught it with her napkin "Where's James?" she asked after swallowing, suddenly noticing that he wasn't at the table.

Mama leaned forward and spoke in a whispered voice. "James is lying on the sofa in the den with a little tummyache. He says it has nothing to do with the empty cookie box I found in the pantry. Someone else ate those, you know."

"Oh, poor James!" Ari replied. "Is he too sick to go to the park today?"

"I'm afraid so, and he's so disappointed."

"Maybe we could all take him this weekend," Papa suggested. "I know you girls are too old for such things, but it would mean a lot to James. Do you have any plans?"

"Not anymore," Ari said, feeling a bit sorry for herself. Mama had little patience for self-pity and was about to say something, but decided to remain silent, knowing her own propensity for showering her daughters with philosophical wisdom when what they really needed was time to figure things out for themselves.

"What about you, Emma. Do you think you could spare a day away from what's-his-name to join us?"

"His name is Roger, Papa, and he's working Saturday at Petrini's Market so I can make it."

"Good, that's settled then. We'll take James to the Aquarium and the Museum of Natural History and then head up to the Cliff House for lunch."

"Could we go to Playland?" Ari asked, trying to show a bit of enthusiasm.

"Why not!"

When the family relocated from Hong Kong, they interspersed their unpacking with excursions around San Francisco to introduce the girls to the culture of their new home and to appease three-year-old James whose patience for unpacking was rather limited. It was on one of those junkets that they visited one of San Francisco's historic treasures, Playland at the Beach—a collection of carnival rides and midway games, a Fun House, food shops, and an original Charles Looff Carousel built in 1906. It was a special place that the Whitney brothers reigned over for nearly fifty years, where generations of young children spent Saturday afternoons and young lovers, Mama and Papa among them, spent Saturday nights and where Captain Fortune, a local TV personality in the '50s regularly held court on the weekends. By the time the family arrived in San Francisco, Playland was in its final decline. The Big Dipper Roller Coaster, one of the old-time wooden works of art, had long since succumbed to modern safety codes, and the other attractions were rusting and peeling and showing their age and neglect. Still it was one of the last urban amusement parks of its kind in America, and worth a visit if only to relive youthful memories or pay final respects.

"I'm going to tell James about Saturday," Ari said. "Maybe it will make him feel better."

Ari slipped quietly into the den. It was a small, cozy room, all soft leather and green and red plaid, just big enough for a sofa, two recliners, some shelves full of toys neatly stored in sturdy baskets, James's wooden trains, which were usually set in some wild configuration on the floor in front of the coffee table, a small stereo set and a large console television. Ari remembered when they first moved to San Francisco. What a novelty American television was then. She and Emma were glued to the TV and never missed an episode of Dr. Kildare. Emma thought Richard Chamberlain was even more dreamy than Troy Donahue, but Ari thought that was going a little too far. By the end of the year, Dr. Kildare was cancelled, the novelty had worn off, and the television was relegated to the infrequent watching of sporting events, Saturday morning cartoons, Ed Sullivan on Sunday nights if someone like the Beatles happened to be on, *Disney's Wonderful World of Color*, and a handful of other programs and movies sprinkled in between.

When James saw Ari, he reached out his arms and began to cry. She sat down close to him, grabbed him up and rocked him soothingly on her lap. "*Ariii . . .*" he bawled, "I'm sick and I can't go to *Golding* Gate Park." He clutched onto her arms and buried his face in her chest and cried until he had made a wet spot on her sweater.

Ari let him cry himself out, just holding him with one hand and stroking his hair with the other. Finally, she said in as jovial a voice as she could muster, "James, I have a surprise for you!"

"For . . . for me?" he sputtered, lifting his quivering little chin.

"Just for you!"

"What is it, Ari, what is it?"

"We're all going to the park. You, me, Emma, Mama, and Papa. All of us together, James."

"Now?"

"No. On Saturday when you're all better and Emma and I don't have school."

"When's Saturday, Ari?"

She held up James's right hand and counted out the days on his fingers. "Today is Tuesday," she began, pointing to his baby finger, and continued until she reached his thumb and Saturday.

James looked dejected again. "That's too many fingers. I want to go in this many." He held up two fingers and smiled at her in that way he already knew, even at his young age, made it hard for people to say no.

"If you go in that many days, James, I can't go with you," she said in mock sadness.

He popped up on her lap and threw his arms around her neck. "It's okay, Ari. You can go. It's okay."

"Oh, thank you, James," she replied with exaggerated excitement. "Saturday will be the *bestest* day of the whole week!" For more reasons than one, she thought to herself.

She plumped James's pillow and snuggled him down under his favorite woolen *"blankie,"* the one that was all balled up and napless from repeated washings, and returned to the others in the dining room.

"Is James all right?" Mama wanted to know.

"He's just fine, Mama. I told him about Saturday."

"Good. I'm sure he'll start feeling better soon."

Ari wished she would feel better soon, but first she had to survive whatever awaited her at school today. "I have to go right by your school this morning," Papa said, reading his daughter's thoughts. "I'm picking up a colleague who lives near there. Why don't I drop you and then Emma can pick you up after school. You only have morning classes today, right, Emma?"

"Yes, I can come get you, Ari."

Ari thought for a moment before answering. "That's awfully nice of you," she said, "but it's probably time I learned to fight my own battles."

"Perhaps you could learn to fight your own battles tomorrow," Mama interjected. "The station wagon's still in the shop, and I have to go to the market for some ginger ale for James. I could really use the other car today."

"Okay," Ari answered, "but we better get going. I don't want to be late on top of everything else."

A car horn sounded outside, announcing Roger's arrival, and Emma said a hurried goodbye and headed for the front door. Ari grabbed her bowl, and the carton of milk on her way out. She opened the refrigerator door and placed the milk on the top shelf, right next to a full bottle of ginger ale. She just smiled thinking about all the times Mama had said that it was her job to help her children, not to rescue them. Even Mama wasn't above a little rescuing every once in a while.

The drive to school was only a few miles through neighborhoods of neat stucco houses with little patchwork lawns and matching ornamental trees planted one to a property. Ari stared out the passenger side window at the passing houses until she was hypnotized by the optical illusion of one pastel house replacing its neighbor in the same space. When the game no longer distracted her from the day ahead, she looked at Papa. He was wearing her favorite navy blue Pierre Cardin suit—the one with the wild burgundy and blue lining in the vest that reminded her of a psychedelic poster from the Filmore West. Papa always wore three-piece suits with notched-collared vests and an etched gold pocket watch Mama had given him as an engagement present. There was an inscription inside the watch that read *My Love for All Time.*

Ari reached over and gently shook the watch chain until Papa's Phi Beta Kappa key lay flat against his vest. "Thanks," he said, glad to have an excuse to start up a conversation. "We wouldn't want the old man looking sloppy."

"You never look sloppy, Papa. Not even when you're wearing a sarong and are covered with sand."

"Well, I'm glad to know you think I'm — what's the word all the kids are using now? Bitchen'?" Ari laughed at the sound of that word coming out of Papa's mouth. Not even she could get used to using American slang after all her years abroad.

They drove on, exchanging small talk about the fog that was lifting early today and pleasantries about their impending outing on the weekend until they reached the yellow house with dark green trim that meant school was only a few blocks ahead. When they pulled up in front of the school, Papa turned off the motor and waited. Ari didn't move; she just sat staring straight ahead, twirling that familiar lock of hair around her finger.

"Who was Jennifer Taylor Winthrop?" she asked suddenly, shifting around to face her startled father.

"Whatever made you dredge up her name?"

"Mama mentioned her last night. She said that she was her Brittany. No, actually she said that she was her *first* Brittany."

Papa didn't respond right away. He was remembering events that had taken years and a lot of help from Mary to put behind him. At last he said, "Jennifer Taylor Winthrop was the girl I was supposed to marry."

"Marry?" Ari exclaimed. "Papa, did you leave her at the altar or something?"

"Nothing quite so dramatic," Papa laughed, his voice resuming its familiar calmness. "Our fathers were close business associates, and they looked upon Jennifer and me as a perfect merger of two fine old families."

"Did you even like Jennifer, Papa? I mean, would you have married her if you had never met Mama?" Ari wasn't sure if her questions were getting too personal, but Papa was always so reluctant to talk about his family. Sometimes she felt like she was missing a whole part of herself.

"I never would have married her under any circumstance, but that didn't keep my father from blaming Mama for ruining one of his biggest business deals."

"It must have been really awful for Mama, with your parents I mean."

"I was their only child, Arianna, the only one who could carry on the family name, and I had the nerve to bring your

Mama into their house and say that I wanted to marry her. They tried everything to dissuade me. They even enlisted Jennifer's help to demonstrate to Mama how she could never fit into proper society."

An audible gasp escaped from Ari's throat as she imagined what it must have been like for Mama, walking into the big Sea Cliff house and being set upon by a savage hoard of Brittanies. Papa had driven Ari by the house once, and she thought it a forbidding place with its iron-gated doors and windows and its thick granite walls. She thought it looked more like a fortress than a home, and in a way it was.

"The last time I saw my father alive," Papa continued, "we were screaming at each other. He said that women like Mama were okay for mistresses but certainly not worthy of bearing Heywood children. He said that if I married Mama, I was no longer his son. I said that I would never forgive him for the way he treated Mama and that he was no longer my father."

"And you never talked to him again after that?"

"No."

"What about your mother?" Ari asked. "Was she ever nice to Mama?"

"I think in her own way she tried to be kind to Mama, but she never was able to stand up to my father. I wish . . ." He didn't finish the thought.

"Mama told me once that you wanted to be an ambassador like an uncle of yours. Was she the reason you never became one?"

"I wanted to be just like my Uncle James. He was my mother's brother. I was closer to him than I ever was to my own father."

"You didn't answer my question, Papa," she reminded him.

"Let's just say that marrying your Mama wasn't the wisest career move a diplomat could make, but it was the best decision I ever made," he replied. "I'm not saying that you should give up everything for someone, but for the right person, some sacrifices are worth making. But let's not mention any of this to Mama. She's not responsible for the circumstances of my career, but she would blame herself if she knew."

"Papa, can I ask you something else?"

"Of course. You can ask me anything. Except female stuff . . . that's all your mama." He laughed and Ari giggled.

"How did you know Mama was the one worth sacrificing for?" Papa sat back in his seat, his blue eyes sparkled and Ari knew his mind was no longer in the car.

"When I met your Mama, I felt like I had known her my whole life. It was unlike anything I'd ever felt before." Ari cocked her head to the side, studying his profile. "I'm sorry I can't give you a better answer, Ari. I just don't have one."

At five past eight the warning bell rang, and Ari and Papa said goodbye. He didn't drive off right away but watched her descend the stairs to the little courtyard in front of the main entrance. She looked so tiny as she opened the heavy glass door and disappeared into the belly of the whale. If only he could vanquish her enemies for her, like when she was his little baby girl and he'd chase away the monsters from under her bed and inside her closet with just a flash of his Eveready "*light-ray.*" Still, there might be something he could do, if only in the background.

Once inside, Ari joined the steady stream of students who were migrating down the wide hallway that separated the offices from the school library, keeping to the edge and staring at the wall as she walked. For a while she busied herself counting the cinder blocks that rose in monotonous gray lines to the acoustic ceiling but stopped when she nearly collided with the glass cabinet that held the school's athletic trophies. Among the gleaming trophies, which Principal Hayes required to be polished weekly, were photographs of the smiling young students, mostly boys of course, whose teams had won the awards.

She continued on, past a drooping rubber tree plant that thirsted for water, an announcement board about college applications, an inspirational banner about school pride that hung over a garbage can, a large portrait of President Johnson hanging on a red, white, and blue background under big block letters that invited boys to join the R.O.T.C., and a hand-drawn poster surrounded by twists of brightly colored crepe paper announcing Friday night's dance after the football game.

When she finally reached the quad, she broke off from the herd and skirted around the edges until she reached the Arts and Humanities building. No Brittany yet. She took a deep breath and entered cautiously. She expected to find a group of students waiting for her at her locker, but there were only a few students in the hall, all retrieving items from their own lockers. They smiled casually as Ari passed but showed no apparent interest in her now well-publicized troubles. Brian Murphy gave her kind of an odd look, but then Brian, or *Murph the Surf* as he was known around school, was one of those hippie surfer types who *smoked* his breakfast and perpetually wore an odd look. It probably didn't mean anything.

She opened her locker slowly, remembering the shock of the previous day, and retrieved her books for her morning classes. Still no Brittany. Perhaps things wouldn't turn out as badly as she feared. Perhaps she might not even run into Brittany today. Perhaps Paul McCartney was going to call tonight and ask her out on a date.

Returning to the quad, Ari took a direct path this time right through the center, stopping here and there to greet the groups of threes and fours who were engaged in a buzz of simultaneous conversation, hoping to give the impression that she had been completely unaffected by yesterday's events. Usually the conversations before school were lively and gregarious and focused on sports or Friday night's dance or which boy was going to ask which girl to the dance. Today the conversations sounded more like the casual small talk in which theatre patrons engage while waiting for the curtain to rise on a memorable production. No one mentioned Brittany.

"Ari, wait up!" a voice called from behind her, and before she could turn around Meghan O'Leary came bounding up beside her.

"Aren't you afraid to be seen with me?" Ari said, a little disappointed that her best friend was nowhere to be found yesterday when she needed her most.

Meghan frowned at the tone of Ari's voice. "Ari, I was absent yesterday. Don't you remember? I had my wisdom teeth pulled on Saturday. I didn't know anything about what happened until I got to school today. Why didn't you call me last night?"

"I'm sorry," Ari returned. "I guess I was afraid you had abandoned me like everyone else. When you didn't call me, and Jen and Jess didn't call, I guess I didn't know what to think. I should have known better," she added.

Meghan smiled her big, toothy smile, making her half dozen freckles dance, and her auburn pageboy bounce. "Didn't you even notice that I wasn't in Government class?"

"No. I spent most of the day looking at my feet!" Ari replied.

"Well, I have to turn in my note at the front office before the bell. Do you want to come with me?"

"That's okay," Ari said. "I think I'll go to class."

"Okay. See you after Government." Meghan whirled around and quick-stepped her way to the office, calling over her shoulder, "Hang in there!" Ari was glad to know that at least one of the fifteen hundred students in her school wasn't laughing at her.

She continued her slow, casual walk to the Math and Science building, hoping that no one would notice the exaggerated length of her strides. She could see the door to the building not twenty yards ahead. Still no Brittany. Maybe she was absent today. She quickened her pace a little until she was only a few feet from the door and the safety of the teachers who were in their classrooms preparing for the day's lessons. That's when it happened.

"Arianna Heywood!" Brittany yelled. Ari turned to face a wildly gesticulating, long-sleeved, bright pink sweater and matching mouth, both of which were way too loud for a school day. Brittany was screaming something about Ari ruining her car, and how she would have to pay for it, and how normal people wouldn't behave like that, and only a stupid, backward native girl from a stupid, backward island would. A gallery of spectators had already formed, some looking horrified, but most smiling and enjoying the show.

"Well, Ari, say something!" Brittany's tone was menacing.

Ari dropped her books on the ground, put her hands on her hips and slowly tapped her right Capezzio while steadily fixing her gaze on Brittany's purple face. She had a vague feeling that something was going on here, something more than a doll and a bit of glue, but she couldn't quite put her finger on it.

"Well!" the pink sweater screamed again.

An abrupt stillness had settled over the quad, much like the eerie silence before a tornado or a volcanic eruption. Everyone was waiting to see what Ari would do next. She dropped her hands from her hips and slowly walked toward Brittany, hoping something really clever would pop into her head on the way. When she was just a foot or two away, she stopped, smiled, and opened her mouth to speak, not having the faintest idea what words would emerge. Before she had a chance to find out, a boy in the crowd shouted, "What are you so mad for, Brittany? You started it!"

Ari watched the color drain from Brittany's face but return just as suddenly.

"I'm sure Ari just figured that if you took all that trouble to buy one of those dolls, you probably wanted it back *permanently,*" the voice added. The emphasis on the word permanently drew laughter from the crowd.

Ari tried to identify the owner of the voice, but Brittany, who had whirled around to face her new adversary, blocked her view. All she could see were snatches of long blond hair hitting the collar of a pale blue oxford button down and one muscular shoulder and one blue eye. She walked forward a few steps more, straining to see around Brittany, who stood motionless, not yet responding to the voice. Finally, Brittany spoke.

"Oh, come on, Jason," she said in a voice turned syrupy sweet. "I know you're only joking, but this isn't funny."

Ari couldn't believe her ears or her eyes once she managed to maneuver through the crowd. The voice belonged to Jason Caldwell. Jason Caldwell—most popular boy on campus. Jason Caldwell—captain of the football team and the boy Brittany most wanted to date. Ari knew Jason. They had spoken often in last period Art class, but Jason Caldwell was untouchable. He went out with a lot of girls but never settled on any one of them for his girlfriend. He had once asked Ari to a party when she first arrived in San Francisco, but she had turned him down. She didn't want to be just another one of his trophies, or anyone else's for that matter. He also had a reputation for drunken parties and fast friends, and Ari wanted no part of that Not that you could find a party where there wasn't some drinking going on. But Jason's parties went over the line, at least so the rumors said.

Now as Ari stared at him in amazement and he smiled back, she didn't know what to think. Maybe Jason wasn't anything like the stories that circulated around the campus. Or maybe this was the work of the Gods. (That would please Mama.) Whatever the case, she'd have to find out later. The final warning bell had sounded. Only three minutes to get to class.

As quickly as the crowd had gathered around the combatants, it dispersed, along with Brittany, to engage in school business as usual. Ari stood motionless, returning the congratulatory smiles of passersby, and the bewildered expression on Meghan, who had returned from the office just in time to witness the strange turn of events. Ari still thought she must be dreaming until Jason approached her. "We better get to class before we both end up in the office with tardy slips," he said with a casualness that belied any of the previous drama. He retrieved her books from where they still lay in a heap on the pavement, tucked them inside his elbow, and led the still disbelieving Ari to class.

They entered the Math and Science building and stood before the Physics room door. Ari could see Mrs. Thomas at the blackboard writing out the problem of the day, and she knew she had a minute or two more before she needed to take her seat. "Thank you for what you did back there," she said. "But why? Why did you do it?"

"I don't know. Maybe because you're never afraid to stick up for other kids when Brittany goes after them. Or maybe because I wish I had the nerve to glue a hula dancer to her car. You're a campus legend, Ari. Everybody knows what you did."

"Really? How could they all know? Brittany was ranting so crazy, I wasn't even sure what she was talking about."

"We all knew yesterday."

"Yesterday!"

"Sure. She drove out of school with the hula dancer bobbing around in her rear window, and every kid in the parking lot saw it. She was just waving and laughing. She had no idea that everyone was laughing at her, not you. You should have been there."

Ari studied him as he walked away. He was broad shouldered and athletic and was just about the closest thing she'd ever seen to Troy Donahue or Steve McQueen. She never thought that a high school boy who looked that good could be that nice. Maybe it wasn't fair to have judged him by the rumors.

"Are you planning to join us today, Ms. Heywood," Mrs. Thomas's voice called from inside the classroom. There was laughter from the class. This time she didn't mind.

Ari could barely concentrate on her classes. A vague feeling of excitement was building in her, the kind that starts in the pit of your stomach and spreads through your insides like a great overture building to a crescendo, announcing that some extraordinary experience awaits you behind the curtains, and you won't know what it is until they slowly draw open and reveal the stage. She couldn't wait to get home and tell Mama and Emma. Even Mama might not believe this one, and Mama thought there were no limits to the possibilities in life.

At lunchtime Ari met up with Meghan and the two of them walked to the cafeteria as usual. "I talked to Jess in English class today, Ari. She and Jen are really sorry they didn't call you last night. They didn't know if you wanted to talk to anyone, and they figured you'd call them if you did. Don't be mad at them."

"I'm not," Ari replied. "I'm too happy to be mad at anyone just now." When they reached the cafeteria, they took seats opposite each other at their usual table overlooking the quad. Ari left just enough room for Jason to sit next to her in case he decided to forgo his customary seat at the far end of the table. She and Meghan were used to watching him there, his surfer blond hair and easy charm making a striking impression on all the girls. It seemed effortless for him, being the center of attention in the group, and Ari wondered if he ever had to think about what he said before he said it or worry about what he said afterward. He just seemed so comfortable with who he was. Ari felt like that whenever she was on the Island. She wished she could feel like that all the time.

Jason arrived carrying his institutional green plastic tray piled high with noodle surprise (everyone joked that the only surprise was that you didn't throw up after eating it) and Jello medley, which was a fancy name for all the different Jellos that were left over from previous lunches. He headed straight for Ari and sat down next to her. It was his first public announcement of his intentions. The first of many, Ari hoped.

The conversation around the table was boisterous and familiar. Mostly, they talked about last Thursday's Government test and how Bruce Danforth had to complete an extra-credit paper by Friday if he hoped to play in the football game that night, and how everyone would help him out because the game was for the conference championship, and he was their quarterback. And they talked about the dance afterward and how the school's social committee had raised enough money from car washes and donut sales to hire a live band and how there was a rumor going around that the band was going to be Country Joe and the Fish. Jason said that it was going to be the best dance of the year because they would all be celebrating their second conference championship in a row, but when he said the part about it being the best dance of the year he was looking straight at Ari. She wondered if Jason was working up to asking her to the dance, and she periodically shot secret glances at Meghan across the table, signaling her excitement.

Suddenly the table grew silent. Ari looked up and saw Brittany and Meredith Sweeny (Brittany never went anywhere alone) standing there with their lunch trays. The kids around the table were fairly spread out, and someone would have to shift over to make room for two more. Ari glanced first at Meghan and then all around the table at the people who were waiting for her to make the first move. "*Take the high road whenever the opportunity presents itself,*" she could hear Papa say. "*In the end, it is always the position of superior strength.*"

Ari moved closer to Jason, who smiled back at the beautiful girl he once thought had some nerve turning him down for a date. Brittany took the space that opened at the far end of the table and the two girls neither spoke to each other nor made eye contact after that, but it was clear to everyone that Ari was in command. When the bell rang ending lunch, Meghan shot Ari a look that said *you better call me tonight,* and Ari and Jason got up from the table, threw their lunch remains in the garbage, and joined the line of students who filed out of the cafeteria. Jason slipped his arm casually around Ari's waist, and she responded in kind. That's when she knew for sure—*he's going to ask me to the dance.*

Emma had arrived at school early in case Brittany decided to ambush her sister when the teachers weren't looking. She was ready to put the little princess in her place if need be. At the very least she wanted to be there so Ari wouldn't have to make the long walk through the courtyard and up the front steps all alone with everyone's eyes on her. When the bell rang, Emma got out of the car, making her presence known to all who emerged through the front entrance. "Well, isn't that typical," Emma said to herself as she watched Ari come bounding through the doors, laughing and animated, surrounded by half a dozen friends. "Somehow she always lands on her feet!"

"Emma, I'll be right there," Ari yelled when she spotted her. She said a hurried goodbye to Jason, who headed to football practice, yelling over his shoulder, "I'll call you tonight," and she signaled Meghan that she'd call her right after. Then she ran up the stairs and jumped in the car, saying nothing until she and Emma were well off school grounds.

"Okay, Ari, give! You seem to be the most popular girl on campus. What happened?"

"You'll never believe it!" Ari exclaimed and told Emma the whole story.

4

THE PHONE RANG and Mama and Papa eyed each other as both their daughters raced across the living room to the tall, walnut secretary in the corner, each hoping that the call was for her. Emma reached the phone first and swooped up the receiver before Ari could grab it, flashing a victorious smile at her sister that quickly turned to a frown when she heard the voice on the other end. She handed the phone over to Ari with a caution not to be too long as she was expecting a call from Roger.

It was apparent to everyone who eavesdropped that the call was from Jason. Ari had her *boy voice* on, even though she didn't know she had one. She spoke a few words into the receiver and then excused herself and bounded up the stairs to the privacy of her bedroom, shouting over her shoulder for someone to hang up the downstairs phone. "Looks like the patient has made a full recovery," Papa teased, pleased that events had favored his little girl.

"Well, I hope there won't be any repercussions for that bit of glue in Brittany's car," Mama commented. "I understand that her father has somewhat of a temper."

"I've already had a call from Mr. Kramer at the office today," Papa admitted.

"Why didn't you tell me? Was he very angry?"

"Yes, but we came to an understanding."

"What sort of understanding?"

"Tomorrow at school Brittany will make a full apology to Ari. A public apology!" Papa said with uncharacteristic vehemence. He said nothing more but just stared silently into the firelight. Mama knew better than to press him for details when that cloud was over him, so she nestled closer to him and resumed her reading.

Ari emerged from her bedroom about an hour later and floated down the stairs to rejoin her family in the living room. Before entering, she stopped at the large vintage Art Deco poster on the wall by the entrance to the room. She smiled at the lady who was walking alongside the Blue train on a platform, elegantly dressed in a long, tapered burgundy gown with fur-trimmed overcoat and long pheasant feathers streaming from her nearly brimless hat. The lady was accompanied by her Russian Wolfhound whose leash she carried in one gloved hand while she carried a small round leather jewel case in the other. She had a smile on her face, not a broad grin, more like a Mona Lisa smile. Ari always imagined she was meeting her secret lover on the train and that he was taking her away for a torrid affair in Venice. "Someday," Ari sighed.

Ari had changed into her long red kaftan, the one with the multi-colored embroidery on the shoulders, that Mama had bought along with several others when they lived in India. Kaftans were just beginning to show up in the hippie fashions that were overtaking the Mod look, but Ari wasn't wearing it to be fashionable. It was just really comfortable. It fell loosely to her ankles just above her bare feet and allowed her to lie on the floor or flop down in chairs or sit in any position she pleased, unlike mini-skirts or even the more moderately short a-lines, both of which she loved for their style but not their convenience.

Mama and Papa were still cozied up together on the sofa, wearing soft, warm, comfortable clothing to match their moods. Emma and James were on the floor at their feet, building an elaborate fort out of Lincoln Logs. There was a warm apple-wood scent enveloping the room from the fire that blazed in the fireplace and just a hint of Papa's pipe tobacco still clinging to his clothes.

"Look, Ari. Look at my fort. It's the *bestest* fort in the whole world. Even Georgie can't build *gooder* forts!" he exclaimed, sticking his little chin out in that funny impression of Papa that he did when he was trying to make a point. Everyone smiled and braced themselves for another eruption of puppy stories that spewed forth from James every time he thought of an excuse to mention Georgie's name, but Ari diverted his attention just in time with a suggestion that he man the fort with his toy soldiers. Then she flopped down on one of the four overstuffed club chairs that bracketed the sofa and the fireplace, leaned her head back, and smiled at the ornate plaster molding that encircled the chandelier, waiting for someone to have the good sense to ask her what she was smiling about.

"So, what did you and Jason talk about for a whole hour?" Mama asked in a mischievous voice.

"I wasn't on the whole time with Jason. I had to call Meghan right after."

Ari was so excited by her accounting of the conversation, especially about Jason asking her to the dance, that she didn't notice the slight change in Mama's expression when she got to the part about how interested Jason was in her life. "Jason said that he thought he'd seen a lot of the world until he met me. He wanted to know everything about the places we'd lived and about the Island."

"Talking about the Island is what got you into trouble in the first place," Mama warned. "Do you think it's wise to be telling Jason too much about it?"

"Oh, Mama, this is different. Jason is different."

"Perhaps." Mama caught the sudden frown on Ari's face. "But why ruin a celebration with such serious talk," she added hastily. "Jason is probably everything you say he is. Just don't expect him to be more than he can be at his age. That's not fair to him."

"I understand, Mama," Ari returned automatically, but Mama knew that she didn't.

5

IT TOOK FOREVER for Friday night to arrive, and almost as long for Ari to choose what to wear for her date with Jason. Finally, she settled on her short red fitted and flared dress—the one that hugged her small waist and floated out at the bottom when she moved. It had a black lamb's wool mandarin collar and matching cuffs and little silver filigree buttons and loops that ran all the way up the bodice and was reminiscent of the romantic period costumes of Dr. Zhivago. Ari looked even more exotic than usual when she wore the dress. She was not unaware of the effect it had on others.

The dress lay neatly on the bed, right next to Jason's letterman jacket that he had given her after school. "You better take this," he had said, slipping it off and handing it to her. "I wouldn't want my girl getting chilled up in the stands tonight."

"My girl." He had called her *"my girl."* Jason always knew the perfect thing to say and do. It was way too soon to give Ari his school ring and ask her to go steady, but when she entered the stadium tonight wearing his jacket, the whole student body would know that she wasn't just one of those girls he took off the shelf for a weekend and then never dated again. She was special and, best of all, Brittany would know it.

Ari glanced over at the jacket and then back at the full-length mirror where she stood wearing only her cream-colored bra and pantyhose and the silk, lace-trimmed petti-pants that had replaced slips when hemlines got shorter. Then she stepped into her black leather boots and pulled up the zippers to her knees and shared a giggle with the image of the Playboy Bunny that smiled back at her from the mirror. She struck a few silly poses and spoke into an invisible microphone in her breathiest voice. "My favorite turn ons are moonlit beaches and picnics by the lake and men who give me diamonds for absolutely no reason at all."

"Better not let Papa catch you," Emma teased from the doorway of their adjoining bathroom. "He'll lock you away in the attic until he marries you off to an old man with a white beard." Ari turned three shades of red.

"Remember when we were really little and used to pretend we were Marilyn Monroe and Judy Holiday?"

"Yeah. We didn't even know who Judy Holiday was, but we liked her name," Ari recalled.

Emma joined her sister in front of the mirror and studied herself in her heather blue V-neck and faded jeans. Nothing exciting about the outfit, but it was comfortable, and it would do for a dark night at the El Rey Theatre. "This old mirror has shared a lot of secrets with us that I wouldn't want leaving the bedroom," she said.

"No kidding," Ari agreed. "I wonder how many lipstick kisses we've left on it."

Before Emma could answer, the door chimes rang. "Roger's here, Ari. You better hurry and get dressed, or we won't have time to drop you at school before the movie." Jason had to suit up for the football game an hour early so Ari was going to sit with Meghan, Jen, and Jess at the game and then go home with Jason after the dance.

"Okay," she called after her sister who had already disappeared into the hallway.

Ari slipped on her dress, pulling the loops over the buttons as quickly as she could and returned to the mirror to fix her hair. She parted it in the middle, twisted a handful of strands on each side and swept them back into a large silver clip that Mama had bought her last summer at a Renaissance Fair. Papa had refused to go with her to the fair, saying that the only thing worse than spending the day with a bunch of mimes was spending the day breathing scented candles with a bunch of mimes in jester costumes. He was uncharacteristically immovable on this point, so Ari had accompanied Mama instead.

The clip was filigree, matching her buttons, and shaped like butterfly wings. Ari regarded it now in the small hand mirror as she held it at just the right angle to catch the reflection of her back in the full-length mirror. "Perfect!" she said, thinking more about her life than her appearance.

"Are you ready yet, Ari?" Emma called from downstairs. "We have to go."

"I'm coming," she yelled back. She grabbed Jason's jacket, turned off the lights, and flew down the stairs.

Mama and Papa were in the living room waiting to inspect their daughters and remind Ari to be home at a reasonable hour. Now that Emma was in college, she no longer had a midnight curfew, and Ari didn't like the sudden inequality. But she'd be eighteen soon enough. "Ari, you look pretty!" James squealed with enthusiasm as she entered the living room.

"Thanks, James. You're pretty handsome yourself!"

James jumped up like a spring-loaded jack-in-the-box from his seat on the floor to give Ari a better view of his new pajamas, knocking over in the process a tall, hastily built tower he had constructed out of some kindling bits he'd found on the hearth. "See, Ari, puppies! Papa bought me puppy pajamas so I could pick out the puppy I get when we don't have to move so much." Ari glanced over at Papa, whose expression she couldn't decipher, and then back at James who was obviously feeling elated over tangible evidence that he was making some headway on his ceaseless quest for his very own puppy.

"Have you picked out a puppy yet?"

"I like this one!" he exclaimed, poking his belly-button and the fuzzy little black and white puppy that covered it. "He's just like Mr. Suti's dog." Mr. Suti was an Island farmer whose tri-color border collie, Masa, herded the chickens and just about anything else that moved, including his children when they were reluctant to return home from the lagoon at dinner time. Ari patted the collie as if it were real, then grabbed James around the waist and tickled his tummy until all the puppies were jumping up and down. When all was calm again, she slid into Jason's jacket, which was almost as big for her body as her smile was for her face and headed for the door.

"You kids be good now," Mama and Papa shouted after

their daughters, and Ari and Emma shouted back, "*You* kids be good now!" It was a family joke. Sort of.

Mama and Papa and James played Candyland and Uncle Wiggly until bedtime. The games had belonged to the girls when they were James's age and had traveled around the world with them. At eight thirty they packed up the games. Then James rode on Papa's shoulders all the way upstairs and down the hall to Mama and Papa's room where he was plopped down into their big bed and told, if he was a really good boy, he could sleep there tonight.

It took a little longer than usual to get James to sleep. He kept interrupting Papa's reading with questions about the new puppy, trying to pin him down to a specific time for its purchase, but, in the end, he accepted Papa's promise that at some vague time in the not too distant future, he would buy him his puppy. After all, Papa always kept his promises.

"Are you sure it was wise to get James's hopes up about a puppy, Ethan? We're years away from settling in one place," Mary observed as she and her husband reclined before the fire on the thick Turkish carpet, enjoying their few precious hours of no responsibility.

"Perhaps, but this is the first really big thing he's ever wanted just for himself."

"All little boys want puppies, Ethan, especially when their best friend gets one first."

"I know, but I think it's more than that. I think James is beginning to feel the changes that are overtaking all of us. Emma's in college now and Ari will be there next year, and we'll probably be moving halfway across the world from them both." Mary heard the sadness in his voice and drew closer to him.

"James is so close to his sisters, especially Ari," he continued. "I think he needs someone to love who won't be leaving him any time in the near future."

"He has us," Mary offered.

"It's not the same. I think James needs somebody that belongs only to him." Mary didn't respond. She knew that Ethan was probably right about James, but right now she was more worried about her husband's disquiet than her son's. He had been brooding about something for a few weeks now, maybe not noticeably to anyone else, but she knew the signs. Perhaps he was experiencing the first pangs of separation anxiety that all parents go through when their children leave the nest.

Ethan stared at his wife as she lay beside him, bathed in firelight, only half covered by her sarong and the wayward strands of hair that fell over her breasts and down to her belly. She was even more beautiful than that moment he first saw her walking through Sproul Plaza on her way to the campus library. He had followed her that day into the library and up the circular iron steps to the stacks. He remembered thinking how surprising it was to see such a beautiful foreign girl gaining admittance to the Honors stacks, a fairly egghead-dominated place at Berkeley in those days. But the moment she spoke, he saw not only her beauty but her intelligence and worldliness as well. He loved her instantly and expected everyone else to love her as he did, but his family never behaved toward her as he had wished. *"That's what we get for not insisting you go to Stanford,"* his father had screamed in a public tirade that hurt and humiliated Mary. Ethan vowed never to let her be hurt like that again. He couldn't keep that promise, of course, and that was the greatest sorrow of his life. "I love you, Mary," he whispered.

"I need nothing more," she whispered back, and they lay wrapped in each other until just before midnight when they would return to being parents again.

6

SOMETHING HAPPENED TO high schools on Friday nights. They seemingly transformed themselves from cold, gray, generic institutional structures that could just as easily have been hospitals or police stations, insurance offices or insane asylums, to places with identity and excitement and anticipation of great things to come. Tonight, the big glass doors were welcoming, not forbidding, and the block walls were majestic. The atmosphere was electric and even President Johnson seemed like a loving uncle smiling down from the wall and not a war chieftain sending young men to die in Vietnam. Papa said it wasn't really fair to blame President Johnson for the war, like it was all his doing. He did need to put an end to it, and right away, but that people should also remember all the Civil Rights legislation he fought for and won. Papa said that presidents shouldn't be judged on the thickness of their hair or the charisma they exuded giving speeches they didn't write. They should be judged on the totality of their actions. Ari guessed he was right, and she smiled at President Johnson as she passed by.

Ari didn't need to watch where she was going. She was part of a river of mostly red and black flowing to a single destination. Along the way she chatted with familiar faces, sometimes friends and sometimes just students she knew from English class or Government or French 4. Everyone noticed the jacket she was wearing, whether they said so or not, and she made sure that her long hair didn't obscure the name monogrammed on the front in script lettering, *Jason*.

Ari and Meghan climbed the bleacher stairs and moved slowly along the walkway until they reached the center section and the shouts of *"up here"* from Jen and Jess who were saving them seats. Ari glanced up at the lights and the thin layer of mist that was gathering in the chill around them and was glad she had Jason's jacket to keep her warm. She could smell the Jade East that permeated the ribbed knit collar even in the outdoors.

The marching band was already on the field trying to form a giant V for victory though it turned out more like a misshapen U. It didn't matter. Everybody cheered really loud anyway. They were playing fight songs and pop music, only a few bars of which were intelligible and, of course, the school song, whose words were known only to a select group of teachers and choir kids.

Suddenly, the pompom girls came screaming out onto the field, shaking their red and black pompoms and anything else that moved. They formed a line opposite the cheerleaders, and with them held a paper banner with a victory sign on it, painted in the shape of a hippie peace symbol. Then a shrill voice came over the loudspeaker to announce the football team coming onto the field. Everyone stood and cheered as the red and black clad football players crashed through the banner and ran toward the fifty yard line. They whooped and hollered and waved their helmets in the air like warriors about to go into battle. Ari searched for Jason in the sea of red jerseys and spotted him by his number. He was facing the stands, and Ari knew he was searching for her. When he found her, he smiled and waved his helmet and then turned to get final advice from the coach.

Ari only saw half the game, the half when Jason was on the field. She spent the rest of the time sending silent signals to him on the bench when their defense was playing or dragging Meghan to the refreshment stand so she'd have an excuse to casually parade her jacket in front of the student body and the line of pompom girls. Meghan didn't mind though. She was always up for just about anything.

The football game was one of those nail-biting, down to the last second games. By the end of the fourth quarter, Jason had already caught several passes, including one for a sixty-yard gain when Bruce Danforth faked a hand-off and the defense went for it. But it was Jason's last second reception in the end zone of a perfect pass from Bruce that ultimately won the game. The fans screamed with voices already hoarse from constant cheering in the cold night air, and Jason and Bruce were mobbed by their teammates. Meghan and Ari were jumping up and down, alternately hugging each other and anyone else in the stands who had temporarily surrendered their *cool* to the unfettered exhilaration of the moment. It was going to be a wonderful dance, and Ari was glad she had worn her sassy red dress.

When they entered the gymnasium, Ari and Meghan headed to the girl's locker room and the long row of mirrors where girls stood three deep fixing windblown hair, reapplying the pale, sometimes even white lipstick that was ushering in the so-called *natural look*, and sharing packs of minty gum that they hoped would make them kissable during the slow dances. "Look at her," Meghan whispered and slyly darted her eyes in the direction of Meredith Sweeny who was busy adding to the Kleenex she had already stuffed in her bra. "She walked in here an A-cup. Bet she walks out a D."

"Oh, you're horrible," Ari whispered back, and joined Meghan in a muffled fit of giggles. Ari was already a 32-C, just like Mama, so she didn't need any padding. And Meghan was one of those wonderfully secure girls who liked her flat chest and everything else about herself, which made it impossible for others not to like her too.

When they had taken their turn at the mirror and were sure that everything was in its right place, the girls reentered the gym and walked to the other side of the room where a group waited outside the Boy's Locker Room for their boyfriends. The gym was undecorated except for some large banners, which had been pre-made earlier that week by the rally committee in hopes of a conference championship and hastily hung around the large room at the close of the game. The band was playing "Get Off of My Cloud" and the girls were gathering on one side of the gym and the boys on the other. The girls were wondering if anyone would make the long walk across the floor to ask them to dance, and the boys were wondering if they would get shot down when they did, and everyone hoped that if the worst happened, nobody else would notice.

There were only a few couples on the dance floor, and Ari watched one of them awkwardly jerking to the beat of the Stones. The boy was so pale that he was nearly albino, and his girlfriend was overweight and unattractive, and together they were the source of much amusement around school. But they were seniors who had loved each other since their freshman year, and Ari envied them their romance. In a funny sort of way, they were like Mama and Papa, but no one else would have understood the comparison.

From behind her, Ari heard voices and she and Meghan turned to see boys coming out of the locker room door. Meghan had a crush on Adam Kent, one of Jason's friends on the team. She had tried flirting with him in English class and periodically over lunch in the cafeteria, but he didn't seem to take any notice.

Five more minutes passed before Ari caught a glimpse of Jason's shaggy, blond hair through the maze of bodies. She could hear his laughter through the clamor of voices all talking at once. She wondered if actually being with Jason would feel half as good as the anticipation. Finally he was there, with cheeks red over tan and hair wet from his post-game shower. He stared at Ari and smiled, "I hope you're looking that beautiful just for me," he said easily, and for just an instant Ari wondered if it was a bit too easy, but she didn't care.

She smiled back at Meghan as Jason took her hand and led her to the dance floor. He was wearing her favorite blue oxford shirt, the one he wore last Tuesday that made his blond hair blonder and his blue eyes bluer. She had casually mentioned that she liked him in that shirt and wondered if that was why he chose to wear it now. Or was it only girls who were that romantic?

They got to the middle of the floor just as the music ended and the first notes of "Johnny Be Good" began. Ari felt a little disappointed. She had been waiting all week to slow dance with Jason. Now she'd have to wait a little longer to find out what it would feel like when he held her and, maybe, kissed her for the first time. After two more fast songs, designed to get everyone dancing instead of standing, the dance floor was crowded with couples.

Meghan was dancing with someone, Ari couldn't tell who, but it wasn't Adam Kent. Then the band called a ladies' choice. She watched Meghan cross the dance floor to where Adam stood with a group of his friends, ladling punch out of the punchbowl. Ari held her breath and waited while Meghan said something to Adam. He got a queer expression on his face, almost startled, and then put his glass down and followed Meghan to the floor. It wasn't until later, when she and Meghan managed a trip to the girl's bathroom that Ari found out what had happened. Apparently, Adam had wanted to ask Meghan out for some time but was afraid that maybe he'd read her signals wrong and would get shot down. After all, she was the sort of girl who was nice to almost everyone. Luckily for Adam, Meghan was also the sort of girl who wasn't afraid to go after what she wanted. So, when the band announced ladies' choice, she marched right up to Adam and, in front of all his friends, announced, "I want to dance with you. Don't tell me I walked all the way over here for nothing."

When Meghan told her this, Ari laughed so hard she cried. "Adam never stood a chance."

The band played the perfect mix of new songs and old, slow songs and fast, the best of the Beach Boys, the Beatles, Johnny Mathis, and the Righteous Brothers and, of course, The Doors' new song, "Light My Fire." When they played "Unchained Melody," Jason stopped dancing and stared at Ari, running the fingers of one hand through her hair and holding her tight with the other hand at the small of her back. Then he moved his hand slowly from her hair, to her cheek and finally to her chin, which he lifted gently until her lips were just a breath away from his, and then he kissed her. It was not a long kiss or a passionate one; the chaperones wouldn't have allowed that. But it was deep enough that Ari knew there was more to come, and that pleased her and scared her all at the same time. Without speaking, she wrapped her arms around his neck and buried her face in his shoulder. He responded by tightening his hold on her.

They danced almost every dance that night, and Ari rarely took her eyes off Jason except to send surreptitious glances toward Meghan, who eagerly received and returned them. And all through the night she tried to imprint memories, as Mama had always done, sensory memories that she would keep for a very long time. The sound of Jason's breathing, the scent of his cologne, the muffled sound of his voice when she listened to it with her ear pressed up against his chest, the heat of his body escaping through his shirt, and the song that played when he kissed her—a song that would remind her of this night every time she heard it again, which would be often because she intended to buy it first chance she got.

The dance ended at ten-thirty, and Ari couldn't remember two-and-a-half hours ever going that fast except on the Island. When the last song was over and the lights went up, she excused herself, and she and Meghan scurried to the girl's bathroom for a freshen-up, a quick exchange, and a promise to call each other over the weekend for all the details. As she and Jason filed out the gymnasium doors with the rest of the student body, she saw Brittany just ahead with a boy she couldn't identify from the back. Ari had forgotten all about her.

"You don't have to be home until midnight. Do you want to go somewhere?" Jason asked as he opened the door of his ice blue Austin Healey and let Ari in.

"Where do you have in mind?" she asked.

"Oh, I don't know. You choose."

Ari knew very well what Jason was hoping she'd say. Half the football team was already parked up on Twin Peaks with their girlfriends. But she still didn't know Jason all that well, and even though his small sports car afforded her some protection, she wasn't comfortable going up there. Instead she said, "I'm starving. I didn't eat much dinner. How about going to Mike's Drive-In. A bunch of the kids ought to be there."

"Great!" Jason said, barely showing his disappointment. "I could go for a burger and fries and a really thick milkshake."

"Me too!"

Jason burst out laughing. "I can see you're not one of those typical girls who plays at being all dainty while nibbling on carrot sticks."

"I'm a lot of things, Jason, but typical isn't one of them."

"You can say that again," he shouted over the noise of the engine as he gunned the little sports car out of the parking lot.

When they reached the drive-in, they decided to take a booth inside. Mike's still employed carhop girls who brought food outside on stainless steel trays that attached to half-rolled-up car windows, but it was a little chilly outside and Jason didn't like risking the trays scratching the paint on his Healey. They found a booth in the back where kids in their cars would be less likely to stare at them through the big picture windows, and they slid into the vinyl seats opposite each other.

Dirty dishes and half-eaten hamburgers still littered the speckled Formica table, but a waitress soon appeared with wash rag in hand to clean up the mess. The girl had a ruddy face and dirty blond hair made frizzy by too many runs to the kitchen. She couldn't have been more than eighteen, and she was spending her Friday night serving French fries to a bunch of teenagers. Ari smiled at her, but the waitress had run out of smiles for her customers hours before. She simply listened to their order without writing it down and disappeared in the direction of the kitchen where a shout to a short order cook produced the sizzle of two more hamburgers going on the grill.

"Why are you staring at me like that?" Ari asked when they were alone.

"I was just thinking how lucky I am to be sitting here with such a beautiful girl." Ari's heart skipped a beat.

"I was just thinking the same . . . well, not the beautiful girl part." Ari blushed and Jason reached across the table to take her hand, stroking his thumb over her smooth skin.

As midnight approached, Ari and Jason sat on her front drive sharing that awkward first date moment when he wanted to kiss her, *really* kiss her, but didn't know if he'd be rejected, and she wanted him to kiss her, but didn't want him to get the wrong idea. In the end, he gave her a long, but proper kiss, and she returned it. Then he walked her to the front door. Papa would be pleased with Jason's manners. She gave him a quick kiss on the lips before saying goodnight and bursting through the front door.

Ari stood by the radiator at the bottom of the stairs with her hands poised over the waves of heat that drifted up from its hissing and pinging metal. When she was sufficiently thawed out, she entered the living room with its pale flickering light that hours earlier had illuminated a good portion of the room but now barely escaped the fireplace.

Mama and Papa were lying on the floor, sofa pillows propped up behind them, an empty wine bottle on the end table, and two purple stained glasses on the hearth. "I don't need to ask you how your evening went," Mama smiled.

"I don't need to ask you how your evening went either, Mama."

"Don't be cheeky, little girl," Papa teased.

Ari slipped out of her jacket and folded it carefully over her arm. "Is Emma home yet?" she asked.

"She's waiting for you upstairs."

"Great!" Ari bent down and kissed Mama and Papa goodnight. Then with one quick glance at the painting over the fireplace, she whirled around and left the room, her sassy red dress flaring out one final time.

It wasn't long before Emma came into Ari's bedroom. She was already in her favorite Lanz nightgown, and she waited for Ari to put hers on, the one with the little red hearts that she had gotten for Christmas last year. Each Christmas Eve, the whole family went to sleep in new sleepwear, unfaded or roughened by laundering, and in fresh, sun-dried sheets that, weather permitting, had been hanging on an outdoor line all day.

"So? Spill it," Emma said and giggled as she settled herself comfortably on Ari's bed.

"Oh, Emma. It was all so wonderful," Ari said with a dreamy gleam in her eye as she prepared to tell her sister all about her night with *him.*

Over the years Ari and Emma had spent so many nights together, sitting on the bed opposite each other with their nightgowns tucked under their feet, sharing important events in their lives and tightening the bonds between them. Like that night in the London house after the horse races when they talked and talked until first light revealed the city's silhouette outside their bedroom window. Well, it wasn't just any old horse race. A friend of Papa's had invited the whole family to Royal Ascot, and it was the first really grown-up occasion to which Ari and Emma had ever been invited. And Mama, who always recognized a memory in the making, decided to go all out.

Several weeks prior to the event, Mama, Emma, and Ari went to James Lock and Co., a milliner at No. 6 St. James Street, which had been making hats for everyone from Lord Horatio Nelson to Hollywood movie stars since 1676. On first visits, clients were fitted with a conformateur, a funny hat-like device used to measure the contours of the head. The measurements were then kept on file so that hats of all types could be custom-made for regular clients without necessitating repeated visits to the shop. Ari remembered fondly the store clerk who set the conformateur on her head and, seeing the horrified expression on her face, discreetly assured her that the odd looking appliance was not the actual hat she would be wearing to Ascot. He was very kind and friendly, not at all what she expected from the stuffy gentleman in the dark conservative suit.

When the call finally came that the hats were ready, Mama hailed a taxi and the three Heywood ladies, as the clerk referred to them, rushed off to Lock's for the ceremonious unveiling. When they arrived, they were greeted enthusiastically by the same bald, stout gentleman. They exchanged pleasantries, and Mama commented on how well he looked despite the long hours of hat-making that always preceded Ascot. He commented on how lovely the young Heywood girls were in their Chesterfield coats and how he wished more young ladies still knew how to present themselves in public. Then he escorted them into a mirrored cubicle in which three extraordinary hats, created in the exaggerated style of Ascot, sat on velvet covered stands.

Ari fondly recalled hers was a pale-yellow straw hat with a large brim and a hatband, made from her floral silk dress fabric, wrapped around the crown then hanging down the back in two long sashes. Beautiful moiré cabbage roses of cream and pink and pale green festooned the front of the crown.

"This could be another all-nighter," Ari said. "You better get comfortable."

Emma stretched out on her side across the end of the bed, grabbed some pillows, and then curled into a fetal position around the pillows. "Now, tell me everything about your date!"

"It was perfect. The whole night was perfect," Ari began. And then she told Emma everything.

"It doesn't take you long to fall in love, does it, Ari," Emma teased.

"Well, I don't know about that, but it was the best first date I've ever been on."

Ari and Emma talked late into the night, about new boyfriends and old boyfriends, and how Emma's first love was Jean-Pierre, the housekeeper's son, who was handsome and dark and oh so French, and how he was sixteen and she was only eight, and how he let her down gently by sending her a single red rose with a note that said, *When you are a woman you will be more beautiful than any other in Paris. I will wait for you.* The rose and the note had their own special page in Emma's scrapbook. "I wonder what Jean-Pierre is like now, and if he's still so handsome," Emma said as a dreamy smile crossed her face, before she burst out laughing. They talked about that day in Singapore when they bought the bottle from the little boy with no shoes and how it was the first time they understood what real poverty meant and how they always felt really lucky after that to be born to Mama and Papa. All of the houses they'd lived in were grand but never so beautiful as the Great House back home on the Island. As the girls reminisced and imagined and giggled, Mama and Papa lay in their big bed, wrapped around their little boy, sometimes quietly reminiscing about celebrations of their own, but mostly basking in the one taking place down the hall.

7

SATURDAY MORNING DAWNED bright blue and crisply cold outside Ari's dormer window. There was a thickness to the air that forewarned a fog bank rolling in off the ocean by late afternoon, but Ari couldn't feel it. She was experiencing that Saturday morning moment when one first awakens and senses there are no responsibilities demanding a hasty departure from the bed. Cosseted under her down comforter and enveloped by its warmth, she felt much like whatever awaited her in the warming drawer of the giant commercial oven downstairs until, that is, James came bursting through the door, his mop of hair trying unsuccessfully to stay where Mama had put it as he ran full speed and hurled himself onto Ari's bed. He was already dressed for the day in his navy blue corduroys and gray woolen crewneck and saddle shoes that Mama had polished with Esquire to hide the scuffed toes.

"Ari!" James shouted. "Get up! I been waiting and waiting forever!" He stood up and straddling her chest, grabbed her right arm with both hands and tugged her into an upright position, falling down on his little round bottom in the process.

"I know, big guy," she mumbled from somewhere in the shadows of her nearly sleepless night.

"Get up, Ari. We're going to *Golding* Gate Park, 'member?" She was becoming fully lucid now. His cherubic face and serious demeanor spoke of a mission not yet accomplished, and she knew that his determination could not be thwarted.

"Get up, get up!"

Ari rolled out of bed and stumbled to the bathroom with James nipping at her heels like the Border Collie he dreamt of last night. When she got to the door, she stopped him in

68

his tracks, knelt to his level, gently grabbed his shoulders, and returned his grin with a big one of her own. "James, if you go downstairs and help Mama get the breakfast on the table, we can leave a lot sooner."

He thought about this for a moment. "Okay," he said cheerfully and bolted for the door.

Breakfast was a light meal of fruit and croissants for the older Heywoods and a bowl of Sugar Pops for James. Everyone knew they were on borrowed time. "It's been way too long since we spent the day together like this," Papa observed, grabbing his coffee cup for a final swallow.

"Best not complain, Ethan. Most teenagers wouldn't deign to be seen with their parents in public," Mama observed. "Especially on a Saturday."

"Oh, that's all right," Ari said. "Not much chance of running into any of our friends where we're going today," she said with a little smirk. In truth, she was glad to be spending the day with the family. Lately it seemed like everyone was dashing off in different directions and sometimes this caused her to miss the predictability of comings and goings from when she was younger.

Once underway, James sat between Ari and Emma in the back seat of the big black sedan, wiggling and jiggling and spewing out a verbal dissertation on the attractions of *Golding* Gate Park to everybody's amusement.

"And we can see the dinosaurs and the snakes and the octopus and the *agilators* and the . . ." But when they crossed Lincoln Avenue and entered the park, he fell silent, straining to see out the windows at everything that passed by. Ari pulled the sleeve of her turtleneck down over her hand and wiped away the condensation that obscured his view. She knew what he was looking for. He wanted to see the buffalo that roamed in a large meadow right in the middle of the park, more reminiscent of Plains Indians and prairie settlers and pioneer wagon trains traversing the heartland than a cosmopolitan city like San Francisco. But the buffalo were only one of the special attractions that brought thousands of city dwellers to the Park each day.

Golden Gate Park was a maze of streets, twisting and

turning through forests and meadows, manicured lawns and formal gardens, around duck ponds where little children fed Wonder Bread to the feathered inhabitants, and circumnavigating a large lake ready for boats and pedalos that could be rented for a day's outing. There was a children's park with a petting zoo and a beautiful old carousel with brightly painted horses, the Japanese Tea Garden with the old humped wooden bridge, and the DeYoung Museum, which housed magnificent art collections. There was also the aquarium, the planetarium, and, of course, the Natural History Museum. Not far from where the park met the Pacific Ocean on its western edge, there was the world famous San Francisco Zoo with its Monkey Island, the seal show, and the children's park filled with swings and gliders and twisty slides and old locomotive engines children spent hours climbing in and out of, much to the delight of sore-footed parents who enjoyed a restful respite on one of the many benches that surrounded the play area. Unsurprisingly, James wanted to visit every attraction in the park, and it would take all of Papa's skills to negotiate a sane agenda.

Finding a parking place at the museums on a Saturday was no easy task, and Ari had to hold tight onto James to keep him from bursting out the door before the car eventually came to a complete halt.

"Hurry, Papa. I wanna see the *pennylum*," James squealed. No one corrected him when he mispronounced words. He would grow up soon enough on his own.

James's "*pennylum*" was actually the Foucault pendulum, a two hundred thirty-five-pound brass ball, hanging from the ceiling in the main foyer in the museum complex. It swung in constant motion above a large round enclosure several yards wide, which had been constructed just below floor level. There was a series of red pegs standing in a circle around the edge of the enclosure, and every few minutes the pendulum struck one of them down. The entire apparatus was designed to demonstrate the earth's rotation.

James stood with his feet planted between iron posts on the bottom runner of the railing that ran all the way around the enclosure, rested his chin and elbows on the top, and waited for the pendulum to swing his way. Each time it did he swayed backwards into Ari whose body served as a kind of retaining wall, keeping him from toppling back onto the floor in a heap. They remained like this for some minutes, swaying back and forth until finally the giant brass pendulum found its next peg. The peg fell over, James echoed his joy off the polished marble walls and then took off toward the aquarium, the family in tow.

In the center of the aquarium's front foyer was another enclosure, rectangular this time, with an iron railing around it as well. But this railing wasn't meant just to keep children out of the exhibit; it was meant to keep the exhibit away from the children. There was a large dirt mound in the middle, lushly planted with tropical growth, and surrounded by a moat, all home to a rather sizable population of alligators. James was absolutely transfixed by the sight. He gave a little squeak every time an "*agilator*" moved and hugged Papa's leg as if the appendage could fend off a reptilian attack. Ari was sure he was reliving scenes from Peter Pan in his head.

Next James led them through the dark gray granite hallways to see the fish, some of which were quite familiar residents of the Island lagoons. Ari always felt a little homesick when she saw the resplendent array of reef fish, but the feeling didn't last long because James never stayed very long at any one window, except when he got to the octopus. The giant orange creature moved fluidly about the tank, more like an alien from outer space than a creature from earth.

James waited impatiently to put his fingerprints and breath marks all over the octopus window, just like the children who had gotten there before him, and Ari stood right beside him, holding his hand and squeezing it periodically. An old man walked by wearing the dark blue uniform of the maintenance crew, pushing a small cart containing brooms and brushes and rags and a bucket of cleaning solution. Ari didn't envy him his job keeping the aquarium glass and granite sparkling clean despite all the sticky-fingered children who came through each day, but from the cheerful tune the old man was whistling, he didn't seem to mind the work.

When James tired of the aquarium, he led the family

across the complex through a series of rooms until he found the displays of the Natural History Museum. Room after room housed pre-historic dioramas of cavemen and extinct creatures against painted backdrops of the Grand Canyon and other similar places. James liked the saber-toothed tiger the best, partly because he liked the ferocious feline, but mostly because he knew that Papa would sneak up behind him and growl like a tiger. He would scream and giggle, sending his voice echoing all over the hall.

When James announced it was time to go, the family left the complex by a side entrance past a skeleton of a giant whale hanging alongside the path. They paused there so that James could regale them with his scientific knowledge, some fact but mostly fiction, which sent Emma and Ari into muffled fits of laughter that they tried to hide, especially when he got to the part about a whale's favorite food being Pinnochio.

"Let's go to Stowe Lake now, Papa," he said, when he had completed his marine lecture. "I wanna drive a boat."

"Not today, James. It's too cold to be driving around in a boat," Papa answered.

"I get to say, Papa. I wanna go to Stowe Lake!" James spoke in a voice that bordered on tantrum.

Papa took his hand gently in his own and silently walked him through an opening in a tall oleander hedge to an empty patch of lawn that was waiting for warm weather and the picnickers that always came with it. He didn't want James to lose his dignity by being publicly disciplined. "James, we're not going to Stowe Lake today," he said emphatically but kindly. "I don't want the whole family getting sick, especially since Christmas is right around the corner."

"It is, Papa, really?" James asked, suddenly diverted from his tantrum.

"Yes, James. So, you understand why we can't risk the lake today. But what do you think about this? What if we have lunch and then head for Playland-at-the-Beach."

"Playland!" James shrieked. He didn't hear the giggles from the other side of the hedge.

"Yes," Papa grinned. "I don't think it would be as windy on

the midway, and if it got too cold, we could always go to the Fun House. Do you think that would work?"

"Yes, Papa, I do!"

"Then let's shake on it!" Papa said, extending his hand. They shook hands in a manly fashion and returned to the rest of the family to share the plan.

"Can we go to the seal restaurant, Papa?" James asked as the car pulled out of its parking place while another family waited, thankful for their good fortune to have come down this row at just the right time.

"Good idea, James," he replied. Actually, Papa had already called the Cliff House Restaurant and arranged for a table by the window overlooking Seal Rock, named for the hundreds of creatures occupying the rock that would hold James's attention long enough for the elder Heywoods to finish a meal.

Papa headed the car down Fulton to the Great Highway and Ocean Beach, where he turned right, and began the steep, windy climb up Point Lobos Avenue to the top of the cliff and the 1950's contemporary structure that perched precariously on its precipice. Ari didn't usually like architecture from this era. After the artistically detailed buildings in Europe and Asia, she found them spare and drab and wonting of character. But there was something about this building that was different. Mama said it had little to do with the appearance of the building and more to do with how the building felt. She said that the Cliff House was one of those special "ghosty" places, where you could just feel the spirits of those who came before you. Mama called that "*Spirit of Place.*" She said that not many people believed in such things, but she knew it was true.

There had been two Cliff Houses before this one, and several remodels along the way due to fires, dynamite explosions, and the ravages of time. The first was built in 1863 by Samuel Brannan, a prosperous Mormon Elder, using salvaged wood that he purchased from a ship that had foundered on the rocks just below the building site. The second was the architectural masterpiece by Adolph Sutro, Comstock millionaire and later mayor of San Francisco. Mark Twain had once praised it as one of the finest establishments of its kind in America. It was an opulent eight story French chateau filled with elegant public and private dining rooms, art galleries, reception halls, countless picture windows to catch the ocean views, and its very own railroad to transport the rich and famous to its doors. When the chateau burned down in 1907, Sutro's daughter Emma, built a neo-classic building in its place, which was purchased in 1952 by Playland's owner, George Whitney, and remodeled into its present structure.

There were two dining rooms in the Cliff House, the Marine and the Pacific, both filled with San Francisco memorabilia, live plants, and magnificent views of sandy beaches or the Dutch windmills of Golden Gate Park or freighters entering the Bay or James's favorite view, the seals that sunbathed just below the restaurant. They could have gone straight to their table, bypassing the others who waited patiently in the foyer for a Saturday afternoon seating. Papa's position and his frequent patronage of the Cliff House allowed for that. But both Papa and Mama believed that there was never any excuse for rudeness, so they waited as usual along with everyone else.

"It feels good to sit down," Mama said, when at last they were shown to their table. Ari didn't hear her. She was glancing at one of the several antique posters of men and women in old-fashioned bathing costumes lounging on the decks and bleachers of the old Sutro Baths, once standing adjacent to the restaurant but now only ruins. She was wondering what it must have been like back then. Certainly not like the over-chlorinated public pools of today where little children ran around screaming because they couldn't go back in the pool for a whole hour after eating. Public baths must have been far more romantic when Sutro and the other robber barons frequented them.

"I miss Sutro's," Mama said, eyeing the same poster as her daughter. "I can't believe it burned down last year."

Ari watched as Mama was idly stroking Papa's hand as she spoke. Papa was watching James, who was standing at the window next to Emma's chair, engaging her in a conversation about the seals and the Great White Sharks they attracted to the Bay. "I'm so glad you took Emma and me to Sutro's when you did, Mama. Otherwise we never would have seen it."

"Well, I always intended to bring you girls there, but at the time I was really just trying to think of a good place to take you ice skating."

"When did they turn the baths into an ice-skating rink?"

"I don't really know. I always thought it was a very clever use of the space though. How many places can you go ice skating where you have to walk through a maze of museum rooms to get there?"

"I know. I remember walking in the front door expecting to see a typical oval rink and some bleachers." Ari replied. What greeted her instead was the first of many steep staircases down which patrons descended from level to level until they reached the steel-girdered enclosure at the bottom of the cliffs where the famous Sutro Baths once welcomed as many as twenty-five thousand swimmers to its pools five hundred feet long. If patrons tired of swimming, there was an amphitheater, a natural history museum, art galleries, and a cultural museum filled with Egyptian mummies, Aztec artifacts, totem poles from Alaska, and countless other treasures, some of which bordered on the unbelievable. Long after the Baths disappeared into history, the Museum remained, perhaps not in its original glory, but still a captivating place for people of all ages who wanted a one-of-a-kind experience. Ari's favorite gallery in the museum housed the Toothpick Carnival—the life's work of an ex-carnival man who spent years building giant rollercoasters and other carnival rides out of nothing but glue and hundreds of thousands of toothpicks.

A commotion brought Ari back to the table and fore-warned that James had tired of seal watching. She turned just in time to see his determined look. "I'm hungry!" he announced. "I wanna eat now, Ari."

"Come sit on my lap, James, and I'll butter you a piece of sourdough to tide you over."

"Okay," he smiled and climbed up. James occupied himself eating out the soft middles of two slices of bread and using the circular crusts to make giant eyeglasses, which he pressed to his face and peered through with a suitably comical expression.

"Your usual Crab Louie," the waitress smiled, setting the plate before Ari and continuing on around the table. Ari stared at the enormous mound of sweet, succulent Dungeness crab, which had been caught that very morning in the Bay, and the mixed greens, boiled egg slices and generous slathering of Louie dressing, and she quickly swallowed the saliva that was gathering in her mouth. "And for you, Mr. Heywood, Crab Louie with enough extra horseradish to cure the common cold."

"Thank you, Dolores. I don't know what I've done to deserve all this special attention," Papa said.

Eventually Mama got around to one of her favorite mealtime games. Ari used to think she played it to keep her children occupied so she could finish her food, but she suspected it was more than that now. "Favorite Saturday afternoons," Mama announced, setting the topic for today's remembrances.

Everyone thought for a moment. "Saturdays at the Louvre?" Emma ventured.

"Oh, I loved those," Ari agreed.

"What was your favorite part?" Papa asked her.

"For sure the scavenger hunts. I loved those sealed envelopes we'd find on our dressers in the morning. I felt like I was being sent on a secret spy mission or something every time I broke through the sealing wax and pulled out the cards."

"I really liked the Paris posting," Ari said. "There was always so much to do."

"It was one of my favorite postings as well," Mama agreed, but she had different reasons for liking it. Paris was more tolerant of mixed marriages than most other places were.

For the remainder of the meal the family continued their reminiscences of past adventures, returning briefly to Kathmandu and the antiquated train they rode that made clickety-clack sounds and smelled of exotic spices and then to the country pub on the River Ouse where the old farmer, who looked like Donald Crisp, came each night with his giant Irish Wolfhound for a pint and a ploughman's or a kidney pie. And there were all those lazy summers on the Island when the most taxing decision anyone had to make was which sarong to wear for dinner in the gardens. Periodically they interspersed stories in which James starred, and this kept him happy for an unusually long time.

Ari looked around the table at her family, all talking and laughing in that animated way people do when they are recalling the happiness in their lives, and she knew that no matter where her life took her, her family would never be very far away. Not really. She was glad that Mama and Papa had stuck with her through her teenage rebellions when there was nothing her parents could tell her that she didn't already know. And she was sure that they were glad she had outgrown the *Attitude*, as they used to call it. But even on her most rebellious days, she wouldn't have traded in her family for anyone else's.

By the time the check came James was wearing more of his hamburger on his face and hands than had ever reached his stomach, so Ari took him to the bathroom for a quick pee and a clean-up before heading down to Playland. Once outside she paused to breathe in the uniquely San Francisco air that swooped up from the ocean and filled her nostrils. It was a blend of salt water and seaweed and thick, cold air with just a hint of the impending fog in it. It was unlike any other sea smell Ari had ever encountered. Native San Franciscans claimed that the unique atmosphere that settled over their city was responsible for the hard crust and soft centers of the famous sourdough bread baked there. She didn't know if that was true; she only knew that she could make a meal out of that bread and never want for anything more.

It was only a short ride down the hill to Playland, which was a good thing because James had done all the sitting he was going to do. A romp through the amusement park was what he needed. They parked the car and entered the midway from the Balboa St. side at Bull Pup's Enchiladas, a San Francisco institution that for over four decades had been selling the fiery treats to customers brave enough to eat them. Papa stopped abruptly in front of the open window and lingered for a moment in the spicy air that floated like a cloud overhead.

"Oh, Ethan, you're not going to eat one of those now are you?" Mama exclaimed.

"No. I was just remembering," he answered smiling and continued on. Last year Ari had bet him that he couldn't eat an entire enchilada with the extra spicy sauce. Never one to

walk away from a bet with his girls, Papa accepted the challenge with gusto. Well, it was more like the enchilada took him
on. Everyone remembered that evening, when Papa discreetly
excused himself and proceeded to spend the next several hours
in the bathroom producing a symphony of sounds that sent the
girls, James, and even Mama into fits of laughter. Papa never
agreed to a food bet again.

An unpredictable breeze was blowing in off the water in
bursts and spits, causing Mama to pull the shawl collar of her
black wool swing coat up around her ears. It wasn't really all
that cold, but Mama's Island blood liked warmer temperatures.
"I think we're on borrowed time out here," she said. "Better tell
us where you want to go, James."

James liked playing the midway games even though he was
too little to get the baseballs to the milk cans or the tennis balls
to the fur-rimmed dolls, but he did get a dime in a dish once
and won a goldfish in a plastic bag and that gave him high hopes
that he would continue his winning ways. He ran from booth
to booth yelling over his shoulder "*I wanna play this one* and *I
wanna play that one*," and they did. Just past the cotton candy
stand he spotted the brightly colored row of monkeys and palm
trees at the Monkey Races booth. This was a game where players rolled balls up a ramp into holes marked with different point
values. Every time a ball went into a hole, that player's monkey
scooted up a palm tree. The higher the points, the further the
monkey scooted. The first player to get the monkey to the top of
the tree won a prize, usually a stuffed monkey.

Papa and Mama sat on stools next to each other and their
children sat on either side of them. Ari and Emma began to
giggle, knowing how competitive their parents got when playing these silly games. Before long they would be knocking each
other's elbows and nudging each other's stools and acting more
like James and Georgie than parents. The starting bell rang and
the monkeys, each dressed in a different colored waistcoat, were
off inching their way up their palm trees. The barker called the
race with all the excitement and seriousness of the Kentucky
Derby, and when the race was over, Papa had won and Mama
was accusing him of cheating. The three children were laughing

uncontrollably. Papa picked out a monkey in a bright red waist-coat and handed it to James. "This is for you, James. It's payment for being such an excellent tour guide today." James smiled, feeling very important.

Next James insisted on stopping at the diving bell to watch it plunge into the tank of water with its young passengers inside. When he became bored with that, he convinced Papa to take him on the miniature cars. They were a sight moving around and around in the bright red fire engine, James madly turning the wheel and clanging the bell while Papa sat entrapped in the tiny vehicle with the knees of his long legs touching his chin. Ari turned to Mama to share a laugh with her and saw her surreptitiously put her small pocket camera back into her purse. She had an odd expression on her face that Ari couldn't read.

"What is it, Mama?"

"Oh, I was just thinking how sad it is to see Playland falling into such disrepair. This used to be a great weekend date place, especially when the Big Dipper was still here."

"It isn't so bad, Mama."

"Perhaps. But I remember when there was no litter on the ground and no rust on the diving bell, and no paint chipping off those beautiful old carousel horses. Still, James seems to be having fun."

Ari saw James running enthusiastically toward them with a smile that filled his face. "Did you see me drive the fire engine, Ari? Did ya' see me, Emma? I went really fast!"

"You sure did, big guy," Ari exclaimed.

James took her hand and pulled her off the bench where she and Emma and Mama had been catching their breath. "Let's go on the merry-go-round," he said.

"It's getting a little cold," Papa observed. "Are you sure we shouldn't head for the Fun House?"

"Just one ride, Papa. Please!"

"Okay. You're the boss. But then you should probably take us indoors."

"Okay," he agreed and ran toward the carousel with Ari's hand still firmly in his own.

They arrived at the carousel just in time to watch it go

round one full revolution so they could pick out the animal they wanted to sit on. It was a difficult decision for young James. There were so many possibilities. There were two chariots shaped like dragons, and gondolas the size of small cars, and sixty-four hand carved animals—horses and rams and camels and giraffes and one very ferocious lion. Each of the unique figures was solid wood, intricately hand-carved and detailed, and covered over in bight paint and shiny glass jewels from Belgium. Ari thought it was more a work of art than a mechanical device. From the two big saucer eyes on James's face, she guessed that he thought it was just about the *bestest* merry-go-round in the whole world.

When the carousel came to a complete halt, Ari sat James up on a big black horse with a streaming mane and tail, cinched the leather safety strap around his tummy, and reminded him to hold on tight to the brass pole. Then she and Emma raced to the giant lion, but Ari got there first. Both of the Heywood girls liked the lion because it reminded them of Aslan and their favorite Narnia stories. Not surprisingly, Mama and Papa grabbed one of the gondolas. The merry-go-round started up and quickly gained speed, and galloping figures whirled round and round faster than any modern-day carousel was built to go. As the music played and the brass poles churned up and down, Ari indulged in a few romantic imaginings about riding the carousel with Jason, hugging tightly to him on the octopus, and standing at the shooting gallery watching him win her the biggest teddy bear there, which she would then proudly carry up and down the midway as a public pronouncement of her boyfriend's love for her.

By the time they finished the carousel ride even James was ready to go indoors, so they headed down the midway at a fast clip, passing by lonely barkers who awaited the few brave souls who didn't mind the now brisk winds and falling temperatures from the fogbank that was beginning to obscure the sun. Papa stopped at the booth to buy tickets for the family while they waited at the front entrance, staring up at Laughing Sal, the giant mechanical fat lady, who slapped her knees and doubled over in laughter that bordered on cackling. James gawked at her through the plate glass window overhead, a horror spreading across his face every time she bent closer to him. Suddenly, he spun around and hugged Ari's leg and buried his face in her thigh. "I don't wanna go there, Ari. I don't wanna go," he wailed.

Ari pried her frightened little brother off her leg, bent down and wrapped her arms around him. "We don't have to go to the Fun House if you don't want to, James, but you really liked it the last time we brought you here."

"I . . . I don't like it now."

"Oh, James, Laughing Sal didn't mean to scare you.

James unburied his face only a little convinced. "Remember the giant barrel inside that goes round and round and makes you roll all over, and horses that slide back and forth, and the giant record player you can sit on and the biggest, *bestest* slide in the whole world? It goes all the way up to the roof, James. Remember?"

The slide did it. James loved slides. "Will you go with me, Ari?" he whimpered between sniffs.

"You bet. I won't let anything bad happen to you. I'll always take care of you, James. You're my big guy!"

"Promise?"

"Promise!"

"Okay, let's go," he said and led the family through the front doors and into the hall of mirrors, still gripping Ari's hand tightly. Ari kept her other hand outstretched in front of her, as she still hadn't learned how to negotiate the maze without smashing her nose on the reflective glass. Finally, they reached the end of the mirrors and squeezed through the giant rolling cloth bumpers that blocked the entrance to all the amusements, and jumped over the final obstacle, air jets that blasted up from the floor.

Once inside, they stood for a moment, adjusting their eyes to the perpetual motion of children, running and shouting and calling out "*Let's go this way*," through the maze of brightly painted wooden surfaces that sea-sawed up and down and glided back and forth and spun round and round and rolled over and over. James led Ari straight to the three-story slide and got in line behind the masses of other children and adults waiting their turn to climb the stairs. When they reached the bottom of the steps, they took a burlap potato sack from the stack that was continually replenished by the sliders who had just finished their descent, and began their own steady climb up the stairs. It didn't take long to reach the top where Ari placed the sack at the beginning of one of the several slippery wooden lanes that bumped up and down on their way to the floor far below. She sat down on the mat and then settled James between her legs in front of her and wrapped her arms tightly around him.

"Ready?" she asked.

"Ready!" he proclaimed.

She nudged forward with her heels and the two of them slid like toboggans on ice, shrieking and laughing and losing their stomachs on the humps, finally crashing in a panting, giggling heap against the heavily padded wall at the bottom of the slide. It took a moment for them to re-orient themselves to the ground—a bit longer for Ari than for James. "Let's go again, Ari. I wanna go again!" he yelled over the other children's voices that echoed off the walls.

"You're the boss, James, but maybe Emma would like to go with you this time. I think she's afraid to go by herself."

"Okay," he replied, running to Emma who was watching them from a nearby bench.

"Come on the slide with me, Emma," he said. "I won't let you get scared'"

"Promise you'll take good care of me?"

"I promise, Emma," he said proudly.

As Emma got up to leave, Ari asked, "Where are Mama and Papa?"

Emma didn't answer. She just pointed. Ari turned just in time to see Mama and Papa come hurling down the slide, screaming like a couple of banshees and acting more like they were on their first date than nearing their twenty-second wedding anniversary.

Eventually James wore himself out and announced it was time to go home. "Did you have fun, James?" Ari asked, picking him up in her arms and nuzzling him affectionately.

"It was the *bestest* day, Ari," he replied, with drooping eyelids and a smile that even his exhaustion couldn't prevent.

8

SUNDAYS IN THE Heywood house were never planned; they were just meant to happen. So, everyone woke when it suited them, did everything or nothing when it suited them, and ate Sunday supper whenever the spirit moved the family to prepare it. The only constants were that Sunday suppers were always served on the fancy china, and everyone's attendance was expected. When Papa was growing up, he always had Sunday dinner at his grandmother's table, and there he learned his Sunday manners, which he often lamented were dying out, at least in the American culture. Ari always smiled when Papa launched into his Sunday manners speech. He spoke so very little of his upbringing and then only in vague references to his eagerness to leave that life behind. It seemed curious that he would insist on bringing this one ritual forward with him into adulthood. But there were many things about Papa's past that were curious. Sometimes it seemed to Ari as if Papa had been born on the day he met Mama and hadn't really existed before then.

Ari woke to distant voices drifting up from the kitchen, unhurried and relaxed, with no children going off to school or father off to the office. Ari thought she heard the sound of the big stainless-steel roaster being taken out of the cupboard. "Hmm, turkey and cornbread stuffing," she thought. She loved Mama's cornbread stuffing. It wasn't dry or crumbly like other stuffing nor was it saturated with too many green spices. Mama's stuffing was golden and gooey and filled her mouth with a delicious taste that lasted long after swallowing. She was glad that it wasn't reserved just for Thanksgiving.

Ari eventually got up, showered, dressed in her favorite

Sunday comfort clothes, and slipped into a pair of slippers to keep her feet warm on the wood floors. Usually she went barefoot, a habit held over from the Island, but Mama and Papa turned the heat down at night and the house had not yet warmed up again. Then she brushed her hair out of the braid she always slept in, cleaned her teeth, and went downstairs to join the family.

As she entered the foyer, she noticed that the front door was ajar. "That's strange," she mumbled to herself and crossed over to have a peek outside. Seeing no one, she closed the door, shutting out the cold, and continued through to the kitchen. "Good morning, Ari," Mama said, glancing up from the bowl of crumbled cornbread in which her hands were fully immersed. "Did you sleep well?"

"Great, Mama," she answered and kissed her cheek. She put her face to the bowl of cornbread and sniffed. "You must have read my mind," she smiled.

"Actually, Papa came home from the office Wednesday and said he'd been thinking about turkey and stuffing all day. I told him I'd make it for supper tonight."

Ari peered across the kitchen to the little dining room where Papa sat with Emma. He was pouring her a cup of the family's favorite dark roast coffee, the steam making little designs in the air as Emma was talking and gesturing. Papa was grinning and munching, totally engrossed in whatever Emma was saying. Emma was still in her floor-length Lanz robe and nightgown and Papa was lounging as usual in comfortable slacks, a t-shirt, and the black silk robe Mr. Nakamura presented to him at the close of negotiations last summer and which Papa adopted soon after as part of his Sunday morning uniform. Sections of the *Sunday Chronicle* were spread across the table between them, supplying, in all probability, the subject of their animated conversation.

"Mama, why don't you come join us in the dining room. I can finish the dinner after breakfast."

"Thank you, Ari. I think I will. I could use another cup of coffee." She lifted her hands out of the cornbread and rubbed them together several times, attempting, without much success, to remove the excess crumbs. Then she headed for the sink to wash up. "You go on in, Ari. I'll just check on James and be right with you. He's been quiet for far too long. There's no telling what kind of mischief he's gotten into," she laughed.

Ari walked into the dining room already filled with mid-morning sunshine streaming in from the gardens beyond the French doors. "Welcome, sleepy head," Papa smiled over the top of his *Sporting Green*. "I made you some of those scrambled eggs with minced onions and peppers that you like so much."

"Oooh, thanks, Papa. How did you know?" She went to the sideboard where Papa had laid out Sunday breakfast for the family in steamers so that their meal would be warm no matter what time they ambled in. The first out of bed on Sundays always started breakfast for the rest of the family, and today that was Papa. Once James woke early and decided that he was old enough to make Sunday breakfast. It took the better part of the day to clean up the Cheerios and peanut butter and Bisquick that covered the kitchen and James in equal proportion.

Ari scooped up some eggs and mounded them on her plate and added a spoonful of hashed browns, two strips of crisp bacon, and half a grapefruit. There was a covered cake plate on the sideboard hiding some scrumptious surprise—maybe Mama's raspberry coffeecake or her buttery croissants or possibly a variety of store-bought pastries from Eickele's Bakery. Mama said that Eickele's pastries were so good that it was hardly worth baking herself anymore. She drove all the way out to Geary Boulevard just to purchase their baked goods and to exchange pleasantries with the hard-working owner of the family business, the jovial man with the graying moustache and Buddha-like physique, who baked the European way and whose pastries rivaled even their Viennese counterparts.

"Bear claws! When did Mama have time to go to Eickele's?"

"She makes time for the really important things," Papa answered, popping a last bite of bear claw into his mouth.

Ari sat next to Emma, grabbed the front section of the paper, and joined in the relaxed rhythm of eating and reading and periodic pauses to savor a particular morsel of food or share an item of interesting news. The Vietnam War covered most of the front page of the newspaper with stories about the mounting war protests, one in particular being planned for the Pentagon, and the military's continued assurances that the war was winding down. There was a nice story about Thurgood Marshall who had just been confirmed as the first African American Justice of the United States Supreme Court. "It's about time," Ari murmured to herself.

"What's about time?" Emma asked.

"Oh, I was just reading about Thurgood Marshall's confirmation to the Supreme Court. She read them the account of Justice Marshall's achievements from the desegregation of professional schools, where he believed the intellectual environment most amenable to the idea, to his tireless fight for racial equality through his work with the NAACP and his appointments to the bench. "Listen to this," she said. "*When asked about his appointment of Thurgood Marshall to the Supreme Court, President Johnson said, 'It was the right thing to do, the right time to do it, the right man and the right place.'*"

"I'd say it was way past the right time," Emma said.

"I agree," Papa replied. "Still I'm glad it's finally come. It doesn't fix everything that's broken, but it's a momentous contribution."

"Now if we could only get women on the Court," Ari said.

"Well, maybe you could do something about that just as soon as you wipe that bear claw icing off the tip of your nose!" Papa laughed.

From somewhere distant in the house, Ari could hear Mama calling for James. She obviously hadn't found him yet. He was probably hiding in his fort under the eaves. The big old houses he had grown up in were custom designed for hide and seekers, and James had become a master of hiding and Mama a master of seeking. It shouldn't be long before . . .

Suddenly Ari remembered the open front door, and a rush of adrenaline shot through her and sent her running out of the room calling, "Did you find James yet, Mama?"

"No," she shouted back in that worried voice mothers use when their young ones are out of sight too long. "I've looked everywhere."

"I think he might have gone outside, Mama. I found the door open when I came down this morning"

Mama appeared at the top of the stairs. "He couldn't have gone far," she said, in a voice more calm than she was feeling. "I better go find him."

"I'll come too, Mama." Ari grabbed her coat and headed for the door.

Papa and Emma came into the foyer having heard the commotion, grabbed their coats and joined in the search for James. They looked like trick-or-treaters on a cold night in their slippered feet and jackets over robes and kaftans and kimonos. First, they searched behind the big old cypress tree in the back yard where James liked to play Robin Hood in Sherwood Forest and then back by the swings and slides and sandbox, but he was nowhere to be found. Then they came round the front again to see if maybe he was hiding among the giant hemlocks and camellias and rhododendrons that separated the circular drive from the street, but still no James. "Ethan!" Mama said urgently, grabbing his arm. "Look! James's wagon is gone!"

Papa looked at the front porch and the corner of the vestibule where James usually parked his wagon. "Where has that boy gone?" Mama asked, exasperated and worried all at once.

"We'll find him, Mary," Papa assured her, and he led the family down the drive to the sidewalk where he turned in the direction of Georgie's house. James wouldn't go the other way. He was too afraid of the Simpson's German shepherd. They walked swiftly down the street past the Davis's Greek revival and the Elerson's French country and the McNab's green shuttered colonial. Still no James. With each passing house their pace quickened until they were walking as fast as they could without breaking into a run, the women taking two steps for each one of Papa's long strides.

Papa was several yards ahead of the others when he reached the Tyler's driveway with the manicured patch of lawn and the English tea roses of their meticulously kept gardens. From there the street curved to the right and made a gentle descent to the intersection below. Papa stopped abruptly and stared straight

ahead. When he turned back toward the others, he had a big
grin of relief on his face. He motioned them silently to hurry
up and when they reached him, he simply pointed straight
ahead with an amused expression. There was James, at his very
Jamesiest, sitting at the corner in his little red wagon. He was
dressed in last year's Christmas pajamas and robe, and he was
singing *Jingle Bells* at the top of his lungs.

Mama ran the half-block to the corner and scooped James
up into her arms and hugged him until she knew he was really
there. "James, I was so worried about you when I couldn't find
you in the house. What are you doing here?" she asked.

"I'm waiting for Santa Claus, Mama."

"Santa Claus! What makes you think he's coming here?"
She was neither mocking nor condescending but sounded interested in whatever information James had to share.

"Because Papa said Christmas is right around the corner. I
wanna see it!"

Mama was dumbfounded, as was Papa, until he remembered his conversation with James the previous day. "Oh James,
honey, that was just an expression, like saying someone is as
big as a house. They're not really that big, they're just fat," Papa
explained, but he knew by James's expression that he was having
little success getting the point across.

"But you said, Papa. You said Christmas is right around the
corner!" he insisted again.

"I know, James, but you'll have to wait for Christmas back
at the house with the rest of us."

"But, Papa, I wanna see Christmas now!" James shouted,
beginning to cry.

Ari didn't see stubbornness in James's expression; she saw
fear, and something from way back in her own childhood suddenly came to the surface, explaining his frantic behavior. "Oh,
James," she said, "are you afraid that Santa won't know we're in
San Francisco for Christmas this year?"

"He won't know, Ari. We already had Christmas here. He
thinks we moved again. I have to tell him." James could only
remember three Christmases and they had taken place in three
different houses—the first in Hong Kong, the next here in San

Francisco, and last year's Christmas at the Great House on the Island.

Papa frowned but managed to force a smile. "Santa is a very smart fellow," he said, tousling James's uncombed hair and wiping away his tears with a gentleness that belied the power in his big hands. He doesn't forget any good children, and you're the best, James! I promise you; he knows where you live."

"Papa's right, James," Mama said soothingly. "Santa would never forget the *bestest* boy on the whole earth!"

Papa's promise and Mama's assurances quieted James. "Okay," he whimpered and hugged tightly around Mama's neck for the return trip home.

Once home, Mama retrieved her fancy gilt-edged stationary and her favorite fountain pen, the one with the fine writing point. She and James were going to write a letter to Santa Claus with their current address. Mama was sure that Santa would write James back, probably by next week, acknowledging the change of address and assuring James that he wouldn't miss the big house in St. Francis Woods. But first, James was going to have a man-to-man talk with Papa in the study about never worrying Mama like that again. Papa wouldn't be too hard on him though. He would be a lot harder on himself for the distress he had caused his little boy.

9

IF SAN FRANCISCO could lay claim to any season, it would be autumn, which was usually sunny and mild with days that could reach the low seventies and evenings that were chilly but not numbing. That was not to say that the weather couldn't turn around in a heartbeat. The most predictable thing about San Francisco's weather was its unpredictability. Still there was a simple rhythm to the autumn—the salmon boats came home and the crabbing boats went out, and the fog shrouded the sun and the sun burned off the fog, and on weekends the Marina filled with picnickers and the zoo with children and the Bay with hundreds of sailors crossing over to Tibouron and Sausalito to drink gin fizzes and gaze at the incomparable city view from the decks of Sam's and the Spinnaker Restaurant.

When football season ended, Ari and Jason fell into a simple rhythm of their own. Jason became a regular at the Heywood house, bringing Ari home after school where sometimes they did homework together, but more often hung out in the kitchen with James and Emma and Mama, rolling up their sleeves and joining in the food preparation and agreeable conversation. Jason got along with everyone in the family, even James whose heart he won over with a football and a team jersey and several trips to the backyard to pass the ball around and tackle each other with Jason always ending up on the ground. Ari liked the way Jason was with James. His affection for him was genuine.

On weekends they went to dances and parties and movies and sometimes out to dinner, just the two of them. Their favorite restaurant was Giuseppi's, which stood near the entrance to the tunnel that ran under Twin Peaks. The tunnel connected the outer districts of San Francisco with the downtown area by way of green and cream-white streetcars with names like the *K-Ingleside, the N-Judah,* the *L-Taravel,* and the *M-Oceanview.* Ari liked the names of the streetcars. They seemed to roll off her tongue like musical lyrics or the last lines of poems. And each conveyed upon its passengers a distinctive identity underscoring the rich cultural diversity of the city.

Ari thought it a bit sad that the streetcars seemed under-appreciated, living as they did in the shadow of the more famous and flamboyant cable cars. After all, work in the city would come to a grinding halt if there were no streetcars. Every morning passengers hopped on board at outlying neighborhood stops and hid behind newspapers, glancing up only occasionally to tell time with each passing of a familiar awning or awakening store-front. As the streetcars converged at the tunnel entrance, silk ties and blue collars and skins of all colors stared briefly at each other through filmy windows before entering the darkness on their way to office complexes or famous department stores at which some went to basement mail rooms and others rode express elevators to exalted floors. Each evening these same passengers returned home along the same tracks in reverse order, and were safely deposited back into their own private corners of the city and into the waiting arms of their loved ones. There was a rhythm to the coming together and the going away of each business day, almost like a heartbeat. Ari thought that's what Papa meant when he said that San Francisco was a city with a heart and soul.

It seemed appropriate that Giuseppi's be situated at the confluence of all the city's streetcars. It was one of those little neighborhood treasures, hidden away from the tourists, where inhabitants of all social, ethnic, and economic strata co-mingled over delicious food. Perhaps it was through word-of-mouth or perhaps through sideward glances out of streetcar windows, but, eventually, scores of locals found their way to Giuseppi's, and this weekend Ari and Jason were among them.

"I thought you were going to a party tonight, Ari," Mama said as she pulled the roaster from the oven and spooned beef juice over the crispy potatoes.

"We were, but we decided we'd rather go to Giuseppi's." Actually, it was Ari who decided, and she and Jason very nearly had their first fight over it.

Ari liked the parties where kids from a lot of different cliques came. There was never any extreme behavior, either too good or too bad. But Meghan and Adam weren't going to this party. Neither were any of Ari's other close friends or even Jason's more responsible friends, the ones who sometimes pretended to be wild in front of the others but weren't really. It was mainly *the Boys*, as Ari referred to them, who would be there—the ones who thought that drinking until you threw up was really cool and publicly parading your girlfriend into a bedroom was even cooler. Ari suspected that a lot less went on behind closed doors than *the Boys* claimed, but she knew she could ruin her reputation for just being seen at one of those parties. It bothered her that Jason didn't seem to care about that. Everything else between them was so perfect.

When Ari and Jason arrived at the restaurant, he opened the door for her, and they breathed in the warm air permeated with garlic and anise seed, olive oil and simmering tomatoes, and all spices green. There were two dining rooms filled with red checker clothed tables and Chianti bottles with drippy candles in them. Moving past several of the tables already occupied by equal numbers of couples and families, they headed to the second dining room where a mural of Venice ran the length of one whole wall and sat at their favorite table.

"Do you think you'll ever really do it? Go to Venice I mean?" Jason asked as they waited for Pietro, their waiter who was busy at a table next to the window, explaining with great dramatic gestures tonight's specials.

"If you promise to go with me," she said. "I mean it, Jason. Will you?"

"Sure," he answered easily, the words sliding out through his smile. "I'd follow you anywhere, Ari."

She regarded him for a moment and thought what an incongruous addition he would be to Venice—the casual blond American. But then there were blond-haired, blue-eyed Italians in the north so maybe he wouldn't appear so out of place after all.

"Tell me what it will be like when we get there," he said, sparking the familiar recitation of the life he meant to live.

"Well, we'll arrive by water taxi down the Grande Canal," Ari began with a far-off look on her face. "The day will be warm and sunny, and there'll be a breeze off the lagoon that refreshes the city and all the people who partied too late the night before. We'll rent a villa in the Dorsoduro near the Campo Santa Margherita."

"What's the Dorsoduro?" he asked eagerly, as he drank the remaining soda in his glass.

"The Dorsoduro is the district across the Grande Canal from the Piazza San Marco. It's where the Salute is. You know, that big domed church that's always on travel posters of Venice. She pointed to the mural and the familiar structure.

"Why the Dorsoduro?"

"Well, it's got all these great tree-lined squares and sunny quiet neighborhoods. It's not quite as closed in as some of the other neighborhoods. Better for finding landscapes. And the best part is the Zattere."

"Zattere?"

"Yeah. That's this long, open dockside full of outdoor cafés with views of a neighboring island. When the tourists all crowd into Piazza San Marco, you can just relax there with a cup of espresso and watch the taxis go back and forth and talk to the people who just come there to stroll up and down. Italians don't sit in front of their televisions at night, you know, at least not in the warm weather. They walk and eat gelato and talk to friends and strangers."

"How do you know so much about Venice? Have you been there?"

"No, but my parents briefly lived there when they were first married, and I've grown up on their stories and photographs. I'll have to show them to you when you come over next time."

He stared across the table at her. She was so beautiful. It didn't matter what she wore. She could have worn a potato sack and she'd still be beautiful. Tonight though she wore her white ribbed turtle neck that hugged her figure and her wool, navy-issue bell bottoms, the ones with the thirteen button flap on the front. He loved the way she looked in those pants.

"So, what will our villa be like then?" he asked.

She thought for a moment. "It will be Tuscan gold and forest green and shades of burnt sienna. And it will have touches of the Byzantine with columns and arches that draw people's eyes to it as they motor by but won't be too big or fancy. On the main level there'll be a courtyard garden that lets the sun in."

He nodded his approval. "And on the second floor," she said, "there'll be a grand terrace overlooking the canal and a bedroom with a large wrought iron bed and a ceiling with old heavy wooden beams." Ari noticed Jason's face as she described the bed, and she felt a small, warm tremble deep within.

"What will we do with ourselves?" Jason asked with a hopeful gleam in his eye.

"Oh, I think that in the morning we'll stroll up past the Rialto Bridge to the outdoor markets and buy fresh fish and pasta and Chianti for the evening meal. We'll barter in Italian like real natives and come home with bags full of food and pockets full of lira. And in the summer, we'll take the vaporetto over to the Lido and lie on the beach all afternoon." Not exactly the answer he had been hoping for she knew.

"At night we'll return to our villa," he continued, "and we'll watch the moon rise over the city from our bedroom and make mad, Italian love to each other." Finally, he had said it out loud, what she knew he had been thinking about for a while. He hadn't tried anything with her, past making out of course. All the kids did that, but she knew he wanted more, and he knew she didn't.

Jason reached across the table and held both of Ari's hands in his. He decided it was time to tell her he loved her. He wanted to move their relationship to the next level. Now was the perfect opportunity. Besides he really did think he loved her. But before he could speak, Pietro arrived with a basket of sourdough bread in hand and the opportunity was lost.

"Buona sera!" he said with genuine enthusiasm. "How is my favorite couple tonight?"

"Hungry," Ari said with a smile, her hands retreating rapidly to her lap.

Pietro set the basket of bread on the table and lit the dark green drip candle that protruded from the empty Chianti bottle. Ari stared at the layers of multi-colored wax that covered the bottle from previous candles that lit the table for other young lovers, and she thought it a simple but beautiful monument to romance.

"So, what are we eating tonight?" the waiter asked, poising his pencil dramatically above his order pad. His smile betrayed his amusement as he began writing their order before the couple uttered a word. Jason and Ari always ordered the same thing— dinner salads, spaghetti Bolognese, and cannoli for dessert. "I don't suppose it would do any good to tell you the specials. Mike has made some delicious veal scaloppini."

"Yes, I can see that," Jason smiled, staring at the stains already occupying the front of the young waiter's apron. "But we'll stick with the usual."

"Then I better get your order in pronto before we run out of pasta!" He smiled and headed for the kitchen, humming a melody from *Rigoletto* as he went.

When the kitchen door swung open, they heard the sounds of knives against chopping blocks, olive oil spitting in iron skillets and the clamor of Italian voices all shouting at once. Above the confusion, they could hear Mike's voice shouting at some poor prep chef, probably his cousin, in his heavily accented English, something about not enough garlic.

Jason began to laugh. "Have you ever noticed how much better arguing sounds in Italian?" he asked.

"Yes," Ari agreed. "If I could, I would argue in Italian, barter in Chinese, make love in French, and speak on all subjects with authority in a British accent." She thought a moment and added, "Actually, I can do all those things, except maybe the Italian." She was not being boastful. She was just stating fact.

"Really?" Jason blurted out, surprised and yet not surprised.

"Really. Mama and Papa thought it was important for us to speak in the language of whatever country we were living in. You know, as a sign of respect. Too many Americans travel to foreign countries expecting everyone to speak English and trade in dollars. After a while, learning a new language seemed pretty easy. It's all just nouns and verbs and phrases."

The kitchen doors swung open and Pietro came gliding out balancing two dinner salads and two large plates of Bolognese on his forearm. Ari liked to have her courses all together so she could move from one taste to another and back again, a habit she had picked up in Asia, and Jason had quickly adopted the habit for himself. As usual, Mike had loaded Jason's plate with an extra helping of spaghetti to show his gratitude for Jason's appreciation of his cooking. Pietro placed the dishes on the table and remained there, beaming over the young couple. That was their cue to take their first fork full of spaghetti and burst out with a stream of accolades for the chef.

"Funny, isn't it?" Ari mused out loud when Pietro had left. "We have a restaurant that is *our place*. Seems like something out of an old movie.

10

NOVEMBER ARRIVED AND brought with it record high temperatures—eighty-five degrees to be exact on the first two days of the month. It was going to be a perfect weekend to pack up paints and canvas and go hunting a landscape. Ari rose early on Saturday morning and came down to breakfast already dressed in her black denim hip-huggers and red tie-dye t-shirt. No one was in the kitchen yet. She got out the juicer and placed it on the island and then halved some oranges and twisted them back and forth on the appliance until she had four perfect little glasses of juice—no seeds, no pulp. Then she put on the coffee and put some pastries in the drawer to warm and was just about to mince some left over ham and throw it in some scrambled eggs when Mama arrived, still in her nightgown and silk jacquard robe, the one that matched Papa's.

"You're up early this morning," Mama said.

"I'm going painting. Jason is coming with me."

"Oh, that's right. Jason's becoming quite a fixture around here."

"I know, Mama. I really like him."

"He seems like a very nice boy."

"Who's a nice boy? Me?" James asked, as he ran into the kitchen followed closely by Papa.

"Yes, you!" Mama exclaimed and gave her boy a bear hug. He nuzzled his face in her silky-smooth hair, which she had brushed out of its nighttime braid and left loose to hang a few inches below her waist. Mama's hair always smelled of jasmine. It was Papa's favorite scent.

James ran around the island and gave Ari a bear hug of his

own. "Pop up on your stool and help me whip the eggs," she said, knowing that would keep him busy for a while. James loved using the odd-looking eggbeater, cranking the handle to super-sonic speeds with a grimace on his face that made it seem like he was constipated.

James was wearing his puppy pajamas. Mama could barely get them off of him long enough to wash them. They were beginning to fade a bit from all the laundering and ball up as flannel will do when it's rubbed against surfaces by a body in constant motion. But James didn't mind. His puppy pajamas were a persistent reminder of Papa's promise. A real live puppy couldn't be that far away.

"I did the eggs," James announced.

"You certainly did!" Ari exclaimed, seeing egg spattered about the island. "Did you leave any in the bowl?"

"Yeah, see?" he said, tipping the bowl and nearly spilling out its contents.

Mama came to the rescue with a wet cloth and wiped off James and then the island. Ari poured what remained of the eggs over the diced ham that Mama already had sizzling on the griddle.

"It's a good thing Emma stayed over at the sorority house last night. We might not have had enough eggs for her," Mama said with a quick smile to Ari.

Papa arrived in the kitchen, a little bleary-eyed Ari thought, just in time to help carry food to the table. At breakfast, Mama talked about the new book she was working on. She had writ-ten several books already. Most of them were children's books and all of them had been published professionally. She said the new one was called *Faraway Places* and was full of adventures, but she wouldn't say any more. She didn't like to talk about her books until they were well underway. Papa was going to take James to the zoo for the morning so Mama could get some writing done uninterrupted, and then they were going to come back home and make a picnic for Mama in the back yard.

"James, maybe tonight we should start working on your list for Santa Claus," Mama said and waited for the eruption.

"Santa Claus! Is it time, Mama?"

"Yes, it is. Before you know it, Grandfather and Mem will be here, and we'll go out and buy the tree and decorate the house and put on the Christmas music and bake the cookies."

The doorbell rang and interrupted Mama's runaway stream of Christmas cheer. "I'll get it," Ari said, jumping up from the table. "It's Jason, I'm sure."

Ari returned a moment later with Jason in tow, smart as usual in tan cords, a navy rugby shirt with one wide baby blue stripe across the chest, and a week's worth of tan that set off his thick blond hair.

"Hi, Mr. and Mrs. H," he said with a smile Mama thought could take him to the highest political office.

"Hi, Jason. Have you had breakfast yet?" she asked.

"Yes, thank you. It's the one meal my mother knows how to cook," he teased. Mama showed no response, but Ari knew that she disliked the lack of parental respect, so she quickly changed the subject.

"Just give me a minute, Jason, to rinse my dishes, and I'll be ready to go." Jason chose an empty chair at the table and waited.

"Ari tells me you're going painting today," Papa said, sipping the last drop of coffee from his cup.

"Yes, sir. Although she's the one doing the painting."

"Nice way to spend a Saturday," Papa observed. "Where exactly are you going?"

"I thought we'd go up to the Napa Valley."

"Well, drive carefully."

"Yes, sir, I will."

Ari said her goodbyes, promised James that she would return in time to read him a bedtime story, and disappeared down the hall.

"Something troubles you about him, Mary," Papa observed. "What is it?"

"Nothing, really. He seems like a perfectly nice boy, and he and Ari seem to have a lot of fun together. Still . . ." She didn't finish her thought because she didn't really know what to make of her vague uneasiness. Perhaps she was just reluctant to see her little girl grow up.

Ari had been to the Napa-Sonoma Wine Country once

before for a charity picnic that one of Papa's associates had hosted. There had been gourmet cooking classes and wine tastings and tables filled with food and flowers, all randomly arranged under giant old oak trees in an idyllic garden on the edge of the vineyard. She and Emma had worn silk dresses reminiscent of Ascot and sipped wines that reminded them of Paris while pleasant waitstaff pretended not to know that they weren't quite legal age. When dusk approached, candles had been lit and Japanese lanterns illuminated and thousands of twinkling little fairy lights switched on in the trees. It had all been terribly elegant.

Ari had always wanted to go back and explore the nooks and crannies of the valley that she had glimpsed out of the car window on the ride up. She had once mentioned this in passing to Jason, and now he was taking her to do just that. She loved that about him. They were headed for St. Helena on the Napa side, a quaint little town with attractive shops and restaurants and interesting neighborhoods full of eclectic architecture. There was an odd mix of colors there that just seemed to work somehow—from the deeply contrasting colors of the Painted Ladies to the soft pastels of the thirties-styled bungalows to the earthy Tuscan shades of farmhouse stucco. For an artist, it was like discovering gold at the end of the rainbow.

The Napa Valley ran north-south and was bordered by two parallel mountain ridges, between which miles and miles of vineyards rolled out like wall-to-wall carpeting on the valley floor. As the mountains ascended, they turned every shade of green, creating a play of light and shadow that was almost mystical, especially when viewed with an artist's eye. The western mountains separated the valley from the Sonoma side and protected it for several extra hours each day from the fog bank that often loomed just over the other side. Ari brought plenty of film for her camera knowing that at every turn in the two-lane road running the length of the narrow little valley, there was another source for a future painting.

As they drove north on Highway 29, Jason and Ari passed by old farmhouses, big estates, and a series of historic little hamlets with names like Yountville, Oakville, and Rutherford.

They didn't talk a lot, and then only in short bursts about the beauty of the passing scenery. There would be plenty of time for conversation once they got out of the noisy little sports car. Ari stared out the window and was mesmerized by the parallel rows of grapevines that periodically peeked out from behind old brick distilling warehouses and antiquated train depots, finally exploding into full glory between townships. She couldn't take her eyes from the vineyards. There was something about them, something other-worldly.

Just passed St. Helena, they cut across the valley floor and wound up a narrow road that ascended the eastern hills. About halfway to the top Jason parked the car in a pullout. Ari retrieved the picnic basket and Jason carried her art supplies and an old blanket from the trunk. Ari briefly wondered if Jason had brought any other girls here before, but she quickly dismissed the thought. Besides, did it really matter?

Jason led Ari down a path that had obviously been used by others before them. The path wound through dense trees and brush for about a hundred yards and then opened onto a grassy promontory from which there was an unobstructed view of the valley floor below and the mountains rising on the opposite side.

Ari stood motionless, trying to take in the magnificence of it all. The panorama was overwhelming in the richness of its colors and textures. But there was more here than just beautiful scenery. As she gazed out over the valley she could almost see the tule Elk and grizzly and brown bear that once roamed freely through the uninhabited grass marshes; the coastal tribes who hunted and gathered here; the Spanish missionaries who forever changed the face of the landscape, for the good some would say, but not all; the Italians and Swiss and Germans and countless other cultures who crossed oceans and prairies and mountains and deserts to plant zinfandel and mission grapes and a variety of others for their world famous wines; the Chinese who worked the fields and built the railroads; and all the young lovers who had ever come here before her to capture this place on canvas or film or just in their memories.

"What are you thinking about?" Jason called from somewhere behind her.

"I don't really know . . . just wondering how many other picnics these mountains have chaperoned throughout the centuries," she answered honestly.

While Jason spread out the blanket, Ari didn't catch the small smirk on Jason's face. She took out her camera again and began snapping pictures of the valley and mountains beyond, making sure to capture both sky and earth. She would need these photos to complete her canvas when they returned home, but she also wanted remembrances of the day.

"I wish I had a better camera," she said, as Jason came up behind her. "You know, one of those with zoom lenses and filters and all. I can get a general idea of the landscape with this one but no details. Like that little farmhouse in the middle of the vineyard down there." She pointed to a building that sat in a small clearing under the shade of a giant oak tree. "I wish I could see that better. It's even hard to tell what color it is from here."

Jason wrapped his arms snuggly around Ari's waist and rested his chin on her shoulder. Following the line of her arm to where it was pointing, he said, "That house is mustard colored stucco with dark green trim."

"How do you know that?" Ari asked in surprise. "Do you have x-ray vision or something?"

"No. I've been there before with my parents."

"What were you doing at that farmhouse?"

"It's only a farmhouse by day. At five o'clock sharp it turns into a restaurant."

"You're kidding!" she said in surprise.

"No, really. A lot of the families in the valley set three or four tables in their front parlors and serve home-cooked meals to the tourists to make a little extra money. The mothers and grandmothers do all the cooking. The sons wait tables, and the daughters wash up. The fathers pour the wine and tell stories of the family's history in the valley. Even kids James's age work by going out back to the family vegetable patch and picking ingredients for each customer's dinner order."

"Wow, talk about fresh food!" Ari said.

"Yeah, it's great. Maybe we'll go there sometime."

"I'd love to, Jason." Ari smiled, lost in the blueness of his eyes.

Ari and Jason sat on the blanket facing each other. After sharing a lunch of cured meats and cheeses with crusty bread, Ari pulled out the fresh cannoli she had carefully packed that morning for them to share. Jason watched as she took one small bite after another, licking the creamy filling from her lips as she went. He shifted uncomfortably on the blanket, his mind wondering what it would be like if she were doing that to him.

Ari lay on the car blanket next to Jason, staring up at the sky while absent-mindedly popping biscotti into her mouth. A little wisp of fog floated by overhead, a seemingly harmless little piece of cotton in a big blue sky dominated by the unusually warm autumn sun, but Ari knew it was the harbinger of gray skies and colder temperatures that lay just out of sight over the western mountains.

"Looks like our Indian summer is coming to an end," she said, but Jason remained silent. She could feel him staring at her, and she knew he was thinking about kissing her. She hurriedly swallowed the last bite of biscotti and pretended not to notice his intentions. In one quick motion, Jason bent over her, slid one hand behind her neck while leaning on the other, and kissed her. At first the kiss was warm and familiar, and Ari returned it with eagerness. Perhaps it was with too much eagerness; Ari was too inexperienced to know. But Jason suddenly took hold of her with both arms, bringing his body down on top of hers, and kissing her with a wildness that frightened her. She worked against his advances, subtly at first, moving her body contrary to his, sending the message that she wasn't ready for this. But obviously Jason wasn't paying attention. His hand slipped from her neck and moved toward her breast and he fondled her in ways that excited her some but frightened her more. With a power she didn't know she had, Ari shoved him off of her, sat up and, adjusting her clothing, stared at him, saying nothing. She just waited for him to speak.

Jason somehow knew his "but I love you" speech wasn't going to work here—the one where he'd say how all his friends were doing it with their girlfriends and they didn't love them like he loved her. In the end, all he could say was, "I'm sorry."

Ari moved closer to him and, with complete calm, kissed him gently on the mouth and said, "I love you, Jason. I'm just not ready for this." And she lay back down on the blanket taking pains not to pose seductively, and grabbed two biscotti from the package, popping one into her mouth and throwing the other at him. They both laughed, making the tension fade away . . . at least for today. Ari had a feeling that she'd find herself in a similar situation again.

The light was illuminating the front porch by the time Jason brought Ari home, and he backed her into the corner of the vestibule behind a giant camellia that sheltered them from the neighbor's view. After a goodnight kiss, he returned to his own home where his presence had been commanded at a gathering of the aunts and uncles. He knew he was late, but that didn't matter. He'd put on some appropriately preppy clothes and turn on the charm in front of the relatives. His father would doubtless forget his irritation and one of his uncles would probably slip him a fifty.

Ari barely had time to hang up Jason's jacket before James assailed her. "Ari, I been waiting and waiting forever," he exclaimed, jumping up into her arms.

"I know, James, but I'm here now. And I'm yours for the whole rest of the night." His excitement over having Ari all to himself gathered on his face and burst out in a giant grin. Ari carried him into the living room and plopped him back down in front of his Etch-a-Sketch and his color forms and sat next to him on the floor.

Mama and Papa were sitting on the sofa as usual, casually clad in the soft fabrics and loose fit of their most comfortable clothes, and fitting into each other's contours like two adjoining pieces of a jigsaw puzzle. "Looks like the fresh air and sunshine agreed with you, Ari. Or is that the rosy glow of love I see on your face?" Papa teased.

"Oh, Papa!"

"Seriously, how was your day?"

"It was the best. Jason and I had so much fun. I can't believe how beautiful the wine country is. I don't know how to describe it exactly—the mountains and the valley and the vineyards and the people." Papa smiled at the speed of Ari's speech, which gained momentum with every syllable.

James began tugging on Ari's arm, having spent long enough out of the center of attention, signaling that the elder Heywoods' borrowed time was up. "Ari," James begged, "read me a story?"

"Okay, big guy. I'll go change my clothes and be right back," she said, standing up and heading for the foyer to a symphony of squeals and giggles behind her.

11

ARI HAD BEEN looking forward to the Christmas break with almost uncontrollable anticipation, and it was finally here. Two whole weeks of absolutely no responsibility for anything other than just being happy. For several nights now she had lain awake in her bedroom, staring into the darkness, playing the Christmas celebration in her head like a feature-length movie. It always began the same way with Papa hauling out the boxes, and the whole family ceremoniously unpacking the Christmas collections and decorations. There were the dishes with the winter scenes on them, the blue ceramic punch bowl with white snowflakes that Papa filled with eggnog and just a bit too much brandy, and the phonograph records of holiday music, the Christmas stockings that Mama had sewn from Island silk, and the original edition of *A Night Before Christmas,* which sent them all to bed each year *"with visions of sugarplums dancing in their heads."* With each unveiling there would be the inevitable sharing of anecdotes of Christmases past and rejoicing in the continuity and comfort that family traditions always brought with them.

Christmas had begun as Papa's holiday, but soon after they were married, Mama joined in with great enthusiasm. It was she who insisted that the family celebrate at least one Christmas in every house in which they lived, with alternating Christmases on the Island, saying that a house just couldn't be a home without family traditions being celebrated there. Mama enjoyed the celebration of faith and the family togetherness it engendered regardless of its religious affiliation or lack of one. She had more genuine *Christmas spirit,* Ari thought, than most Christians. She inherited that from Grandfather and Mem, who had never missed a single Christmas since the first year Mama was married, and who celebrated the holiday not as disinterested spectators but as eager participants.

"Is it hard for you, Grandfather, Christmas I mean?" Ari had once asked.

"Why should it be?"

"Because you believe in your Gods, not Jesus."

"Oh, child, the true celebration of faith uplifts us all to a state of kindness and compassion and humanity. It is irrelevant who guides our faith—God or Jesus or Jehovah or Buddah or Allah or my Gods, or Mother Nature for that matter. It only matters that we make the journey."

"Then why is there so much religious prejudice, Grandfather?"

"Because too many people have confused faith with religion. You can have faith even in the total absence of religion because faith is about what you feel inside, not what church you attend or what Bible you read or even if you read a Bible."

Grandfather and Mem were arriving from the Island tonight, and rather than spend a wasted day of pacing and clock watching and fidgeting, the family was going downtown to view the decorations and to take James for his annual sit on Santa's lap. James had already sent his wish list to Santa, making Mama take him to the post office to mail it rather than entrust it to Harry, the mailman, who was really nice and always took time along his route to share a friendly word with the neighborhood children, but he was too old and out of breath, James thought, to carry his letter all the way to the North Pole.

Ari hurried to finish dressing, knowing that she had taken longer than she should have to get moving this morning. She couldn't help it. She was still thinking about last night and her goodbye dinner with Jason at Giuseppi's. Jason was going to his grandparents' house in Vermont for the holidays and wouldn't return until New Year's Eve when, he announced with great dramatic emphasis, Ari would be in for the best night of her life. He wouldn't tell her anymore. She already missed him terribly, but in an odd sort of way, she was glad to have this time with her family. She was on her way to college next year, and there was no telling where Mama and Papa and James might be posted, and there wouldn't be many more years before she and Emma were alternating Christmases at the in-laws. Things were changing and this was the only Christmas she could count on being the way Christmases had always been.

Ari pulled her red wool turtleneck over her head and slipped into a box-pleated wool mini skirt in red, white and black plaid. She opened her lingerie drawer to grab a pair of pantyhose but settled instead on a pair of festive red tights that would add extra warmth. Then she slipped on her soft, black leather t-straps, the ones that felt more like bedroom slippers and provided far more comfort than the platform shoes that were coming into fashion, gave herself one last glance in the mirror and, satisfied that she was smart enough for downtown San Francisco, joined the family in the little dining room.

"Ari!" James cried as he spied her entering the room. Ari smiled back at the inevitable continuation of his greeting. "I been waiting and waiting forever!"

"I know, but I'm here now."

The family had nearly finished eating by the time Ari arrived. Outside the French doors a thick mist had already settled on the lawn. "I'm glad to see you all dressed warmly. The fog has settled in early today," Mama said, surveying her family.

"It might be sunny downtown, Mary. You know how different the weather can be from one side of Twin Peaks to the other, but still it will be cold," Papa added. He sipped from his favorite coffee cup and peered over the top of his newspaper. "So, let's map out a route through the city today. We don't want to miss anything special."

The excitement around the table was palpable as everyone first suggested potential destinations and then began shouting them out like they were bidders at an auction. San Francisco really knew how to celebrate Christmas, and there was no end to the possibilities. Department store windows were decked out like the elaborate stage sets of Broadway musicals, cable cars were draped in shiny aluminum garlands, the famous little corner flower stands were bedecked in ribbons and bows, hotel lobbies were transformed into the Palace of Versailles at Christmas time, and the night sky over Fisherman's Wharf was illuminated by the fishing boats whose masts and wheel houses were all lit up with strings of colored lights. The boats looked like jolly drunken sailors when they bobbed up and down in their moorings. There were carolers at Union Square and the Christmas Eve concerts at Grace Cathedral and the Nutcracker Ballet at the Opera House, and the myriad other performances by the little theatre groups and singing chorales and dance troupes that populated the city. It seemed that all of San Francisco engaged in one big family celebration, which commenced each year with the unveiling of the City of Paris Christmas tree, a gargantuan live tree that soared several stories high, all the way up to the stained glass dome ceiling.

"One at a time," Papa admonished.

"I wanna see Santa Claus," James called out, not waiting for anyone else to grab the floor.

"You will, James. I promise, but Santa wants to see you after you have seen the other decorations, so you won't have to rush off before he's through talking to you."

"Okay, Papa," James replied amiably and went back to stuffing spoonfuls of cereal into his mouth as fast as he could.

"Why don't we just head out and see what treasures we can discover," Mama suggested.

"I wanna see Santa Claus!" James repeated more vehemently this time, afraid that Mama might go off on one of her adventures and forget the most important reason for going downtown.

"Of course, we must go see Santa Claus," Papa reassured his son who smiled in reply, causing a dribble of milk and cheerios to escape his mouth and fall back into his bowl.

"Uh-oh!" James said, and went back to eating, undaunted and unaware of the amusement he caused around the table.

"There's the City of Paris tree, of course," Papa continued thinking out loud "and you girls love seeing what Macy's does with its window displays and I hear Robinson's Pet Store has an excellent . . ."

"Puppies!" James exclaimed. "I want to see the puppies. Ari, hurry up!" James ordered, his words garbled by one last mouthful of cheerios that should have been two.

"I've just started my breakfast, James. You'll have to be

patient." Ari sighed at her baby brother who had already climbed down from his chair and was standing beside her with a plaintive expression that would have melted the hardest heart.

"Okay, big guy, you win," she said. "Why don't you pick me out a muffin while I help clear the table, and I can eat it on the way."

"I'll pick a muffin for you, Ari," Mama said congenially. "James, you go to the bathroom before we leave. And don't forget to wash your hands and face. Santa doesn't like for messy little boys to make his suit all dirty," she smiled.

"Okay, Mama," he shouted back as he ran out of the room, nearly tripping over his shoelaces that flew in every direction.

When James was well out of earshot, Mama put down her coffee cup and turned to the girls. "I didn't want James to hear," she began, "but Papa's offered to bring him home when he gets tired, and the three of us can take ladies' luncheon at the Fairmont."

"Ladies' luncheon!" Emma and Ari squealed in unison. "It's been a long time since we did that," Emma added.

"Too long," Mama returned, "but we're going to rectify that today." Mama had instituted *ladies luncheon day* several years ago as a special gift to her daughters—a gift of fine food, elegant surroundings, and intimate conversation, all intended to make her girls feel quite grown up. At each new posting, Mama and the girls explored the city to find just the right place for their special dress-up afternoons. In London, it was tea at the Ritz, in Singapore, it was luncheon at Raffles, and in San Francisco, it was buffet at the *Crown Room*. Sometimes they went to their special place to celebrate an event and sometimes Mama took Emma and Ari there simply because they needed a lift to their spirits. Whatever the occasion, all three looked forward to the afternoons with equal enthusiasm when, for just a few hours, they could be women together.

By the time James returned, the table was cleared, the food put away, and the dishes stacked in the sink where Mama said they could stay until they got back home. "Hurry up now, ladies. It always takes you so long to get out the door," Papa teased, and winked at James who attempted a wink of his own but could only scrunch up his face until it resembled a prune. Ari affectionately referred to it as James's scrunch face and would frequently ask him to give her his scrunch face, which always resulted in both giggling at one another. James, as many little boys do, thought it was so hilarious, he often went around asking anyone who would take the time to listen, "Wanna see my scrunch face?"

Mama and the girls went to the under stairs closet and retrieved their long woolen chesterfields. Emma's coat was black, but Mama and Ari's were traditional gray herringbone, which kept their black hair from disappearing into the fabric. Each of them accessorized to coordinate with the clothes they wore beneath. Ari chose her cashmere scarf, leather handbag, and kid gloves in an elegant shade of red that was not overly bright or flashy. Emma's accessories matched her baby blue velveteen jumper, the one Ari thought emphasized her slender figure. Mama's accessories were green and black.

Papa helped James on with his John-John coat and mittens and double-knotted his shoelaces before donning his own overcoat. Then with a quick inspection of his handsome family he said, "I think the Heywoods are ready for high society," and he led them to the front door.

Papa opened the door wide for his family and waited for them to all go through. Then he hesitated, turned around and headed for the powder room off the foyer, calling over his shoulder, "I'll just be a minute."

"Men!" the girls said simultaneously which set the three Heywood women to giggling. Without fail, Papa would push them out the door after teasingly telling them to hurry up, only to turn around himself for one last visit to the bathroom.

The family piled into the Town and Country station wagon and drove down to West Portal where they parked on a side street. There was no sense bringing the car downtown during the Christmas rush. Even the huge underground parking garage at Union Square would be full. Then they hurried up the street toward the nearest trolley stop, the air of excitement mounting with each step that brought them closer to the commencement of the long-awaited Christmas festivities. When they reached the narrow strip of pavement next to the tracks, Ari held onto James's hand, and they waited for the distant clickety-clack of metal wheels against the rails to announce the impending arrival of the trolley. Ari could feel the electricity coursing through James's little body, and she remembered, a bit sadly, what it used to feel like when she still believed in Santa.

They didn't have long to wait before a streetcar arrived, and they jumped on board, dropped their coins into the rectangular glass coin box, and grabbed seats opposite each other. Ari held James on her lap, and he wiggled and squealed as the street-car lurched forward toward the tunnel three blocks ahead. She peered out the window at the neighborhood businesses until the trolley made its final West Portal stop in front of Giuseppi's. She smiled at the familiar entrance and the warm images it conjured, and Mama smiled too, but Ari didn't notice. Then the streetcar moved forward once more, closer now to the tunnel entrance.

"Ari, Ari, we're going inside the tunnel," James screeched. "See!"

"I see, James," Ari said, giving her precious little brother a squeeze, as the lights came on and the trolley was gobbled up by the mouth of the tunnel.

The entrance to the tunnel was a big, dome-shaped open-ing that turned pitch black just a few feet in, after which the only sights were the equally spaced white lights and occasional red and green ones. It reminded Ari of going through a portal into some new time dimension like something out of *The Twilight Zone*. She often thought someone could write a great science fiction or fantasy novel about traveling into the tunnel and coming out the other side into some other land or maybe into San Francisco during the Gold Rush Days. Maybe she would suggest the idea to Mama.

As the streetcar exited the tunnel on the Market Street side, they were greeted by a profusion of light from the sun that had not yet been shrouded in afternoon fog. After another fif-teen minutes of stops and starts and exchanging of seats, they finally reached Fourth Street and disembarked, but not before Mama and the girls obtained transfers for use on the Powell

Street Cable Car that would take them from Union Square to the top of Nob Hill for lunch.

Crossing Market Street, the family joined the throngs of shoppers making their way to the stores. They came first to Macy's Department Store, which stretched a full city block. It was difficult to gain entrance to the store because so many people were stopping to read the progressive story being told in elaborate mechanical displays in the store windows. "Look, Mama, it's *The Night Before Christmas!*" James shouted.

Mama smiled at Papa. She knew he shared her thoughts. They had done well raising their children for all three found such joy in simple things. Life would never be wasted on them. Mama came up between her daughters and slipped her arms affectionately through theirs, and they began reading the first verse of the story aloud to James, who sat perched on Papa's broad shoulders.

When at last they had finished viewing the windows at Macy's, they decided to forego the decorations inside and leave them to the masses of frenzied shoppers. They headed instead to The City of Paris to see the giant Christmas tree, a sight that could not be missed regardless of the crowds. The tree stood in the middle of a multi-storied rotunda at the store entrance, which ran all the way up to a domed stained-glass ceiling depicting Neptune and ancient sailing ships in elegant shades of gold and bronze. Each floor above street level was open to the rotunda and afforded close-up views of the decorations to droves of shoppers who hung over the marble balusters. There were thousands of decorations several times normal size in keeping with the scale of the tree, all brightly colored and appearing to have been hand-made by Santa's elves. There were intricately decorated glass balls, giant wooden fire engines, soldiers with drums, dolls that were perhaps real porcelain and hand-painted glass Santas from Europe. There were angels with shiny gold dresses and wings like spun sugar and mice dressed up as furry little elves and garlands made from brightly colored all-day lollipops. There were so many decorations that it was impossible to see them all from the ground floor, so the family joined the other onlookers in climbing the stairs to the upper levels. By the third floor, James had seen enough ornaments and was ready to move on, so Papa picked him up and said that he could choose where to go next.

"I wanna see the puppies, Papa!"

"Okay, James, Robinson's Pet Store it is!"

Once outside Papa led the family across Geary and up Stockton Street until he reached Maiden Lane, a broad pedestrian alley with chic shops lining each side. "Do you know why they call this Maiden Lane?" Papa smiled.

"Oh, Ethan, not in front of the children!" Mama teased.

Papa set James down, pointed him toward the pet store window and let him run out some of his restlessness. When the rest of the family caught up with James, he was standing pressed up against the center window. In the background there was an elaborate scene of Santa delivering kittens and puppies and birds to good little children around the world, while in the foreground live puppies sporting Christmas bows romped and played or sometimes just sat staring with big eyes at passersby, hoping to go home with the next little boy or girl.

"Papa, I want that one," James said, pointing to a fuzzy tri-color collie puppy who sat all alone with his nose pressed up against the window. "Please, Papa, I want him!"

"You know that's not possible, James. We move around too much, sometimes to countries that won't allow dogs. You wouldn't want to get a puppy and then have to give him back again, would you?"

"I don't care, Papa," James said, thinking only about today as young children do. "I want that puppy!" he insisted again. "See, Papa, he's looking at me. He wants me too!"

"I know, James," Papa said, and his voice suddenly sounded tired.

Ari came up beside Papa and put her arm through his. "Papa," she said gently, "maybe you didn't give me puppies, but you gave me the whole world. I wouldn't trade that in for all the puppies on earth, and neither will James when he's old enough to appreciate what he has."

Papa turned to his daughter and gave her a big hug.

"Sometimes I wonder who's raising whom," he said, and his mood turned more celebratory.

It was becoming obvious that James was getting tired. It had to be difficult being such a little creature among so many big people, seeing little more than a forest of knees coming at you. So the family decided to take James straight away to I. Magnin to see Santa, stopping only briefly at Podesta Baldachi's to peek inside the front door at the spectacular floral scenes of Christmases around the world, which Emma said reminded her of a miniature rose parade. They would have to forgo the St. Francis Hotel until later.

The family entered I. Magnin and walked down the marble-floored aisles past expensive perfumes and exquisite jewelry until they reached the bank of elevators where they stood with a crowd of customers waiting for the next available car. It took three elevators before there was room for all the Heywoods, so Papa held the impatient James, and Mama distracted him with questions about his Christmas list for Santa. Finally, it was their turn to enter the car.

"Please move to the rear. Please move to the rear," came the emotionless voice of the elevator lady in the taupe-brown dress. When the car was filled to capacity, she held her baton across the entrance to signify to the customers outside that they must wait for the next car. As the elevator arrived at each floor she spewed forth a recitation of that floor's departments in a weary monotone, and Ari felt a bit sorry for her, this woman who obviously did not feel any joy at the Christmas holidays. When they reached the eighth floor, the family said *Merry Christmas* to the attendant and to Ari's surprise she smiled back an enthusiastic *and the same to you*. Perhaps she wasn't apathetic after all; maybe she was just feeling invisible.

Holding tightly to James's hand, Papa led him to the back of the line where James fidgeted and squirmed his way toward Santa who sat on a giant golden throne surrounded by elves in red and white striped tights and long green velvet tunics. Mama waited with the girls just outside the ropes with camera ready. When it was finally James's turn, he went bounding up to Santa and flew into his arms, landing on his lap with an audible thud.

"Well, son, what's your name?" Santa asked in his most jovial voice.

"I'm James Heywood. Don't you know me?" he asked with an innocence so beguiling that Santa broke into a belly laugh that nearly tumbled James off his lap.

"I'm sorry, James. Of course, I know you. You've been a very good boy this year, haven't you?"

"Yes, Santa," he replied, smiling his joy at being personally known to Santa Claus.

"So, James, what is it you want Santa to bring you for Christmas this year?"

"Don't you know? I wrote a letter."

"Of course you did, James. But often boys and girls think of new things after their letters are sent. I want to make sure I know what you really want most."

"I want a puppy, Santa," James announced.

"A puppy!" Santa repeated, looking at Papa for a sign of approval. Papa hesitated before shaking his head in the negative.

"Well, James, it might be a little tough for me to bring you a puppy. Our puppies were born late up at the North Pole this year, and they might not be ready to travel by Christmas Eve. If they're not ready for Christmas, what else can I bring you?"

James looked up at Santa with a forlorn expression, his big blue-green eyes welling up with tears. "Nothing, thank you, Santa," he said mournfully. Without saying another word, he climbed down from Santa's lap and ran to Papa's waiting arms where he burst into tears, unable to contain his disappointment any longer.

Papa did his best to console his son, but James's disappointment in discovering Santa's limitations was more than he could bear. He just laid his head on Papa's chest and sobbed in silent disbelief. Santa arose with some difficulty from his throne, his sizeable girth being genuine, and walked over to James. "Good little boys like you should never be sad about Christmas, James. Now dry your tears, and I'll tell you a secret."

"A se-secret?" James replied through his sobs.

"Yes, James, a very special secret."

"What?" James asked, just a hint of a smile creeping onto his face.

"Sometimes it's not possible even for Santa to grant every wish. So when I can't grant the wish of an especially good little boy or girl, then I go down to a secret hiding place under the North Pole where the very most magical presents are kept. These presents aren't made by my elves, James. These presents are made by me personally!"

"Really, Santa?"

"Really, James. And I promise if my puppies aren't old enough to travel on Christmas Eve, I'm going to give you one of my really special presents. Okay?"

"Okay," James replied, wiping his face on his sleeve. "Papa, Santa's going to give me a magic present. Did you hear?"

"Yes, James, I heard. You must be Santa's favorite little boy," Papa whispered so no other little boys could hear, and James just smiled the biggest smile his mouth could make.

Santa returned to his throne, and Papa shot him a grateful glance before gathering his family and heading for the elevators. As they stood waiting for the next available car, Mama put her arm through Papa's and said, "It will be all right, Ethan."

"Yes," he said after a while. "I will make it all right." And Ethan always kept his promises.

12

MAMA STOOD BETWEEN her girls on the back platform of the Powell Street Cable Car as it clanged and strained its way up Nob Hill toward the Fairmont Hotel and the glass elevator that would whisk them skyward to the Crown Room, the rooftop restaurant where impeccably dressed patrons shared good food and an exquisite view. She had watched Ethan walking on Market Street, carrying their exhausted little boy in his arms, his weary gait signifying the weight of the world he carried on his shoulders. She knew he was worried about James, of course, but there was something more on his mind—something he simply wasn't ready to share with her. Well, she wouldn't think about that now. There was nothing she could do from the platform of the cable car to change anything and worrying would only ruin the memory of ladies' luncheon with her daughters, so she locked her concern away, planning to bring it out again when it might do some good.

At first glance, the Crown Room seemed like an odd choice for ladies' luncheon given its more traditional and opulent predecessors. After all, it had only been erected six years ago as part of the contemporary tower addition to the Fairmont Hotel, and many longtime residents thought it an effrontery to the prestigious old San Francisco treasure. Still, when Ari and Emma learned of the colorful history of the Fairmont, they couldn't think of anywhere else they'd rather go, and the incomparable view from the Crown Room won them away from the more traditional surroundings of the restaurants in the old building.

The Fairmont Hotel had been purchased by the Law brothers only twelve days before the 1906 earthquake heavily damaged it. Most of San Francisco had been destroyed in the quake, and what little remained was in danger of being dynamited by the fire department's attempt to thwart the raging fires that burned out of control. Within days of the devastation, however, the indomitable inhabitants of San Francisco were already hard at work on plans to rebuild the city and when the hotel opened with a week of gala celebrations and fireworks displays sponsored by the Merchants Association, the cream of San Francisco society attended, including Mrs. M. H. deYoung, whose patronage almost guaranteed the hotel's success. Many of San Francisco's wealthiest families then moved into the hotel, having lost their homes in the earthquake, and some remained there until the 1940s, watching from their illustrious confines as San Francisco arose once more from the ashes.

During those early years, fashionable ladies spent their afternoons taking tea in the palm-filled Laurel Court while their children attended the hotel's elementary school or amused themselves in the outdoor playground under the watchful eyes of matronly nannies. In the evenings, wives joined husbands in a procession of Paris silk and diamond studded black ties and tails to the hotel's lavish dining room where they supped for hours on multi-course banquets, retiring afterwards to gossip in the ladies' lounge or to cigars and politics in the gentlemen's bar. On Sundays, after church services, some residents and guests attended concerts given by the hotel orchestra while others frolicked with the likes of Helen Hayes in the indoor plunge. To all outward appearances, the Fairmont Hotel was a place of refinement and gentility, of elegance and affluence, of power and prestige. Yet the walls whispered secrets, widely known but never spoken, that the wealth that created this *Snob Hill* community had been amassed in large part by the robber barons, a group of tenacious scalawags and scoundrels who had fought and gambled and bamboozled their way from the gold fields of Placerville to the saloons of the Barberry Coast to the respectability that only millions of dollars could bestow. The Fairmont Hotel was a contradiction in terms, and Ari was captivated by the irony and by the ghosts in whose company she and Emma and Mama would soon be dining once more.

"We're here, Mama!" Ari shouted over the screeching breaks of the cable car as it came to a halt at the California Street stop. The ladies disembarked and watched for a moment as the trolley continued on its way to Fisherman's Wharf. Then they ascended the hill, negotiating the steep grade slowly after a morning of chasing James around Union Square. When they reached level ground, they paused to catch their breath and admire all the landmarks that made Nob Hill famous. To the left was the Mark Hopkins with its renowned glassed-in rooftop bar, The Top of the Mark, where, during World War II, camera girls in short-skirted costumes took pictures of young couples saying goodbye for maybe the last time, she in her fanciest dress and he in his dashing uniform. Across the street was The Pacific Union Club, the all-male bastion of the city's rich and powerful. It was rumored that much of California's history was directed from behind the Club's massive front doors. Beyond the Club was Grace Cathedral, a listed tourist attraction known for its stunning architecture, stained glass windows, and organ concerts. And, of course, crowning the bounty of historical treasures that reigned over the city from their exalted height was the Fairmont Hotel.

The hotel's front entrance was lined with colorful flags representing the original member countries of the United Nations, and they made an impressive sight against the ornate, colonnaded architecture. Once inside, visitors were greeted by a large lobby of bronze and black marble and gold leaf ornamentation, red and black patterned carpets and massive crystal chandeliers. The centerpiece of the lobby was an imposing grand staircase that descended from the mezzanine above, a staircase fit for the royalty who had stayed at the Fairmont over the years.

"Every time I see the staircase, I imagine Grace Kelly descending it in one of her Edith Head gowns," Mama said.

"Every time I see it, I think of Jack Lemon tumbling down those stairs in *Good Neighbor Sam!*" Ari laughed.

"Oh, Ari, you'd probably go tumbling down those stairs right now if we weren't here to stop you," Mama joked.

"No, I wouldn't," Ari retorted feigning offence. "But I might slide down the banister," she added, and flashed that devilish grin that always made Mama laugh.

They strolled across the lobby, stopping here and there to admire the ornately festooned Christmas trees and extravagant decorations in all of their turn-of-the-century glory. There were massive live garlands draped from the banister of the grand staircase and encircling the marble pillars. More garlands ornamented the doorways. These were decorated with brass musical instruments and giant silk bows in burgundy and antique white satin with shiny gold trim for sparkle.

They paused for a moment to read the directional signs for the glass elevator and then entered a hallway lined with exclusive shop windows displaying silk suits and alligator handbags. They joined the group waiting for the car to return from its express trip to the restaurant. It was an attractive crowd filled with distinguished men, who seemed to have just stepped out of a Brooks Brothers window, and smartly dressed women in tailored suits, stylish hats, and dress gloves. Mama removed her coat, revealing her emerald green knit sheath, which hugged her graceful figure and drew glances, as always, from men who still dreamed of such exquisite women. She wore her black hair in a twist that was held in place with a silver clip sculpted in the shape of a Bird of Paradise and adorning her throat just above the scoop neck of her dress were the multiple strands of silver beads that Papa had bought her in Taxco. A wide black suede belt rested loosely on her hips, it too fashioned with a silver buckle, accentuating Mama's perfect curves. Mama was beautiful but more than that, she was elegant—as elegant as Grace Kelly.

The elevator doors opened and disgorged several passengers, all overfed from the feast that waited above. When Ari entered, she stood by the railing and braced herself for the dizzying ride. As the elevator ascended the side of the building, the hills of San Francisco revealed themselves above the neighboring rooftops, bumping up and down and finally flattening out before reaching the water's edge. Ari searched the panorama for those invisible lines separating one neighborhood from another, and then she traced the skyline from the low buildings of old San Francisco to the towering skyscrapers of the new city. When the elevator reached the top floor of the tower, she turned from the view and followed Mama and Emma into the restaurant.

The Crown Room was refined and understated, the designers knowing they could not compete with the majestic view out the big picture windows. The only major ornamentations in the room were two large topiary trees adorned with giant gold balls, which stood sentry on either side of the elevator. The walls, ceiling, and carpet were all done in a rich green-gold, with only a scalloped and tasseled valence of gold and white stripes encircling the room to interrupt the monotone. Scattered about the perimeter were several tables, strategically placed to catch the view and covered in starched white linen tablecloths meant for fine dining. The centerpiece of the room was a large, round revolving bar at which patrons could sip fancy drinks while enjoying the view from the California Street side of the hotel to the Sacramento Street side without ever changing seats or turning their heads. Sometimes, when the restaurant wasn't busy, the maître d' let Arianna and Emma join Mama in non-alcoholic beverages at the bar before going to their seats, but today it was packed with holiday shoppers and was, therefore, an imprudent time to stretch the rules.

"How nice to see you again, Mrs. Heywood, and you, Miss Heywood, Miss Heywood," the maître d' said, nodding at each of the ladies in turn. "I have your usual table waiting."

They followed the maître d' to a table by the window where he gathered their coats and first seated Mama and then came around to seat the girls on the opposite side. He paused for a moment to ask after the welfare of the family and then withdrew to tell the waiter to bring three iced teas and a loaf of sourdough, which the waiter did without delay.

"I hope the holidays find you all well," Arthur, the gray-haired waiter said as he filled the glasses and placed the basket of bread in front of Ari.

"Last time we were here, Ari," Emma said as she cut into the loaf, "you practically ate a whole loaf all by yourself."

"I'll try to show a little restraint," Ari responded as she cut a huge piece for herself and began liberally spreading it with butter.

"We're going to need another loaf," Mama said with amusement. The girls turned their attention to the view, but Mama just gazed admiringly at her daughters, thinking once more how delightful it was that beauty had so many ways of expressing itself. Emma's beauty was as soft and seamless as a Monet painting while Ari's was wild and dramatic and full of contrasts, and each foretold perfectly the beauty that waited within. Emma was her dancer who with grace and elegance floated through life on delicate tiptoe, never landing too heavily, never bumping into obstacles. She worked with the world as she found it and then carefully choreographed her steps to ensure she would get everything she ever dreamed of. Emma was so like Ethan, thoughtful, pragmatic, sure of the dream she wanted to achieve. Ari was her adventurer who soared through life experiencing all its possibilities and making new ones for herself if she found the world lacking. She wasn't impulsive or capricious; she simply accepted no limits—well, few limits anyway. Emma wanted to be the next Teacher on the Island, Mama knew, and she had set about gaining all the knowledge and skills and experience necessary to make her the most obvious choice for the position. If Ari had wanted to be the next Teacher, she too would have prepared herself thoroughly, but then she would have marched right up to the Elders and informed them of their golden opportunity. Mama smiled inwardly at her happiness, a smile so immense that it spilled out onto her face, but her girls didn't notice.

Ari glanced around the room at the other patrons who were all speaking in the subdued voices that accompanied fine dining. There was a threesome at a nearby table—an attractive woman in her early thirties accompanied by two young girls who appeared to be about six and eight. The girls were outfitted in matching navy blue dresses with white polka dots, lace-trimmed socks and patent leather Mary Janes. They sat primly proper, napkins in their laps, feet dangling quietly, while doling out extra helpings of "*please*" and "*thank you*" to the waiter who smiled back his appreciation.

"We're not the only ones enjoying ladies' luncheon day," Mama said, smiling at the scene that had caught Ari's attention.

"They do remind me of us, Mama, the first time we went to Raffles together. Remember?"

"I remember. You girls were so sophisticated, so well

mannered, that the manager came to our table to compliment me on my impeccable young daughters. As I recall, when we got home that afternoon, you two undressed, threw your dresses on the floor, put on your play clothes, climbed to the top of that gnarled old tamarind tree out back, where you, Ari, promptly fell out of the tree, and we spent the rest of the afternoon getting your broken arm set in plaster!"

"I guess culture didn't stick on us very long back then, Mama," Emma laughed.

"I wouldn't change a thing about my daughters," she replied proudly.

Arthur returned to refill the glasses and ask if there was anything he could bring them. Then, satisfied that all was in order, he left to attend to his other patrons, but his gaze never left the Heywood table for very long. When the ladies rose to fill their plates at the buffet, he quietly brushed the breadcrumbs from the starched white linen tablecloth, lest the ladies feel embarrassed at their untidiness. By the time they returned to their table, their plates filled with just a taste of a dozen different delicacies, Arthur had once again discreetly faded into the background.

"Mama," Ari began, but swallowed a last morsel of deviled egg before continuing. "I'm worried about Papa. Is he alright?"

"I'm not really sure," Mama answered honestly. "Why do you ask?"

"He just looked so sad when James was begging him for that puppy. And later at I. Magnin, I thought Papa was going to cry or something."

"I thought so too," Emma agreed. "I wanted to say something to him, but I didn't know if I should."

"Something's been troubling your Papa for a while now. I think he's beginning to feel like he's losing his family. I don't think he wants to be halfway around the world from you girls, and I know he worries about uprooting James when you two are no longer in the house."

"I've been thinking about the same thing," Ari admitted. "I mean, I'm really excited to go to college, and I know I'd just die if I had to stay in high school another year. Still . . ."

"Change is difficult for people, even when it's a good change."

"Yes, but it's not a very good change for James, is it? Emma and I always had each other. In all the new houses and all the new schools, we never felt alone or scared. But James . . ." Ari didn't finish her thought.

"Is there anything we can do?" Emma asked.

"I don't know. You can't stop growing up, and your Papa wouldn't want you to. He gets so excited just thinking about what awaits his girls."

"You know, Mama, if James needs a little brother . . ." Ari began with a devilish air.

"Perish the thought!" Mama exclaimed in a voice louder than she intended.

The next few minutes were spent in silence, alternating thoughts of Papa and James with delicious bites of food and glances out the window at the slow progression of the fogbank now inching its way toward the bay. Ari was a bit sorry for having brought up the subject of Papa. She didn't mean to dampen the festivities with somber conversation. She glanced across the table at Mama, whose pensive expression had caused her little worry wrinkle to appear on her forehead. Still, she looked scads younger than the other middle-aged women in the room.

There was nothing on Mama's face that revealed her years; her skin was smooth and evenly bronzed, her neck was firm, and her beautiful almond eyes and full lips were usually smiling. Perhaps, she was so young and vibrant because she never worried about her age. For Mama, every year was the best year of her life.

It was Emma who finally broke the silence. "When did you know you were in love with Papa, I mean really in love?"

"I knew the moment he looked at me," Mama began in the breathy voice that always emerged when she spoke about Papa and the memories they shared. "I was sitting in the stacks at the campus library, cramming for midterms, when I glanced up and saw your Papa's blue eyes staring down at me." Lost in the memory, Mama paused, and a dreamy smile gently spread across her face. "I remember thinking his eyes were the purest blue I'd ever seen. Like the waters that flowed from the highest mountain lagoons on the Island. It was almost as if he recognized me, but I'm certain we had never met . . . not in this life anyway."

"What do you mean, Mama?" Emma asked.

Mama took a sip from her water glass and gently brushed away the condensation that had dripped onto her lap. "My people don't believe in death in the way most do. To us, death isn't an ending, it's just the beginning of a new chapter. You don't simply cease to exist; your spirit just moves on."

"Like reincarnation?" Ari asked.

"Yes, in a way." Mama answered. "But there's more." Ari and Emma sat forward, eagerly awaiting the secret that they knew Mama was about to share.

"They also believe that two spirits can be bound forever, destined to find each other again and again with each new chapter."

"So, you knew Papa in a previous life?" Ari asked. She was certain the Gods wouldn't waste a love like Mama and Papa's on a single lifetime.

"Yes, I believe so," Mama answered.

"You're saying we are all destined to be with one particular person then?" Emma asked, a small frown forming on her face.

"No, not exactly," Mama answered. "The Islanders believe the Gods give us opportunities, but it is up to us to write our own stories. Life is what we choose to make of it." Mama thanked the waiter as he refilled her water glass before continuing.

"Love at first sight. It's all so romantic," Ari sighed.

"Oh, Ari," Emma laughed. "You always are a hopeless romantic." Ari playfully threw her napkin at her sister, who threw it right back at her.

"Girls," Mama said sternly, but the wicked smile on her face gave away her amusement. "It's much more than love at first sight, Ari. As unromantic as it might sound, you need more to make a marriage. It's the love you feel at second sight and third and fourth that makes a marriage. While I am certain it wasn't a mistake that Papa and I met, it was up to us to determine which path we would choose. We chose to live life together. Not even the Gods can force someone."

"What made you want to marry Papa?" Emma asked.

Mama answered without hesitation. "It was Papa's intelligence that continually broadened my curiosities. It was his humor that made me laugh. It was his constancy that told me he would always be there for me and for our children. It was the values we shared and the friendship that grew from them. But mostly, it was Papa's passion for . . . well, just for everything, especially me. He still makes me feel like I'm the sun that fills his skies in the morning and the stars that fill his skies at night and that every breath he takes is just so he can spend one more moment on this earth with me!"

"Wow," both girls sighed in unison.

"I hope I find someone like that when the time comes," Ari began, "but . . ."

"But what?"

"What if I don't . . . or what if I choose wrong?" Ari knew a lot of people whose parents divorced, and it was becoming more and more common.

"I was in love once before I met your Papa," Mama said. "It could have been the beginning of a new love story, but I wasn't ready."

"What do you mean . . . ready?" Ari asked.

Mama resettled herself in her chair. "You must have the self-confidence to know that you deserve the best a man has to offer and the self-reliance to know how to be happy with or without a man. You mustn't let a man define who you are. Oddly enough, those are the women who men are most attracted to over the long haul. Don't misunderstand. I adore Papa, and I would be devastated if I ever lost him. I know that neither of us would ever be as good alone as we are together. But we bring two complete individuals to our relationship."

"So, what happened to the first guy?" Ari asked.

Mama rolled her eyes. "I was young and refused to see what was really happening right in front of me. He had this amazing ability to be sweet and romantic when it suited him best. But then I found him in . . . well let's just say a rather compromising position with my roommate."

"Oh Mama! How awful," Emma exclaimed.

"Yes, it was at the time. I was devastated, but worse, I

forgave him! I fooled myself into thinking it wouldn't happen again like he promised. Fool me once, shame on you. Fool me twice..."

"Shame on me," Ari said.

"Exactly. You can't always choose what happens to you in this life, but you can choose how you respond to it. It was a blessing in disguise really. It forced me to take stock of myself, really examine myself inside, and I didn't like what I found. I had let him define who I was. Without him, I felt lost. That's why I tried to make it work even though what he did was unforgiveable. Now I'm grateful for it. It gave me the perspective I needed to decide who I wanted to be as an individual, not as someone's girlfriend. That's when I found my Sanctuary."

"What's Sanctuary?" Ari asked.

"It's different for everyone, but for me it was the place where I finally discovered who I was, or at least began to. And coincidently, right as I realized I was okay being on my own, I met Papa."

"I don't understand," said Ari.

"You will when the time comes," Mama answered.

13

THE TROLLEY EMERGED from the tunnel in near darkness and groped its way through the mist, its headlamps resembling eerie praying mantis eyes on the nearly invisible conveyance. Inside, passengers stood three deep, arms laden with packages and feet throbbing from the day's shopping. Mama and the girls had given their seats to an elderly couple at the Castro Street stop and were thanked profusely in one of the heavily accented versions of English that contributed to San Francisco's international flavor. By the time the screeching of wet metal announced that the first West Portal stop lay just ahead, Mama and the girls were ready to be home.

It was a few moments before they located Papa and James through the crush of disembarking passengers. If it weren't for a single downlight illuminating the damp wood slat bench where they were sitting, Mama and the girls might have missed them altogether. "There they are, Mama," Ari said, pointing to the huddled pair.

James was cradled in Papa's arms, looking all sleepy-eyed from a nap obviously interrupted. He was wearing his puppy pajamas under his John-John coat and his hair still had the impressions made by his pillow. When he saw Mama, he suddenly lost his sleepiness and began waving wildly. "Mama," he called, "Mama, Mama!"

"Hello, James," she returned as Papa set him down and sent him hurtling toward her outstretched arms. As with most preschoolers whose siblings spent their days at school, James's world revolved around Mama. He didn't much like being away from her for too long—except when he was on the Island. There he could go for hours playing with the Island children without needing Mama for anything, and this both pleased and saddened her. He was an Island child, like Ari; perhaps that's what wove them so tightly together.

By the time the station wagon pulled into the drive, the fog had turned to drizzle on its way to steadily falling rain. "I hope the plane will make it in on time." Mama said, closing the heavy front door against the cold and the damp and the thought of her parents flying through them.

"They'll get in all right," Papa said with authority. He gave Mama's shoulder a gentle squeeze. "John's never lost a passenger yet."

"I know. He's the best company pilot we've ever had. Still . . ."

Ari helped James remove his coat and lifted him up so he could hang it on the brass hook that was still a couple of years out of his reach. Then she set him down and watched him scurry off to the living room, smiling at the preschooler's waddle he had not quite outgrown. In some ways she wished James could stay this age forever. He was so innocent, so completely uncomplicated, and he did make her laugh. But then he also could be so exhausting at times, as could any active little boy who had yet to learn that he wasn't the center of the universe. Perhaps the Gods were wise to let five-year-olds be five for only one year, she thought.

Upstairs in her bedroom Ari changed out of her sweater and skirt and tights, to which the dampness still clung, and replaced them with a warm woolen kaftan, her green one this time, sniffing the fabric first to ensure its freshness.

Ari had descended nearly to the first landing before she heard the voices coming from Mama and Papa's room. They were loud, angry, unfamiliar voices. She couldn't hear what they were saying, but that didn't matter. Mama and Papa were fighting, and that's all Ari needed to know to be distressed. It's not that they never disagreed about anything or never argued. But the arguments were always respectful—never personal or hurtful. Mama and Papa never took their relationship for granted as so many other married couples did. They had nearly lost each other once, during Ari's birth, and they never forgot what that felt like. Besides, Mama was raised on the Island. Couples treated each other differently there.

The bedroom door suddenly flew open, and Ari could hear Mama clearly now. "Ethan, how could you make a decision like that without talking to me first!" He didn't answer. He just stormed down the hallway and blew by his daughter without a word. Ari turned back and got a glimpse of Mama's tear-stained face just before she closed the bedroom door. A moment later the front door slammed, and the noise reverberated throughout the house.

Forty-five minutes passed before Mama emerged from her bedroom. She too had changed into a kaftan. She had taken the silver clip from her hair, brushed it out smooth and parted it in the middle, letting it fall unfettered past her waist. Her red, puffy eyes were barely visible behind the lustrous strands of hair that partially obscured them. She moved silently to the fireplace and stood barefoot on the flagstone hearth, warming herself at the blaze Ari had set in anticipation of her appearance in the living room. As she breathed in the sweet Applewood aroma of the fire, she thanked Ari. "I think the damp got clear down to my bones."

"I made the fire too, Mama," James exclaimed proudly. He held up both hands to show off the black stains that covered them. "See! I squished up all the paper."

"I see, James. It's so nice to have two big, strong men in the house."

"But it's only me in the house, Mama. Papa went outside. Where did he go?"

"He went to take care of some last-minute Christmas shopping," she lied.

"For me, Mama?"

"Perhaps. So, you better get all that newsprint off your hands before he comes back. It wouldn't do to get smudges all over your Christmas presents."

Ari heard the weariness in Mama's voice. "Come with me, James, and you can show me how you wash your hands all by yourself."

"Okay."

Mama watched after them as they left the room, James

holding tightly to Ari's hand. She smiled, and Emma was relieved to see a familiar expression returning to her face. "Mama," she ventured, "are you and Papa all right?"

"We just had a disagreement about something and both handled it very poorly." She offered no further explanation.

It was two hours before Papa returned. He strode into the living room carrying a bouquet of butter yellow orchids surrounding a half dozen Bird of Paradise. The expression on his face was calm and just a bit tired, Ari thought.

"I would have been back sooner, but you can't believe how hard it is to find these flowers at Christmas time in San Francisco. I had to drive all the way back downtown to Podesta Baldachi's and got a whopper of a parking ticket for my troubles." He smiled.

He handed the flowers to Mama, whose face was showing just a hint of a smile in her relieved expression. She opened the card and read it silently. Her smile broadened. "Oh, Ethan," she said and rose to hug him. Ari and Emma shared matching expressions of relief mixed with more than just a little curiosity.

"What about me, Papa? Did you buy me a present?"

"As a matter of fact, I did, James. But you'll have to wait until Christmas to open it up. I promise you, though, it's really, really, really worth waiting for." The smile on Papa's face grew so broad that James couldn't help but smile too.

"Okay, Papa," he nearly shouted, and returned to the Lego town he and Emma were constructing.

Mama and Papa and the flowers disappeared upstairs for an hour. It took about half that long before Ari's curiosity got the best of her and she read the gift card that Mama had left behind on the coffee table. "Oh, Emma. Listen to this," she said, and read the card aloud. *Can you ever forgive the old fool who loves you?*

"Oh, Ari, do you suppose anyone will ever love us like that?"

"Well, if what the Islanders believe is true, there's definitely a possibility." They both smiled, settling into the warm comfort of the couch and each staring into the fire lost in the imaginings of who he might be.

14

THAT NIGHT THE family nibbled on leftovers while sitting around the fire and reading away the time until Grandfather and Mem arrived—all except James who had tired of his Lego town and was now busy building a space station with his erector set, which spread from one end of the Turkish carpet to the other. It was an odd little scene— the futuristic aluminum structure on the Middle Eastern antiquity—but then the living room was one of those delicious British Colonial rooms that invited family gathering and the varied leisure activities that accompanied it. Not like those *Louis the Whichever* rooms that were so pastel and gilt-edged that you were afraid to put your feet up on the furniture or drop crumbs on the floor. Somehow the British just knew how to design rooms that were formal and opulent while being comfortable and inviting at the same time.

Mama and Papa sat together on the damask sofa. Her legs were draped over his lap and he aimlessly caressed her slender ankles with one hand while holding his volume of Solzhenitsyn's new book, *Cancer Ward*, with the other. Mama was perusing an old *National Geographic* but she spent more time staring at the front door than at her magazine. Ari and Emma sat opposite each other in the overstuffed club chairs that sat two on each side of the sofa. They looked like identical bookends, their knees drawn up to their chests, their chins resting on their knees, both staring at books, which balanced precariously between fingers at the end of outstretched arms.

Ari had pulled down the old leather-bound volume of her favorite Dickens, *A Tale of Two Cities*, hoping it would divert her from the sounds of the grandfather clock, which she was sure ticked much louder and more slowly tonight. *It was the best of times, it was the worst of times, it was the age of wisdom, it was the age of foolishness.* She didn't know why exactly, but those words had always captivated her ever since Papa first read them aloud in the Hong Kong house. Maybe it was the idea that the world could be so many different things all at the same time, or maybe it was that the range of possibilities made free will really important. Arianna liked the notion of free will. While it had sometimes made her stubborn and petulant when she was younger, Mama and Papa always said that if she learned to use it for its true purpose, it would serve her well one day. She had begun to prove them right.

A sigh of impatience arose from the sofa. Mama was holding her magazine in front of her face, shielding herself from the front door, which stubbornly refused to swing open. "Ethan, do you think we should call the airport for an update?"

"Oh, Mary," he laughed, "you sound like the children on long drives. *How many more miles? Are we there yet?*"

"I guess I do," Mama admitted, "but I've been waiting so long to see Grandfather and Mem, I'm getting a little impatient."

"I know," he replied, "but they'll be here soon." He bent sideways and planted a gentle kiss on her cheek. Then he returned to his novel.

Ari tried to concentrate on her book, but to no avail. She found herself glancing up more and more at the painting over the fireplace or at Mama's glass bottle collection on the mantle or at the jade Quan Yin from Hong Kong or the framed Erte from Paris or the carved wooden screen in the corner, which Papa had paid a local artisan to recreate for Mama's birthday as she had so admired the original at Raffles. Finally, she got up and crossed to the credenza behind Mama's head, retrieved the little family album, and plopped herself down in the empty chair next to Emma.

The picture album had been a gift from Mem to Mama on her wedding day. Mem had found it in a musty little antique shop on the Mainland—one of those unnamed back alley emporiums where the only indication that commerce was being conducted inside was the collection of artifacts from past lives carefully displayed behind filmy windows. Mem had spent weeks traversing the interconnected maze of alleyways in search of the perfect wedding gift, and when she spotted the emerald velvet album lying on a parson's table amidst bits of silver and glass and one over-embellished opera fan, she knew she had found it. "Once upon a time this album held the memories of a very happy life," she told the elderly proprietor.

The little wisp of a man raised his head from his wrapping and tying and replied in whispered words that barely escaped his beard. "It shall again."

"Put the album between us, Ari." Emma put down her book and scooted over in her chair.

Ari rested the album on the arms between them and opened to the first page. There were no pictures, just an inscription written in Mem's delicate, flowing script. *May your life be filled with memories worth keeping.* After an appropriate interval, Ari turned to the next page, and she and Emma began browsing through the pictures they had reminisced over so many times before.

"I love this one," Ari said, pointing to the photograph of her parents on their wedding day. Mama and Papa were standing together against a backdrop of jungled mountains and azure seas and stately palms and lush tropical flowers where one day the Great House would rise. Papa was so handsome in his white silk shirt and linen trousers. They perfectly set off his bronzed skin and the strand of green tea leaves and butter yellow orchids and Bird of Paradise that hung around his neck.

"If it weren't for Papa's brown hair and blue eyes, you'd think he was born on the Island," Emma observed, but Ari wasn't listening. She was staring at Mama's wedding dress handed down to her by Mem. It would reappear at Emma and Ari's weddings. The dress was made entirely of pale crème silk, dupioni for the strapless bodice and floor length under sheath and sheer silk for the overlay that covered Mama's delicate shoulders and slender arms and nearly bare back and floated out in gentle gathers from the empire seam to the graceful train that elegantly trailed behind her. A single carved jade teardrop adorned Mama's forehead and hundreds of tiny jade beads twisted and turned throughout her long black hair. The only other embellishment was a bouquet of flowers matching Papa's lei, which rested gently in Mama's upturned palms.

The dress still hung in Mama's closet at the Great House where Ari retrieved it each year when they returned to the Island and stood in front of the full length mirror and waited as Mama carefully slipped the tiny loops around each of the twenty-one pearl buttons that ran the length of the back, counting *one, two, three* . . . while Ari's eyes would trace the thousands of tiny seed pearls the Island woman had hand-sewn into intricate ancestral patterns on the throat and bodice and hemline and into a liberal scattering of tiny clusters on the overskirt, and she would measure her progress toward womanhood in the fit of the dress and dream of the day the dress would belong to her.

"Ari . . . earth to Ari," Emma teased.

"Oh, sorry," she replied and turned to the next page in the album. These were the pictures of Mama and Papa in Italy, where they honeymooned at Lake Como before Papa took up his posting in Venice. There were pictures of them at the lakes, descending the cobbled, stair-stepped streets of Bellagio, and taking tea on the manicured lawns of the Grand Hotel Victoria in Menaggio, and there was one of Mama standing barefoot in front of a brightly painted red house at the water's edge in Varenna. But Ari's favorite picture was of the two of them enjoying a romantic dinner at one of the moonlit terrace restaurants that dotted the shoreline, where the only illumination came from candles on the tables and fairy lights in the trees and from the occasional flashbulbs of cameras held by genial waiters who were only too happy to oblige young lovers with keepsake photos.

From Venice there were pictures of Mama and Papa at the Grand Hotel des Bains Beach Club on the Lido, which always reminded Ari of an Esther Williams movie, and pictures of gondola rides and fancy-dress Carnivale balls and sipping Bellini Cocktails at Harry's Bar after midnight.

"What are Bellini Cocktails, Papa?" Ari asked.

"Hmm?"

"What are Bellini Cocktails?" she repeated. "It's written

under this picture in the album. See?" She turned the album around and held it in Papa's direction. "*Sipping Bellini Cocktails at Harry's Bar after midnight,*" she read aloud.

Papa put down his book and leaned forward for a better look, nearly toppling Mama to the floor in the process.

"Ethan!"

"Oh, sorry," he smiled and helped her reposition herself so she could see as well.

"The Bellini Cocktail was the invention of Harry's Bar," he began. "I believe they're a mixture of Prosecco, which is a local sparkling wine, and fresh white peach juice. Kind of like a Mimosa, but better."

"Much better!" Mama echoed.

Finally, the company car pulled up on the front drive and Mama shouted with a child's voice, "They're here!" They all darted for the foyer, like a pack of excited teeny-boppers who had just spotted the Beatles' limo approaching. Papa swung open the door and Grandfather and Mem blew in with the rain and in seconds, everyone was hugging and kissing and asking questions about the flight and sharing observations about how the children had grown and, of course, how James's best friend, Georgie, had just gotten a brand new puppy.

The driver brought in the suitcases and, with them, several Christmas presents beautifully wrapped in fibrous paper decoratively painted in red and green Island designs. Obviously, Mem had made the paper. She liked to add a personal touch to everything she did. Ari and Emma were so excited to see their grandparents that they barely noticed the colorful packages, but James couldn't take his eyes off of them, asking repeatedly if the biggest one was for him.

"Is it, Mem? Is this one for me?" he asked again, trying without success to put his arms around a giant box three feet square and twice as tall.

"No, James," Mem answered. "That package is for your Mama and Papa. But don't worry. There are some very special packages for you too. And you know what they say, James."

"What, Mem?"

"That the best things come in small packages."

"How do you know that?"

"Because, James, you're a small package and you're the best!" she exclaimed, poking his tummy and swooping him up into the arms that had been aching to do just that all the way across the Pacific.

Ari stepped back and soaked in the happy confusion that always accompanied long-awaited reunions, and she heard Mem's sweet, melodic voice, which could have been the voice of the Island breezes were they able to speak, and Grandfather's eloquent tenor, always steady, always confident, always sure of exactly what it wanted to say, and that feeling came over her again, as it always did when the whole family came together, that life was perfect and everyone and everything was in its right place.

"It is perfect, isn't it," Mama whispered from somewhere beside her. Ari turned her head in the direction of her voice and smiled.

When the greetings subsided, they all went into the living room and sat around the fire. Grandfather reposed in one of the club chairs nearest the hearth and looked, Ari thought, like a benevolent emperor holding court. He was wearing his midnight blue Nehru Jacket and creased grey woolen slacks, which made the slight silver at his temples appear even more distinguished than usual. He and Papa were deep in conversation.

They were discussing Grandfather and Mem's plans for a new science laboratory at the Island School to nurture their students' interests in physics and engineering. Papa was saying that his company's educational foundation might be interested in a project like that and that he would make inquiries. Grandfather smiled and thanked him and flashed him a look that Ari couldn't quite discern but seemed kind of amused and admiring all at the same time.

Mem was reclining on the sofa with Mama. She had already kicked off the shoes she wore as little as possible and was far too relaxed and comfortable for someone who had just flown across an ocean. She was wearing her traveling outfit, as she liked to call it—a long peach tunic and loose-fitting white linen pants and strands of pale green and pink and yellow beads around her neck. It made Ari think of a cool dish of rainbow sherbet, and she loved seeing her arrive in it each visit, but always hated seeing it come out of the closet again for the return trip home.

Eventually the conversation got around to next spring's Celebration Night and who would be dancing for the very first time. "Emma, you're out of high school now and of age. It's your right to dance, you know, if you choose."

"I know, Mama," she replied. "But I don't know if I'm ready for that just yet."

"There are, of course, girls who choose to dance just for the experience; however, I am glad I waited for your grandfather," Mem said with a fond glance at her husband and remembering. "I would have hated to waste such an important moment on someone I didn't really love. But then different generations view these things in their own way, I suppose."

"It only matters what's right for you," Papa interjected seriously. "But for what it's worth, I'm glad Mama only danced for me."

Suddenly James popped up like a spring-loaded jack-in-the-box and shouted, "Hey, everybody, look at my space station!"

"Oh, James, I can see that's a fine space station," Grandfather replied. "Why don't you show us what all those different rooms are for." As he spoke, he slid onto the floor with the agility of a child.

Ari was glad for the interruption. She didn't like talking about Celebration Night, at least not about Emma dancing. It wasn't that she begrudged her sister the opportunity or even remotely wanted to dance herself; she was way too young for that, and she was pretty sure that Emma felt the same. She just hated those transition times when her older sister embarked on a new stage in life and left her behind at the end of the old one. Like the day Emma came home after school and announced that she was too old to play dolls with Ari anymore, and when she graduated to high school and then to college, leaving Ari to fend for herself in their old school. Through each transition, Mama was there filling the void with companionship and special outings designed to make Ari feel like she was growing up too. It helped some, but Ari still couldn't shake her uneasiness.

"Ari," Mama said, leaning in and whispering, "if Emma decides to dance this year, would you be my Adi?"

"Oh, Mama, I'd love to!" she whispered back. "But what about Kemala?" Kemala was Old Batara's granddaughter, and Tao's wife and Mama's best friend. They had served Adi for each other ever since their second Celebration. First Celebrations were always reserved for the family matriarch.

"It will be all right. We always intended to serve Adi only until our own daughters were of age."

Ari's excitement was palpable. The Adi was the woman entrusted with making all preparations for a dancer on Celebration Night. Only the closest personal friends or family members were ever asked to perform this service. It was an honor to be asked and an acknowledgement of Ari's woman-hood. And, best of all, it meant admission to the Women's Hut before the ceremony.

"You are my Island Child, Arianna. I feel everything you feel. I always will." She reached for Ari's hands and stared deeply into the reflection of her own face. "I *always* will," she repeated.

The Westminster chimes struck ten and drew yawns from everyone who suddenly remembered their exhausting day, and they all agreed that it was time for bed. With Grandfather and Mem's arrival, the Christmas festivities had officially begun, and there would be a lot to do tomorrow, beginning with Papa handing down more Christmas boxes from the attic, hopefully without stepping through the ceiling of Emma's bedroom this time.

"Looks like one Heywood has beaten us to it," Papa said, smiling and pointing in the direction of the floor. James was on his stomach, his knees folded under him with his eyes shut tight, his head resting on the box of unused construction pieces. "I thought the room had quieted some in the last few minutes."

"Well, it is rather past his bedtime," Mama added. "Ari, take Grandfather and Mem to the guest room and make sure they have everything they need. I'll get this little boy to bed." She scooped up James, adjusted him in her arms so that his head rested firmly on her shoulder, and headed for the stairs. They all followed, each carrying a suitcase, and after depositing them in the guest room, everyone said their goodnights again in the upstairs hallway.

Ari turned down the covers on the old iron bed, laid out the extra down comforter from the cedar chest, checked the towels, and filled the water pitchers on the nightstands. "Is there anything else you need?" she asked.

"Just another hug from my granddaughter to make sure I'm not dreaming," Grandfather said, throwing his arms around Ari with a gentleness and a strength that were not often possessed by the same person. They hugged, and then opened their arms inviting Mem to join them.

"I'm so glad you've come," Ari whispered.

"We're never very far from you, child," Mem whispered back.

15

THE NEXT MORNING they all packed into the station wagon right after breakfast, warmed on the inside by Mama's waffles and Papa's cheesy eggs and on the outside by wool and flannel and tightly squeezed bodies. Papa had already retrieved the Christmas boxes from the attic, without mishap this time, and then had led the family in a sherpa-like procession up and down the stairs until all the boxes had been neatly deposited on the foyer floor. Now they were on their way to buy the Christmas tree.

Ari sat between Mem and Mama in the back seat and held tightly onto James, who wiggled and giggled and squirmed and chattered as usual all the way to the big Christmas tree lot near Lake Merced.

"Oh, Ari, look! Look!" James shouted as Papa pulled the car into a space next to an old black Cadillac with giant fins. James's unbridled joy at seeing all the Christmas trees infected the whole family with heightened anticipation. Everyone in the car was remembering those fleeting moments when long-awaited events finally arrived, like crossing the threshold at Disneyland, or descending the stairs in an exquisite new prom dress, or hearing the first drum beats of Celebration, or seeing Grandfather and Mem walk through the door last night.

"Isn't it exciting, James?" Ari said and squeezed a terrific giggle out of him.

Mem waited to open the back door while a large family filed out of the adjacent Cadillac and slid between the parked cars with some difficulty given their voluminous clothing. "Hurry up, Mem!" James commanded. "They're going to get our tree."

"Don't worry, James, there's a special tree waiting just for us. No one else is allowed to buy it," Ari assured him.

For the next half-hour the family strolled and sniffed and examined and compared indigenous pines and farm-raised fir and blue spruce. Periodically, one or the other would call James over and ask, "Is this our tree, James?"

"No. Keep looking," he would say. This tree was too skinny, and that tree was too pointy and the next tree had *holes* in the branches, but James continued undaunted because Ari had promised that there was a special tree waiting just for them. She was beginning to regret it.

"I found it! I found it!" he shouted at last in a voice way bigger than he was, but not half so big as his excitement. His voice must have echoed all over the lot because soon the whole family appeared, and James proudly presented his tree—a ten-foot tall, densely-branched blue spruce that smelled as if it were still growing in the forest. It truly was the most magnificent tree, worthy of the cherished ornaments the family had collected all over the world and had made by hand each year. "See, everybody, I found our tree!"

"It's the most perfect tree I've ever seen," Mama said, warming him with her smile. "Thank you, James. We couldn't have found it without you!"

Papa paid for the tree and watched as four muscular men in soiled plaid woolen jackets hoisted it on top of the car and tied it securely to the roof rack. He wondered for a moment how the family would get the majestic tree down off the car and into the house when they got home, but he knew they would manage somehow. Grandfather and Mem arrived at the car soon after with a cart load of fresh green garlands, and Mama and Emma appeared carrying little sprigs of mistletoe, which would surely find their way to every doorway and archway in the house. Ari and James were nowhere to be seen, but one familiar whistle from Papa brought them scurrying out of the trees with James holding a red and white striped candy cane that he promised not to open until later. When the garlands were loaded and "Merry Christmas" exchanges made, they all climbed back into the car and headed for home, with one quick stop at Eickele's

Bakery on the way back to pick up some Dutch Crunch rolls and assorted baked goods to munch on during the day.

They got the tree into the house with everyone's help—well, six of them anyway. James tried to help, but all he could do was hang onto the end of the trunk with his short little legs dangling in the air until he tumbled off onto the front lawn with a thud and a belly laugh.

Papa pulled out two red velvet elf hats with white balls at the tips. He set one on James's head and put the other on his own all askew and then bent way down so James could fix it for him. A flashbulb popped, and Mama disappeared down the hallway. Papa could only hope that none of his coworkers would ever get a glimpse of that photo. "Ready, partner?" he exclaimed, thrusting out his hand to James.

"Ready!" he returned, shaking Papa's hand with a grin. Another flashbulb burst and a whole lot of giggles floated into the room.

Papa and James were in charge of preparing the house for decorating. It was their job to make the tree stand and hang all the lights and tree garlands so that later the whole family could join in hanging the ornaments. Papa had already cut large, sturdy pine boards just the right size for the stand. All that was left was the driving of the nails, which he did, except for the last, most important nail, which he left for James.

Everyone was relieved when the tree was finally in place and secured to the little handmade tree stand Papa had made for Mama on their first Christmas as a married couple. Last year, the tree had been a disaster. As Papa had carried the tree through the front door, most of the needles fell off, creating a mess and eliciting a few choice words from Papa, who immediately apologized upon being scolded by Mem for using *that sort of language* in front of the children. The tree was clearly from the prior year's Christmas and had been spray painted green to look fresh and new. Papa would not stand for being taken advantage of and immediately drove down to the tree lot to demand his money back. He and Ari had then found a different lot with an honest proprietor and brought home a new tree, which James proceeded to knock over as he was flying through the living room in all of his Superman glory. *"That's it, no more Christmas trees!"* Papa had proclaimed, which sent James into a fit of hysterics, but everyone else knew Papa would never follow through with his threat.

Grandfather was busy in the long hallway that led to the dining room, untangling and laying out the large, multicolored lights for the tree and the small, twinkly fairy lights for the garlands. No matter how carefully the lights had been packed the year before, they always seemed to come out of the boxes in some sort of tangle. It required the patience of a saint to straighten out the several yards of wire and find the one or two lights that prevented whole strands from lighting. It was mutually agreed that only Grandfather possessed the patience required for the job.

In the kitchen the warm air was already filling with the scents of cinnamon, nutmeg, cloves, ginger, and vanilla. It floated up from the big gas ovens and spread out in all directions, permeating the whole house with familiar Christmas smells emanating from the mélange of Christmas cookies Mama and Emma baked each year. Some were to be kept for the family, but most were to go to others—this year to the elderly at the Laguna Honda Home. There were stars and trees and Santas and bells and giant gingerbread boys and girls ready for the family to decorate with several colors of creamy, sweet icing. And they baked Ari's favorite pfeffernuesse, those delicious little balls filled with cloves and cinnamon and covered all over in powdered sugar. Ari didn't know what she liked most about the pfefferneusse—how they slowly disintegrated in her mouth, spreading their sweetness all over her tongue, or how they set her to giggling every year when James, his face covered in powdered sugar, stood in the kitchen with his tiny little fists on his hips and insisted that he wasn't the one who ate all the *"pfeffernoonies"* off the platter.

While Mama and Emma mass produced cookies, Ari and Mem sat at the other end of the butcher block island stamping out angels with ornate cookie cutters that left imprints in the salt clay of delicate facial features and rows of lace on dresses and outlines of feathers on wings, all of which required painting by an artist's hand after the angel ornaments were removed from the oven and cooled. Mem had called last month as usual to plan this year's ornaments. Sometimes they made them out of wood, sometimes out of paper, sometimes out of dough as they were doing this year. But every year they painted them in festive designs and signed them with their initials and the year they were made, chronicling not only the products of their labors but the memory of making them together.

When the garlands were hung and the tree lights untangled and tested and the cookies and ornaments were cooling on their racks, everyone convened in the living room for a brief rest and another cup of cider before unpacking all of the Christmas boxes that had been waiting for them to open. "It's after five. Would anyone like something a little stronger than cider?" Papa asked. "I've got some twelve-year-old single malt."

"I think I could use one after untangling all those lights," Grandfather replied. "I seem to be fresh out of serenity!"

"Anyone else need a glass of serenity?" Both Mama and Mem nodded. He walked over to the tall black lacquer cabinet standing on the end wall bracketed between two giant palms in porcelain fish bowls and opened it up revealing a collection of glasses and liquor and mixes all hiding behind the ivory and soapstone figures that covered the massive Asian antique. He pulled four short glasses out from a row of similar ones, all engraved with the emblem of Raffles, placed them on a butler's tray, and poured a finger of Glenlevit's in each. Then he returned to the group, all reclining comfortably around the fire and handed out the drinks.

"You're a good son-in-law, Ethan."

"Why thank you, Joseph," Papa replied and hoisted his drink. "Cin Cin everyone!"

Ari looked around at the little gathering. It all felt so warm and familiar. The waiting, the anticipation, the animated faces and joyous exchanges and moments of introspection, the rich Christmas aromas yielding now and then to the faintest scent of Mama's jasmine and Papa's special Dunhill blend. "I wonder which box we should open first," she said, when everyone had settled in with their drinks.

"The soldiers, the soldiers!" James shouted to no one's amazement.

"Okay, James. Go see if you can find the box that says *Soldiers*."

He scurried into the foyer and Emma followed. "Do you know what letter soldiers starts with, James?"

"*S,*" he replied proudly.

"That's right, James. But Santa also starts with *S* and we have a whole collection of them too. How are you going to tell which box to get?"

He thought for a minute, scrunching up his face and then breaking into a broad smile. "I'll ask you! You know how to read, Emma."

Emma smiled, along with everyone else, at the simplicity of his solution. "That's right, James, I do," she said, and she proceeded to find the appropriate box, wholly unconcerned that James didn't follow along with her original lesson plan.

They returned to the gathering, box in hand, and sat down together on the carpet. "Here, Emma," Papa said, handing her the swiss army knife he'd brought out to slit open the tightly taped boxes. Then he slid back onto the sofa next to Mama, prepared to enjoy the quiet time that James's reunion with the tall wooden soldiers in the red British uniforms afforded the whole family. Emma handled the knife carefully, remembering her first experience with it and the tears and bandages that followed.

Papa had found the soldiers several years ago in a little military shop in the mews near Buckingham Palace. An elderly man, confined to a wheel chair since Gallipoli, owned the shop, and he had filled it with military memorabilia and hundreds of miniature soldiers he had made since confined to his chair, some for toys, some for holiday decorations, but most for use in the battle scenes depicted on tabletops scattered about the shop.

James's soldiers never failed to win great battles before taking their places on the Christmas tree. He lined them up on the living room floor opposite the collection of Christmas mice dressed in Dickensian costumes that were used to decorate the staircase garland. Mama had cleverly decided to pack them in the same box with the soldiers last year. He spit out rifle noises and cannon noises and systematically knocked over the mice, one with each noise, until his soldiers had won an overwhelming victory. Papa watched his son, smiling inside and out, and decided he'd take James to the little military shop in the mews when his son was old enough to distinguish between the romance of war and the realities.

"So, Ari," Grandfather said, over the quiet chit-chat and occasional *ratta-tat-tats* coming from the floor, "do you have all your applications submitted for college yet?

"Yes, I do."

"Where have you applied?"

"I applied to the University of California. My first choice is Berkeley and my next UCLA. And I did a back-up application to San Francisco State. I really want Berkeley though. If I don't get in there, I think I'll go to State until I can transfer."

"You could always apply to Mainland University and come live near us," Mem suggested only half in jest. "Tao's son, Joseph, is there now."

"Joey Ahmanjaya? I didn't know he followed his brother there." Tommy was the oldest of Kamela's two boys and the one closest in age to Emma. "I haven't seen Tommy in ages. Ever since his parents moved the family to the Mainland to be closer to their medical practice, he didn't get back home much."

"Well, Joey became interested in football and girls."

"That sounds like him," Ari laughed. "So, how is he?"

"He's just fine. He's pre-med, you know. He says he wants to join the family practice when he finishes med school."

"I'd love to see him again. We used to get into such mischief together when we were younger."

"As I recall," Mama said, "you two were almost inseparable as youngsters."

"Is Tommy well?" Emma asked casually, without looking up from the current battle in which her mice were getting slaughtered.

"Quite well," Mem smiled. "In another few years, he'll have his MBA. That will come in handy. Island commerce is growing."

They paused their conversation for a moment to "*ooo*" and" *aah*" over James's impending victory and watched him lead

Emma by the hand to the kitchen so she could get the Bosco off the top shelf for him. He loved making chocolate milk with Bosco. When he returned, Mama cast her eye at his glass of almost black liquid with an amused expression. "Any milk in that chocolate syrup?"

"A little, Mama," he assured her, licking the dark moustache off his upper lip.

"So, what do you think of my idea, Ari, about applying to Mainland University?" Mem asked, resuming conversation. "Joey is a very handsome man!" She rolled her eyes and gestured her amusement.

"I don't think that's the criteria I'm supposed to use for selecting a university, Mem. Still . . ."

"It's all a moot point. You'll get into Berkeley," Grandfather declared. "From what your Mama tells me about your grades and test scores, your acceptance should be automatic."

"Well, I'm not going to count on anything until the acceptance is in my hands, and that won't be till next spring."

A loud *caboom* from the carpet alerted the family that the British Army had just sustained a final and overwhelming victory over the mice, and James was ready to move on. Emma traipsed with him to the bathroom so he could wash the stickies off his face and hands, and then they returned to the family, who by this time were all sitting on the floor around the perimeter of the rug each with a different box in front of them. Mama was busy unwrapping the rest of the contents of the box with the Christmas music in it, pulling out paper-wrapped music boxes, brass bells, snowflake wind chimes and piano sheet music of familiar Christmas Carols. "Oh, Ethan, remember this one," Mama said, holding up a snow village in which the Christmas tree turned, and two miniature skaters whirled around in each other's arms to the skater's waltz. "We found this in that little shop at the end of the promenade in Bellagio. Remember?"

As each box was emptied and its contents neatly lined up on the floor, the family flattened out the sheets of newspaper and returned them to the box where they awaited the repacking after the holidays. Then they carried the empty boxes out to the foyer and came back with full ones waiting to be unpacked.

There were the hand-blown colored glass ornaments from Murano, and the brilliantly painted glass Santas and bells and snowmen from Switzerland. There were the angels dressed in crème silk and lace that Mama had found in the little shop on the Left Bank in Paris. There were the collections of colorful glass balls, and wooden toys and brass musical instruments made in the States. And there were the yards of embroidered gold brocade from Asia for encircling the tree with a festive garland. But mostly there were the happy reminiscences of a family who knew how to make memories and were making one now.

By the end of the evening, everyone was exhausted by a good day's work. The tree was fully loaded with decorations, all but the new ornaments still left for Ari and Mem to paint tomorrow, and the garlands were all decked out in their burgundy and gold ribbon, foil packages and Dickens mice. When it was time to put the angel on top of the tree, the honor went to James who sat on Papa's shoulders as he climbed the step ladder while Mama held her breath below. James strained forward and placed the angel firmly on the top point of the tree. Then wriggling against Papa's powerful grip, he said, "Let me down, Papa. We have to hang the stockings."

When the stockings were hung, James marched down the length of the fireplace stopping at each one to read the names out loud. "Ethan. That's you, Papa. Mary. Emma. Arianna. James. That's mine! Joseph. Mem. They're all here," he announced. There was an additional stocking that didn't have a name on it. James examined it curiously. "Whose stocking is this, Mama?"

"I'm not sure, James. Perhaps Santa has a surprise for you," Mama answered as she glanced over at Papa, which clearly indicated they privately shared a little secret that would be revealed shortly to the rest of the family.

"Okay, everyone. I think we're ready for the light show," Papa announced. Grandfather went to the main switch and Mem and Mama went to the switches for the garland lights, and Papa stood at the switch for the tree lights. "Ready?" Papa shouted in dramatic excitement. "Go!"

All at once the room went dark and all the Christmas lights came on. It was like a fairyland. There was a moment of silence in which everyone restarted their breathing and then broke into simultaneous congratulations. Still, they were nowhere near finished yet. Tomorrow they would get out the collections of satin-robed and beaded Santas that would greet visitors on the foyer table, and Christmas dolls in Victorian dress that would be displayed throughout the house, and the wooden nutcrackers and candlesticks and snow globes and potpourri and the Dickens Village that grew by one new building each year and would this year light up the grand piano, having outgrown the card table it had once sat on.

The clock in the foyer struck eleven. "We have a lot to do tomorrow," Papa announced. "Perhaps it's time we call it a day." He grabbed up James and lifted him high over his head before cradling him affectionately in his arms. Then he led his weary family upstairs where they paused in the middle of the hallway to say goodnight before dispersing to their own rooms and the big feather beds that awaited their aching muscles.

16

CHRISTMAS EVE FINALLY arrived and found James kneeling at the base of the tree, trying in vain to count the burgeoning mound of gaily wrapped Christmas presents one last time . . . *nine, ten, one-teen, two-teen, three-teen, four-teen, five-teen* . . . All week long packages had mysteriously made their way to the tree from bureau drawers and closet shelves and from under beds and inside hat boxes. On more than one occasion, Ari heard the squeak of the attic stairs being lowered and footsteps of someone rummaging around storage boxes, searching for gifts they had secreted away. She only hoped they wouldn't stumble across the boxes she had left there.

The men were responsible for Christmas Eve dinner. It was always a light, casual meal, something to offset the heavier formal dinner when they would inevitably over-indulge on Christmas day. This year Papa and Grandfather had chosen to make a seafood fondue out of shrimp bisque, aged cheddar and mounds and mounds of succulent crab they had purchased early that morning, fresh off the boat at Fisherman's Wharf. It always amused Ari to hear the furious sounds of the men in the kitchen and the excited banter. The air was full of authoritative directions, as if they were cooking up some great military campaign rather than a one-pot meal. But this year was even more amusing with the inclusion of James, who was deemed old enough to join the men for the very first time, and with the periodic sounds of dishes crashing to the floor and the inevitable "*uh-oh's*," which followed.

When James appeared in the living room wearing a sprinkle of shredded cheese in his hair and more than just a splash of milk on his shirt, it was difficult to keep a straight face, but the ladies managed somehow and, with his announcement that dinner was served, dutifully followed him into the little dining room. When they arrived, they found Grandfather pouring chardonnay into each of the wine glasses (except James's, in whose plastic stemware he poured white grape juice). Papa was standing beside the rolling cart holding a large wooden bowl and a linear series of ingredients in preparation for the Caesar salad he was about to make tableside. James seated each one of the ladies in chronological order of their ages, as Papa had instructed him, beginning with Mem who praised him profusely for his gentlemanly manners.

Dinner became more like a hockey match than a meal. When the salad was made and distributed, the family dove into the fondue pots, fighting for the best lumps of crabmeat, nabbing them on cubes of sourdough and whisking them to their mouths before anyone else could steal them away. Even James got into the spirited play, squealing *I got it* every time he won a lump of crab away from a would-be usurper. By the end of the meal, there was a trail of cheesy drops on the tablecloth leading from the pots to each of the place settings and a whole lot of large, gooey spots where James's food had fallen off his fork.

After dinner, Papa went to his study for a bowl of his favorite Dunhill Blend, Grandfather and Mem decided on a stroll around the neighborhood, and Mama and the children cleared the table and reset it with the festive winter dishes for Christmas breakfast. Then they retrieved the bright red pottery punch bowl from the top shelf of the pantry, set it on the island and surrounded it with a selection of the cheeriest mugs from the mug rack. Tomorrow, after breakfast and presents, Papa would make his infamous eggnog, not from that watery over-sugared bottled stuff with the funny smell, but from scratch with fresh eggs and cream and more than just a little bit of *Christmas Spirit*. Mama set out a second bowl, her bright green ceramic mixer, for the children's virgin eggnog and hoped that this year there'd be no confusion over the two, although she had to admit that the look on James's face last year when he spit out the *"nasty eggynod"* was pretty funny.

"Tell Papa we're almost done, Ari," Mama said as she set out the little condiment dishes for the nutmeg and cinnamon and cloves and then surveyed the total arrangement.

"Sure, Mama," she said, and hurried off.

She knocked on the study door and waited. There was no reply. She knocked again, more forcefully this time. Still no reply, so she put her ear to the door and listened. Faint little drifts of one-sided conversation seeped through the heavy wood—just enough to know that the conversation was serious but not enough to know what was being said. She did hear Papa say the name, "*Arthur,*" and knew that he must be speaking to his boss, Arthur Ramsey, and suddenly a vague uneasiness came over her—the kind that lacks form or substance but arises when someone close to you behaves uncharacteristically. Nothing could be more uncharacteristic than Papa conducting business on Christmas Eve.

Eventually the study went silent, so Ari slowly opened the door and peeked in. There was a slight haze lingering in the room, the aftermath of Papa's Meerschaum, and it stirred slightly as she entered. Ari liked the smell of Papa's tobacco—the way it hung on his sweaters like his own personal signature and the way its sweet, cognac-scented leaf blended so harmoniously with Mama's jasmine. But mostly she liked the gentle, subtle fragrance created by the blending of Mama and Papa, and how, over the years, it had gradually filled each strange new house with a familiarity that soothed and comforted and made the house a home.

"Papa," she said quietly, finding him deep in thought in his wingback chair. He didn't answer. He just continued frowning at the Toby Character Jugs on his mantle. "Papa," she repeated a little louder this time.

"What is it, Ari?" His voice sounded flat and tired.

"We're ready for you."

"I'll be along in a moment."

Ari didn't leave. Instead she slumped down in the chair opposite Papa and waited. "What are you thinking about?" she asked at last.

"I was just remembering all the wonderful junkets your

Mama and I made into the English countryside collecting those mugs." He walked over to the mantle and retrieved a jug, an original Dick Turpin with a green jacket and mask uplifted to reveal its face. "We found this one down in Devonshire in a little village called Widecombe on the Moor." He handed Ari the jug for her inspection.

"I remember you and Mama talking about Widecombe and some man that you met there."

"Andrew Thatcher. He owned a little curio shop in the village. At least it looked like a little shop until he led us down these dark, creaky stairs into an underground root cellar filled with hundreds of Tobies."

"In the middle of nowhere like that?"

"It surprised us, too, but apparently Andrew was well known to collectors. He had several discontinued mugs and even a few pre-wars. I found this mug there," he said, gently tapping the Dick Turpin.

Ari got up out of her chair, pushing herself up carefully with one hand while cradling the Toby to her stomach with the other. She replaced the jug on the mantle and then tried to follow Papa's gaze, but it didn't seem to land on anything in particular. "You know what Mama always says—*only memories, no regrets.*"

There was a gentle knock at the door. "Are you two all right in there?" It was Mama.

"Couldn't be better," Papa returned and swung open the study door. "Are we ready?" His voice was energetic and familiar.

The family assumed their traditional Christmas Eve places in the living room. Papa sat in one of the club chairs nearest the fire, turning it slightly to face the sofa where Grandfather and Mem were already curled up together. Mama and the children sat on the rug at Papa's feet. As everyone settled themselves into comfortable positions, Papa opened the large leather-bound volume of *The Night Before Christmas* and began to read, his deep baritone voice resonating through the air that surrounded them all. "T'was the night before Christmas and all through the house . . ."

By the time Papa reached the end, James was getting sleepy.

It was time to open the Christmas Eve packages and put him to bed. After all, there was still work to be done. "Can we open our presents now?" James asked through a yawn that was just forming itself in the back of his throat. "Please, Mama," he added thinking the please might get him a *yes*.

James opened his package first to reveal brand new flannel pajamas covered all over with a new crop of puppies, which obviously delighted him. Mama's package contained a very sexy green negligee of pure silk with a low back and a slit up the side and a matching kimono-styled robe that went all the way to the floor. "Oh, Ethan," she laughed, "not in front of the children!"

Papa got silk pajamas in dark greens and blues and golds, which elicited that smile Mama knew and the girls were guessing almost always preceded foreplay. Emma and Ari opened their packages last. After all, it wasn't like they didn't already know what was inside them. Or so they thought. It was Emma who first held up her new silk negligee and uttered a long, breathy, "Thank you."

"You girls are practically women," Papa answered. "Mama and I thought it was time you were treated like young women." It was Papa who had bought the negligees, searching until he had found ones that were appropriately feminine without being sexy. After a lunch hour spent at the City of Paris wading through dozens of necklines that were too low and slits that were too high, he had finally found the lace-trimmed gowns of pure vanilla, with robes whose Victorian necklines rose to the throat.

Ari turned to James to show him her new nightgown and tell him how handsome she thought his new pajamas were, but he was sound asleep. "I think sugar plums are already dancing in his head," Mama smiled. "I'll get him to bed, and we can get started." Mama carried him up to bed, dressed him in his new pajamas, tucked him into his freshly laundered sheets, kissed both cheeks, and returned downstairs to finish the night's work.

Papa had already retrieved the big box from the garage, which contained James's new two-wheeler, and was laying out the pieces in logical order on the carpet. He and Mama were going to put the bike together, but not before the inevitable argument over Papa's insistence that there was a right way to do things and that all directions must be thoroughly read and strictly adhered to and Mama's desire to launch right in and see what happens.

"Who's going to help me take one bite out of each cookie?" Ari asked. They all raised their hands.

"I'll drink half of the milk from the glass," Emma said, knowing her sister wasn't a fan of milk except in cereal.

"And I'll make the trail of cookie crumbs to the fireplace," Mem offered.

"I guess that leaves me to spread the ashes on the hearth and leave a boot mark in them," Grandfather said. "Ethan, do you still keep your work boots in the garage?" Papa nodded while straining with one of the bolts on James's bike.

When their work was finally done, everyone stood and surveyed the results. The bicycle stood in the middle of the room where James was sure to see it from the stairs, and Mama was sure to get a picture of his face when he did. Santa had tasted each of the different cookies and had drunk half the milk. His cookie crumbs were left, his boot mark made, and all that was left was to write Santa's note to James.

"Who's going to write the note this year?" Mama asked.

"May I?" asked Grandfather, and Mama handed him the special stationary she kept hidden for the occasion.

Grandfather wrote out the note and then read it aloud for everyone's approval. "Dear James," he began. "Thank you for being such a good boy this year. I'm glad you're learning to say please and thank you and that you listen to your Mama and Papa when they ask you to do something. I'm not mad at you for lying to your Mama about who ate the *pfeffernoonies* that were in the refrigerator. Nobody's perfect. Just try a little harder to tell the truth next time."

Mama smiled at this. Grandfather continued, "Thanks also for the cookies and milk. I was sure hungry. I hope you don't mind, I took some extras for my reindeer. Sorry I had to eat on the run; I still have a lot of packages to deliver. Hope you like your new bike."

"Could you add just one more line, Joseph?" Papa asked.

"What's that?"

"After *hope you like your new bike,* would you add *I made it especially for you with my own hands.*"

Grandfather did as he was asked, signed it with love from Santa, and then sealed the letter in the gilt-lined envelope and placed it in the basket of the shiny red bicycle. Everyone applauded. Grandfather bowed with a sweeping gesture of his arm and then they all agreed that it was time for bed. Once inside her bedroom, Ari put on her new negligee and stared at herself in the mirror. She was sad and elated all at once not to be thought of as a little girl anymore. She walked over to her bed and slid between the new sheets that had hung in the fresh winter sun all day and breathed in the fragrance that few people knew anymore. She would always hang her sheets in the sun she decided.

Before long Emma came in, looking older, Ari thought, and jumped under the covers. "Well, Emma, you've never said. Are you going to do it? Are you going to dance this year when we go to the Island?"

"No way!" she said without hesitation. "When I'm on the Island, it seems like the most natural thing to do, but when I'm here it seems like the thing only cheap girls do or girls who have dated the same guy for a really long time."

"Do you ever think of doing it with Roger?"

"Sometimes," she answered honestly. "We've been dating for a long time now."

"That doesn't sound like much of a reason."

A smile crept across Emma's face. "No . . . it's not, is it?" she murmured. She didn't say anything else for a full minute, and Ari waited. "What about you and Jason?" she finally asked.

"Well, Jason wants to. I don't know though."

"I asked Mama once how you know when you're ready," Emma said.

"What did she say?"

"That I wouldn't have to ask if I was. I'm not sure that's true, but I do know that I'm not ready now, so I guess I'll just be watching the Celebration this year."

"Mama and Papa will be glad," Ari observed. She didn't tell Emma how relieved she was as well.

Both girls lay silently for a few moments, both trying to imagine what it would really be like their first time, neither coming anywhere close. "Remember the first time we sneaked out of bed and watched the dancing?" Ari asked. "I didn't want you to know, but it kind of scared me. I don't think I was old enough, but I didn't want you to think I was a baby either, so I went with you."

Emma started to laugh. "I didn't like it any more than you did, but I was trying to act so grown up."

"Well, we may not be completely grown up yet," Ari said, "but we're making progress. At least the thought of sex doesn't make us sick anymore!"

17

THE STEREO BLASTED out the first notes of "Joy to the World" from downstairs as Mama and Papa shouted *Merry Christmas* up the stairwell. Ari and Emma came running downstairs together, dressed in their new gowns and robes, with James dangling between them, his small hands held firmly in theirs, his feet not even touching the treads. When they reached the step that afforded a view into the living room, the girls suddenly stopped and shouted in feigned surprise, "Oh James! Look what's waiting for you in the living room."

"A bike! A bike!" he screeched with joy enough to fill the room. The sisters continued holding his hands to the bottom of the stairs averting a sure accident. Then they let go and James ran into the living room and climbed up on the bicycle seat, only tripping once along the way on his new puppy pajamas, which were just an inch too long.

"Oh, Papa," James beamed proudly, ringing the shiny chrome bell on the handlebars, over and over and over. "Do you like it?"

"It's the best bike I ever saw." Papa shouted over the noise.

When James tired of ringing the bell, Papa set him down and together they found the remains of the cookies Santa had eaten, and the footprints he had left on the hearth. Then Papa read James the letter that Santa had left for him. James's expression showed no signs of disappointment at Santa's inability to bring him his long sought-after puppy, but then he was distracted by all the other presents under the tree. Maybe he thought his puppy was waiting for him there.

Ari viewed all this from the living room entrance as if she

were a distant observer watching the scene unfold on a giant television screen. She envied James a little. Not that Christmas wasn't still magic for her too.

"Do you wish you still believed in Santa?" Mama whispered, startling Ari who hadn't seen her come up beside her.

"A little," she admitted. "I still remember the day I came home from school and told you and Papa that Michelle Depardeau said that Santa wasn't real, and I asked you if that was true."

"I think that day was as sad for me as it was for you. James was still an impossible dream, and if the doctors were right, it was the end of an era for Papa and me."

Ari looked at Mama and studied her face and saw the serenity and contentment that was almost always there. "How do you do it, Mama, cope with endings, I mean?"

"By letting go."

"What do you mean?"

"Well, every time I find myself starting to feel sad at the passing of time, I think about the day you and Emma will join me in the women's hut at Celebration. And how we'll wait for the drums to call us to the Gathering Place, and how we'll tell stories about our lovers and share secrets only women are meant to know." Mama paused for a moment to play this scene out in her mind. "I might not have my little girls much longer, but soon we will be three women together. Once I let go of the past, I can enjoy the present and begin anticipating the great joys that wait for me right around the corner."

The children enjoyed the lion's share of the packages, James ripping open his gifts, barely noticing what was in the first in his excitement to get to the next and the next, and Emma and Ari opening theirs ever so slowly, knowing that the anticipation was half the fun. There were gifts filled with new clothing that Ari and Emma delighted in and James tossed aside in his determination to root out all the toys, a new hair dryer for Emma, and a portable phonograph for Ari, and a junior baseball glove and bat and ball for James so he could make his first foray into the alley down the street with Papa to teach him and protect him. By the time they were through, the three youngest Heywoods were surrounded by stacks of open boxes and mounds of wadded up wrapping paper, and James had nearly disappeared in the debris.

Finally, it was time to open the *big* gifts. "I wanna go first!" James shouted rising from his seat on the floor and hurtling himself toward the tree. He would have toppled headfirst into the lower branches if Papa hadn't intercepted him and grabbed him up in his arms. He sat him down gently, but firmly in his lap.

"Today, James, you must wait until the last. Do you know why?" Papa asked. James just shook his head. "Because, we're saving the very *bestest* present for last, and it's really, really, really worth waiting for. I promise!"

Emma opened her gift from Mama and Papa first. It was a large bisque porcelain carousel with horses and lions and tigers ornately decorated like Victorian carousels from the turn of the century. She had nothing like it in her already substantial music box collection.

"Oh, I love it. This is a real collector's piece. Wherever did you find it?"

"You remember last spring when Papa and I flew over to Switzerland for a few days for Papa's meetings? That's where we found it—in a little clock shop in the old city in Lake Lucerne," Mama answered.

Ari's was a big package with several parts to it. Inside one long narrow box was a brand-new professional easel. Inside a smaller rectangular box was a wooden case filled with tubes of watercolors and expensive brushes. There was also a large, flat parcel, obviously a book of some kind that Ari assumed was a *How To* book on painting. When she opened it, she found instead a beautiful hardcover coffee table book featuring a collection of works by her favorite artist, Maxfield Parrish. Slipped inside was an envelope containing tickets to the Parrish exhibit at the Museum, which had sold out long before it ever opened. "You said you tried to get tickets, but they were all sold out!" Mama and Papa just smiled. "Thank you," Ari smiled back.

Grandfather and Mem opened their gift next—an antique picture frame, which Mama and the girls had found hiding behind several bolts of silk fabric in an Indonesian import shop on Union Street and had filled with a collage of photographic memories of events the grandparents had missed. "I know exactly where this is going," Mem said.

"The end table next to the lounger in the gathering pavilion?" Ari surmised.

"Exactly!"

When Mama and Papa opened their gift from Grandfather and Mem, they too were overcome with emotion, even Papa who rarely veered too far from center. It wasn't the large Chinese fishbowl that moistened his eyes, nor the pinks and purples and greens of its exquisitely crafted ancient designs. It was the majestic Bird of Paradise that ballooned out from its loamy soil, shooting a dozen regal purple and orange heads skyward.

"This is from our place, isn't it, Mem?" he said, referring to the lagoon by which he had lain with Mary on Celebration Nights—and where all three of his children were conceived.

"We grew it from cuttings from the bush at the top of the twin waterfalls," she replied.

"Thank you, Mem, and you too, Joseph," he warmly returned, and Mama reiterated the appreciation.

Next Papa opened his gift from Mama and the children. It was a beautiful velvet piped smoking jacket and twelve hand printed tickets giving Papa permission to smoke his pipe anywhere in the house he chose, one day a month. He laughed, saying it was about time they admitted that he was king of his castle, if only for twenty-four hours at a time.

Then it was Mama's turn to open her gift from Papa and the children. James climbed down off Papa's lap. "Open the card, Mama. I made it all by myself!" he proudly announced.

"Really, James? How wonderful!" she gushed. She slipped the card out from under the gold satin ribbon and read aloud the words that James had laboriously copied down with Ari's help and limitless patience. *"Merry Christmas to our favorite author. You make our dreams come true every day of the year."* It was signed by each member of the family. "Thank you, James, for my beautiful card."

Everyone watched as Mama untied the ribbon and pulled loose the scotch tape and slid the paper from the book until it alone rested upside-down on her lap. Slowly she turned it over revealing the cover. Ari had pictured this moment all those weeks she had painted kings and queens and castles and knights, and lazy summer swimming holes and Santa's Workshop full of toys. Mama gasped in disbelief.

"It's your book, Mama," James said.

Mama ran her fingers over the embossed gold leaf letters on the cover. *Dreams for All Seasons by Mary Heywood.* She opened the book, and the family watched in silence as she perused each page, running her hands over Emma's calligraphy, delighting in each new image in Ari's illustrations and loving Ethan more than ever for making possible this most cherished gift.

"Well, I guess that's all," Papa teased, knowing the rise he would get out of his young son. He wasn't disappointed.

"No, Papa! You forgot me! I want my big present." There was nothing frantic in his voice. Papa had promised him a gift *"really, really, really"* worth waiting for, and Papa always kept his promises. Even Papa needed reminding sometimes though.

"That's right," Papa smiled. "Now where did we leave your present? Have you seen it, Mama?"

"Somewhere," she joined in the game. "Now where can it be?"

"James, look under the tree and see if it's there," Papa directed. James scurried over to the tree, got down on his tummy, and peered under the low hanging branches for the missing present.

"It's not here, Papa."

"Well, Mary, maybe we left it in the under stairs closet. Try there."

James did as he was told, and the rest of the family followed him. He opened the closet door and crawled inside, feeling the floor under the coats for his present, but nothing was there either. He emerged from the darkness looking a little forlorn.

"Think hard, Ethan," Mama commanded. "I'm sure you'll remember where we put James's gift *this* time." It was time for the teasing to stop, but fathers rarely understood the importance of such things.

Papa bent down on one knee facing James. "Give me your

bestest bear hug, partner, and I'll bet that will pop the memory right out of my brain." James put his arms around Papa's broad chest just as far as he could and squeezed, grunting and groaning and scrunching up his fat little cheeks until they were almost purple. "I've got it!" Papa announced. "Remember, Mary? We left James's big present on the front porch."

James dodged past Grandfather who was blocking his path, reached up, pulled the big wrought iron lever and swung the door inward. "A puppy! A puppy!" he screeched, loud enough for the whole neighborhood to hear him. "You got me a puppy!" Tied up to the railing was the little tri-color collie puppy that James had seen in the window of Robinson's Pet Store. He still wore the big green Christmas ribbon around his neck, but now there was a tag hanging from it that read in big bold red letters, *For James Joseph Heywood.*

"He is the *bestest* present, Papa! He is!" James sputtered through wet doggy kisses and equally wet nose nuzzles. James couldn't stop laughing—big robust belly laughs that sounded as if they came from someone several times his size. Papa grinned from ear to ear. Mama smiled from behind her camera.

"What are you going to name him, James?" Emma asked. James put two fingers to his chin, deep in thought.

"Tippy!" he proudly proclaimed.

"That's a wonderful name," Mama said. "Let's go write it on his stocking, shall we?" Ari was right. The mysterious extra stocking signified a new member of the family was soon to arrive, and she wondered what that sudden arrival meant for the rest of the family.

That night the family sat longer than usual around the festive dinner table, even little James, whose puppy sat in a box on an empty chair next to him, right in front of the place card marked *Tippy.* The only light in the room came from three large cut-crystal bowls filled with floating candles, whose flickering flames periodically sent prismatic designs flashing about the walls, and from the thousands of tiny white fairy lights strung over archways and French doors showing off Grandfather's skill at untangling lights and hanging garlands. They all talked and joked and laughed as usual, except maybe Papa. Ari couldn't put her finger on it exactly, but there was something different about his rhythm. It was like he was a half beat off from the rest of the orchestra, not all the time, just every once in a while. Papa definitely had a secret he wasn't ready to share with the family, and this troubled Ari a little. But she wouldn't think about that now. No use spoiling a perfectly wonderful Christmas dinner by brooding over something that might be nothing at all.

When at last the family got up from the table, unbalanced from the excess of rich foods—beef wellington, apricot glazed carrots, buttered croissants, roasted potatoes and black forest cake, they immediately began clearing up. All except James, whom Mama had wisely deposited out of the way on the kitchen floor with his new puppy while everyone else carried the good crystal and heirloom dishes.

The phone rang and Emma and Ari both ran to answer it, hoping it was their boyfriend. Ari got there first. "Hello."

"Ari?" the familiar voice on the other end asked.

"Hi, Jason. Merry Christmas!" He could hear in her voice how glad she was that he called.

"Merry Christmas, Ari. Are you having a good one?"

"The best! How about you?"

"Well, it's what I expected."

"Oh, Jason, I'm sorry. You don't sound very happy."

"That's all right," he said flippantly, "I don't care. It's only a holiday. At least the skiing's good."

"Has something happened?"

"Nothing special. Just the usual. Mom's overly festive. Dad's overly miserable. And my grandparents just sit in the corner and complain how the world's going to the dogs."

"I'm sorry," she said again. She didn't know how else to respond to all the negativity.

"Well, at least New Year's Eve is going to be great."

Jason's cousin, who was a freshman at San Francisco State, was having an Open House. The party was up on Twin Peaks, and Jason said that you could see the lights of the city, all the way to the Bay, from the picture windows that ran the entire length of the two-story living room.

"I can't wait to see you," Ari said. "I miss you."

"Me, too." They spoke for a few minutes more about the presents they received and their plans for the rest of the week, and they thanked each other once more for the gifts they had exchanged that last night at Giusseppi's—the photograph of the Grand Canal in Venice that Ari had blown-up from a snapshot and had professionally framed and the heart-shaped silver locket he had given her with a note that said, *Keep me close to your heart.* Ari had cut out a picture of Jason that she had taken in the Wine Country and had placed it in the locket. She hadn't taken the locket off since except to shower.

When Ari hung up the phone, she joined everyone else now in the living room lounging comfortably or uncomfortably depending upon their food consumption. She must have had an odd expression on her face. "Who rained on your parade?" Mama asked.

"What? Oh, I'm sorry. I was just thinking about something Jason said. Nothing important." The smile returned quickly to her face, perhaps too quickly, Mama thought.

18

IN THE DAYS between Christmas and New Years the family settled into a quiet routine, rising when the mood struck them, every day a Sunday. James learned to ride his new bike without training wheels in only two days, and Papa said that was a good thing because he was tired of chasing James's wiggly little behind down the street. Mama had less success helping James housebreak his new puppy. She said that the puppy needed a lot more than two days before *his* training wheels came off.

When Emma wasn't out somewhere with Roger, she was at the piano, serenading the family with *Misty*, whose sheet music she found rolled up in her stocking on Christmas morning. Grandfather spent long afternoons reading in the club chair nearest the piano. He had just finished a re-read of *The Mayor of Casterbridge* and was about thirty pages into the latest J. T. Keenan mystery. Grandfather never put on airs when it came to literature. He loved a good who-done-it, and Keenan was his favorite mystery writer. At least that's what Ari thought. Grandfather's bookshelves at home contained every volume Keenan ever wrote.

Mem and Ari spent their days in Mama's writing room, chatting about everything and nothing while applying paint to canvas and paper. It was a perfect place to paint. The sun streamed in through the glass walls all day, filling the hexagonal room with light from all directions. You could hardly call it a room. It was more like one of those Victorian conservatories with a white-washed tongue and groove ceiling that soared to a point in the exact middle and masses of tropical trees and shrubs and orchids randomly placed around the furniture.

Mama's writing desk faced the doors to the living room. Its lines were simple and organic, but the polished rosewood gave it elegance, what little you could see of it under the old typewriter and stacks of loose-leaf paper. A white wicker settee, matching rockers at the far end of the room, a few small tables, and an old-fashioned chaise, which faced a little pond and the graceful cutleaf Japanese Maple that bowed and swayed and fluttered in the breezes beyond the windows, were the only other furnishings.

Ari hoped that the lush, tropical surroundings would offer her some much needed inspiration for her painting of the Island. "I don't understand why I can't get this painting right," she said in exasperation one day. "You'd think the Island would be so easy for me to paint." She watched Mem who was effortlessly applying paint to canvas, her brush seemingly painting the picture by itself. It was a portrait of Grandfather gazing at the horizon from the Sunset Bench. Mem was painting from memory.

"Technically your painting is excellent, Ari. But it's not your best work."

"I know, Mem, but why?"

"Well, it's only my opinion, of course, but I saw *you* in the paintings you did for Mama's book. I don't see you here." She said this with an honesty that Ari valued over the false praise most adults offered. Ari threw down her brush in defeat, causing a tiny splash of green water to fall on the black and white tiled floor.

Mem put down her brush and palette and turned to her granddaughter. "Ari, when you painted the illustrations for Mama's book, what inspired you?"

"Mama did," she answered in a voice that said the answer should have been obvious.

"But, Ari, you didn't just do picture versions of Mama's words. Your illustrations were alive, like you were the little girl in those paintings and you had actually lived each of the dreams. You invited the readers to live the dreams with you, not just look on as bystanders."

"In a way I had lived them, Mem. I remember every one of those stories from when I was a little girl and Mama used to tell them to Emma and me in bed. After a while, we knew the stories by heart, and we'd beg her to tell us our favorites over and over."

"But those stories were more than that to you, weren't they, Ari? Think, child!" Mem was wearing that odd, almost ethereal expression that Ari had seen come over her from time to time.

"Well . . . perhaps there was something," she began. She thought a bit more before continuing. "The first night we slept in a new house, I'd always feel kind of scared. Well, not scared exactly, but kind of spooky. There'd be boxes everywhere, and our bedroom wouldn't be set up yet. It was all so unfamiliar and chaotic and . . . I don't know. It wasn't our home. And then Mama and Papa would come up and tuck us in as they always had, and Mama would spend an extra long time storying us to sleep, and everything would just feel right somehow."

"Those stories were Mama's gift to you and Emma," Mem said, with obvious admiration for her daughter. "She was giving you a part of herself through the telling of them, a part that comforted you then and will still be with you when you are ninety. Mama found her voice with words. Your voice is in your paintings." Mem picked up the water can in which several brushes were soaking and handed it to Ari. "Now, speak to us!"

Ari thought about this for a moment. "I *think* I understand, Mem, but I don't know where to begin."

Mem reached over and removed the photograph of the Island that Ari had taped to her easel just above her painting. "Perhaps, by putting it away for a bit until the Island speaks to you again. Maybe you are trying to capture something that you haven't experienced yet," she said.

Ari spent that evening lounging on the chaise in the conservatory pouring through her Maxfield Parrish book. "I thought Alma watered the plants on Thursdays," Ari said when Mama entered the room carrying a brass watering can. Alma was the housekeeper who came in three days a week to put a shine on the house but never to pick up after the children. That was their responsibility.

"She does," Mama replied. But she's been off since my Bird of Paradise came, and I noticed it was looking a little thirsty." Ari looked at the majestic plant in its ancient Chinese pot and the masses of slender green leaves and flamboyant blooms and the single new bud that would soon burst forth into orange and purple brilliance, and she saw no signs of it needing water. But Mama swore that plants talked to you if you only listened. Perhaps she was right. Plants thrived under her care. Ari, on the other hand, could kill a spider plant, and usually nothing could make those die.

She watched as Mama finished watering and left the room, leaving behind a small puddle of water on the floor as evidence that she had been there. Not that this room required any more evidence of Mama's presence. It was everywhere, from the writing desk with its clunky old black Underwood and scraps of paper scattered about with hastily scribbled ideas that wanted remembering to the lush tropical flora that snaked and vined and umbrellaed and billowed about the room to the dozens of family photos that peeked out from end tables and door jambs and window frames to the slight scent of jasmine that always hung in the air. Few women could fill a room like Mama could.

Ari leaned back until she felt the plump paisley cushion fill the space behind her. Then she rested her elbow on the single armrest, and her cheek on her hand, and stared out into the gardens, replicating the pose in which she had so often found Mama when she tip-toed into the room. Mama said that she reclined on the chaise whenever she needed to *gather ideas*. That there was just something about the softness of it that welcomed the curves of her body and made her stop over-thinking things.

Ari wriggled herself into the indentations Mama's body had left in the feathery cushions, in hopes that the magic chaise might mistake her for Mama and send her an epiphany. Then she closed her eyes and waited. Nothing happened. All she could see was blackness followed by little bursts of lights and darks, which eventually grew into showers of glittery colors bursting up and cascading down in slow motion, like her own private fireworks show. But then images began to play themselves in her head, like one of Papa's slide shows projected on the portable white screen. They were fuzzy at first, overexposed in the light, but gradually they came into focus, and she was seeing the Island, not as a bare landscape, but with the people she knew there and loved.

She saw Grandfather and Mem standing on the steps of the Island School, bathed in early morning light and smiling at the eager children who emerged from the palm groves in answer to Grandfather's old brass bell. And she saw the water babies, too young to answer the bell with little James among them, kicking and thrashing their way out to the reef to swim with the sea creatures as if they were one of them. She saw Old Batara and Maru on their daily stroll through the fields and Old Willie, the fisherman, in his faded red skiff. Kemala and Tao were carrying mango pie and fresh berry tarts to pot-luck at the Great House. And then she saw Emma, crouching beside her under the old banyan tree, her hair in the single French braid she used to wear when she was young, staring out at the Gathering Place and stifling giggles. Mama was in the Gathering Place, dancing her slow, undulating dance for Papa, so graceful and serene and seductive. And the look on Mama's face when she called Papa to her, was the same look she wore on Christmas day when she first saw the giant Bird of Paradise in its ancient Chinese Pot.

Ari opened her eyes, and the Bird of Paradise stared back at her from the carved mahogany plant stand that elevated it above the rest of the jungle. It seemed to be smiling at her. Suddenly, she bolted from the chaise, maneuvered through the maze of plants and furniture and ran through the living room on her way to the stairs. "Where's the fire?" Mama laughed.

Ari didn't answer. She just ran upstairs and changed as fast as she could, not stopping to fold or hang up or put away her clothes. Then she went down to the storage room off the kitchen where she kept her painting supplies and grabbed a fresh sheet of fibrous watercolor paper. Running through the living room with paper in hand, she nearly knocked Mem over.

"Oh, I'm sorry, Mem," she said as they righted themselves. "Are you all right?"

"I'm fine, Ari," Mem laughed. "I'm not that fragile. Where are you off to in such a hurry?"

"I know how to paint the Island," she exclaimed. "I

know . . ." Ari stopped in mid-sentence, not wanting to take the time to explain and knowing that she didn't need to.

She headed for the writing room, closed the door behind her, and turned her easel around so that it faced away from the living room and the glass doors through which someone could see her painting before it was finished. Then she replaced the old painting with the new paper, put fresh water from the spicket just outside the garden door in her can of brushes, laid out her tubes of paint on the little plastic work table she used for her supplies, and settled on her stool. "I'm ready," she smiled at the blank paper.

For the next few days Ari worked furiously, only stopping to take a brief meal or an abbreviated night's sleep, or a much needed shower that Mama insisted upon, she said, before Ari permanently ruined the fragrant air in her writing room. Mem joined her for several hours each day but spoke only infrequently and never asked to see the painting that now sat with its back to hers. On the few occasions when Ari arose from her easel, she covered the painting with a cloth, telling everyone she wanted it to be a surprise. But that wasn't exactly true. It was really that she wanted to see if she could get this painting right all by herself—no clues from those who already knew what she was just now discovering.

When the painting was finally completed, Ari stood back and surveyed it. It was the best work she had ever done—even better than her illustrations for Mama's book. She signed the painting *Arianna Elizabeth* as she always did and dated it before she covered it back up. Then she joined the family gathered in the living room.

"Have you returned to us for more than five minutes?" Papa asked good-naturedly.

"Yes," she answered, both tired and exhilarated. "The painting is finished."

"You are obviously very pleased with your work," Mem observed.

"How do you know that?"

"Because you have the look of someone who has discovered a great secret."

"When do I get to see it?" Mama asked. "After all, I did donate my writing room to its production."

"Well, I was going to unveil it on New Year's Day, but I can't wait that long to show it to you. How about after dinner? I need to get cleaned up first and have something to eat. I'm starving!"

"We'll have an unveiling party," Mama said, never missing a chance to celebrate and then added, "Where are you going, Ethan?"

Papa, who had just risen from his chair, replied, "I'm going to get the camera. I believe we're going to need it tonight." And he winked at his daughter as she ran by.

Ari showered and put on a fresh shirt and some comfortable slacks. Then she clasped her locket around her neck while surveying herself in the full-length mirror. She opened up the locket and looked at Jason's picture for the first time in three days she suddenly realized and wondered if that meant anything.

Ari barely noticed the egg rolls she ate that night or the Wor Won Ton or Char Siu Bow. Usually she gushed over Mama's Asian cooking, but she was too excited at the prospect of unveiling her work. She knew how James felt all those times he had to remain at the table and wait patiently for the rest of the family to finish their meals before he got up from his hastily emptied plate. Tonight, it seemed as if even James was eating slowly. Of course, he was eating for two now, every other bite of eggroll making its way to Tippy under the table.

Finally, dinner was over. Papa sent James into the living room to save a big club chair for them to sit in and then he went into the writing room to retrieve the easel and painting. Mama and Emma took up places on the sofa and Grandfather and Mem occupied the two chairs opposite Papa's. Tippy lay sound asleep in his cardboard box at the edge of the carpet.

Ari stood by the easel in front of the fireplace and, when everyone was settled, she announced, "I call this painting *The Gift*," and she pulled away the cover with drama befitting the occasion.

"It's Mama!" James shouted over an audible gasp from her. "Ari, you painted Mama! Paint Tippy next, okay?"

Ari had painted Mama reclining on the chaise in her writing room. Her back was to the door and she was leaning back in her thinking pose, gazing past the Bird of Paradise in its ancient Chinese pot and through the windows beyond. Her hair hung loose in cascades down her back and she was wearing Papa's favorite sarong—the multi-colored silk with the Bird of Paradise pattern that, much like the Scottish tartans, was the family's personal signature. Mama wore that expression she reserved only for Papa.

Instead of painting the San Francisco garden beyond the windows, Ari had painted the lagoon with the twin waterfalls and the original Bird of Paradise billowing out from the precipice above. She had never been to their special place, but Mama had shown her a picture of it once, and she had never forgotten its beauty. There were two figures lying in the grass at the water's edge, barely perceptible in all the greenery. And in the shadow of the doorway just behind Mama's head there was the faintest suggestion of a little girl with long black hair. She, too, was staring out through the windows, and she, too, wore the signature silk and her Mama's expression.

"Oh, Ari," Mama murmured. "It's . . . it's . . . " She couldn't think how to finish her sentence. Tears spilled over her lashes and down her cheeks.

19

JASON AND ARI sat at the corner of Broadway and Columbus in North Beach, waiting for the light to change. It was cold outside, but the waves of heat floating up from the floor vents in the little sports car warmed Ari's legs and sent whiffs of Jason's Jade East cologne her way. Her body responded, as it always did to his cologne, with that familiar sensation in the pit of her stomach that began like an adrenalin rush and then slowly spread a tingly feeling all the way to her fingers and toes. She had never felt anything like it before, not until the very first time she and Jason slow danced, and he held her close, and she put her head on his shoulder and nuzzled his neck, losing herself in the music and the scent of him.

The sidewalks were already crowded with New Year's Eve revelers who had come to the ethnic neighborhood for its authentic Italian cuisine and for the numerous clubs and topless bars for which the district was famous. Phinnochio's, the drag club where young men transformed themselves into beautiful divas for the pleasure of high society patrons, would be packed tonight, as would Enrico's Coffee House and the Bocce Ball and the world famous Condor Club where Carol Doda exposed the breasts that Lloyds of London had insured for 1.5 million dollars. Of course, Broadway was not a good place to bring a high school girl on New Year's Eve, and Ari was relieved when the light changed, and Jason headed the Healy down Columbus Avenue toward the Wharf.

"Are we going to Scoma's for crab?" she asked.

"You'll see," Jason smiled, suddenly turning right and beginning the steep ascent up Telegraph Hill.

"What restaurants are up here?"

"You'll see," he repeated.

Ari cocked her head to see Jason's expression as he stared straight ahead. He was obviously quite pleased with himself. She put her hand on his shoulder and squeezed the soft wool of his navy blue blazer and moved her hand to his collar and ran her fingers through the fringe of blond hair that hung over it. He looked especially good tonight. After two weeks of skiing in Vermont, he was tan and vigorous and could have been mistaken for one of those Scandinavian ski instructors who frequently appeared in romantic comedies. That tingly feeling ran through her again. "I've missed you," she sighed.

"I've missed you too, Ari," he said. He reached over and squeezed her knee and quickly returned his hand to the gear-shift knob just in time to downshift before making a sharp left turn onto a street of upscale houses. Ari stared out the window at the tall, narrow dwellings tightly packed together on the scarce San Francisco real estate. They were multi-level structures, clinging precariously to the hillside, each with its own unique architecture, but all sharing one thing in common—the mag-nificent panoramic view of the City by the Bay. Her eyes darted from one building to the next, from doorways to alleyways to street signs, but as hard as she tried, she could find no clue to their ultimate destination.

Jason had called Ari earlier that day to tell her to "*dress fancy.*" He wouldn't tell her where they were going before the party. Just that it was a big surprise and she was going to love it. It was all so romantic. So she had drawn a bath instead of show-ering and had lain for almost an hour in the jasmine scented bubbles from Mama's amber glass decanter. Then she had spent an extra-long time with Emma in the feminine pre-date ritual of running back and forth between bedrooms borrowing shoes and jewelry and the inevitable pair of panty hose, which Ari always needed after discovering at the last minute that all hers had runs in them.

At six o'clock Mama had come into her bedroom carrying the blue velvet box that held the emerald stud earrings and the platinum and emerald hair combs that Papa had commissioned for Mama's fortieth birthday. The combs each had three stones in them, which Papa said represented the blessings of their three children. "The earrings are just a bonus and are in no way indicative of my desire for two more children!" he had added.

"Mama, are you sure you want me to wear these?"

"Special evenings require special preparations."

Mama had helped her slip into the black chiffon cocktail dress, hidden all week under the Christmas tree in the shiny gold I. Magnin box, and into the black satin swing coat with the green shawl collar and cuffs that matched the green trim of her dress. She had artfully twisted two locks of Ari's lustrous hair and firmly secured them in the tortoiseshell teeth of the exotic combs. A final hair brushing and slip adjusting and make-up blending, and Mama stood back and surveyed her work. "You look beautiful."

"Thanks, Mama. I feel beautiful. I feel . . . I feel almost as if you were serving Adi to me."

"Not quite, Arianna. And don't you forget it!" Mama half joked. While she was fairly confident in her daughter's ability to make smart decisions, she remembered high school boys and how their decision-making was often driven by something other than their brains.

Jason slowed the car at an intersection to allow a group of noisy merrymakers to cross the street. They were laughing and blowing party horns and had obviously begun their celebrating some time ago. They were heading for a German restaurant on the corner, one of those special San Francisco eateries that hid among houses in largely residential neighborhoods but were somehow well known to locals who had a way of ferreting out restaurants in obscure locations if the food was good and the service friendly. Ari wondered for a moment if she and Jason would be eating weiner schnitzel tonight, but when the last reveler passed by, he gunned the engine and continued on.

Finally, Jason pulled the car into a tiny parking area at the end of the street. Ari strained to see the restaurant from the diminutive front windshield but could see only the legs of a tuxedo-clad figure approaching her side of the car. Her door opened and a gentleman with what sounded like an Italian accent said, "Welcome to Julius' Castle" and offered his hand to pull her effortlessly from the low sports car.

"Where did you say?" she asked in disbelief.

The man smiled. "Oh, I see. You did not know you would be coming to the Castle tonight. Well, it is our good fortune that you have," he said, eyeing her in that way Italian men had of admiring beauty without being offensive.

Ari knew all about Julius' Castle. It was Mama's favorite restaurant in the City. Lovers had been coming to its intimate, candlelit dining rooms since 1922 when Julius Roz, a restaurant counterman and Italian immigrant, first built the cherished old San Francisco landmark high atop Telegraph Hill. Over the years, couples had dined on lobster tails and rack of lamb and fresh seafood while watching history being made outside the panoramic picture windows. The building of the Bay Bridge and the dredging of Treasure Island for the World's Fair, the parade of battleships and destroyers going out to meet the Japanese Navy, and the clockwork comings and goings of the ferry boats with their little band of sea gulls trailing behind in hopes that the galley cooks might be generous that day. The Castle had witnessed them all. It was no wonder that San Franciscans celebrated their most special occasions at Julius' Castle. It was where Papa proposed to Mama all those years ago.

"Oh, Jason, I can't believe you did this."

"I wanted to do something really special for you, Ari. You're the best thing that has ever happened to me." He grabbed Ari up in his arms and held her close to him. The Italian man stood a discrete distance away and waited.

At the door, the maître d' greeted them and took Ari's coat, revealing the elegance of the sheer silk over empire sheath, which hugged her curves just enough to accentuate her beauty. "You are a lucky man, Mr. Caldwell," he said, momentarily forgetting himself.

"Yes, I am," Jason smiled. He linked Ari's arm with his and together they followed the maître d' up a narrow flight of stairs.

Ari had woken up that morning a teenager, and she would wake up tomorrow feeling the same. But tonight, as she entered the dining room at the top of the stairs, she was aware of every pair of eyes that followed her to their table. She felt like an exotic princess making a grand entrance into a ballroom filled with admirers who had waited for hours in line just in the hopes of being noticed by her. She returned their smiles graciously as if this night were no different than any other in her life. *I can't wait to tell Emma*, she thought to herself.

The maître d' led them to a table by the window that faced directly on the lights of the Bay Bridge and seated them adjacent to each other. "I hope this table suits you," he said, unfurling Ari's napkin and placing it on her lap.

"Very much, thank you," she smiled.

When they were alone, Jason took Ari's hand. "Well, are you surprised?"

"Overwhelmed," she answered honestly.

"Then you're pleased?"

"Oh, Jason, no one has ever done anything like this for me before. I love you," she said without thinking.

"I love you too, and tonight I'm going to show you how much."

At just the right moment, the waiter approached with menus in hand, which Jason said were unnecessary. "If you agree, Ari, I think we'll start with the crab and artichoke appetizer, followed by the Caesar salad, rack of lamb, and the chocolate soufflé with raspberry sauce."

"Wonderful choices, Mr. Caldwell." The waiter finished writing and promised to return shortly with sparkling cider and sourdough bread. He didn't remove the wine glasses.

"You've been here before, Jason." She tried to say this as casually as she could, not wishing her mild disappointment to show in her voice. She let her mind briefly wonder how many other girls Jason had shared this table with, promising to show them *how much he loved them*.

She searched his face for some sign of insincerity but couldn't find any, so she forgot her disappointment and let the romance of the Castle sweep her away. The warm woods and crystal chandeliers and stiffly starched linens, the whispered voices that floated on classical concertos through the dimly lit room, the elegant seclusion of the hilltop hideaway that felt more like a private home than a commercial establishment, and the magnificent view—of hills and water and bridges and tiny white lights of far-off automobiles moving up and down the streets of San Francisco. Ari understood why Mama loved this place so much. Julius' Castle was more than a restaurant; it was a celebration, and no one loved her celebrations more than Mama.

The food was exquisite, and the service an art form. Their waiter's name was Enrico—at least that's what he said it was. It may have just sounded better than *Irving*. Still, he knew exactly how to flow with the rhythm of their romance. All night long, the water glasses were filled, the bread basket replenished, and the coffee kept hot by the unobtrusive gentleman who seemed to appear and disappear as if by magic, never interrupting important conversation nor the silence of romantic glances. The only time he took center stage was to prepare the Caesar salad at tableside with great flair and artistic presentation.

It was late by the time Ari and Jason finished dinner, but they were in no hurry to end this part of the evening. They talked on about their vacations and about where Jason would take Ari painting next now that she was so well equipped. "I really would like to take you to Venice one day," he said. "You could paint the Grand Canal from the piazza of our villa and then paint the villa from a gondola on the Grand Canal."

Ari imagined him lying back in a gondola, his hair bleached white in the hot summer sun, his bronze chest peeking through his unbuttoned shirt, and his deep blue eyes seeing no one but her.

It was nearly nine o'clock when Enrico brought Ari her coat, and Jason helped her slip it on. Then he held her hand and led her back through the dining room, but instead of descending the stairs they had previously climbed, he took her up to a higher floor and through a private dining room to a door on the other side where he ushered her through.

Ari found herself on a rooftop patio—a lofty sanctuary hidden away from view—except for the handful of inhabitants who lived in a nearby house and the wayward flocks of seabirds that occasionally passed overhead. Jason slid his arm around Ari's waist and guided her toward the wall on the far side. For

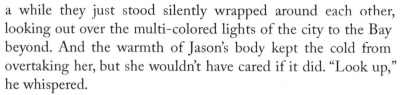

a while they just stood silently wrapped around each other, looking out over the multi-colored lights of the city to the Bay beyond. And the warmth of Jason's body kept the cold from overtaking her, but she wouldn't have cared if it did. "Look up," he whispered.

"What?"

"Look up behind you," he whispered again.

They turned around together, never taking their arms from one another, and he lifted her chin and waited. For several moments she just stared straight up, too awestruck to speak, not sure if what she was looking at was real or some giant projection superimposed on the sky. Jason could feel the slight trembling of her body as she struggled to fathom the enormity of what she saw. "Dream Castles," she murmured. "Dream Castles."

Ari was staring up at Coit Tower, not from a distance that put it into scale with the rest of the city, but right beneath it where her proximity to it made it soar to colossal heights. There was a small crescent moon peeking over its roof, almost fragile in comparison to the giant monolith, yet with a brilliance worthy of a harvest moon. Together they seemed to be reigning over the city like benevolent monarchs. Ari stared up at them with an expression on her face that Parrish could have painted—of happiness and contentment and anticipation for all the secrets that waited to be discovered.

Ari turned toward Jason, wrapped both arms around his neck and stared silently into the eyes that were barely visible against the night sky. She waited as he felt through the darkness to her lips, and they kissed, gently at first, and then deeper, with a passion that sent shivers through her body.

By the time Jason and Ari arrived at the party, it was in full swing. People were packed into the large vaulted living room, milling around the center and leaning against walls and lining the wide staircase, hanging over the second story railing and cramming onto the balcony that ran the full length of the house just on the other side of the two-story glass wall. Every windowsill, ledge, table top, and stairway step was already littered with discarded beer bottles and potato chip bowls and ashtrays stuffed with those cigarette butts that managed to avoid the marble floors. Despite the open glass doors and the cold night air that flowed through them, the house was already beginning to smell of smoke and sweat and stale beer and a sweet odor Ari had smelled somewhere before but couldn't quite identify.

Ari had been a little nervous about coming to the party ever since Jason had told her about it. She didn't know Jason's cousin, Brian, or a lot of the people who were going to be there. For that matter, Brian didn't know a lot of the people who were going to be there either. When his parents decided to go out of town for New Year's Eve, he posted a notice on the Student Center bulletin board at State: *OPEN HOUSE, NEW YEAR'S EVE, GREAT HOUSE ON TOP OF TWIN PEAKS, BYOB.* He had told Jason to spread the word among his friends as well. If only Meghan were in town.

Ari had only been to a college party once before. Emma and Roger had invited her to come along to Emma's pledge party at the sorority, which was co-sponsored by the fraternity around the corner. Emma had told her to keep in sight at all times and to never go upstairs at the frat house no matter how nice the boy seemed to be. Ari had followed her sister's advice and had had a wonderful time. Perhaps it was childish to feel nervous now. After all, she had given Papa the address and telephone number of the house before she left home, and she was going to be in college herself next fall. Besides, Jason was here to take care of her. If the party got too rowdy, they could just leave.

"Let's put our coats away," he shouted over the music and the exuberance of the wall-to-wall party guests. He took Ari's hand and led her into a guest bedroom off the front foyer where a pair of beds were already stacked several layers high with discarded coats. That sweet odor was heavier in here and seemed to be coming from the half-open bathroom door. Before long, a dozen people filed out of the bath, straight faced and quiet until a sideward glance erupted into giggles, which spread like a communicable disease throughout the group. "Jason, they're smoking grass!" she whispered.

"*Jason, they're smoking grass!*" one of them mimicked and the laughter erupted all over again.

Jason got a sheepish look on his face and remained silent until the others had left the room. "Ari, it's just a few kids smoking weed. None of our friends will be doing that. Besides I don't know what the big deal is with pot anyway. It's probably a lot healthier than drinking."

"I know, Jason. You're probably right. But it's still illegal. And I'm only seventeen. And if the party gets out of hand, and the neighbors decide to call the police . . . well, they might understand a little underage beer drinking maybe . . . but drugs?"

"Oh, you worry too much. Loosen up, Ari. I'm not going to miss the best party of the whole year because you're afraid of a little pot." She thought she detected just a little bit of irritation in his voice, but if she did, it quickly disappeared. "If things start getting out of hand, we'll go somewhere else. I promise. All right?"

"Okay." He hugged her and planted a kiss on her forehead, and he felt so warm and familiar that she forgot her anxiety. She sometimes wondered after that night what would have happened if she had made Jason leave right then. Maybe things would have turned out differently. Probably not.

They paused at the living room entrance to get their bearings and then proceeded through the crush of bodies making their way to some familiar faces from the football team on the other side of the room. As they inched and side-stepped and squeezed their way through, Ari took a good look at the house. It was one of those ultra-contemporary houses, open-planned and free flowing; perfect for parties like this, but with minimal furniture and hardly a photograph or personal memento in sight. The expansive empty white walls surrounded a lot of chrome and little color, and the only interruption in the smooth surfaces and rounded corners was an occasional oversized abstract oil, mostly done in reds and blacks, and a gray stone fireplace occupying the entirety of the north wall. Ari could only imagine how cold and cavernous and lonely this house must feel when only the family was in residence.

Beth Miller was there with her boyfriend, Mike, as well

as a couple of the other pom pom girls. Ari had hoped Geena Thompson and Mary Kay Shipton would be there. They were both living proof that you could be a pom pom girl and be really smart and nice and beautiful all at the same time, but she didn't see them or their boyfriends. In fact, she didn't see Bruce Danforth or Adam or any of the kids she liked best. Mostly, the only high schoolers she saw were Jason's drinking buddies and a handful of girls from what was known around campus as the *slut patrol.*

"Hi, Ari," Beth said. "Nice dress."

"Thanks," she returned. "You too."

"It's about time you showed, Caldwell," Mike slurred. "We're already three beers ahead of you."

Just then Brian appeared dangling several paper cups of frothy beer from between his fingers and one from his tightly clenched teeth. He was followed closely behind by his girlfriend, Carol Kennedy, who carried a large pitcher of refills. Jason grabbed a couple of beers. "Well, I guess I better start catching up. After all, I did pay for half of this." Ignoring Ari's obvious surprise at his last remark, he gulped down the first beer and was halfway through the second before he stopped to take a real breath.

"Aren't you going to introduce us?" Brian asked, leering at Ari in a way that was more predatory than admiring.

Jason threw his arm around Ari with his beer hand, spilling some on her new cocktail dress. He didn't apologize. "This is my girlfriend, Ari Heywood."

"I've heard a lot about you, Ari. A lot!" He leered at her again.

Another round of beers and the boys raced each other to the bottom of their cups. They laughed too loudly and dribbled beer out their mouths and wiped their chins on the back of their sleeves and called the slow drinkers *Homos* and repeated the whole process without losing a step. Some of the girls joined in the drinking and some just joined in the laughter. Ari was still holding the first beer she had been handed, having put it to her lips only a time or two for show. She was growing increasingly quiet and Jason could feel her uneasiness.

"Ari, drink your beer."

"I am, Jason."

"Faster, goodie-two-shoes." He was just joking, but there was an edge to his voice Ari didn't like. She put her cup to her lips and sipped slowly.

"Come on, Ari, it's New Year's Eve," Jason pressed. He grabbed her cup while it was still at her mouth and tipped it to a more severe angle, causing a gush of beer to fill her mouth and splatter all over the front of her dress and onto her shoes. Ari coughed and shoved the cup back at Jason. Everyone laughed. She wasn't the exotic princess anymore.

"Jason, you've had enough!" She never would have said that in front of his friends, but she was getting angry now.

"What are you, my mother?"

Amid the laughter that surrounded them, one sneering voice rose above the rest. "No trouble between the love birds, I hope."

Instinctively, Ari wrapped her arms around Jason's neck and kissed him. He was already beginning to taste of stale beer. "No trouble here, *Brittany*," she said.

Jason smiled at her and returned the embrace. For a moment she stopped feeling like just one more trophy on his bedroom shelf.

"Will you take me out to see the view?" she asked in her sweetest voice. Brian made some lurid, drunken remark about her intentions and that was enough to make Jason comply.

When they were outside, they stood silently for a moment, the sea of lights spread out before them to the blackness that must be the Bay. "Jason, I'm sorry for snapping at you in there, but ..."

"That's okay," he interrupted. "Let's dance." He grabbed her and twirled her back into the living room.

They danced until almost midnight, and for a while things seemed to be returning to normal. Jason held her tenderly, never taking his hand from the small of her back. He wasn't being possessive, he was simply staking his claim, daring anyone to make a move on his girlfriend. In a funny sort of way, it made Ari feel more comfortable—for a little while anyway. And when

"Nights in White Satin" came on the stereo, and the lyric voices of the Moody Blues floated across the room on the strings of the London Symphony, she and Jason were for a brief time back on the rooftop of Julius' Castle.

But then the song ended, the arm on the stereo lifted, and the next album dropped down the spindle onto the pile. It was The Rolling Stones and by the time the needle moved to "Let's Spend the Night Together," Jason and several of his friends were dancing their girlfriends in the direction of outstretched cups and grabbing them up and chugging them down all in time to the seductive rhythms of the music. Between the drinking, the beer that inevitably found its way to her new dress, and the obnoxious rites of male bonding that proliferated as the album wore on, Ari could barely remember the boy who had swept her off her feet only a few hours before.

By eleven thirty, she had had enough and was just about to tell Jason so, when his cousin came by with another load of beers, and this time Jason refused him. "I've had enough," he said, smiling at Ari. She was so relieved to hear him say that. She had never seen him drink like this before. Maybe something could be salvaged of the rest of the night.

"Come with me. There's something I want to show you," he said. He led her through the dancers, most of whom were just leaning on each other and swaying to the music and proceeded to the stairs on the other side of the room.

"What do you want to show me?" she asked, not liking where this was heading.

"You'll see," he answered. She thought of refusing him, of just getting her coat and threatening to leave with or without him. But then she thought, maybe, if she could just get him alone, away from the adolescent friends who strutted and bragged and coerced one another into going along with the group, maybe they could end the evening the way it had begun.

When they reached the top of the stairs, they maneuvered their way down the hallway through several couples who were making out as if they were the only ones there. The hallway was open to the living room below and even through the din Ari could hear the trashy remarks being sent their way. She knew that Brittany was downstairs somewhere spurring everyone on, so she ignored the remarks as she had been ignoring them at school ever since Meghan first came to her and told her what she overheard in the girl's locker room after P. E. one day.

"Ari, Brittany and Meredith Sweeny were telling everyone that you are going all the way with Jason, and that you did all sorts of weird things that only Island girls would do. You've got to say something. I told them to go to hell, but you have to tell them too."

Meghan was so mad that day, and Ari loved her friend all the more for it, but she wasn't going to dignify Brittany's attacks by getting into it with her. "Don't worry," she had said, "Everyone knows me. They won't believe Brittany. And if anyone does, Jason will set them straight."

Jason led Ari to the end of the hallway and through a pair of doors to the master bedroom. It was similar to the living room, oversized, white-walls and glass, a minimum of furniture and devoid of the *objets d' art* or photographs or personal paraphernalia that would have indicated that somebody actually lived there. There were no dressers, just drawers built into the walls, and the only furniture was a single club chair, an arching chrome floor lamp and a king-size bed with shiny black lacquer headboard and gray silk bedspread. The bed was all the more formidable for the absence of competing furniture. No wonder Jason's cousin was such a bore. He came by it honestly.

"Come sit down," Jason smiled, pulling Ari toward the bed.

"I'll stand, thanks."

"Ari, don't be mad at me. You know how much I love you."

"Jason, I . . ." She couldn't get anything more out before Jason's tongue was in her mouth and his hands were pinning her shoulders against the wall. She shoved him as hard as she could, extricating herself from his drunken clutches with little difficulty and putting a safe distance between them. "Why are you treating me like this?" she demanded to know. She was visibly angry now.

"Like what, Ari?" he slurred. "I love you. I thought you loved me."

"I do, Jason, but I've told you I'm not ready for this."

"What better way than this to say Happy New Year to each other," he said, becoming more insistent. He came at her again, this time shoving her back up against the doors, knocking her purse from her shoulder. He clumsily grabbed at her breast with one hand while holding her fixed against him with the other. She broke free once more.

"Jason, stop this right now," she yelled, "or I'm going home and you can kiss yourself at midnight!" Ari was really angry now, and she didn't care who knew it.

"Go ahead," he yelled back, too drunk to stop the words from coming out of his mouth. "I promise you, Ari, I won't be alone at midnight if you go."

That wounded her, he knew. And he felt victorious and miserable all at once. She picked up her purse and stormed out of the bedroom and down the hall past rooms full of animal noises. She just wanted to find her coat and get out of the house as fast as she could. She had already been hurt and humiliated enough for one night. As she reached the bottom of the stairs, Jason caught up to her and grabbed her. "Ari, calm down!" he ordered.

By now, they had attracted attention. "Not getting any tonight, Jason?" one of his teammates teased. "I thought you told us your island girl was easy!" said another.

Ari froze. She just stood there, barely breathing, staring at Jason, too stunned to speak. "So, it was you," she said finally. Jason just stared back at her through bleary eyes, saying nothing in denial or defense of her honor.

Ari turned to the boy who had made the remark. "It's funny you should say that," she said without emotion. "Jason always claimed he was a virgin just like me." The room erupted into laughter, and Ari saw a look of animosity on Jason's face she never thought she'd see. She wheeled around to go and walked slowly, but deliberately toward the door. *Dignity* she thought to herself. But then she stopped and turned back toward Jason once more. He smiled, thinking she had changed her mind, and started weaving toward her. "Jason, I'm sure a big man like you won't have any trouble finding another girl to wear this," she said abruptly, and ripped the silver locket from her neck and threw it at him. She could be dignified tomorrow!

This time when she turned to go, she did not come back. She walked into the downstairs guestroom where the coats had been laid on the bed when they arrived. There were two people on the bed she didn't know. She yanked her coat out from under them and started for the door but had second thoughts. She returned to the bed, grabbed Jason's blue blazer and removed the car keys from his pocket and slipped them into her purse. As she opened the front door she turned, curious to see if Jason was still there. She caught just a glimpse of him as he and Brittany ascended the stairs. "Whore," Ari shouted, and slammed the door behind her.

Once outside, she stood for a moment too dazed to get her bearings or feel the cold of the damp air that surrounded her. Then she turned right and headed for the end of the street in the direction of home. It was only about three miles away and all downhill. Maybe she'd walk. No. Mama and Papa wouldn't like that—a teenage girl walking alone in the city on New Year's Eve. She had to admit the idea didn't sound all that good to her either. How could Jason let her leave alone like this? Didn't he know it was dangerous? Didn't he care? She was getting angry all over again.

Ari pulled her shawl collar up around her for warmth and headed for the Flying A Station on the corner. There was a telephone there and the station was still open for business. She could wait safely inside until Papa picked her up. She dropped Papa's dime in the telephone, the one he always gave her before she went out on a date, dialed her number, and waited for someone to answer. She would sound calm. Papa answered the phone. "Papa," she said, and burst into tears.

"Arianna, what's wrong? Are you all right?" Mama bolted to his side at the alarm in his voice.

"I'm okay, Papa," she assured him. "Could you come and get me? I need a ride home."

"Where are you?"

"I'm at the Flying A Station at the top of the hill." And knowing how worried he must be, she added, "The station is open, Papa, so I'm safe here."

"I'll be right there," he said and hung up the phone.

Ari waited inside the office with a pimply-faced boy about twenty-one, she guessed, who was working the graveyard shift. He was stocking the shelves when Ari entered but paused to ask her if he could be of any help. She thanked him and said that everything was all right. Her father was on his way. The boy stepped into the back room for a moment and emerged with two Coca Colas and offered one to Ari. He smiled a sweet smile and raised his bottle to clink it with hers in a mock toast. Ari thought of Julius' Castle, which now seemed like forever ago, and was about to cry again when suddenly the Peaks were alive with the sounds of party horns and cheering and invisible party makers yelling "Happy New Year." Ari and the boy just stared at each other, he wondering what a beautiful girl like this was doing in his station alone at midnight on this night of all nights, and she thinking how sad that this kind boy couldn't get a date.

When Papa's car pulled into the station, Ari ran to meet him. She flew into Papa's arms and didn't let go. He was like the safe harbor in that children's game where as long as you were touching the safety spot, no one could tag you out. Papa held her securely and waited until he felt her hold on him ease a bit. Then he asked her just one question. "Did Jason *hurt* you, Arianna?"

"No, Papa. Not the way you mean. I'm all right."

"Then everything else will take care of itself. I promise," he said.

When they arrived home, Mama and Grandfather and Mem were waiting anxiously. "I'm all right," Ari said. "There was just a lot of drinking at the party and college kids I didn't know, and things were getting out of hand, so I left." She didn't tell them about the pot. She had already exercised enough bad judgment, she thought, just by staying at the party as long as she did.

"Why didn't Jason bring you home?" Mama wanted to know.

"He was having a better time than I was, Mama."

"He was too drunk to drive, wasn't he?" Mama persisted angrily.

"Yes. But he won't be driving anywhere tonight. I took his keys."

Papa smiled at his daughter's good sense. He pretty well had figured out what had happened between Jason and Ari, and he knew his daughter was angry. He was proud of her for seeing the bigger picture at her age. He made a mental note to tell her that in the morning. "I think Ari's had enough for one night," Papa observed. "I think she'd like to go to bed."

"Thank you, Papa, for understanding and for picking me up." She gave everyone a kiss and turned to go upstairs, glancing at the painting of the Island over the fireplace as she went. *Nothing bad ever happens to me there* she thought, and she ascended the stairs.

When Emma came home, her night had obviously gone much better than her sister's. She gave everyone the highlights and said she'd fill in the details in the morning. Papa told her about Ari's night and suggested that she might want to pop in on her and see if she wanted to talk. Emma went upstairs straight away.

She stopped to listen at Ari's door before knocking. She couldn't hear anything—no crying, no movement about the room. Ari must be lying on her bed. Emma knew she wouldn't be asleep. She quietly opened the door and peeked her head through. "All right if I come in?"

"Sure."

Emma entered the room. There was only the soft light of aromatic candles glowing. The air was filled with the soothing scents of tropical flowers and sea breezes and, of course, jasmine. Ari was lying across her bed. She had gotten undressed and had put on an old Lanz flannel gown. Her cocktail dress was carelessly thrown across the arm of her rocking chair, and her shoes and pantyhose and slip were on the floor right where she had taken them off, but the earrings and hair combs had been carefully replaced in their blue velvet box. "Did Papa tell you?" she asked and began to sob before Emma had a chance to answer.

"Only that he had to pick you up. But he didn't know what happened exactly. Are you all right, Ari?"

"Yes. I mean . . . I will be. Jason didn't do anything

like . . . you know. If that's what you're asking."

Emma waited until her sister had gathered herself before continuing. "But he tried, didn't he?"

"Yes, but that's not why I'm crying. He was so drunk that it was easy to get him off me." She sat upright, wiping the tears from her mascara-stained face with her sleeve and motioned Emma to sit with her. "Oh, Emma, the night started out so perfect. Jason took me to Julius' Castle for dinner."

"The Castle!" Emma exclaimed. "You must have been thrilled."

"I was. He knew I would love it. And it was even better than I had ever imagined it. We had this wonderful little table by a window that overlooked the entire bay. And we sat with our backs to the rest of the room and it was like we were dining all alone. Everything was just like it had always been between us, but even better. After dinner he took me up on the roof and we looked out over the Bay and then we turned around and Coit Tower was practically on top of us. He was holding me and saying such romantic things. It was all so perfect." The tears started again.

Emma waited. "Then what happened?" she asked at last.

"Then the party happened. When we got to the party, everything changed—he changed. He started drinking and got really drunk. And he got kind of obnoxious in front of his friends, you know, the way boys do sometimes. Then we went upstairs . . ."

"Ari!" Emma exclaimed in surprise.

"Oh, Emma, I wasn't going to do anything with Jason. I just thought if I could talk to him in private, I might be able to fix things. I was wrong. It just got worse, so I left." Ari paused to let a few more tears fall before continuing.

"There's more, isn't there," Emma said, knowing her sister well.

"Yes," she answered and recounted the details of her parting. "Turns out it was Jason who was spreading rumors about me all over school. I guess all this time he's been bragging to his friends about what he and I had supposedly been doing together. I had no idea. I . . . I thought it was just Brittany all this time." Her voice trailed off into more tears.

"Boys can be such assholes sometimes," Emma observed.

"Sometimes," Ari returned, remembering all the lovely times she and Jason had shared, which were lost to her now.

"What are you going to do?" Emma asked.

"Just try to salvage as much dignity as I can, I guess," she said and added jokingly, "and hope that Papa gets another transfer real soon." They both laughed, but neither thought there was much to laugh about.

"So, how was your night?" Ari asked, changing the subject. "I hope it was better than mine."

"It was, but maybe you don't want to hear about it right now."

"Of course I do." So, Emma recounted her night with Roger. Their dinner that wasn't as fancy as Ari's but was special anyway because of how hard Roger had to work to make the money for it. She told Ari about the party with the live band and all the kids dancing. No liquor had been served at the party because some people were under age, but a lot of people came with their own beer, and how the lights all went out at midnight leaving only the twinkling holiday lights on, and how everyone kissed and hugged. It all sounded so perfect to Ari, so innocently romantic.

"Why do my friends think they can't have a good time unless they get drunk?"

"Oh, Ari, it doesn't sound to me like any of *your* friends were at that party tonight."

"You're right. I should have known when I walked in the door and saw who was there that I didn't belong at that party. I don't understand why the boys had to act so stupid. I don't remember the boys in our other postings being like that. Well, in Hong Kong anyway. I guess I wasn't old enough to know the difference anywhere else."

"I don't know, Ari. Maybe because in other countries kids grow up having an occasional glass of wine with dinner so drinking isn't this forbidden thing they can't wait to do behind their parents' backs. At least that's the way it's always been with me. Forget the fact that the wine Mama and Papa gave us was so diluted it was practically grape juice," she laughed.

"I wish I had been at your party, Emma. If I had, maybe Jason and I would still be together."

"Would you?"

"Well, he wouldn't have gotten drunk like that."

"Ari, he wasn't drunk when he told all those lies about you."

"I know," she admitted.

"Don't make excuses for him, Ari. What he did was deplorable."

"I know," she said again, "but he doesn't really mean to be like that. When we're alone . . ." she said and began to cry again.

Emma didn't say anything more. She knew that Ari needed to be emotional tonight, not rational. Still, she worried about her.

When Ari had gathered herself enough to speak, she said, "I keep thinking about all the wonderful times we had together. I'm going to miss Giuseppi's and the wine country and all the conversations about Venice. If only I knew what to do. Maybe I could have . . ."

"Changed him?"

"Well, maybe."

"Ari, you can't make someone into somebody they're not."

"I know you're right, Emma," she said dejectedly. She sat up and wiped her tears on the back of her hand. "You know what the worst part is? Now I don't even know what was real about our relationship. Jason probably just took me to Julius' Castle tonight so he could get me into bed!"

Emma could hear the anger in her voice when she said this, and she was glad. "Well, if Brittany was as drunk as Jason was, they may have made something *really* real tonight!" she said.

"Emma!" Ari exclaimed in feigned shock, but she had to admit the possibility.

20

THE NEXT MORNING Ari arose early, not having slept much the night before. She dragged herself out of bed and stopped at the full-length mirror on her way to the bathroom. Her eyes were red and puffy from the intermittent bouts of anger and crying, and her cheeks were uncharacteristically blotchy. She slipped into the bathroom quietly, not wishing to disturb Emma, whose steady breathing she could hear through the door that stood slightly ajar. When her face was washed and her teeth brushed, she returned the toothbrush and Ipana to the medicine cabinet and clicked the door quietly shut. With one last glimpse of herself in the mirror and after promising the slightly improved face that she wasn't going to let Jason spoil her last day with Grandfather and Mem, she whirled around and headed for the stairs.

The table in the little family dining room was already set with the country scene dishes and festive green glasses, so Ari launched into breakfast preparations. First, she prepared the fruit chillers with melon balls, strawberries, and grapes, all grown in southern climates, and slices of mango that Mem had picked fresh from the trees that grew along the front path of the Great House. Next, she took the dough that Mama had prepared the previous day and rolled and twisted it into plump round cinnamon rolls that would go from oven to glazing to the table in a matter of minutes. For Ari, these sticky, melty treats were the highlight of their New Year's breakfast. Then she put on the coffee. She knew the robust aroma of fresh ground beans for espresso would find its way upstairs, and it wouldn't be long before the rest of the family joined her.

They came down in ones and twos that morning, beginning

with Grandfather who grabbed a finger full of icing, planted a sticky kiss on Ari's cheek and headed for the gardens and his morning stroll. Halfway to the door he smiled at her. "You're not the first teenager to have better judgment in the morning than you had the night before, Arianna," he said kindly. *How did he know?* She knew Papa wouldn't say anything. Perhaps it was true what the Islanders said—the old man really did "*see all and know all.*"

As Ari was taking the bacon and eggs from the refrigerator, Mama entered the kitchen closely followed by James and his constant companion, Tippy. "I wanna beat up the eggs!" James yelled.

"You don't have to scream, big guy," Ari smiled. "I was just getting everything ready for you."

James climbed up on his step stool and waited for Ari to bring him the eggs and beater so he could perform his customary breakfast job. Tippy lay at his feet, where he had already learned at his tender puppy age that the best food scraps always fell.

"Good morning, Ari," Mama said, when she could finally get a word in. "Did you get any sleep last night?"

"Not much, Mama."

"I'm sorry," she said. "I wish there was something I could do to make it better."

"Me too. But I'll live."

Despite her night, Ari enjoyed breakfast, everyone talking easily, reminiscing about past breakfasts and anticipating spring break when they would all be together again on the Island. Afterward, Emma accompanied James outside to walk Tippy in the garden for another wee and to continue the daunting task of house breaking the young pup. Ari glanced out the window at James in his robe and slippers and car coat, beseeching Tippy to lift his leg on the old cypress tree. Tippy was, of course, too young to do anything but squat, but Georgie's puppy, Ralph, had already lifted his leg so Tippy was going to follow suit. James waggled his finger at Tippy and tried every manner of pleading and plying and coercion he could think of. Finally, in total exasperation, he got on all fours, lifted his leg and pretended to wee on the tree. This set Ari to laughing so hard, she lost control of the coffee in her mouth and it ended up back in her cup.

Having already taken center stage at the table, she decided it was time to tell the family what happened last night. She told them everything. There was no scolding, no criticizing for bad judgment. They just listened to Ari describe the evening. "I'm sorry things didn't end for you the way they began," Mama said. "I know how disappointed you must be."

"You and Papa never wanted me to go to that party, did you, Mama?"

"What makes you say that?" she asked.

"I don't know. Just a feeling I got when I told you about it."

"We were nervous about you going to your first college party alone on New Year's Eve," Papa said. "But we thought that it was just going to be your friends and some of Jason's cousin's friends, and that with the party being just up the hill, it wasn't a bad way to broaden your experience before going off to college next year. Had we known it was an open house, we wouldn't have let you go. You never know who's going to show up at one of those or what they'll be bringing with them." He didn't chastise her for not telling them, but the message was clear.

"Jason didn't tell me right away. But when he did, he said that the party was at his cousin's, and he knew Brian's friends, and he said that I would really like them. I know I should have thought twice about going to an open house, but I guess I thought Jason would take care of me if anything happened."

"You're the only one who can ensure your own safety. You shouldn't trust a boy to do it for you," Mama said.

"But you trust Papa."

"He's proven himself trustworthy time and again." The admiration in her voice was obvious.

"I wish you *had* forbidden me to go," Ari said. "I probably would have squawked a little, but at least I'd still have my boyfriend."

"Well, your Papa and I decided a long time ago that our children needed to make their own mistakes to learn from them and that we would only interfere if we thought that any of you might make a mistake you couldn't take back."

"Like what exactly?"

Papa answered this time. "Like driving in cars with people who drink. Or getting involved with drugs or people who do them. Or dropping out of college to become a Las Vegas showgirl."

Ari laughed. "Well, no worries about the first two. Not after last night. But I can't make any promises about the Las Vegas showgirl!" she joked.

Just then the patio doors flew open and James came bursting through with Tippy in his arms and Emma close behind. "I wanna 'nother sticky bun! Please?" he said as an afterthought.

"Take off your coat, James, and climb up on your stool, and I'll get you one from the kitchen," Ari said. She returned with a plate of buns and handed one to James and added one to her plate.

"So, Ari, what are you going to do now?" Mama asked.

"I don't know. Never leave the house as long as I live?"

"Seriously, Arianna, I hate seeing you hurt like this. What are you going to do?" Mama asked again.

"Well, for one thing, I'm not going to any more parties where I don't know the people, at least not while I'm still in high school. And I'll think twice before I ever date anyone like Jason again," she added.

"You were very happy with Jason until last night."

"But the way he spread lies about me, Mama. I could never forgive him for that."

"That's understandable."

"I guess he never cared about me the way he said he did. He was only using me because of what I told him about the Island. You were right about that, Mama."

"I'm not so sure," she said. "I think Jason cared about you very much."

"Are you saying you think I shouldn't have broken up with him?" she asked in amazement.

"No," Mama replied emphatically. "I think you should most definitely break up with him—not because he didn't love you but because his behavior was more than just the immaturity that all boys suffer through."

"I agree," Papa interjected.

"Listen to your Papa, Ari. He's an expert on immature behavior," Mama teased.

"What do you mean?"

"Tell her, Ethan."

Papa looked embarrassed. "Well, I hate to admit it, but there was a time when my behavior wasn't all that different from Jason's. Not that I ever tried to force myself on a girl. That goes *way* over the line. I don't care how drunk he was."

"Oh, Papa, I can't imagine you treating anyone like Jason treated me."

"Well, there's something about a high school locker room that turns hormonal teenage boys into obnoxious beasts. Something in the foul-smelling air, I suppose. Unfortunately, I had given my girlfriend a music box instead of a locket. When she threw that at me, it nearly knocked me out!"

"Oh, Papa, you're kidding!" Ari laughed.

"It's the truth, I'm sorry to say. But then I met your Mama, and maybe I was ready to grow up or maybe she just brought out the best in me."

"Then why couldn't I do the same thing for Jason?"

Mama answered this time. "Because there are two kinds of people you never want to fall in love with—evil people and weak people. Your father is neither of those, but I think Jason falls into the second category, which makes things more difficult for you. He can be so loving at times, but only those times when it's convenient for him. Any effort required and he'll let you down every time."

"But people can change, can't they?"

"Sometimes. But they have to really want to. And they must have the strength to do it, and I don't think Jason will ever be as strong as your Papa. Besides, I suspect he has something else going against him."

"What, Mama?"

"The disrespect he showed you. That went *way* beyond locker room talk." Mama was getting angry again and calmed herself before continuing. "That was learned behavior, Ari. I suspect if you had ever been invited to his home, you would have heard his father being disrespectful to his mother and to women in general. Babies pick up the language that is spoken in their homes with no special lessons. And the process continues throughout childhood on many different levels. The fact that you were never invited to his home should tell you something."

"But, Papa," Ari said, turning to him now, "you came from a home where your parents weren't very nice to each other. How did you turn out so different?"

"I had my Uncle James to show me the way. He practically lived in our house when I was growing up, and he was my mother's big brother, and they loved each other. Uncle James spent more time raising me than my own father did. Even later, when his duties took him abroad, I could always count on him."

"Was he ever married?"

"Once, when he was young. But she died in a tragic accident, and he never remarried."

"Oh, I didn't know." She didn't say anything else until she had reached the bottom of her coffee cup. "Mama, I had no idea you disliked Jason all this time."

"Oh, Ari, I never disliked him. In fact, I found his company very pleasant. But there were always things about him, things which only time would determine if they were youthful immaturity or life-long character flaws. Well, after last night, time's up!"

"I know you're right, Mama. Give me a week, some chocolate chip cookie dough, and a few Troy Donahue movies, and I won't even remember Jason's name!"

"That's my daughter!" Mama smiled.

21

IT WAS MID-AFTERNOON by the time Jason got up the nerve to call Ari. He probably wouldn't have even then, but his father had ordered him to retrieve his keys. He hoped Ari would answer the phone and not either of her parents.

"Hello," came the voice on the other end. It was Emma. Jason could hear several voices talking in the background and guessed the family had congregated in the den for the afternoon. He could hear the television broadcasting a bowl game and he wished he were in front of his TV right now.

"Hi, Emma, is Ari there?

"May I tell her whose calling?"

"It's Jason. Please, I have to speak to Ari."

"Ari, it's Jason on the phone," Emma shouted over the television. "Do you want to talk to him?"

He waited nervously to hear Ari's answer, but it didn't come right away. Finally, he heard her shout back, "I'll take it in the study."

"She'll be right there."

A minute passed while Ari traversed the house. "Hello," she said.

"Ari, its Jason."

"I know. What do you want?" There was no emotion in her voice.

"My father said I had to call you to get my keys back."

"Oh." He could hear the hurt in her voice now. "Well, you needn't have bothered. My father was going to deliver your keys later this afternoon." Jason didn't say anything so Ari continued, "I only took them because you were too drunk to drive. I didn't want you getting in an accident, no matter what I thought of you."

"Thank you," he said more gently. He had convinced himself that he was glad to be rid of this girl who delighted and troubled him more than any other he had ever known. But his conviction melted away at Ari's concern for him.

"Is that all?" she said coolly.

"No. Ari, I want to see you," he blurted out suddenly. "I don't know what happened to me last night. It must have been the beer. I just started acting crazy, and then I couldn't take anything back. Please, Ari, will you let me come over?" Jason pleaded.

"Perhaps we should talk about this in person."

"I'll be right over."

Jason arrived wearing his pegged cords and blue oxford cloth shirt, and Ari wondered if that, too, had been calculated to elicit a positive response. It had the opposite effect. She was wary of him now, and he knew it. "Thanks for letting me come over, Ari. I know I'm the last person you wanted to see today." She didn't reply. She just turned and started walking toward the writing room.

He followed her, pausing briefly at the bottom of the stairs when he glimpsed his letterman jacket hanging over the banister. This wasn't going to be easy. At least her family was still in the back of the house. He didn't relish running into them today. Perhaps next week he'd send flowers to Mrs. Heywood and a sincere note of apology to Mr. Heywood. But first he'd need to smooth things over with Ari.

He entered the writing room a few steps behind her. "I've never been in here before," he said.

There was an awkward silence, more awkward for him than for her. "Oh, Ari, can you ever forgive me for last night? I don't know how I could have treated you like that?"

"I don't know how you could either, Jason. You really hurt me, and I never saw it coming."

"I know. I promise it'll never happen again."

"That's right. It won't."

"Oh, Ari, don't be mad." He grabbed for her hand, but she

pulled it away. "Ari, you gotta understand. I never would have acted like that if it wasn't for the beer."

"Jason, *you* have to understand. Last night was bad, really bad. But it's not what made me break up with you."

He knew what she was referring to. "Ari, it's the other guys. They're always expecting me to be the Big Man on Campus. They never let up." His words struck a familiar chord, and suddenly she understood that vague uneasiness that had always loomed somewhere in the shadows of their relationship, like that funny, unidentifiable taste that starts to form in the back of your throat when you eat something that's not going to digest well.

"Oh, I see. It was all their fault."

"I didn't mean that. But, Ari, I don't ever act like that when they're not around."

Ari didn't say anything, and he knew that he wasn't getting anywhere with her so he tried another approach. When he spoke, his voice was soft, almost philosophical. "I don't know why I do what I do sometimes. Remember, I told you on our first date that I couldn't be myself in front of the guys. I can't even be myself in front of my own family. Sometimes . . . sometimes I'm so jealous of the way you are with your family. It just doesn't seem fair."

As Jason spewed out his soul in a series of plaintive *if only's*, Ari almost began to feel sorry for him, but then she remembered last night and the anger and humiliation. And she remembered seeing Jason and Brittany going upstairs before she had even left the party, and she heard the words ringing in her head, "*I thought you told us your island girl was easy.*"

"Was it worth it, Jason, going to bed with Brittany?" she asked evenly, keeping the anger from her voice.

"How did you know?" he asked, astonished.

"I watched you two go upstairs."

"Oh god, Ari, I'm so sorry," he said, and this time he meant it. There was no going back. "If it makes you feel any better," he muttered, "it was horrible. All Brittany and I managed to do upstairs was pass out but not before I threw up all over her fancy white dress." Ari started laughing uncontrollably.

"It's not funny," he protested, but Ari's laughter was infectious, and he soon joined in. "Some Big Man on Campus! I don't know how I'm going to show my face at school again."

"I was thinking the same thing," Ari said. "Brittany's going to be lying in wait for me. I assumed you'd be standing with her, Jason.

"Please believe me, Ari . . ." He was about to tell her that he could change, that he didn't care what anyone else thought, that he'd never treat her like that again. But then he knew it wouldn't do any good. Besides, why should he have to choose between her and his friends? "So, where do we go from here?"

Ari thought about this. In a way she still wished things could go back to the way they were—Giusseppi's, school dances, painting in the Wine Country, long talks about all their plans for the future, Venice. Perhaps it was talking about Venice that she'd miss the most. But she couldn't go back even if she wanted to. Mama and Papa would be so disappointed in her. At least that's the excuse she gave herself for being strong.

"Jason, if you mean what you say, we can still be friends."

"Oh, you're not going to give me the *let's be friends speech*, are you?" he asked anxiously.

"No," she laughed. "But think about it. What was it about our relationship you liked the most? It couldn't have been the sex!" They both laughed, and for the first time they relaxed just a little.

"No, it wasn't that, although I'd give anything to kiss you right now," he said. He stood for a moment, his eyes darting this way and that at the air that surrounded him, trying to sort the memories. "I think what I loved most was just talking to you, Ari, and not being afraid that I might say the wrong thing. I miss feeling like that. We could talk about anything. And we did talk, for hours."

"Now who's giving the *let's be friends speech*?"

"What?"

"Jason, friends talk to each other. And they're never afraid to say what they really think. We can still do that."

"But there's one thing you have to do for me first."

"Anything."

"You're going to have to tell your friends the truth about me. I'm not going to have people talking behind my back anymore. Jason, it's the *only* way." She wasn't angry when she said this, just determined, and she liked the way that felt.

"I promise, Ari. First thing when school starts."

Ari walked Jason out to his car. He slid into the driver's seat, put his letterman jacket on the seat next to him, turned the key and revved the engine. Before driving off he said, "Ari, how about I pick you up for school on Monday. It might stop everyone talking." And then he added, "Just one friend giving a ride to another."

"I don't think so, Jason." she said.

"Why not?"

"First you need to act like a friend. Then I'll treat you like one."

"But I am your friend, Ari."

"Not until you tell everyone the truth."

Ari didn't wait for Jason to drive out of sight. She didn't stand at the bottom of the drive waving to him as he waved back. She didn't listen for the two toots of his horn as he turned the corner and sped toward home. She just returned to the house and never looked back. Once inside, she headed for the den, glancing at the art deco poster as she passed by. "Guess I won't be going to Venice anytime soon," she said to the lady in the nearly brimless hat.

"Are you all right, Ari?" Mama asked.

"Yes, I think I am actually."

"You do know, Ari, that Jason has no intentions of being just friends. He's still hoping to get you back once the dust settles," Mama observed.

"I know," Ari said, and she smiled a victorious smile that Mama didn't miss.

22

ARI WATCHED HER grandparents disappear down the drive, and she felt that familiar sadness when an event so long awaited was so quickly over. It was barely light out, and she was still in her nightgown and robe. She wasn't ready for the holidays to end, much less for school to begin. But they had ended as they always did, with tearful good-byes, promises to write soon, and the little family album having grown larger by several cherished memories.

Winter progressed in pretty ordinary fashion. After a few days of awkwardness, Ari came to realize that Jason wouldn't, or couldn't, keep his promise to her and that keeping a polite distance from one another was the best course of action. It took about a month for the temptation to take him back to subside. It didn't happen gradually, but all at once when she came around the corner of the art building one day and found him and the new girl from Washington making out. That's when she realized that she had been pining away for a relationship that never really existed.

Brittany, of course, was hoping to make the most of Ari's New Year's Eve troubles. She made a few feeble attempts to ambush her, but quickly relented when Ari yelled across the quad, "Hey, Brittany, get the vomit out of your New Year's Eve dress yet?"

Emma was spending a lot more time on campus this quarter. Ari missed having her around, and Roger if it came to that. He was always so nice to her. Never treated her like a little kid or anything. Emma said she and Roger were both carrying heavy loads at school this winter and were seeing each other whenever they could. She still came home on weekends—it was a quieter place to study, she said—and at least one night during the week so things weren't so terribly different.

Mama began writing a new children's collection of stories about faraway places, but she wasn't to the point where she was saying much about the book yet. Papa was deep in negotiations with a group of Asian bankers, and he wasn't talking about his work either. Several nights he came home uncharacteristically late, even missing dinner on a few occasions, and Ari had to teach James to count different numbers of chimes on the grandfather clock. James was in negotiations of his own with Tippy over house training, but Tippy got far more dog biscuits out of the deal than his three accidents a day deserved.

One Friday in early March, Ari came home and found Mama and Emma waiting at the front door for her. Their broad smiles told her not to be alarmed. "What's going on?" she smiled back. Mama pulled a thick white envelope from behind her back. It had a University of California logo in the top left-hand corner. "Oh, Mama!" Ari exclaimed. She bolted forward and grabbed the envelope. "A thick envelope usually means good news," she said, but she didn't make a move to open it.

"Open it, Ari," Emma pleaded. We've been waiting for two hours for you to come home."

"What if the envelope's thick because it has information about my second choice campus, not Berkeley?"

"You won't know until you open it," Mama said.

Ari dropped her purse and binder on the floor and held the envelope in both hands, flap side up. Slowly she worked her forefinger under the flap, ripping it open and removing the contents. She looked at the greeting and read, "Dear Miss Heywood . . . It is with great pleasure that we offer you admission to the University of California at *Berkeley*." She nearly shouted the last word. The packet dropped from her hand and she lurched toward Mama, threw her arms around her, and hugged and squealed and jumped up and down and grabbed Emma and did the same all over again.

The merriment sent James hurtling into the foyer from the den, closely followed by his constant companion. "What's happening? What's happening?" he shouted.

Ari swooped him up in her arms. "I got into Berkeley with Emma. Now I'll be really close to home next year and we can see each other all the time, big guy!"

"Oh boy!" he giggled. Even Tippy joined in the excitement, jumping up and down and barking his little puppy barks until Emma picked him up and placed him in James's arms.

That night when Papa came home, they told him the good news. Sounds like we need to celebrate," he said. "Let's go out for dinner tonight."

"I was hoping you'd say that, Ethan, because I was too excited to cook anything."

"Where shall we go?"

"I think Ari should choose," Emma said.

Ari didn't need to think about where she wanted to go. "Giuseppi's," she said. "I've been wanting to go there for a long time."

"Are you sure," Mama said. "I don't want it bringing up bad memories for you."

"I'm way past that, Mama. Jason's already gone through a bunch of girls since me. Besides, I'm so happy, nothing could spoil the way I feel now!" She didn't see the cloud that cast a shadow on Papa's face; he swiftly willed it away. But Mama saw.

When they returned home that night, Papa went straight to his study and didn't come out again. He had been jovial at dinner, too jovial Mama thought, even speaking Italian to the waiter and again when he went to the kitchen to tell Mike that he hadn't had food that good since he lived in Venice. But no one else seemed to notice, so she tucked away her apprehension until later, not wishing to spoil the celebration with serious thoughts.

When James and Tippy were safely in bed and the girls upstairs making plans for being schoolmates again, Mama went to the study, knocked on the door, and entered without waiting for a response. She found Ethan sitting at his desk, staring into space. "What's troubling you, Ethan?"

"Why do you ask that?" he replied, but still stared into space.

Mary walked over to him, slid into his lap, and gently turned his face toward hers. He returned her smile. "I know my husband after all these years. Can't you tell me what's on your mind?"

"Not just yet," he said.

She looked deeply into his still brilliant blue eyes, those eyes that first captivated her all those years ago in the stacks at Berkeley. "It's time to tell the children, isn't it?"

"It will keep for the weekend. I don't want to spoil Ari's happiness."

23

PAPA WAS THERE to greet them when Ari and Emma returned home from school on Monday, which was a bit unusual.

When Emma opened the front door, Papa was just coming down the hall from the kitchen wearing some loose khakis and an old Berkeley sweatshirt, and he had James in one hand and James's baseball equipment in the other. "What are you doing here?" she asked in surprise.

"I live here, remember?"

"You know what I mean, Papa. It's awfully early for you to be home."

"I had some family business to attend to. I'll tell you all about it when Ari gets home." He brushed her cheek with a kiss as he went by, and he and James disappeared out the door.

An hour later, Ari pulled into the driveway in the little green Ford Fairlane. It was the car she and Emma shared for getting to and from school and for running around with friends. It wasn't very sexy. Ari called it her *old lady car*. "Well, you might as well dye my hair blue," she teased good-naturedly the first time she saw it. But Mama and Papa had specifically told the company not to send a fancy car for the girls. It was enough that they had a car at their disposal for necessary driving. They didn't want the girls growing up with feelings of entitlement because of Papa's position or Mama's increasing celebrity as an author.

Ari was bent over the bench seat, retrieving her binder and thinking about the spring holidays on the Island, which were only a few weeks away now, when Papa and James came sauntering up the drive. "Papa! What are you doing home so early?" she asked when she glimpsed him through the front windshield.

"James and I had an appointment in the alley," he replied. "And I had some family business I wanted to discuss with all of you."

"Is everything all right?"

"Yes," he assured her. "I'll tell you all about it after dinner. But now James and I have some puppy walking to do. We want Tippy thoroughly trained by the time we reach the Island." The mention of the Island made her forget all her questions.

Ari followed Papa and James into the house. She could hear the uneven rhythms of the old Underwood typewriter clicking away in Mama's writing room. It sounded as if her stories were going well today. Papa sent James to retrieve Tippy from the kitchen where they had left him sound asleep on the brick floor, basking in the sunshine that poured through the windows, warming the masonry. Meanwhile Papa traversed the living room to the writing room door and stood silently peering in through the glass. He remained motionless, just watching Mary work. With every click of the keys on the faded brown ribbon, she added a new dimension to herself. Mary was always fresh, always new, yet always familiar. He would never tire of her.

That night everyone brought their dishes to the sink, but they left them soaking there and went into the living room. Mama came in last carrying a tray of juice and fresh date nut bread that she and James had baked only that morning. Papa motioned for everyone to sit in front of the fireplace while he removed the coffee table and set it behind the sofa. Then he disappeared into his study. When he re-emerged, he was wheeling the giant world globe that had waited three long years to be rescued from the obscurity of the corner. Ari and Emma shot each other a glance but said nothing. So many things were beginning to make sense now.

Papa took a seat in one of the overstuffed chairs, the ladies sat together on the sofa and James joined Tippy on the floor at Papa's feet, being too wiggly to remain seated on furniture for long.

"All right, Ethan, the floor is yours," Mama said wearily.

Papa had thought for some time how he wanted to present

this to his children. All through the holidays he had brooded over this decision, and he and Mary had had several discussions about it, which had always ended unsatisfactorily. Now, as he sat looking at his little family assembled before him, he wondered if he was doing the right thing. "I have been thinking for a long while now that perhaps it is time for our family to settle in one place. We have had a great adventure living around the world, but you girls are almost full-grown and will be leaving the house soon. I don't want to be halfway around the world from you while you're in college. And I don't want to be dragging James all over the globe with no siblings to keep him company. The Great House on the Island will always be our real home, and one day Mama and I will retire there. But for now, we have been very happy in this house, and I wish to remain here. What do you all think?"

"That would be the best news ever," Ari replied, "But then . . . what's the globe for?"

Papa resettled himself in his chair. He was obviously uncomfortable with what he was about to say. "I've approached Mr. Ramsey about the possibility of being permanently assigned to company headquarters here in San Francisco. He says it can be arranged if . . ." Papa inhaled deeply, wishing to finish the sentence in only one breath. "If I am willing to take one last field assignment." He paused to look at his children for some reaction before going on, but they seemed neither alarmed nor excited. "I don't feel that under the circumstances I can refuse," Papa continued. "It would be a short assignment. We wouldn't even have to move anything from this house. We'd just pack enough items to make our new house a home."

"But it's not that simple, is it, Papa?" Ari observed.

"No. I'm afraid not. The posting begins in April, right after Spring Break. I'd have to fly directly there from the Island, and all of you would have to return to San Francisco without me.

"But, Papa, we always keep the family together! Isn't there some other way?"

Papa glanced at Mama, who remained expressionless on the couch. "I'm trying to keep our family together, permanently," he replied. "We'd only be apart until the end of the school year, and then if it looks safe, you can all join me for a while in the summer before returning to the Island."

"What do you mean *if it looks safe*?" Ari asked, unable to keep the alarm from her voice.

"The country they're sending me to has had a lot of unrest over the past few years, and some significant anti-western feeling. But there is a new government in place, a decidedly pro-west government, and they have been literally begging us to bring our businesses back to their country."

"Then what's the problem, Papa?"

"Before I let any of you come over, I want to be certain that things have really changed there. That the unrest is over and no one harbors any lingering feelings of hatred for Americans or Europeans. I'm not sure if people can suddenly stop hating someone just because the government changes its mind."

"But, Papa, if it's not safe for us then it's not safe for you either," Ari observed.

How like Mary she was, Papa thought. "I'm not saying it's unsafe, Ari. In fact, I've been assured that it's very safe. There's an enclave in the middle of the city where most of the European and American families used to live. You know, tree-lined streets and big bungalows with beautiful grounds. And the clubs are right there and the schools. You really never have to leave there if you don't want to. Some old friends are going to be there the same time we are. You remember Miles Pembroke?"

"From London?" Mama asked, breaking her silence.

"Yes. I spoke with him today. He's going over at the same time I am and Sophie and the boys will follow in the summer. He says that things have been pretty peaceful there for some time now, and he feels confident that it will continue."

"Then why can't we go with you?" Emma wanted to know.

"Well, I don't want you missing the third quarter of your freshman year, Emma, and Ari would miss graduating from high school with her class and . . . and I'd feel better if I personally checked things out first. That way I could get us all set up in the Quarter and have a staff arranged. I'd just feel better."

"Would you be able to spend the summer with us on the Island?" Ari wanted to know.

"Not the whole summer."

"Papa, you've always gotten a summer sabbatical."

"I know, but not this summer. However, I will be able to get away from time to time and join you there. And next fall, you two girls will be in Berkeley together living, I imagine, in the off-campus apartment you intend to wheedle us into renting for you." Ari and Emma smiled at one another.

"How did you know that, Papa?" Ari laughed.

He didn't answer but continued where he left off. "And Mama and James could join me for the fall, and then we'd all meet up again on the Island at Christmas and then go back to San Francisco and unpack for good."

"There's no other way to stay together in San Francisco?" Emma asked.

"No. No other way. So how about a show of hands. Who thinks we should take the new posting?" Ari and Emma raised their hands because, despite some reservations, this was obviously what Papa wanted, and it really meant just a short separation now rather than an inevitably long separation later. James raised his hand because Ari did; he didn't even know what he was voting for. And, of course, Papa's hand went up. But Mama's hands didn't leave her lap where they had been folded ever since Papa began to speak. She just continued to sit in silence, struggling to keep the emotion from her face.

"Mary, please," Papa pleaded, "I can't do this without your support."

"Then I shall offer you a compromise," she said calmly.

"What is it, Mary?"

"If we decide *as a family* that it is too risky for us to join you in your new posting, or if once we get there, we feel uncomfortable in any way, then you must return with us to San Francisco. Your job be damned!" she said with uncharacteristic vehemence.

Papa took in a deep breath and let it out slowly. "My job be damned," he repeated, and Mama smiled at him, melting away the tension that had pervaded the family meeting.

"So, we're agreed. I take this one last assignment. We go to the Island for the spring holidays, and then we all meet up again this summer in . . ." Papa gave the globe a mighty spin and got that familiar sly smile on his face—the one he used when he knew a secret and it was the family's turn to guess. "Round and round and round she goes, where we stop, only Papa knows!"

"Let me guess, Papa, let me guess," James shouted with that unbridled joy of the very young who only understand the adventure but none of the pitfalls.

"Okay, James, step up here to the globe," Papa said. "Now, your first clue is—the equator runs through this continent. Can you point to the equator, James?"

"That's in the middle, isn't it, Papa?" James said, excited that he knew such important information about geography.

"Yes, James," Papa concurred. James stood for some time, hands on hips, contemplating his very important assignment. There were so many lines and he didn't want to point to the wrong one. He spun the globe around a couple of times, pretending to read the different labels, unaware of the stifled giggles around him, and finally pointed to his choice.

"This is the equator, Papa. It's the line with the *E word* on it!" James announced proudly.

"That's right, James," Papa exclaimed, giving him a manly handshake. The family applauded and everyone took seats on the floor around the globe, having been caught up in James's enthusiasm. Even Mama seemed to be in the spirit of the game.

"Now, James, there are seven continents on the globe. Continents are really big pieces of land. Maybe Ari could point to the different continents for you, and you could tell us if the equator runs through them."

"Okay, Papa," James said eagerly, and everyone listened as Ari read the names of each continent and pointed them out to her little brother. James never took his pudgy finger from the equator line on the globe, fearful he might lose it if he did.

"This is North America where we live right now. See, James, here's San Francisco. Does the equator run through the North American continent?" Ari asked in a businesslike manner.

"No," he answered, and waited for the next choice.

"Okay. Now here's the continent of South America. Does the equator run through this continent?"

"Yes," he screeched. "Are we going to live in South America, Papa?" he asked exuberantly.

"I can't tell you that, James. You and your sisters will have to figure that out with more clues." James looked disappointed with this answer, but his expression changed when Papa added, "You have to tell your sisters which continents to look on for our secret destination."

Ari continued pointing out the major landmasses and James continued running his finger along his chosen line until, at last, he and Ari had narrowed down the list of continents.

"Emma," Ari began, "James says we should look in South America, Africa or Asia. Right, James?"

"Right, Ari!" James returned, happy to be consulted by someone so much older.

"Well, Papa, I'm glad to know we're not going to Antarctica!" Ari joked. "Of course, I don't imagine there's been much unrest there in recent years, unless there was a penguin revolt I didn't hear about!"

Papa laughed. "Second clue," he said, resuming his serious countenance. "Our trip to this country will be over seventy-five hundred miles. Emma, can you narrow down the possibilities from that?"

"I'll need the atlas, Papa," she answered. "It's easier to work on a flat map." She crossed over to the tall bookshelf behind the pair of burgundy duck chairs and ran her finger along the rows of book spines until she found the thick red Rand McNally. Then she returned to the floor and laid the book open on her lap, turning the pages until she found the world map. She studied the map for some minutes while everyone else enjoyed some more juice and bread. When she had finished her calculations, she announced, "We're not going to South America. Buenos Aires is the furthest destination on that continent that would likely offer you an assignment, Papa, and it's not quite seventy-five hundred miles away. We must be going to either Asia or Africa."

"That's right!" Papa announced as if he was a game show host. After a moment of dramatic silence, he continued, "Your next clue is—we will arrive at our destination sooner if we fly west instead of east."

Ari and Emma began counting meridians. James joined in, but he had no idea what he was counting. "Oh, darn it," Ari blurted out. "I thought we might be going to Egypt. I knew there was trouble in the Middle East in recent years over Israel and the Suez Canal. I thought Egypt might be it. I've always wanted to see the Valley of the Kings."

"Well, I don't think you'll be too disappointed in where we're actually going," Mama assured her. And she said nothing more for fear of giving the destination away.

"Hmm," Ari said. "This could be somewhere you and I have discussed, Mama." Ari looked to Mama for the slightest clue in her expression, but she got none. Mama was good at this game; she had played it so often.

"So we're going somewhere in Asia," Emma said, getting the game back on track. "What's our next clue Papa?"

"Your next clue is—if you like islands, you'll like our destination."

Ari and Emma smiled. They did love their islands so. Looking at the globe, they started calling out possibilities. "There's Japan, the Philippines, and Indonesia," they began.

"Don't forget Formosa and Hong Kong," Ari added. "But we've already been to Hong Kong, and besides, there hasn't been any trouble there to speak of."

"I'm not sure all these islands are further than seventy five hundred miles." Emma interjected. "In fact, I know Japan isn't that far," she said, removing it from the list. Then she looked back at the globe once more. "Oh, Ari," Emma suddenly looked worried, as she pointed to a region near the Arctic Sea. "What if Papa was assigned to one of these islands north of the Soviet Union!"

"But Mama said that we wouldn't be disappointed in our destination," Ari reminded her.

"Oh, that's right."

"You know, Emma, Papa didn't actually say we were going to an island," Ari said. "We could be looking for a place on the mainland that is near a lot of islands."

After several calculations, multiple trips to the encyclopedia, and Papa's clues about terraced rice patties, Gamelan music and dances, Wayang Shadow Puppet plays, carved masks, and peanut sauce, Ari and Emma arrived at their answer. But before saying it out loud, they wanted to give James a chance to be in on it. So they gave him one clue they were sure would tip him off.

"James, you won't believe where we're going!" Ari exclaimed in dramatic fashion. "We're going where they have your favorite animal on the whole earth!"

"Puppies!" James squealed, his ear-to-ear smile making his dimples stand out even more than usual.

"No," Ari laughed, realizing how temporary favorites were with five-year-olds. "Your other favorite animal."

James thought for a minute. "Komodo Dragons?" he asked, excited that he could say such a big word just right.

"Yes, James," Ari answered. "You're going to see Komodo Dragons where they live in the wild."

James suddenly got a frightened look on his face and scurried to the safety of Mama's arms. "Oh, Mama, are there gonna be dragons in our house?" he asked with a tremulous voice.

"Of course not, James. The dragons live way out in the country, and we're going to live in the city. You'll be perfectly safe," she assured him, and he relaxed instantly on Mama's say-so.

"So, children," Papa said, once more resuming his role as game show host, "for $64,000, what is the name of our destination?"

"Indonesia!" the girls shouted in unison, as James shouted, "Komodo Dragon Land" and Mama and Papa applauded and laughed.

"Papa, will we be living in Djakarta?" Emma asked.

"Yes, in the enclave I told you about. And our house is quite close to the Club. You'll be able to walk there and go swimming and play tennis and go to dances and have lunch with the other families." Mama lowered her eyes and withdrew from the excitement, and Papa saw this and came to her. He knelt down on one knee in front of her and grabbed her hands and held them tightly in his own. "Mary, it's different than before. No one will ever again tell you to leave a place because it's for whites only."

"Mama, why would someone say that to you?" Ari asked in astonishment.

"To a large part of the world—the colonial world in particular—I am a woman of color. Or so I was informed by the chairman of the club in Singapore. But your Papa put him straight as I remember," she said smiling down at him now.

"What did he do, Mama?" Emma asked.

Mama raised her eyebrows and crinkled up the corners of her mouth in such a funny expression that it made everyone smile. "He announced at the top of his lungs, *Well, sir, after seeing your flabby white ass, we'll leave gladly!*"

"Oh, Papa!" the sisters exclaimed.

"Mama said a bad word!" James squealed in surprise.

Mama sat up straight and tall and looked quite serious. "You're right, James," she said matter-of-factly. "I promise not to do it again." Then she covered James's ears with her palms and added, "unless we run into that man's flabby white ass in Djakarta!"

Part Two

The Island

24

ARI OPENED HER eyes and stared at the dimly lit cabin. It took a second for her vision to adjust and another second for her to register her disappointment at finding the airplane still bathed in darkness. She had hoped that maybe this time she would have slept through more of the long flight across the Pacific. It took about twenty hours for the company jet to reach the Island from San Francisco, more if they were delayed during the Honolulu refueling stop. Today, at least, everything had gone smoothly. They were on the ground for only an hour, just long enough to stretch their legs, buy some macadamias from the cheerful, rotund native who grew them in her backyard and take Tippy for a much needed walk in hopes that he might not need the newspapers that had been laid out for him on the floor of the second lavatory.

James was sound asleep in the seat next to Ari. He was all curled up under his favorite blankie, his arms and legs carelessly spread around his furry companion. Tippy didn't seem to mind though. He never minded anything James did.

Mama was in the galley at the back of the plane brewing another pot of coffee when Ari came up beside her. She looked a little tired, Ari thought, or perhaps she was just anxious to be home again. Mama never slept on the way to the Island. She said the quiet hours gave her a chance to catch up with herself, but Ari knew that wasn't the reason. When Mama saw her approaching, her expression brightened.

"Well, at least I got a little sleep this time," Ari said. "How long was I out?"

"About three hours."

Ari frowned. Mama smiled and took down two mugs from

the overhead bin, poured steaming, aromatic coffee into each one and placed them on a tray. Then she motioned Ari to follow her to the bench seat at the front of the plane. Halfway down the aisle she stopped to glance at Ethan and Emma who were lying next to each other in identical positions, fully stretched out on their sides and hugging their pillows. They looked even more genetically connected than usual. But that wasn't surprising. Not for Ethan and his Little Shadow.

"Mama?" Ari whispered from somewhere behind her. "Are you all right?"

"I couldn't be happier," she murmured.

As the hours droned on with the jet engines, Mama and Ari played *remember when*, trying both to make the time pass more quickly and to recapture that feeling of familiarity most people lose when they leave the ground. They reminisced about the early years on the Island, before the Great House was built, when they used to stay in the guest pavilion at Grandfather and Mem's. And they spoke about the first time Ari swam in the lagoon without Papa's strong hands holding her up, and rode her own horse bareback across the valley, and hiked to the High Plateau with Grandfather and Mem to learn the secrets of the rain forest. And still, the hours droned on with the jet engines.

"Remember the summer we returned to the Island from Singapore?" Mama asked.

"That was the year we came home to find the Great House finished, wasn't it, Mama?" The Islanders had spent months helping to build the Heywood's new home on the Island. The Island was special like that. It wasn't like other places, where people helped others only if it didn't interfere with what they wanted first. The Island had a true sense of community that had been lost in the hustle and bustle of the outside world.

Mama didn't reply. She just sat there, rolling the ends of her braided hair between her thumb and index finger until she felt them tangle. Then she smoothed them out again before speaking. "I can remember everything about that day, Ari. How everything looked exactly the same, but different somehow, how the air was especially pure and fresh after the night showers, and I can still hear the song the birds sang that morning. You know, the one that when you were a little girl, you thought sounded like they were hiccupping at the end."

"I still think they sound like they're hiccupping," Ari laughed.

Mama stared at her for a moment, scrutinizing her face as if she was searching for something she had lost, or perhaps had planted there. "Have you ever experienced a moment so significant that you don't just remember it—you live it over and over again?"

Ari thought for a moment. "No," she replied. "I don't think I have. That day we came home from Singapore was like that for you, Mama?"

"Yes," she sighed. "When I think of how they were all there waiting for us. They were all there, Ari. All the families. They had come from farmer's fields and doctor's offices and court houses and factories and fishing boats and . . ." She stopped to wipe a tear from her left cheek, and for a moment she looked more like Mem than usual. "It meant so much more than just a house."

Ari had only fleeting memories of the family's return from Singapore—just vague feelings and impressions really. Some of seeing Mama cry and knowing that she wasn't sad. And a lot of hugging and smiling and rejoicing. She remembered Mama and Papa sitting on the front steps of their new home, and the Islanders filing by in some sort of greeting. And how each of them placed a single orchid at their feet, but when it was Grandfather and Mem's turn, they didn't give Mama and Papa an orchid, but gave them instead a small cutting from a Bird of Paradise, which over the years had grown into the large plant in the painted pot that stood in the middle of the gathering pavilion.

But she had a much clearer recollection of the weeks that followed; how old Mr. Padua, the sculptor, came to the house every day and worked atop his rickety old ladder. And how she sat at his feet, listening to him hum the ancient melodies and waiting for his signal to gather up the curly little wood shavings that showered down from above. When he arrived one day with his paint pots, she remembered watching in amazement how deftly his gnarled hands applied the delicate whispers of pale teal green and saffron yellow and coral pink to each of his newly made crevices. Ari didn't know it then, but Mem did, from that very first day she stood in the shadows and watched her three-year-old granddaughter staring up at Mr. Padua, tracing each stroke of his brush with eyes that barely blinked. That's when Mem knew that Ari was born to be a painter, just like her.

It was Mama who first noticed the pale gray haze through the windows. Ari looked out the window nearest her. At first there was nothing. Just water and sky and one large sailing ship probably on its way to the Mainland harbor. So they waited, and they waited, until finally it was there—that faint little irregularity way off on the distant horizon. They stared at it for a very long time, barely breathing or blinking, for fear it might prove an illusion. But it was real. It was always real. And they knew that finally, after all the months, and the piling into the car, driving to the airfield and the packing up the plane, and the settling into the cabin, and the hours of listening to the engines drone on and on . . . they were almost home.

James came stumbling down the aisle with his blankie trailing behind him, his round little tummy protruding out of the pajama bottoms that had gotten twisted all around in his sleep. His eyes were still half-closed, and his hair was all matted down on one side. Ari thought she detected a slight glistening on his left thumb where it must have found his mouth sometime during the night. "How much longer, Ari?" he asked in a thin gravelly voice as she put right his jammies.

"Not long. Do you need to go to the bathroom before we get there?" He nodded, and she walked him (and Tippy, of course) back to the lavatory, stopping along the way to retrieve some fresh clothes from their overnight bags neatly stowed under their seats. They returned some minutes later, freshly scrubbed and ready for deplaning.

Papa was seated next to Mama. His arm was around her shoulders, and he was leaning in toward her window. Emma was sitting in the facing seat. Before joining Mama, they had discarded the wrinkled clothes they had slept in and had replaced them with fresh shorts and cotton camp shirts. They were quietly conversing about the weather, and how glad they were to see the sun, which meant that the Island wouldn't be shrouded in clouds today as they flew by on their way to the Mainland airport. Their calm exteriors only barely concealed the excitement that threatened to burst out of them at any moment.

The excitement in the plane was palpable. It pulsed through and between the members of the family like an uninterrupted electrical circuit. It felt to Ari as if at that moment they were all just one body, one mind. But she knew that as they approached the southeast corner of the Island that each would immerse themselves in their own private coming home ritual, searching out those landmarks that assured them that nothing had changed in their absence.

Ari looked out the little oval window of the airplane and began her ritual of saying hello to her Island home. She started as always at the Dolphin Lagoon, the perfect little crescent of warm amber sands and sparkling waters that rested serenely between jungled cliffs, directly behind the Great House. It was easy to locate the little c-shaped indent on the eastern coastline. The valley, which ran west to east across the Island, ended there and provided one of the only interruptions in the miles of jagged cliffs. She briefly scanned the waters inside the reef for the tell-tale gathering of dorsal fins, which signified that the dolphins were already in residence, but she couldn't find any. So, she turned her attention inland to the peaky roofs of the Great House pavilions, peering out from behind the clusters of coconut palms that separated the gardens from the beach.

The plane banked left and skirted around the eastern headland, passing by the waterfall that plunged from the mountain lagoon at a great height and circling around the Sunset Bench waiting patiently for the return of Mama and Papa. It was only a moment more before South Bay came into view and behind it the ellipse of rugged, emerald mountains that descended from the High Plateau at the center of the Island. The sun was just high enough to reflect little sparkles of light off the Pashmari Falls that spilled over the Plateau and fed the lagoons and rivers and waterfalls below. The Pashmari always reminded Ari of

Niagara Falls. Smaller maybe, and certainly less fierce, but every bit as breathtaking.

From the falls she followed the jagged contours of the mountainsides until they gave way to the terraced valleys that led to the little village that stood on the edge of South Bay. She located the green expanse of the Gathering Place and the wooden columns and blue tiled roofs of the Island School on its western edge. Then she looked for the banyan tree on the opposite side and followed the winding path behind it that led back to the Great House. She could see the irregular contours of the house that had been built around the natural vegetation, not through it, but she could only see little bits of the gardens. The palms and frangipani and banana trees obscured her view.

There were a number of small figures scurrying toward the long wooden pier that protruded out into South Bay on its western edge. Ari knew that among them were Grandfather and Mem. For now, they were just ants on the landscape, but soon they would be life-sized figures, warm and radiant and welcoming her home. She strained to see them as long as she could before the western headlands came between them, and then she turned away from the window, her ritual completed, and settled back in her seat for the short trip to the Mainland airport.

The pilot's voice came over the intercom again. "We've been cleared for landing," he said.

Ari set James down in his own seat and strapped him in. "What about Tippy? He needs a seat belt too," James informed her.

"I'll hold onto him, James," she returned. "I promise I won't let anything happen to him." She picked up the puppy with some difficulty. He wasn't a furry little ball anymore. She set him on her lap facing her little brother, who proceeded to recite Mama's instructions about staying in your seat during the whole landing. Tippy listened intently, cocking his headfirst to the right and then to the left, in the earnest effort to understand every word. Perhaps he did. He laid down on Ari's lap, rested his chin on the armrest and didn't stir again for the rest of the flight.

The plane was coming in from the north today so the town

wasn't visible out her window, but Ari could see the commercial harbor where a freighter was being loaded with something that looked like sugar cane, and beyond that she could see the beginnings of the neatly planted plantation fields that spread out for miles in patchwork green squares. Then the plane swung around in a wide arc and headed south. Not far ahead was the pink stucco terminal building of the little airport, the smattering of commercial jets littering the tarmac, and the dual runways running parallel to each other at the water's edge. Ari listened for the sounds of the landing gear clicking into place and the raising of the flaps and the slowing of the engines. Finally, the plane floated over the end of the runway and gently returned to earth.

It took only a few minutes for the baggage handlers to unload the plane, even though there were several boxes of Christmas decorations on board, and only a few minutes more for the customs official to stamp them all through.

It was a ten-minute shuttle ride to the docks where Tao Ahmanjaya stood ready on his boat to ferry the family to the Island. He looked the same as always—tall, bronzed, dark-eyed, with maybe just a touch more gray in his thick black hair. He was wearing his Mainland casuals, khaki hiking shorts and a madras shirt. His beaming smile broadcast his pleasure at seeing the family again, especially Mama, whom he had known since they were children together. It was once thought that Tao and Mama might be married one day, but he had always been the brother of Mama's heart. She couldn't risk losing the only brother she had ever known, or at least that's what she told herself until she met Papa. Then she understood why everything was as it was.

"Welcome home!" Tao shouted.

"Tao!" Mama cried, throwing her arms around him in greeting. "You look wonderful!"

"Well, perhaps Kemala keeps me a little too well fed," he laughed, patting his barely rounded stomach.

"I've missed Kemala so much. How is she?"

"She couldn't be happier. She's been running around like a chicken with her head cut off, preparing for your return, Mary.

You know Kemala. She's already cooked ahead enough food to last for the next two weeks."

"I don't know where she stores all that energy. She's such a tiny little thing," Mama laughed.

"You two do look a little like Mutt and Jeff when you're together, Mary," Papa interjected.

It was true. Kemala was so unlike Mama, except for the long black hair and bronzy skin. Mama was tall and curvy and statuesque, and her motion was graceful and elegant. Kemala was more like Tinker Bell—a diminutive little fairy who flitted from place to place with barely enough mass to leave footprints in the sand. She was inches shorter than Mama and very petite with a beautiful, fine-boned face, straight contours and those dark, almost black eyes that were typical of all the Islanders except for Mama's family, whose emerald eyes were a genetic mystery. But she and Mama couldn't have been closer if they had been identical twins. For any other two women it might have been difficult, one loving Tao in silence while he loved the other. But it was Mary who turned Tao's face toward Kemala all those years ago, and it was Tao and Kemala who thanked her for it every day since.

"Uncle Tao, Uncle Tao! Did you see my dog?" James asked, tugging on his godfather's shorts.

"James!" Tao beamed. "He must be the most beautiful dog in the whole world! What's his name?"

"Tippy!"

"Ah, a perfect name for a perfect dog." Tao grinned, and gave both James and the pup a pat on the head.

When the suitcases and boxes had been properly stowed, the family jumped aboard Tao's boat, took seats on the sun-faded blue canvas cushions that encircled the aft deck and steadied themselves for the twelve mile crossing to the Island. "We appreciate you picking us up, Tao," Papa said as he handed him the aft line, "but won't your patients be missing you at the office?"

Tao laughed. "It's Saturday. Remember, Ethan?"

"I lose all sense of time when I come home."

"That's the idea," he replied and headed for the Captain's

chair.

The boat moved slowly through the harbor, sailing past little fishing boats with single masts, peeling paint, and jovial sailors flashing warm smiles. They were already done fishing for the day, having gone out before dawn to bring in the day's catch, most of which they sold in the fish stalls at the open market down the wharf. But they always saved a few of the biggest ones for the owners of the ever-increasing number of opulent yachts who loved engaging in the native bartering ritual whenever they left *civilization*.

Ari waved to Old Willie as they passed by. He was sunning himself in the back of his boat, his weathered face and bare chest positioned perfectly to catch the morning rays. He had a juicy slice of mango in one hand and a thick leather-bound book in the other, which probably looked incongruous to anyone who didn't know him. But Old Willie was always reading something. In fact, Ari could barely remember a time when that old khaki rucksack of his wasn't filled to the brim with books, many of which he distributed to the Island children whenever he happened upon them. Willie looked up from what was obviously one of his treasured classics, and his big toothy smile broadcast his pleasure at seeing the family again. "Welcome home!" he shouted across the water.

Welcome home. There they were again. Those sweet words that heralded the family's return to everything familiar. The warm sun, the fragrant air, the gentle waters in constant motion. And those friendly sounds of commerce, which drifted out each morning from the wooden sidewalks and tin-roofed plantation buildings that had, for the last two hundred years, crowded the old Mainland wharf.

Mrs. Yao was standing in front of her little café, watering the ferns that hung over her freshly washed windows and issuing a stream of instructions in Chinese to her children who listened intently and then scurried away. Mrs. Prada and her son, Manuel, were just leaving the Mercantile with their pushcart full of provisions, wheeling away, clickety-clack, clickety-clack, down the warped wooden boardwalk toward the sailing yachts moored in the harbor. And there was old Mrs. Kanjeera, sitting at her corner just completing a transaction for one of the beautiful batik sarongs she had learned to make as a child and had been selling in the open market for nearly fifty years.

They motored on past the last of the fishing boats and made their way between the rows of sleek sailing yachts that had grown so numerous over recent years a whole new marina had been built to accommodate them. They were bigger than the old sailing vessels and certainly more modern, but Ari could barely tell one from another. It bothered her a little, the scarcity of teak and brass and spar-varnished artistry. These boats looked like big white plastic apartment houses whose owners valued size and price tag above art.

Once free of the harbor congestion, Tao turned the boat due east and gunned the engines full speed, setting James to giggling and whooping like a rodeo cowboy. "Faster, Uncle Tao, faster!" he yelled over the roar of the twin engines.

"If we go any faster, James, we'll fly right off the water!" he yelled back.

The remainder of the crossing was made in silence. Even James confined his activity to staring at the Island as it grew larger and more distinct. Gradually, granite outcroppings took shape, and the shadowy monoliths which protruded from them grew into coconut palms, the narrow white vertical stripes into waterfalls and the verdant green blotches, which filled every crevice, into giant primordial-looking ferns whose growth was unfettered by clay pots or improper watering. Ari couldn't see any people yet. The western side of the Island was all uninhabitable cliffs. But soon they would turn south and skirt around the western headlands. South Bay would come into full view, and with it, the beach and the pier and the smattering of friends and family who had gathered there to welcome them home.

Ari glanced at Mama who was sitting adjacent to her on the port side bench. Her shoes had already disappeared into her straw bag and her long, loose hair was slightly airborne, having been liberated from its traveling braid before the wheels of the jet had even touched down. Her arms were securely wrapped around James, and Ari noticed that she had already removed her watch, which would not reappear again until she was back in San Francisco. "What do I need with a watch on the Island?" she would ask. "I have the rising sun for an alarm clock, and the dolphins to tell me when it's time for my morning swim, and the red sky to call me to the Sunset Bench, and the night birds to tell me its dinner time. I can figure out the rest for myself."

By the time she looked up again Tao was maneuvering the boat into South Bay toward the pier and a scene for which she was wholly unprepared. "Oh, Mama, look!" she shouted. "Look!"

Mama was looking toward shore. She had already seen all the Islanders who crowded onto the long wooden pier and had quickly scanned the length of the wide crescent beach and found all the people who waited there too. She had searched the gamut of signature silks that identified each of the families and could find none missing. "They're all here!" she shouted with a child's voice. They've all come back to the Island!" She looked at Ethan, who was standing next to Tao at the wheel. He was obviously feeling quite pleased with himself. "You knew, didn't you? You knew they'd all be here," she cried.

Ethan grinned and for a moment looked just like James. "Well, Tao and I . . . well, we thought . . ."

Mama looked to her old friend. "Tao, what's going on?"

"Actually, it was all Ethan's doing. It's been so long since all the families have gotten together at one time for a Celebration. It seems like lately, one family or another is always missing, or kids and grandkids have moved off-Island and can't make it back. So, your husband started rounding us all up some months ago."

"Oh, Ethan, I . . . I . . ." Mama began to cry.

Papa came to her and sat beside her. "I know this doesn't make up for the worry I've caused you, Mary, but I thought if maybe we got *all* the families together for Celebration this year, that maybe you could lock your worry away in one of those little compartments of yours and see past Djakarta to what awaits us on the other side." He smiled at her.

"Are Tommy and Joey coming home?" Ari asked Tao.

"They're on their way up from the university," he replied. "Old Willie's waiting to bring them home."

Ari felt an unfamiliar pang in her stomach when Tao said

this, and it surprised her a little. Maybe last Christmas, when Mem had talked about Joey, the seeds of something were planted in her subconscious, or maybe it was the excitement she was feeling over the big reunion, or maybe it was just being back home again. Ari didn't know for sure, but she would have two whole weeks to figure it out.

25

IT DIDN'T TAKE long to locate Grandfather and Mem. They were standing with Old Batara and Maru on the beach at the base of the pier. From offshore they looked like the seismic epicenter of a rippling of activity that extended out from them in all directions. Several of the families had obviously just arrived and were still tying up their boats, while others were in various stages of assembly-line unloading and suitcase carrying and shirt unbuttoning and shoe removing and old friend greeting. There were several children already frolicking among the brightly colored coral formations spanning the Bay, and their laughter and shrieks could be heard over the gentle purr of the engines as Tao slowly maneuvered the boat toward its appointed slip.

It took forever to traverse the last fifty yards of the journey from San Francisco, but Ari didn't mind. She used the time, as she always did, to let the *Island feeling* wash over her before she took her first step onshore. It was like going through an invisible doorway to a magical world, where life was simple. No cars or paved roads and where time passed slower than on the Mainland. In short, it was Paradise.

It was Mem who first saw them coming today. And Mem who waved her arms wildly in the air and called out, "Mary! Ethan! Children!" Then she ran down the pier maneuvering in and out of clusters of Islanders, her long braid fluttering behind her like the tail of a kite, until she reached the slip into which Tao was deftly guiding the boat. Ari didn't wait for him to cut the engines, but leapt onto the pier and into Mem's arms, holding on until she was sure she wasn't dreaming again.

"Oh, Mem . . ." was all she could say, but it was enough.

In moments they were all together on the beach, shoeless and worry-free, hugging and greeting and crying just a little. Kemala was there and she and Mama were already bantering away like a couple of schoolgirls. Grandfather was hoisting James in the air and threatening to throw him in the ocean, and James was yelling, "Throw me, Grandfather, throw me," because he had been *waiting forever* for someone to say that it was time to go swimming, and this was the closest he had come. Eventually, Kemala's fourteen-year-old niece, Tia, offered to take James swimming while the rest of the family unpacked and unwound from the long journey. Mama gratefully accepted.

Old Batara and Maru were waiting a discreet distance away. They resembled a pair of granite statues from Easter Island, Ari thought, large and solid and stalwartly looking on. Their snow-white hair was the only clue to their advanced years, but nobody knew how old they actually were. Ari had asked Mama once and she said she didn't know, but that they must be pretty old. They were the only Elders anyone could ever remember, including Mrs. Padua, and she was ninety-six.

"I am pleased to see you both looking so well," Mama greeted them in the ancient language.

"As are we to see you, Daughter," they replied and then continued conversing in a patois of old and new languages with a liberal helping of English.

Finally, it was time to go home. "Everybody," Papa said, "Grab some suitcases. Ari, you take Tippy home or he'll end up in the Bay with James." Tippy was sitting motionless at the end of the leash Papa held. He was staring in the direction of the children's laughter, and his sadness at being left behind by his best friend was apparent in his down-turned head, forlorn eyes, and unusually quiet tail.

"Don't worry, Tippy," Ari said in a soothing voice, "James hasn't forgotten you." She picked up the gangly pup and rocked him and stroked his head, assuring him again and again that James would be back soon. Then she set him down and joined the tail end of the barefoot procession that was already disappearing into the thick stand of coconut palms that separated the beach from the Gathering Place.

They passed Tao's brothers, Herry and Paku, on the way, coming in the opposite direction and dragging some long, heavy-duty extension cords behind them, the other ends of which were plugged in at the school. They appeared to Ari like two giant stuffed teddy bears, their faces sewn into permanent smiles. "Beach Party. Tomorrow night," they shouted.

There were several Islanders setting up tables on the lawns, which extended some fifty yards out from the steps of the school to the banyan tree on the other end. By tomorrow night they would be laden with local delicacies—pulled pork, fresh yellowfin, mango chutney, flat breads, fruit salads, curried rice with raisins, and sen lek, Mrs. Gupta's rice noodle dish made with peanut sauce and miniature purple couri berries that grew up on the Plateau and tasted a little like raspberries only sweeter. By now Kemala would have organized every child on the Island to take a turn at cranking the ice cream makers filled with fresh coconut, sugar, and cream. But Ari would have to wait until Celebration Night to taste Mrs. Tanji's kiwi tarts. Mrs. Tanji was the curator at the Natural History Museum on the Mainland and her long hours didn't permit the baking of the labor-intensive tarts for just a beach party.

"Hello!" several Islanders shouted at once. "Glad to see you back!" But they didn't detain the travelers any longer than that. There would be time enough later for a really good chat.

From the banyan tree a narrow path circled in wide arcs through the shade of a Mimosa grove. The earth there was cool and damp and soft underfoot and was a welcome respite from hot sands and warm grasses. Only dappled sun managed to filter through the fern-like leaves, making this part of the path a perfect home for shade-loving hostas and the pink and purple star-shaped blossoms of creeping impatiens. Another hundred feet and the path would come out into the sun again and make its final turning toward home. Ari would get her first glimpse there of the giant-leafed philodendrons and feathery ferns and exotic blooms of Mr. Bashira's beautiful gardens and the sparkling waters that played hide and seek there. There would be resplendently feathered peacocks who strutted and preened there, and the exquisitely crafted pavilions of the Great

House that rose from the earth like the majestic palms, waiting patiently for the return of the family.

At last, they stood on the covered veranda, gazing at the tall glass doors, whose graceful serpentine-like filigrees Mr. Padua had lovingly fashioned from rosewoods found on the Plateau. "Open the house, Mama. Open it," Ari urged.

Mama put her hands on the two wooden handles carved to look like blooms of the Bird of Paradise, and she whispered ancient words of homecoming. Then she swung the heavy doors inward to reveal the Great House beyond. Ari smiled, thinking as she always did at the opening of the house about that scene in the Wizard of Oz when Dorothy opened the door of her farmhouse and discovered the colorful world of Oz on the other side. Except that this time she was looking at an open-air courtyard and the covered walkway that wrapped around it, and the filigree balusters that kept James from falling into the foliage, and the elephant ears, the blooming hibiscus and the trailing purple bougainvillea that had wrapped itself around one of the heavy carved pillars some years ago and had migrated around the porch roof until it had triumphantly met up with itself again. The little stream that trickled over the stones and out through the stilts that elevated the house was flowing just a bit more rapidly than usual. There must have been a recent rain up on the Plateau, Ari thought.

Mem handed Ari her suitcase in exchange for Tippy's leash. "I think this young man and I shall take a walk around the property and discuss the appropriate places for conducting his business." Ari watched the two of them walk down the veranda and descend the steps to the side gardens and head out toward the big jacaranda tree outside Mama and Papa's quarters. Its low spreading branches were already filled with the purply-blue flowers Mama loved so much. "You don't want to go here, Tippy." Ari heard Mem say. "This is a people tree."

Ari never knew what Mem did after that, but from that day forward, Tippy always took himself outside when he needed to go, and went deep into the bushes where his leavings would never be underfoot, and if the house was closed up and he needed help, he would sit at someone's feet and yip twice—never once, never three times, always twice. It had long been whispered among the Islanders that Mem could talk to the animals and that when she did, they always listened. Perhaps the whispers were true.

26

IT WAS GIDHRA Kandiri, the architect, and Mem's lifelong friend, whom the Council of Elders had charged with designing the Great House. Before ever laying pencil to paper, she and Mem had walked the Island together, through the valleys and mountains and rain forests, until she was sure she knew all that the Island wanted of her.

When Mem first saw the final renderings of the Great House, she cried. Two of her tears still stained the lower right-hand corner of the top page. Mem had replied simply, "Mary and Ethan will be so pleased." Nothing else needed to be said.

Ghidra had designed a cluster of magnificent pavilions in the Balinese tradition around an interior courtyard, each pavilion dedicated to a different daily activity—sleeping, cooking, gathering—and each connected to the others by covered walkways. The exterior walls were largely glass with wide mahogany mullions that picture framed the view, and all were movable for a fluid transition between the house and the surrounding gardens. The rich woods and the coppery-veined stone and even the green tiled roofs were all indigenous to the Island, giving the house the appearance of having grown there rather than of being constructed.

Ari's bedroom was one of three that lined the north side of the courtyard. It was identical to the others in structure—large, multi-leveled, with the sleeping area when you first walked in and a sunken sitting area that looked out over the gardens. To the right of the sitting area was an archway that led to an enclosed W.C. and vanity, both tiled in the classic mosaic tradition, and beyond to a small walled garden in which the bath and shower hid among the lush vegetation in the open air. All of the sleeping quarters had high, peaky wood ceilings and polished wood plank floors and paneled walls with insets of silk or woven matting as personal taste dictated. All were embellished with just enough filigree and columns and carvings by Mr. Padua to balance the organic simplicity of the architecture without overpowering it.

"Hey, Ari, have you finished unpacking yet?" Emma called as she entered her sister's quarters.

Ari looked up from the floor where she knelt in front of the tall Chinese armoire, putting her things away. "Almost," she smiled. "Will you wait for me?"

"Sure." Emma crossed over to the platform bed, lay back, dangled her legs over the end and stared up at the graceful translucent silks of saffron and crème that billowed down from the ceiling to the four corner posts. She had already changed into her bathing suit and sarong and the emerald dupioni coverlet felt cool against her skin. "It'll be great to see Tommy and Joey again," she commented casually. "I mean, it's been a long time."

Ari felt that pang again. "Yes, too long," she replied in a measured tone.

"I wonder if they've changed much."

"I hope not!"

Emma laughed. "You mean you hope nothing's changed about Joey not having a steady girlfriend since the last time you saw him!"

Ari really hadn't thought about this, not in her conscious mind anyway, but now that Emma said it out loud, she pondered the idea. She stopped unpacking and looked over at her sister who was now sitting upright and looking back at her. "I think I would be disappointed if Joey had a girlfriend. I don't know why. I never really thought about it before, but I just would."

"Well, we'll soon see, won't we?" Emma's voice was full of giddy teasing and Ari suspected she was wondering the same about Tommy.

It didn't take long for Ari to finish unpacking. She never brought much with her to the Island. There was always a full supply of toiletries in the bathroom, and a hairdryer and shampoo and the special oils she used to replenish her hair when it dried out in the salty sea. As for clothes, she spent most of her time in bathing suits and sarongs and occasionally in shorts, particularly if she was going to hike or ride, and of course, she had some fashionable outfits and a couple of dresses for evenings on the Mainland. "There," she said, and gently closed the doors of the armoire, taking care to ensure that the palace garden scene, which had been meticulously hand-painted on the yellow lacquered Elmwood, fitted together as closely as a hundred-year-old antique would allow. "I'm officially home."

"Not quite yet," Emma smiled, pointing to the glass walls that wanted opening.

Ari descended the pair of stairs to the sitting area and pushed back the heavy glass and mahogany panels until they accordioned all the way to the corner posts. The room seemed to inhale when she did this. Fresh breezes wafted in and lifted the gauzy curtains from their resting place, and gently fluttered the silks over the bed bringing with them tantalizing fragrances and the languid melody of birds calling and waters spilling and palms swaying.

"It's so good to be home," Ari sighed flopping down on the bed next to Emma.

"I know what you mean," Emma replied. "I mean, our house in San Francisco is beautiful and everything, but it's not . . ."

"Home?"

Mama was just coming out of her quarters on the opposite side of the courtyard when the girls emerged from Ari's room. She was wearing her turquoise sarong tied low around her hips and a short purple cotton tank top, loose fitting, that revealed her midriff. She was not wearing anything underneath. She rarely did on the Island. Ari watched her as they headed toward the gathering pavilion, little bits of her peeking out from behind the banana trees and the wayward stems of magenta bougainvillea that floated freely down from the overhang. There were no signs of fatigue from her sleepless journey nor of the worry that had pervaded her dreams ever since Papa made his announcement about Djakarta. Mama was happy—supremely happy. Mama was home.

They met up at the entrance to the gathering pavilion, where family and friends came together nightly to continue the many animated discussions begun around the dining room table or to relax in companionable silence, book in hand, letting the sounds of the Island wash over them. They were greeted as usual by the two ancient stone statues, a man and a woman, whose smiling faces, Ari thought, looked a little like Grandfather and Mem. But, of course, it couldn't be them. The statues were hundreds of years old.

"Where is everybody?" she asked.

"Papa and Grandfather are waiting at the service road for the truck to come with all the boxes, and Mem went back to her house to pick up something she prepared for our dinner tonight. I was just getting ready to open up the rest of the house."

"May we help?"

"Well, if you girls wouldn't mind opening up the gathering pavilion, I'll go on through to the kitchen," she replied and headed there without further comment.

The gathering pavilion was a large room, bordered on two sides by an elevated gallery. It was accessed from the courtyard through an intimate little library that was tucked into the west wall of the gallery under a low, flat ceiling. The end walls of the library were covered in books and the smooth plank floor in soft Tibetan carpets and overstuffed rattan club chairs and the little butler's tables with magazines and reading lamps and, of course, the burled wood humidor Grandfather presented to Papa in a show of male solidarity over the ongoing crusade to allow pipe smoking indoors. It was a cozy space, separated from the drama of the grand pavilion by a filigree railing and a series of hand carved posts at eight-foot intervals, a place perfect for curling up on rainy days with a really good read.

Beyond the gallery, the ceiling soared to a great height and was supported by massive, hand-hewn beams from which rows of single palm-bladed Punjab fans hung down and, when switched on, gently swayed back and forth stirring the air. As with the rest of the house, the gathering pavilion's furnishings were a perfect blending of Asia and the Tropics with just a smattering of British Colonial thrown in. But the colors were borrowed from the Island—from the soft turquoise seas and the steamy green jungles, to the deep rich earth, and the saffrons and paprikas and other aromatic herbs and spices that grew there in abundance. Mama called it *Paradise.*

Ari watched Mama as she passed through the library to the opening in the railing, descended the three polished wood stairs and traversed the stone floor to the far side of the room. Along the way she stopped to plump a pillow here and there on the soft-cushioned sofas and chairs, glance at photographs on the Shantong altar table, and test the dryness of the soil in three of the giant porcelain pots that were home to the palms and philodendrons and citrus trees and one particularly beautiful Bird of Paradise.

The gallery ran the full width of the courtyard and continued around the north side of the pavilion, past a little guest bath hidden in an alcove, to the company dining area where the exterior wall jutted out an extra fifteen feet to accommodate the large round rosewood table. Emma headed there first to open the glass walls and switch on the ceiling fans before retrieving the watering can from under the powder room sink. Ari remained in the library to open the louvers over the half wall that overlooked the courtyard.

The simultaneous opening of walls caused a sudden crossbreeze to blow in from the back gardens, scattering to the floor a stack of pamphlets that had been neatly piled on one of the butler's tables. They were announcements of Mem's upcoming exhibit at the Fujiri Gallery on the Mainland. Ari gathered them up and placed them on the green felt game table under one of the polished stones Mama kept in the fishbowl near the stairs. Then she checked the bookshelves for any dust that Mrs. Nari's cleaning service may have left behind, though of course there was none, and descended into the main part of the gathering pavilion where she fitted the dozens of odd candle sticks and glass lanterns with the candles that Mama kept by scent in the drawers of the old lacquered step tansu.

"There," she said, fitting a spice-scented candle into the last of the character lanterns. "Are you almost done, Emma?" she called, not sure where Emma had gotten to.

"Just finished," Emma called back from the guest bath.

"Then let's go."

Mama was sitting at the center island, writing a grocery list when the girls entered the cooking pavilion. She had thrown open the two movable walls to the back patio letting in the gentle sounds of rippling water off the lily pond and two blue dragonflies now playing chase over her head. "All finished?" she asked.

"I think so, Mama," Ari answered. "Do you need anything else before we go swimming?"

"Well, I'm making a list for Mr. Prada. I thought I'd call it in, and he could send over our order on the evening launch. Is there anything you girls want in the house? Besides a year's supply of Mrs. Yao's steamed dumplings, of course."

"Oh, you know what we like, Mama," Ari replied, and Emma nodded.

Mama looked up and smiled, and Ari noticed a little bead of sweat forming itself on her forehead. She whisked it away with the back of her hand before it traveled too far. "It's a warm one today, isn't it," she remarked. "Or, perhaps San Francisco requires a bit more re-acclimating than Hong Kong used to."

"A little of both, I think," Ari returned. "Why don't you come swimming with us?"

"Yes, Mama, please," Emma chimed in.

"Well, I have to get the list finished first."

"We can wait."

Mama glanced around the pavilion for anything else that might still need attention. The pilots on the oven and cooktop were lit, the cover on the outdoor Japanese Hibachi had been removed and the cook surface seasoned with peanut oil, the sealed spice jars filled, and the pots and pans removed from storage and hung overhead. There wasn't much more to do except the list. "If you wouldn't mind setting out the cushions on the patio furniture, I'll just call Mr. Prada and go grab my suit."

"Okay, Mama."

It didn't take long to retrieve the green duck cushions from storage or hang the striped Mayan hammock from its wooden stand. Mrs. Nari's crew had already cleaned off the big stone table, which shared the shade of a giant bhodi tree with the cooking pavilion, and had arranged around it the deep, rounded-back chairs that invited prolonged lounging under the stars. There wasn't much else to do except fall back into one of the gliders and wait.

Ari and Emma sat together, their bare feet planted on the irregular stones, gently swaying back and forth. Their long hair hung over the backs of the cushions allowing the breeze to find the hot spots on the back of their necks. They didn't talk but just stared up at the sky whose blue perfection was, as yet, still unmarred by even a single wisp of a cloud.

"Look who I found," Mama called, as she entered the patio from her quarters.

Ari and Emma both turned round to see her coming toward them, still wearing her turquoise sarong but over her matching floral print bikini this time. She carried a stack of beach towels over her right arm and a wet, wiggly James in her left. The girls smiled to cover their disappointment at losing a few quiet moments with her.

"Mama says we're going swimming at the Dolphin Lagoon!"

"Haven't you had enough water yet?" Emma asked, already knowing the answer.

"I wanna go swimming," he replied.

"And we want to go swimming with you too, don't we girls," Mama said with a wink.

James squirmed out of Mama's arms and ran ahead toward the footbridge to the beach. They followed quickly after him. He scurried past the lamppost with the double Kyoto lanterns that marked the path to the guest pavilion, past the Quan Yin statue peering out from beneath a shower of delicate yellow golden chain, past brilliant red flamboyants and New Zealand fern trees and spiky heliconia, finally disappearing around a cluster of giant green banana trees. "Oweeee!" they heard him scream and ran to see what kind of trouble he had gotten himself into this time.

They found him lying on the grassy path, holding his right knee in his hands. A peacock was standing nearby, his feathers in full regalia. "He made me fall down, Mama," James wailed, pointing to the bird that was more flustered than mad. "He pu . . . pushed me!"

Mama knelt and cradled James in her arms. When she spoke, her voice was neither critical nor babying. "Oh, James, he didn't mean to. You just scared him coming around the corner so fast." She gently stroked his shin and kissed his knee before saying "all better."

"Remember, we have to move slowly through the gardens so we don't frighten the creatures who live here."

James peered up at Mama, and for just an instant, they resembled Madonna and Child. "Okay, Mama," he sniffled and got up and limped past the peacock.

By the time James's feet hit the sand, his limp had magically disappeared, and he ran full steam toward the water. "Wait, James!" Mama called. "You can't go in the water by yourself." Mama handed the towels to Emma and quickly untied her sarong and let it fall to the sand. Then she grabbed James's hand and together they dashed away and splashed into the water, quickly disappearing beneath the sparkles of sunlight that danced on the surface.

Mama was still so beautiful, Ari thought, as she watched her slide into the water. Her body was a near perfect original of the one she had handed down. Perhaps her stomach was just a bit more rounded from having had three children, but it was still smooth and firm and not at all fleshy. Most women Mama's age would have jiggled chasing after James, but not her. It was James who jiggled. His soft little body was noticeably leaner than when he was only four, but he still had a way to go before he outgrew toddlerhood completely. Right now, he mostly resembled a giant bouncing orange in his flashy new bathing trunks.

Mama and James were already well out on the reef by the time Ari and Emma submerged themselves in the lagoon. The girls swam in tandem for a while, skirting effortlessly along the shallow bottom, wrapped in the silence of the sea except when they surfaced for intakes of air where they caught odd syllables of James's shouts and hoots and hollers. When the bottom dropped away, they joined schools of iridescent yellow tang and black and silver angel fish and striped butterflies and pencil-thin trumpeters who were maneuvering through the coral canyons and in and out of the rutted formations.

Ari remembered the first time Papa fitted a mask on her face and swam with her to the reef, holding her hand in his and gliding easily alongside her thrashing body. She remembered the way the sun illuminated the coral through the crystal clarity of the water, and how surprised she was by all the different shapes and textures. She thought how deliciously familiar this all felt now; how comforting and secure. The continuity of the past blending into the present and pointing toward the future. Maybe that's what coming home was really all about.

That night the family sat around the old stone table, bathed in the cool evening breezes and the soft light of patio torches and stars and the ascending moon. There was no pretense of table manners. Bodies reclined, legs draped over chair arms, cheeks rested on hands, elbows firmly planted on the table. The conversation was happy and laughter-filled with the relaxed cadence of those who had nowhere else to be but exactly where they were.

Periodically, Ari would withdraw from the conversation and let it float somewhere outside her hearing, and she would look around the table at the animated figures of her family as if she were watching a silent movie in which subtle gestures became exaggerated and noticeable. The way Mama tossed her head back slightly before letting out a laugh replicating the same gesture from Mem only a moment before, and how Emma curled her hair around her finger whenever her thoughts strayed, and how Papa reclined full out in his chair, carefree and contented, only moving from elbows down to lift a chilled drink to his lips or emphasize a point for Grandfather's illumination. Grandfather was in a reflective mood. Ari could tell by the way he stroked his chin with the forefinger of his left hand while listening intently to the conversation, speaking some but mostly just interjecting from time to time with, *I wonder*. Mama, though, was in anything but a reflective mood. Ari could tell that, too, by the way she stared at Papa and the single drop of perspiration that travelled down his bare chest, trickled into a deep crevice in his muscles and disappeared into the fabric of his linen shirt.

"Ari . . . Ari!" Papa called across the table, returning her from her reveries. "Where have you been?" he laughed.

"Right here, Papa. Sorry, my mind must have wondered somewhere."

"That's what evenings on the Island are for, my child," said Mem. "Life without daydreams is no life at all, you remember that."

James listened attentively to the conversation, his fatigue keeping the interruptions to a minimum. Eventually, he crawled down from Ari's lap where he had been resting in the crook of her arm and circled round the table until he stood next to Papa. He tapped Papa's forearm with the tip of his finger until he got his attention. "What is it, James?" Papa asked.

"You said when I was a big boy I could swim with the tanks. I'm a big boy now, and I can swim really good. Honest, Papa."

"James is right, Ethan," Mama interjected. "He swam all the way out to the point today without any help from me."

Papa bent forward and picked up James and placed him on his lap. "Well then, son, I guess it's time we tried on those tanks."

James's eyes grew huge and his mouth flew open, but no sound came out. "When, Papa, when?" he finally shrieked. "Can we go now?"

"Whoa, James," Papa chuckled. "Not now. Tomorrow when it's light." James looked a bit crestfallen. "I promise, James. Tomorrow we'll take out the tanks and the masks and the fins and we'll try them on. Right after my morning calls."

"But you talk forever and ever, Papa."

"Sorry, James, that's the best I can do."

"Okay," he replied and continued without stopping for breath. "And then we can swim with the tanks, right, Papa?"

"Well, that depends upon you. You may not like the tanks as much as you do snorkels. A lot of grown-ups don't."

"How come?"

"Because the tanks are heavy and sometimes divers who like to really zoom think that the tanks slow them down too much."

"Oh." James thought about this for a moment, scrunching up his cheeks and squinting his eyes the way he did on those rare occasions when he stopped long enough to try and think something through. Then he looked up at Papa, and beaming with pride and admiration, he declared, "I don't care, Papa. I can zoom with the tanks . . . just like you!" Papa grabbed him up and squeezed him in response, and Ari wondered to herself if there was a male equivalent of Madonna and Child.

James disappeared into the house to go to the bathroom and the conversation turned to Mem's show at the Fujiri and how everyone would be there, including Old Batara and Maru, who rarely left the refuge of the Island. They talked about their excitement that all the families had gathered for Celebration this year, and how much fun the beach party would be tomorrow night. And how Mem had run into Joey Ahmanjaya when she had gone back to her house to pick up the lobster salad and how pleased he had looked when she told him that Ari had already arrived. "I have it on good authority," Mem purred, "that there hasn't been a serious girlfriend for quite some time now."

Ari was just in the process of rolling a fresh strawberry in some confectioner's sugar, and she quickly popped it in her mouth, glad for the excuse not to respond. She couldn't stop her cheeks from blushing bright red though. She had been distracted by thoughts of Joey all day and with remembrances of all the firsts that come with new romances. The first time he smiles at you, and makes excuses to talk to you, and asks you out to something the whole gang is going to, and kisses you in that special way that you know the first kiss will not be the last. Jason had become a distant memory. One that she would learn from, but wouldn't think back upon often, if ever.

Suddenly, a loud crash diverted everyone's attention to the side of the house. It was followed by an *uh oh* and a slapping sound that seemed to be coming toward them. Mama giggled from behind her hand and then put on a serious expression and waited. Before long, James appeared around the corner of the cooking pavilion. He was wearing a mask and a pair of bright lime green fins and a weight belt wrapped twice around his waist, and with each labored step he grunted, and the fins flapped against the stones and the belt pushed his bathing trunks even further below his already protruding little bottom. He was such a comical sight that everyone had the worst time trying to keep their serious expressions, but when James announced in a pinched-nose, nasal twang, "See, Papa, I told you I was a big boy now," the laughter erupted out of all of them, causing a whole chorus of night birds to join in.

It was late by the time Grandfather and Mem returned home. Despite the long journey, no one wanted the evening to end. "Would you like me to put James to bed?" Ari asked, looking over at her brother who was curled up on a lounger next to where Tippy lay. He was no longer wearing his mask and weight belt, but the lime green flippers had never left his feet.

"That's all right," Mama replied. "Papa and I will put him to bed. If you wouldn't mind finishing up out here?"

"No problem, Mama." She watched them stroll away—Papa carrying James in his left arm and holding Mama close to him in his right. James's head was slumped on Papa's shoulder and his arms hung loosely around his neck. Tippy followed slowly behind them.

When the dishes were all washed and the leftovers stored in the refrigerator, Emma and Ari made one last check of the counters and the island and the table tops and the stones around James's chair for any crumbs that might attract insects. "Looks good, I think," Emma said. "So, what now, Ari? Are you ready for bed?"

"Not yet," she replied, with that look Emma knew so well. "I was just thinking . . ."

"Thinking what?" Emma parroted.

"Well . . . you really shouldn't go to bed on a full stomach, you know. Don't you think we should take a little walk to work off our dinners first?"

"And where did you have in mind?"

"Oh, I don't know. Maybe we should go over to the Gathering Place and see if they've finished setting up for tomorrow night. Maybe they still need some help."

"*They*? Since when did Joey Ahmanjaya change his name to *They*?" Emma teased.

"Since he came home with his big brother, Tommy!"

Now it was Emma's turn to blush.

27

ARI OPENED THE top drawer of her armoire and pulled out a fresh sarong in a leaf pattern of several shades of green interspersed with large pink and purple orchids. It would only take a minute for her to change. She and Emma had already freshened up from the beach, having excused themselves before dinner to wash the sea water out of their hair and apply the aloe lotion to their skin that the Islanders had been producing for years and were just now marketing on the Mainland with great success under Papa's direction.

Standing naked in front of her full-length mirror, Ari held one corner of the sarong next to her stomach and carefully wrapped it around her hips several times before knotting it. Then she rolled the knot inward and tucked it inside the folds, causing the sarong to be pulled down at an angle across her stomach, just low enough to reveal her navel. "Can you imagine what Brittany would say now?" she asked the topless girl in the mirror. Then she put on her cropped purple cotton tank and headed for the side yard and the wrap-around veranda that enveloped the sleeping pavilions.

At James's quarters Ari peeked in to make sure he was all right. James was sleeping peacefully on his platform bed, lying in a fetal position. Tippy lay curled up in his grooves. A single night light on his side table illuminated his face. He appeared to be smiling. She kissed his forehead and whispered *"Sweet dreams, big guy."* Then she tiptoed back out the way she had come and found Emma waiting for her on the veranda outside her quarters. "Is James all right?" she asked in a whispered voice.

"He's out for the night."

Emma had also changed into a new sarong. She had taken

the clip out of her hair that had held it up off her neck during dinner and had let it fall in layers of soft, shiny chestnut waves down her back. Ari thought she smelled just a whiff of Shalimar as she followed her around the front corner of the house.

"When do you think we ought to ask Mama and Papa about sharing an apartment next year?" Emma asked when they were far enough down the front path that their voices wouldn't carry into the house.

"I don't know. I was thinking about maybe asking them while we're here on the Island. They're always in such a good mood. But I'm a little afraid of what they might say, and I really, really don't want to live in the dorms next year and, no offence, but sororities just aren't me."

"Well, they're not really me either, which is why I want my own place next year, but I have to say, I have made some nice friends there."

"I know you have. Still, sororities remind me of summer camps. But I don't know if Mama and Papa will go for it, and it would be awful if we got into an argument about it here. Ari wanted to say something but wasn't sure exactly how to say it. "Emma?" she ventured at last. "I never asked you if you minded sharing an apartment with your little sister. When you said that you didn't want to live in the sorority next year, that you wanted your own place, I just sort of horned in on the idea. Maybe you have a best friend at school that you'd rather room with."

They had reached the banyan tree, and Emma leaned back against its giant trunk. "Ari, you *are* my best friend. You always have been. You know that. And as far as sharing a room, half the time we stay up so late talking to each other that we fall asleep in each other's rooms anyway."

"Oh, Emma, this is going to be so much fun! I can't wait. We just have to get Mama and Papa to say yes. We just have . . ." Ari was interrupted by a sudden fluttering of leaves, followed by a flurry of birds and a voice calling from somewhere in the darkness.

"What's going to be so much fun?" the voice asked.

Ari felt a shiver run through her even though the breezes had stilled and the night was unusually warm. It was his voice, older and deeper perhaps, but still so familiar. "Joey, is that you?" she called.

"It's me. Stop hiding behind the banyan tree and come out into the light where I can see you," he ordered.

Ari came around the knurled trunk and overhanging branches to where Joey was waiting for her. He stood several inches taller than the last time she had seen him, with no hint remaining of the gawky, adolescent body she remembered. He had his father's thick, black hair and dark eyes, but his mother's fine-boned features, and put all together they made him strikingly handsome, movie star handsome, *James Darren* handsome. Ari heard the sudden intake of her own breath. "It's been way too long," she heard herself say, and she hugged him, hoping he wouldn't feel her heart beating through her chest.

Emma waited until Joey stepped back and then she came out of the shadows to greet him. "Emma! Good to see you," he smiled, and two delicious dimples formed themselves in his cheeks.

"Good to see you, too."

"I see your goofy little sister finally outgrew her braids," he teased, running his fingers the length of her long, loose hair.

"Oh, you're so mature," Ari shot back. "You're only two years older than me. That may have meant something when you left me behind in lower school, but I think I've caught up with you now."

"And then some," he said without thinking as his eyes trailed the length of her body.

Ari glanced at Emma. She thought she saw disappointment hidden behind her placid expression. "Where's Tommy tonight?" she asked on her sister's behalf.

"They're at the beach. I was just on my way there to join them," he said.

Them? Did Tommy bring someone home with him? A girlfriend maybe. Oh, that would ruin everything. Ari had started imagining how romantic the next two weeks could be. But it wouldn't be the same if Emma weren't part of it. Of course, there was Roger and all, but Ari had been sensing for some time now that things were different there. Maybe they were still in love, but then why was Roger's picture back in San Francisco on Emma's dresser. She had always taken it with her before.

"I'd love to say hello to Tommy," Emma said casually.

"Then let's go."

A number of Islanders were still strolling on the beach when they got there, couples mostly, but a few of the families were there as well. Periodically, they would stop to chat with this old friend or that before continuing on their way to nowhere in particular. Old Willie and Mallory were there talking to Gidrha, and Herry and Paku were just coming out of the water after a night swim. "Hi, Uncle Herry, Uncle Paku!" Joey called. "Have you seen Tommy?"

"Yeah. He's over there with your mom and dad," Paku answered, pointing toward the pier.

Ari and Emma exchanged glances and then chased after Joey who was already several long strides ahead of them. "Tommy, look who I found wandering around," he yelled across the sand. His brother looked up and even the flickering torch-light couldn't hide his happiness to see them approaching.

28

FIRST LIGHT HAD barely begun to creep across the rooftops when James came barreling into Ari's room and dragged her from her bed. For a moment she was unsure whether she was dreaming about Joey or thinking about him, but whatever she was doing it ended abruptly with James's pudgy little finger pulling up her eyelid. "Are you awake, Ari? You promised we could go swimming."

"Okay," she mumbled. "Let me brush my teeth and . . . get my swimming . . ."

"Ariiii! Wake up!" he ordered and shook her into sitting position.

She rubbed her eyes and blinked several times until the sleepiness left her. Then she began to laugh. "Oh, James, you got dressed all by yourself this morning, didn't you," she exclaimed.

"How'd ya know?"

"Because you've got your bathing suit on backwards!"

James glanced down at himself. "Oh, yeah," he said and promptly removed his suit and put it right . . . well, almost right anyway.

Grandfather and Mem were already in the lagoon when Ari and James arrived. They began every day there, swimming laps and then floating for a time over the reef. Mem said that she and Grandfather liked to welcome the sun back to the Island each morning. She said that it was their way of showing appreciation for the sun's loyalty. "I guess no one likes to be taken for granted," Ari had once said. "Not even Mother Nature."

According to the ancient Island culture, there were two Gods of Nature, one male and the other female. Ari didn't know

256

much about them. In fact, she only knew smatterings about the old ways. Mainly that everything was pretty much based on common sense, like having both a Mother and a Father Nature. It certainly must have taken both their efforts to create the Dolphin Lagoon to such perfection. The verdant cliffs that rose out of the sea on either side were just tall enough to be impressive without making the small lagoon seem claustrophobic. The palms were clustered into a perfect ellipse and the sands were soft and finely sifted. The cool turquoise waters moved just enough to make lazy little lapping sounds against the shore.

"Good morning!" Mem's melodic voice called from the reef. "Come join us."

"Good morning, Mem. Good morning, Grandfather," Ari called back. She slipped off her flip-flops and sarong, dove into the water and followed James's bubble trail all the way to the reef.

By the time Emma straggled out, carrying a pitcher of fresh-squeezed juice, Ari was already back on her tatami mat, having deposited James in the safekeeping of her grandparents before taking a long, peaceful, solitary float over the reef. Her eyes were closed now, but Emma could tell she was awake. She was aimlessly tracing little squiggles in the sand with her fingertips.

Emma unfurled her mat next to Ari's and flopped down on it almost in one motion. For a while they just lay on their backs, eyes closed, enjoying the stillness of the early morning, which hadn't given itself over yet to the breezes or the birds or the swaying palms. Occasionally, the silence was broken by playful shouts coming from the reef. "Throw me, Grandfather, throw me!" they heard James command.

Ari opened one eye and kept the other closed against the brilliant sky and rolled over on her stomach. A whiff of wet matting filled her nose, and she smiled to herself. It wasn't a particularly fragrant smell, but it was an Island smell. Like salty water and charcoaled meats and Coppertone on sweaty bodies. Smells that triggered happy memories no matter where you were when you smelled them again.

It was another hour before Mama and Papa made their way to the beach. Mama carried a picnic hamper filled with chilled fruits and warm pastries and a carafe of iced expresso. Papa's arms were draped with masks and fins and he was dragging two air tanks behind him in the sand. Ari and Emma jumped up to help them with their loads. "I thought we might take breakfast at the lagoon today," Mama said.

When they were alone, Ari and Emma talked in subdued tones about the Ahmanjaya brothers who were going up the mountain that morning to bring down Mrs. Padua who still lived in her little house at the trailhead to the Pashmari Falls. Ari told Emma how great it had been to see Joey last night. How at first, she had worried that their conversation might be strained or awkward. After all she wasn't the little *kid sister* anymore whose hand he held when they dove the deep-water reef or slid down the waterfall at the mountain lagoon or ran headlong into battle against the evil wolves and witches of their make-believe Narnia. But from the moment he had hugged her hello, she knew that the easy-going relationship they had always known was still there, except that now the teasing had evolved from who was tougher or stronger or faster to more sensual things. Sometimes she thought Joey was flirting with her, but she couldn't tell for sure. The only thing she was sure of was that the friendship she had felt for him all those years had grown overnight into a strong attraction.

Emma didn't say much about Tommy. Oh, she said how she thought he was really cute. How you could tell instantly that Tommy and Joey were brothers; how they were both tall and dark and way too brawny to have come from little Kemala. But Tommy had much more of his father's solid bones, like he had been constructed by an engineer. Joey, she thought, looked more like he had been sculpted by an artist. Ari knew there was more on Emma's mind.

"Emma?" she ventured at last.

"Hmmm?"

"Can I ask you something?"

"Ask away."

Ari rolled over on her side and propped her head up on her elbow. "Did something happen last night, you know, with Tommy?"

"Why do you ask that?" Emma replied evenly.

"I don't know exactly except that you two disappeared for a long time last night, and you're awfully quiet about him this morning. You always get that way with a new boyfriend. And . . . well . . . we don't see as much of Roger around the house anymore, and you didn't take his picture with you and . . . well, things just seem different."

Emma rolled over and put her face close to Ari's. "Something did happen last night but, in a way, it really happened years ago."

"What do you mean?"

"Oh, Ari, I've had a thing for Tommy Ahmanjaya ever since we were little kids together."

"Why didn't you ever do anything about it?"

"Well . . ." She hesitated, as if she started to say something, but changed her mind. "What was the point? We lived so far away from each other."

"And Tommy feels the same way about you now?"

"Yes." Emma couldn't keep the smile from spreading across her face.

"You and Tommy," Ari repeated. "Well . . ." In the silence that followed, Ari rolled the situation over and over in her mind until she got hold of it. In a way, it just seemed the most natural thing, Emma and Tommy. They were always close, even after long absences. Of course, she and Joey were too. But she had never thought of Joey like that . . . until now, maybe. "What makes things different now? I mean, you and Tommy still live a million miles apart." Ari wasn't sure if she was asking for information about Emma or for a roadmap to her own relationship with Joey.

"I don't know. I think it's just that we're older now, and there's not all that much time before we're out of school and free to do what we want, where we want."

"But what about Roger?"

Emma paused to gather her thoughts, such as they were. "Things have been different with Roger for a long time now. I know that happens a lot to couples who dated in high school. They go off to different colleges and make new friends and sometimes they grow apart or . . . or just outgrow each other. It just seems like lately every time Roger and I get together with his friends or mine, one of us feels out of place. Bored even. I don't know. I really love Roger. He's such a great guy and everything, but I don't think I'm *in love* with him anymore. When I think about it, I probably never was, and I feel really bad about that."

"So, what are you going to do now, about Roger, I mean?"

"Well, there's not really anything I can do until I get back to San Francisco. But I don't like the idea of starting something with Tommy before ending things with Roger. It feels like cheating."

Ari thought about this for a moment. She and Emma had always said that they'd never be the kind of girls who started a new relationship before ending an old one. "Emma, I think this is different. I mean things are already ending between you and Roger. Right?"

"Well, yes."

"And I don't think just because of you, Emma. I mean, Roger doesn't seem to be calling as much. And he seems to be busy an awful lot lately."

"Well, we both had midterms and were busy." Emma fell silent and began curling a strand of hair around her finger. Ari waited until she was ready to start up again. "You know, Ari. I hadn't really noticed it before but . . ."

"But maybe Roger has been feeling the same way as you, and he doesn't know how to tell you either," Ari offered.

"Maybe. That would be kind of ironic, wouldn't it?"

"Emma, even if you and Tommy spend no time together, you and Roger are going to break up. Right?"

"Yes."

"Then this is not cheating."

"How do you know that?"

"Because you're not breaking up with Roger because you met up with Tommy. You met up with Tommy because it's time to break up with Roger. Besides, if Tommy lived in San Francisco, you'd be doing everything in the right order."

That was about as serious as the day ever got. For the rest

of the time leading up to the beach party, Ari and Emma slept some and talked some, heated up on their mats and cooled down in the lagoon, and joined Mama in catching up on the latest Island gossip with Grandfather and Mem. But the best part of the day was watching Papa and James. Papa fitted the scuba tank on James's back, who immediately fell backwards and thrashed in the sand like a giant tortoise. They listened to James's laughter echo between the tall granite cliffs when Papa affixed an air tank to a float and a long air hose and mouthpiece to the tank and showed James how he could scuba dive under the water for thirty feet in any direction without the weight of the tanks on his back.

It was Papa who finally dragged the reluctant James from the lagoon that day. Ari watched James walk back toward the house, holding Papa's hand and chattering away about all their adventures. He seemed older somehow. There was something in the way he walked or maybe in the way he talked. There was none of that need to get the grown-ups' attention, no interrupting or whining or tugging on arms. James had taken a giant step toward being in Papa's world now, and he knew it. "I can really, really zoom now, Papa, can't I," he proudly announced.

"You sure can, son! You sure can."

That night Ari tried on half the sarongs in the old Chinese armoire before finally settling on what she had intended to wear in the first place—a white on white, gardenia-patterned silk sarong with a strapless ruby red crop top that fitted snugly around her torso without revealing more than it should. Her long black hair hung in one lustrous sheet all the way down to the small of her back, and its only ornamentation was a single white gardenia, which she wore behind her right ear.

"I thought you might like to wear these," Emma said, handing Ari a small silk brocade pouch, obviously Chinese.

"Oh, Emma, is this what I think it is?"

"Open it and see," Emma said with a laugh. Ari pulled at the drawstrings until they loosened sufficiently to get her hand inside the pouch. As she suspected, when her hand emerged, she was holding her sister's sculpted ivory earrings and matching necklace, the ones with the tiny little flower buds that had been meticulously hand-carved by Mem's friend who lived in Macau.

"Emma, are you sure? These were a gift from Grandfather and Mem. They're so special. Don't you want to wear them, Emma?"

"They don't go with my dress. I was thinking maybe I could borrow . . ."

"My coral jewelry?"

"If you don't mind," Emma smiled.

Grandfather and Papa were sitting together in the library when the girls entered the gathering pavilion. They had just returned from the Sunset Bench where they had gone a little earlier than usual with Mama and Mem to do whatever it was they did up there every day. Grandfather was wearing a crisp white cotton tunic and trousers and his long hair was swept back and held at the base of his neck by one of the multi-colored friendship chords that the children liked to trade on the playground. Ari wondered if it was a gift from one of his students or a prize confiscated from an inattentive child. He had just taken his first draw off his burled bulldog pipe—a long, deep draw—and was watching the pattern of the smoke as it rose up and dissipated outwards into the Punjab-circulated air. When he saw his granddaughters enter, he lowered his pipe and smiled. "You girls look lovely," he said. "No sarong tonight, Emma?"

"Not tonight, Grandfather. I thought I'd wear a sundress for a change." Mama had bought Emma a new sundress last year for her nineteenth birthday. It was a halter-topped sheath dress in paisley cotton, reminiscent of Carnaby Street and Mary Quant. There had been a few times in San Francisco, some of those eighties days that seem to pop up out of nowhere there, that Emma could have worn the dress, but she had decided to save it for the first really special night on the Island. She was glad she had.

It *was* going to be a special night, Ari thought—a cool-breezed, starry-skied, exotically romantic night. At least that's how she had been imagining it all day. And when she *finally* heard the drums calling the Islanders out of their homes, she imagined Joey leaving the family bungalow and walking down the road past Grandfather and Mem's house and on past the school to the Gathering Place. She imagined him waiting for her there, dressed in the red and yellow signature print of his great grandparents' clan, making small talk with the others but all the time looking toward the banyan tree, anxious for his first glimpse of her. Of course, that could all be just wishful thinking on her part.

Mama and Mem appeared in the gathering pavilion carrying two large wooden salad bowls. They were both dressed in bright multi-colored sarongs and strings of matching beads. Obviously, they were both in a festive mood. "Can we help you with the salads, ladies?" Papa asked, rising from his chair.

"Thank you, Ethan. We've got them, but perhaps James could hold your hand."

There was a large quilted picnic blanket folded neatly on the game table. Ari grabbed it before following the others through to the courtyard. On the way out, Mem popped into James's quarters to have a little talk with Tippy. She emerged again almost immediately and told James that Tippy was all curled up on his bed, and that he would wait there for him until he got home. "Oh, and he told me to tell you to have a really good time!"

The Gathering Place was buzzing with activity by the time the family arrived, and more people were pouring in from all directions. Old Batara and Maru were sitting on the school steps with Mrs. Padua, receiving a steady stream of Islanders wishing to pay their respects. Behind them in the central hall of the school, Kemala's niece Tia and several of the teens were laying out mats for the younger children, whom they would take turns babysitting until their parents came to collect them at the end of the party. There were Islanders arranging food on the long row of tables that bordered the north side of the lawn and others who were lighting the torches and carrying wood for the bonfire that would burn on the beach after sunset. Everywhere vivid colors were mingling and meandering amid a steady hum of conversation and the intermittent laughter of children who had been told at the end of school on Friday that their spring holidays would commence on Monday, not Wednesday, in honor of the festivities.

The scene spread out before Ari was like an illustration in a cherished book from childhood, which had been read and reread until it was permanently etched in memory. "Oh, Mama," she said, squeezing her arm, "it's so good to be home!"

"It is good, isn't it, Ari. And I think it's about to get even better."

Ari looked in the direction of Mama's gaze and found the cluster of bare-chested men in yellow and red sarongs. And she fixed her eyes on the tall muscular one with the fine-boned face and watched him speak to his uncles and greet Tommy and Tao when they returned from their torch lighting. She mused at his familiar habit of running his fingers through his shaggy black hair until he had removed it from his eyes—well, most of it anyway. She waited breathlessly for him to feel her presence and to turn and look at her, and when he did, she knew from the smile that spread across his face that they were about to add a whole new chapter to that cherished old children's book. But how their story would end, she couldn't even begin to imagine.

29

IT WAS ONE of those perfect sunsets, with just enough clouds to make a really orange sky. Ari and Joey sat watching it from one of the big, flat-topped boulders that lined the eastern edge of the Bay. They had sat there often as children, basking in the warmth of the sun-heated stones. They talked to one another now as easily as they did then. "Do you remember when you taught me to dive from this boulder?" Ari asked.

Joey had just finished the last swallow of wine from his goblet and was licking away a wayward drop from his lower lip. For some reason, that made Ari smile. "You couldn't have been more than five," he answered at last.

"Four, actually. You and Tommy and your cousin Sammi were cliff-diving that day, and I wanted to dive with you, but Sammi said I was just a baby."

"Some cliffs. We were only about five feet above the water."

"I know. But I didn't care how high it was. I just wanted to do what you did."

"I remember that you ran away and hid under the banyan tree."

"And you found me there and wiped my tears away telling me not to mind what Sammi said. Then you brought me here and taught me how to dive."

"You were so fearless." Joey smiled at her.

"Or reckless. I don't know which. I was probably lucky I didn't break my neck."

"I wouldn't have let anything happen to you," Joey said with a hint of longing in his voice.

Ari leaned back on her hands, closed her eyes and put her

face to the sky. Joey just watched her, bathed in the glow of the sepia light, tracing with his eyes the curve of her cheekbone and the delicate upturn of her nose, before stopping at the fullness of her lips. He continued down her long neck and along the prominent collarbones that accentuated her elegance. Her feline body—so sleek and graceful yet built for power and speed all at the same time. He felt himself overwhelmingly attracted to her.

Joey slowly leaned in toward Ari, until his lips were just an inch from hers. His kiss was long and warm and silent, expressing much more than just a kiss. And when they opened their eyes again, neither looked around to see if anyone was watching. It didn't matter.

Mama watched them from a distance, sitting on her picnic quilt down the beach. Papa was with her and Grandfather and Mem and Kemala and Tao, who had laid down their quilts next to theirs. "Mary, if you stare at them any harder, your eyeballs will pop out of your head," Papa teased.

She looked at him when he said this, but he had already turned away and was staring at the couple himself. He had an odd expression on his face, one she hadn't seen before. "Perhaps you should worry about your own eyeballs, Ethan," she replied. She slipped her arm around his waist and held him close to her. She didn't let go for a very long time.

After that, Mama took turns with Kemala, stealing little glances at Ari and Joey. They would have watched after Tommy and Emma as well if the pair hadn't taken their plates to the far end of the pier where the boats obscured their view. Mama didn't have to tell Kemala what she was thinking because she knew that her friend was thinking it too. How when they were little girls together they used to talk about the boys they would marry, how they would live next to each other, have their children together, and how one day their children would grow up and marry each other uniting the families forever. Well, it might not have turned out exactly that way, but they were both exquisitely happy with their husbands. Perhaps the younger generation would fulfil their dream. If tonight was any indication, there was a good chance that a union of the families was in the winds.

When the sun disappeared behind the western head-lands, the bonfire was lit. The eight track was switched on and the Beach Boys ratcheted up the festivities to an excited pitch. Mama and Papa disappeared for a while, as did Grandfather and Mem. When they reappeared, they joined the multi-gener-ational crowd dancing on the beach.

It was some time before Tommy and Emma appeared. They were immersed in stories about high school and college and how different everything was now. Emma couldn't believe how easy it was to tell Tommy about all the things she hadn't even told Ari until today. When she returned with Tommy to the beach, she wove her way through the maze of dancers until she found her sister.

When the music shifted to Johnny Mathis and the Righteous Brothers, teens began pairing off, and parents con-tinued sneaking off. Ari heard only the slow seductive rhythms of the music, and saw only Joey looking down at her, feeling the movement of his body against hers and the ever so faint shifting of the sands under their barely moving feet. As her head found the perfect place to rest itself against his shoulder, she thought *he's not the little boy I wrestled to the ground all those years ago.*

As the hour headed past midnight the crowd began to thin out a bit. By one o'clock Mama and Papa decided to take James home to bed and call it a night themselves. "I'll walk you home," Joey said, when Ari could no longer stifle her yawns.

She wrapped her arm around his waist, and they walked in silence all the way to the Great House. When they reached the front steps, Ari turned to face Joey. This time, she was the one who kissed him. "Promise me we'll never go so long without seeing each other again. No matter what happens between us," she said, when she opened her eyes.

A smile flashed across his face, causing his dimples to go so deep that they were visible in the moonlight. "No matter what," he said, and they kissed one more time. As the kissed deepened, an unknown feeling washed over Ari's body. Reluctantly bid-ding Joey goodnight one more time, she let herself into the Great House, a small smile on her face.

30

IN THE DAYS that followed, the whole family settled into Island life. Each morning they awoke at first
light, and they lingered in their beds for as long as they
liked before ambling down to the Lagoon for a swim and then
joining Grandfather and Mem for breakfast. The cool waters
provided a sort of communal awakening for the family. When
they were fully refreshed and feeling hungry, they strolled
back again to the Great House and began their day as they
knew it would end—gathered around the table under the old
bhodi tree.

"So, girls, will you be spending the day with the Ahmanjaya
brothers *again* today?" Grandfather asked one morning over
breakfast. He couldn't help accentuating the *again*. After all,
Emma and Ari had spent every day since the beach party with
Tommy and Joey, diving the outer reefs together and riding
horses to the western egress of the valley to picnic by the pools
there.

Emma was wrapping her lips around a juicy chunk of
fresh pineapple, so Ari answered Grandfather first. "Joey and I
thought we'd go into town today. He and Tommy promised Mrs.
Padua to fix a leak in her roof, and they need some supplies."

"Good boys," Mem murmured, but said nothing more.

Ari grabbed the coffee press and poured herself a second
cup. It was her favorite coffee, brewed from the rich, dark beans
that grew up on the highest terrace of the mountain. The coffee
was freshly roasted and a freshly picked single vanilla bean,
which lay slit open lengthwise on the bottom of the pot, ensured
that nowhere else on earth was there better coffee. Mama tried
to have the coffee and vanilla beans shipped from the Island to

wherever they were living, but it was never quite the same, she said.

Ari took a long, slow sip from her cup and let the coffee swirl around her tongue until she had gotten the last of its flavor. Then she leaned back and listened to the family's day unfold.

After breakfast the family cleared the table, cleaned the dishes, and straightened the cooking pavilion like a well-synchronized colony of ants. They were all anxious to start the day. When they were done, Ari went back to her quarters, showered, changed into her white pants and pink striped shirt and put on a pair of comfortable sandals. She and Joey would have a lot of errands to run in different sections of the town. They didn't mind. It's just what Islanders did for each other, and Ari was looking forward to spending another day with Joey.

"Ari," Mama called from the courtyard door, "may I come in?"

"Of course, Mama."

"Would you mind running a couple of errands for me while you're in town?" she asked.

"Sure, what do you need, Mama?" Ari put down the towel she had been using to dry her hair and took a list from Mama's outstretched hand.

"Would you give this list to Mr. Prada for me, please? It's provisions for the weekend. Tell him I'll be in on Monday to order what we need for Celebration."

Ari smiled when she heard the word *Celebration*. She always had ever since she was a very little girl. She didn't know why, but then she started to notice that Mama did the same thing every time she heard it and it all made sense. "Anything else?"

"Well, Grandfather asked if you could stop by the library for him. His books have come in from the Main Branch. And if it's not too much trouble, could you stop by Mrs. Kanjeera's booth at the Open Market? She's got two parcels waiting there, one for me and one for Mem."

"What are you getting from Mrs. Kanjeera, Mama?"

"I'll show it to you when you come back," was all she said before turning on her heel and heading for the door. "Thanks," she added as she disappeared.

Joey was already at his father's boat when Ari arrived at the pier. He was wearing faded jeans that clearly had seen better days and a sage colored t-shirt. Despite his well-worn look, seeing Joey waiting for her on the pier made Ari's heartbeat speed up ever so slightly. He was barefoot, but Ari knew that his brown leather topsiders wouldn't be too far away. When he saw her approaching, he smiled and waved enthusiastically and then kept loading the boxes of produce delivered to the pier fresh from the fields that morning. They were being handed down to him by Herry and Paku.

"Good morning," the uncles grinned.

"Good morning," she returned. "Is there anything I can do to help?"

"No thanks," Joey answered. "We're almost done. Why don't you step aboard?"

Ari stowed her bag below and grabbed a fresh towel from the drawer next to the galley sink. She wet it and brought it up to Joey who was just setting down the last of the boxes from the pier.

"Thanks," he said, wiping the sweat from his face and the back of his neck before deftly easing the boat out of the slip. He pointed it toward the open sea, and they motored away.

Over the years the town had grown, gradually spreading out from Old Town on the wharf toward the distant mountains to the west, and its evolution could be traced through the layers of architecture that radiated out like rings on an ancient redwood. It was Grandfather who first introduced Ari to the town, buying two tickets on the High Street Trolley and riding with her all the way to the end and back again. It was Grandfather who taught her to see the beauty in the faded mansions of the old merchant class and the simple pastel houses of the post-war settlement. Then there were the modern downtown skyscrapers that challenged the mountains for dominance over the skyline. But it was Old Town that Ari loved best. Grandfather was secretly glad for that.

Old Town was a maze of streets and alleys filled with wooden sidewalks and with buildings whose architectural styles were as confused and colorful as the immigrants who had built them during the last two hundred years. The tin-roofed plantation buildings of the first settlers still stood along the wharf. Their plank floors sagged and creaked, and their plaster was a bit peeled, but that only added to their charm. Some people thought they were a little plain next to the gingerbread facades of the Victorian storefronts that Barberry Coast shipping merchants had built further along the High Street. They certainly weren't as impressive as the solid fortresses of the venerable old British firms on Wellington Square. But the plantation buildings had been built on virgin ground, unpopulated by even the indigenous natives who preferred the more bountiful fishing grounds to the south, and, as such, Ari thought that they deserved respect, or at least appreciation, from all the Johnny-come-latelies.

The most prominent structure on the wharf was the Open Market, a large wooden warehouse. Long ago bales of wool from the interior sheep stations awaited the arrival of tall-masted ships in the harbor. Now it was home to dozens of vendors who came early each morning to fill their stalls with fresh fish or produce or a variety of locally made goods. Ari liked the Market. There was always a kind of rhythmic hum in the air that changed as the activity progressed from setting up the stalls to selling to the early customers, mostly locals, to bartering with the tourists whose habit it was to rise late in the morning after an evening of partying in one of the bars or bistros that were appearing around town with ever-increasing frequency.

Mr. Gupta's eldest son, Kenji, was waiting with two of his brothers at the dock in front of the Market when Ari and Joey arrived.

"Thanks for bringing over the rest of today's orders," he called to Joey and Ari across the short expanse of water that still separated them.

"Glad to do it," Joey called back.

When Kenji and his delivery van were well down the High Street, Ari and Joey headed for Prada's Mercantile to turn in their orders. Except for the electric lights and the radio whose broadcaster was announcing the sides for tomorrow's rugby match in a deep baritone voice, Prada's could have been used for the stage set of any TV western. Wood floors and walls, yardage

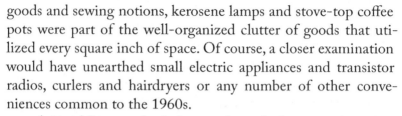

goods and sewing notions, kerosene lamps and stove-top coffee pots were part of the well-organized clutter of goods that utilized every square inch of space. Of course, a closer examination would have unearthed small electric appliances and transistor radios, curlers and hairdryers or any number of other conveniences common to the 1960s.

Ari and Joey made their way through the grocery section, past the displays of tinned and boxed goods and the baskets of fresh produce. There was a cold cabinet filled with meats and cheeses and a long counter at the back of the store where Mr. Prada stood at his old National cash register ringing up an order for two elderly women who appeared to be sisters. Behind him were wooden shelves, built floor to ceiling, containing all manner of marine supplies, samples of which were displayed in the front windows next to the new line of rods and reels that arrived last week on one of the big freighters in the northern harbor. Ari could smell the spicy aroma of the hard salamis hanging over the meat counter and the hot yeasty smell of freshly baked bread. She could hear Mrs. Prada's familiar sing-song humming coming through the curtained doorway that separated home and workplace.

"And what may I do for you fine young people today?" Mr. Prada asked in an accent Ari could never quite identify.

"My brother and I need a few roofing supplies for tomorrow, sir, and Uncle Herry is running low on varnish," Joey began.

"Hasn't he finished the canoe yet?"

"Not quite, sir. One more coat of varnish and he says it's done."

"Well, hand-carving, it takes time, I think," Mr. Prada observed. "And his work, is it not magnificent?"

"Yes, sir. We all think so."

Turning to Ari, Mr. Prada said, "And you, young lady, have you an order for me as well?"

"Yes, sir. I have Mama's weekend list."

Mr. Prada took the list from Ari's outstretched hand and squinted at it until he had read each item. "Your Mama is planning for company, I see," he said.

"Yes, sir. Joey's family is coming to dinner tomorrow night."

"Any particular reason for the families coming together?" he asked with a sly smile at the couple.

"Just dinner, sir," Joey piped in.

Mr. Prada looked disappointed. "Oh, well, perhaps one day soon then. I just thought with Celebration coming . . ." Ari's face grew several shades of red.

A sudden noise diverted their attention, and they turned to see a man in denim trousers and canvas shoes standing near the tinned goods. There were two soup cans rolling away from his feet down the old slopping floor.

"Sorry," he called and chased after the cans, managing to grab them just before they reached the front door.

By the time the man reappeared at the back counter with his armload of purchases, Ari and Joey were getting ready to leave. "Thank you, Mr. Prada. I'll tell Mama to expect the order on the evening launch," Ari said and, wheeling around, collided with the man in the denim trousers, nearly spilling his soup cans on the floor again. "Oh, I'm sorry" she said, "I didn't see you behind me."

"That's all right," he smiled, but made no move to step aside. "Did I hear you say something about a Celebration?" The last word was accompanied by the smell of stale beer, and Ari began to feel a little uncomfortable.

Before she could reply, Joey inserted himself between her and the man. "Yes, sir, you did," he said.

"Then you must be from the Island. We've heard about your *Celebrations.*" There was that tone again.

The man shot a lascivious look past Joey to where Ari peeked around his left shoulder. Then he spilled his purchases onto the counter, shoved his hand into his pocket and pulled out a roll of paper money. "How much for an invite for me and my friends?"

Ari saw the look of anger spread across Joey's face. She grabbed his arm and gently stroked it and waited. "Sir," he said at last, "there are some things money can't buy." Then he took Ari's hand and together they slowly walked out, much to the relief of Ari and Mr. Prada, who was prepared to give a good thrashing to the man in the denim trousers and canvas shoes but was glad he didn't have to.

Once outside, Ari turned back toward High Street without a word to Joey. Her stride was long, her pace quick.

"Ari, wait up," Joey said from just behind her. She didn't stop. "Ari, wait up!" he repeated. This time he grabbed her arm, whirling her around, pulling her into one of the dozens of dark little alleyways that hid in the shadows of Old Town. There were tears in her eyes. He grabbed her up in his arms and held her, gently stroking her hair and shoulders until he felt her body relax and her arms slowly slide around his waist.

"I'm sorry, Joey," she stammered. "People like that just make me so mad! They think just because we don't treat sex like something dirty that we're all fast or something. I'm not like that! Mama's not like that! None of the Island women are like that!"

"I know," he said gently. "I know."

Joey waited until he knew her tirade was over before he spoke again. "Have you ever thought about it? At least a little, anyway?" he asked softly.

She looked up at him, and he was smiling. That beguiling smile that made his dimples go deep. She didn't feel mad anymore. "Of course I have. I am human, you know."

He wasn't going to ask the next question, but the words came falling out of his mouth before he could stop them. "Have you thought about it . . . with me, Ari?"

Joey's question took her completely by surprise, and suddenly she felt the difference in their ages. Well, maybe not their ages exactly, but certainly the fact that she was still in high school, and he was in college, and she was sure that he had already slept with a whole bunch of girls there. "Joey, we can't," she exclaimed. "You know the Elders would never allow it. Not to mention my parents."

"I know! I wasn't saying that you should . . . I mean, that we should . . . Oh, you know what I mean."

Ari did know. It had been on her mind all week. Not weighing on it or anything, but just there. From that very first night at the beach party when Joey held her close to him and they spoke in whispered phrases that didn't need completing. Every day, every night, there was a moment when she wondered what it would be like to make love to him. She knew it was too soon, and she knew she was too young. Still, each morning, when Joey came striding across the gardens to collect her, she knew that it was only a matter of time before she would experience that exquisite moment of wondering all over again.

"What are you thinking, Ari?" he asked when he could no longer bear the silence. She didn't answer him. She just looked at him with that same far-away expression he thought he'd seen on her face a few times before. "Ari?" he prodded again.

"I was just thinking how glad I am that you decided to come home for Spring Break this year," she said. Then she took his hand and led him out of the alley, and together they strolled back down the wharf, leaving Prada's and the man in the denim trousers and canvas shoes far, far behind.

Ari and Joey boarded an eastbound trolley that would take them to the Wellington District and their next destination. The District was known for its Houses. Not the mansions that lined its broad tree-lined avenues, but the Merchant Houses that bordered the manicured lawns and English gardens of its central square. There was Morgan House, purveyors of fine silks, and the House of McFaddon, the sugar and spice traders, and the House of Glendon-Smythe, the Mainland's largest wool merchant. In fact, the District was riddled with British Houses whose families could trace their Mainland roots back several generations. The one exception was the House of Lim, whose teas could be found in the finest shops around the globe and in many of the world's royal dining halls. The Lims were the only Asian family to leave the obscurity of Old Town for the grandiose lifestyle of the District, and this caused no end of whispered disapproval from those who knew that Old Mr. Lim never would have condoned such a move if he were still alive.

The sun was high overhead, and the park was filled with smartly-tailored businessmen sitting straight-backed with legs neatly crossed on park benches, reading belated copies of *The London Times* and pinched-nosed nannies whose expressions were only slightly less stiff than their crisply starched aprons pushing prams. They weren't angry or cold—just terribly proper . . . or *wonderfully English* as Mama would say.

A block north of the Square was the Mainland's second largest branch of the Public Library. It was a foreboding brownstone building with heavy mahogany doors that made no noise when you opened them and four bulgey-eyed gargoyles who peered down from the rooftops at everyone who entered. As a young child, the gargoyles had scared Ari. They seemed to her to be guarding the books against anyone who might want to borrow them. But Mrs. Talapaka, the head librarian, said that the gargoyles were just guarding the books against anyone who might want to *steal* them because they loved little children and wanted to make sure that their favorite books would always be there when they came.

Inside the atmosphere of the library wasn't frightening at all. It was elegant and grand. There were speckled green marble floors, rows and rows of crystal chandeliers the size of miniature hot air balloons, and long polished tables with walls of fitted bookshelves filled with the most marvelous literature. "Arianna!" Mrs. Talapaka warmly greeted her. "What a pleasant surprise. I don't usually get to see you on your short breaks."

"No, ma'am, but I make up for it in the summers I think."

"You certainly do. I believe you set the record for checkouts of *The Lion, the Witch and the Wardrobe*. Until someone bought you your own copy." She turned to look at Joey. The smile never left her face. "And you, young Joseph. It's not surprising to see you at all. Not with Arianna here." Joey got a sheepish look on his face.

"We've come to pick up Grandfather's books," Ari interjected.

"Oh, yes. Of course. The books. Only two have come in I'm afraid. I expect the others the beginning of next week," Mrs. Talapaka said, handing Ari two hardbound volumes that she had ready. "Tell your grandfather I'll call when the rest come in."

Ari read the titles. *The Portrait of a Lady* by Henry James and Michael Grant's *Annals of Imperial Rome*. "Hmmm, I bet Grandfather's got the traveling bug again," Ari said to herself. "Thank you. He'll be very happy to have these."

Out on the sidewalk, Joey took the books from Ari and slipped them under his arm. "Mrs. Yao's?"

"You bet. I'm starving!"

"You're always starving," Joey teased.

"Well, then the walk to Old Town should do me some good," she laughed.

Ari and Joey headed east toward the wharf. They moved at a brisk pace, not hurried or frazzled, but more like a matched pair of spirited carriage horses enjoying a promenade down wide avenues of stately mansions on a sunny afternoon. When they entered Old Town the streets abruptly narrowed, and the sunlight had to pick and choose where to shine among the cobbled alleyways and storefront awnings. The trappings of wealth and power were gone—no more manicured lawns or embellished verandas. But in truth, the most powerful families on the Mainland resided in Old Town, running vast empires from their simple clapboard businesses whose names were twice painted on window glass in ancient languages and their English translations. Maybe the McFaddons had made a tidy fortune off of the spice market over the years, but it was Mrs. Yao who had systematically bought up all the sugar cane fields, and Mrs. Yao who owned the biggest ships in the harbor. It was she who had shrewdly negotiated and relentlessly worked until she had acquired a fortune rumored to be larger than all the British Houses combined—a fortune that capitalized business ventures, amassed real estate holdings, secured university educations for every Yao descendent, and even financed the campaign of the first Yao ever to sit in the State House.

Ari and Joey zig-zagged through the labyrinth of back alleyways along a route they had known since childhood. They didn't need a sign to tell them when they had reached their destination. The aroma of ginger and the sound of Mandarin Chinese told them they had arrived at Mrs. Yao's back door.

"Come in! Come in!" Mrs. Yao waved exuberantly when she spotted them. "I've been wondering when you two would come!"

"Oh, Mrs. Yao, we couldn't go too long without your delicious food," Joey beamed.

Mrs. Yao knew the compliment was genuine. "Do you want your usual?" she asked.

"Please," Ari replied. "And could you also prepare three boxes of Char Siu Bow to go? We'll steam them at home."

"My pleasure."

Mrs. Yao led them through the kitchen and the glass-beaded doorway that separated it from the tables filled with boisterous patrons. She seated them at a table in the front window. "It no be long," she said to the couple in the clipped pigeon English she used routinely in front of *Foreigners,* (which included almost everyone outside the family). "You eat soon," she added and disappeared.

Joey set Grandfather's books on the extra chair, and Ari laid her purse on them. "Heavy?" she asked.

"I'll say. Doesn't your Grandfather ever read paperbacks?"

"Not often. He likes the feel and the smell of leather and old paper, and he says that books should weigh something in your hands."

"I know. He used to tell us that a lot in First Form. Come to think of it, he told us in Second and Third as well."

"You know, I get kind of jealous when you talk about going to the Island School. I wish I could have had Grandfather and Mem for my teachers," Ari said.

"But they have been your teachers, Ari. You just never had to sit in a classroom to learn from them."

She smiled. "I guess you're right. Besides, if I had to choose between them being my teachers or my family, I'd choose family."

Just then Mrs. Yao's sixteen-year-old great granddaughter, Lili, arrived at the table carrying two chilled glasses of iced tea on a tray and a plate of steamy pot stickers with ginger sauce. She was a striking girl with a beauty that belonged to a woman. She had full lips and liquid eyes and flawless skin, and her petite figure was already perfectly proportioned.

"She's going to be a real knockout when she grows up," Joey observed.

She thinks you're pretty cute, too, Ari thought, but she didn't say so out loud.

Joey and Ari lingered over lunch, their legs finding each

other under the small table and their fingers intertwining between courses, as they talked and talked about all the years they had known each other. About the carefree days of swimming, hiking, riding, sailing, and lazing on the beach. And the nights when their two families gathered around the old stone table while the grown-ups talked well past midnight and the children played in the garden because there was no bedtime.

They stared at each other for a time, neither saying anything, until they found something in the other's expression they had not seen there before. It was then, while sitting at Mrs. Yao's, that Joey knew for sure he had fallen in love with Ari. Perhaps he had always known. And that's when Ari knew that she had loved Joey ever since that day he had comforted her under the giant banyan tree before teaching her to dive.

Ari had always imagined that when true love hit her, she would be strolling on the beach under the stars or gliding down the Grand Canal in a gondola in Venice, but never did she imagine it would hit her sitting across an oil-clothed table in Mrs. Yao's tiny restaurant with a plate of half-eaten pork buns.

On the way back to the launch, Ari and Joey popped into the tobacconist to pick up a tin of Papa's favorite blend. It was waiting for them when they arrived, all neatly wrapped in the non-descript brown paper, which was supposed to mask the contents from wives who didn't appreciate the delicate aromas of smoke air in their houses.

At the Market, they found Mrs. Kanjeera just completing a transaction with a fortyish-looking woman with blond hair. She had a pleasant face and a slim figure that was slightly rounded at the middle from childbearing and age. She was buying one of Mrs. Kanjeera's lovely silk sarongs. Ari imagined the woman back home around a swimming pool, probably Beverly Hills, her friends there for a barbecue, everyone talking and laughing just a little too loudly from the batches of frozen daiquiris that appeared like magic every time a glass emptied. The woman feeling like the most elegant hostess in her beautiful silk sarong. By the time Ari and Joey reached Mrs. Kanjeera, the fortyish woman had left and was on her way back down the harbor toward one of the big yachts that was moored there.

"Hello, children!" Mrs. Kanjeera called when she saw the couple approaching.

Ari smiled at the rotund woman with the silver hair. "Good afternoon, Mrs. Kanjeera," she replied. "Mama asked me to stop by and pick up a couple of packages."

Just then Mrs. Kanjeera's grandson, Tedi, appeared with the parcels. "Tedi will take the packages to your launch. It appears that you already have many purchases to carry," she said.

"Thank you," the couple said in unison.

"You're welcome, children. And please thank Mem and Mary for allowing me the honor of creating these," she added, pointing to the bundles, one small and one very large. "Perhaps I will have the honor of creating them for you one day, Arianna," she said, and turned to greet a new customer before Ari could reply.

Back on the boat, Joey and Ari motored slowly out of the harbor and onto the open sea. It was still a perfectly cloudless day, but something in the air alerted them that a rainstorm would visit the Island by late evening. They stood side-by-side at the wheel. Their free arms wrapped securely around each other. They didn't try to talk over the engine noise. They just silently savored the day, the sunshine and the breezes, the revisits to old haunts, the time together no longer taken for granted. Suddenly Joey pulled back on the throttle until the boat idled in place. The Island was in sight but still a few miles away. "Ari," he said, steadying his feet and grabbing her up in his arms. He kissed her with that vague desperation of lovers whose time together is short, until the horn of a passing yacht and the cheers of its passengers brought them back to their surroundings. They smiled sheepishly at the passersby and feigned a little bow. Then Joey throttled the boat forward again, and they continued their journey home, both knowing that their relationship had changed that day, and they could never go back.

31

THE RAIN HAD begun as a mist in the air and didn't come pouring out of the sky until well after darkness had settled on the Island. Ari was glad for the rain. It meant a quiet night at home with the family—well, quiet except for the steady patter of rain on the roof tiles, the splishes and splashes in patio puddles, and the periodic whooshes of air that flickered candles and fluttered leaves sending gauzy curtains dancing around the perimeter of the living pavilion. Some people wouldn't have called that quiet at all, but to Ari's way of thinking, it was the very best kind of quiet. The kind where Nature talked and people listened.

It had been awhile since the family had snuggled down for an evening together, and even James seemed glad for the respite. It was the first time Ari had seen him out of his bathing suit all week. "Look, Papa," he said, pointing to the tropical fish book opened out across his knees. "We saw this fish at the reef today."

Papa and James were all curled up together on one of the overstuffed loungers in front of the fireplace. James was sitting on Papa's lap, legs out, his head resting on Papa's big chest, his little round tummy hidden behind Papa's muscular forearms. "It's called a yellow tang, James. There are lots of them in these waters."

"Oh, yeah . . . yellow tang," he mimicked.

Mama sat across from them on the long sofa, feet-to-feet with Emma who stretched out from the opposite end. Periodically she looked up from her book and smiled in the direction of her men. She was smiling at them now. "James," she called softly, "perhaps you could take me out on the reef tomorrow and teach me the names of all the fish. I get them mixed up sometimes."

"Sure, Mama. I could teach you."

"And could we bring the fish chart and see how many of them we can find?"

"Yeah, Mama. Let's bring the fish chart."

"I'm not so sure I want to give up my scuba buddy even for a morning," Papa chimed in, "but as long as it's Mama, I guess I can share you, James."

"You could come, too, Papa," he replied, not wanting to hurt anyone's feelings.

"Well, why don't I get some work done in the morning and join you after. How does that sound?"

James nodded and continued pointing out fish in his book.

Emma had been quiet all evening. In fact, she had been quiet ever since Ari had come home from town and found her sitting alone in the gardens on the little bench near the Quan Yin. She had offered up a few words about her day with Tommy. Emma and Tommy had taken Mr. Gupta's Arabians and ridden out to the far end of the valley to swim in the pools there. But there was more that Emma wasn't saying. Ari knew there was more. "Emma . . ." she began.

Emma cut her off. "Why did Grandfather and Mem go home early tonight?" she asked Mama.

"Mem said she had a few last-minute details to attend to before next week's opening at the Fujiri."

"Has she sent her paintings over yet?" Ari asked.

"They're going over on Sunday. Why? Were you thinking of going to see them early?"

"I thought I might," Ari replied. "Joey and Tommy are repairing Mrs. Padua's roof tomorrow. I'm on my own."

"Too bad the rain came early," Papa commented. "I hate to think of Mrs. Padua getting wet tonight."

"Don't worry, Papa. Joey and Tommy headed up to Mrs. Padua's this afternoon to put some plastic on her roof until they can fix it tomorrow."

"Oh, so that's why I have the pleasure of my daughters' company tonight," Papa smiled.

Ari smiled back. "Actually, I'm glad to have a night just for the family. It's going to be awhile before we can do this again."

That was the first time anyone had said it out loud. Everyone had tried to lock away the impending separation, but now Ari had brought it out in the open, and she was instantly sorry.

Mama came to the rescue. "I hope Joey and Tommy are planning to spend the night at Mrs. Padua's. The road back down to the valley floor can be treacherous in the rain."

"They are, Mama. They told Mrs. Padua that they were coming early because they were craving her chicken pie for dinner, but I think she knew the truth."

"Those are good boys," Mama said almost to herself. "We are very lucky I think."

A look passed between Ari and Emma. They said nothing. In due course, everyone returned to their books, though Ari spent more time staring at the page than reading the words.

The rains were still going strong when the family turned in for the night, so strong that Ari didn't hear Emma's gentle footfalls when she entered her quarters from the open veranda. "Ari, are you asleep?" It was barely an audible whisper.

"No, what's wrong?" Ari whispered back. She scooted over and positioned herself on her right side and she waited for Emma to mirror her. Emma sat quietly, looking at her knees tucked up to her breastbone.

"So, what's going on with you and Tommy?" Ari asked eventually. Emma said nothing, she just sighed. It wasn't a sigh of sadness, but one of pure remembrance. Ari could tell that Emma's mind was far from the cool comfort of the cotton sheets upon which she sat. "Well, are you going to tell me?"

Emma shifted slightly and ran her fingers through her sun-reddened curls until they all fell neatly over her left shoulder. "I've decided. I'm going to ask the Elders for permission to dance for Tommy at Celebration."

Ari bolted upright. "What! What made you change your mind?"

"Shhhhh. I don't want to wake the whole house."

"Are you sure, Emma?" Ari asked, returning to a whisper. "I mean, you and Tommy have only been together a week."

Emma sat up, crossed her legs and leaned in toward Ari. "Not really, Ari. It's actually been much longer . . . well kind of."

"I don't understand."

"Remember that summer we came home from Hong Kong about five or six years ago? It was the summer you got really mad at me because you said I was always doing things with Tommy. That was the first time Tommy ever kissed me."

"There were other times?"

"Yes, but then it just got too hard trying to go steady long-distance."

"You started going steady?"

"For almost two years, until we got transferred to San Francisco. After that, Tommy stopped coming back to the Island when we were here. He said it was just too hard to see me knowing that we could only be friends."

"I had no idea, Emma. Why didn't you tell me? That first summer, I mean."

Emma could hear the slight hurt in Ari's voice. They had always shared everything with each other. "I don't know really. It just seemed easier not to talk about it, but I've always known. Tommy has always been the one, I just wasn't ready to admit it until now."

Ari's mind flashed back to the lunch they had shared with Mama at the Fairmont several months prior. "Do you really think he's the one?" And when Emma didn't say anything, Ari continued, "You know . . . what Mama was saying at lunch . . . about former lovers destined to find each other again?" Emma remained silent. "So . . . what now?" Ari asked.

"Well, we're going to see each other as much as we possibly can for the next couple of years. Then when school's over I'm going to come back here to the Island to live, and I'm going to ask Grandfather and Mem if I can teach at the school with them when they think I'm ready. I'm going to talk to them about all the courses to take and everything. And by the time I graduate, Tommy will be back here, and we can really start a life together."

"You've thought a lot about this, haven't you," Ari observed.

"Actually, Tommy and I have spent the whole week talking about it."

"A lot has happened in a week."

"I know it seems like that. That day we talked on the beach about Tommy and Roger and everything . . . I don't think even I was ready for how strong my feelings were. I mean, I'm supposed to be the practical one, the slow, steady plodder—the one who thinks everything through before taking action. I couldn't admit, even to myself, that just one look at Tommy Ahmanjaya and I was head over heels in love! You're supposed to be the love at first sight sister!"

"I am, aren't I?" Something made her uneasy about that, but she didn't know what. "Actually, it's not like this is really love at first sight. I mean, you said yourself that you've loved Tommy for years. And, apparently, he's loved you for years, too. It's not like you're suddenly going to discover something about him that would make you two incompatible or anything. You've been friends since you were in diapers." Ari noticed a smile slowly creep across Emma's face, and it was clear that Emma's mind had slipped once again into a pleasant daydream.

"Do you think Mama and Papa will approve of your dancing now? Not to mention the Elders."

"Oh, I'll have no trouble with the Elders. I'm already of age. And I have a feeling that Mama and Papa have known about Tommy and me for a long time now, probably even before I knew myself. I think they'd be disappointed if I decided to dance with someone just for the sake of dancing. But with Tommy, I know Mama won't have any problem."

"And Papa? You know how fathers are when it comes to their little girls. It's easy to talk about the right and wrong of things in the abstract, but when reality hits home . . ."

"Well, that probably depends upon which side of Papa I'm talking to, the Eastern half or the Western half, but in the end, at least, I know he'll be happy for me. Tommy and I are so good together."

There was a long pause while both sisters tried to grab hold of everything that had passed between them. "Are you sure you're really ready for this, Emma? I mean, aren't you a little scared about . . . about . . . you know?"

"I am a little nervous. But with Tommy, it just feels so right. I want him to be my first and my last."

"But you could wait until this summer. It's not like it's that far away or anything. That would give you time to really prepare yourself for all this." *Or am I the one who needs time to prepare myself for all this?* Ari considered silently. She felt the sadness of the real possibility that Emma was moving on without her.

"I'm tired of locking my feelings away, Ari, and always being the practical one. Maybe it's time I trust my feelings instead of trying to analyze them all the time. And, Ari, I know this is going to sound strange, especially coming from me, but I've just had this feeling—no, it's stronger than that. It's almost like a premonition that this is our time, Tommy's and mine. That there'll never be a more perfect time for me to dance for Tommy for our very first time than this Celebration. Maybe it's because all the families have come together after so many years, or maybe it's because our family will be separating soon, or I don't know . . ."

"Or maybe you've finally answered the big question."

"What question?"

"How do you know when you're *really* in love, like Mama and Papa?" Ari smiled.

"Mama was right. When you are, you don't have to ask."

32

ARI AWOKE TO a sparkling morning. Rain that had come down in torrents just last night now lay gently in swollen ponds and newborn puddles and in tiny droplets that clung to leaves and flower petals and delicate blades of grass. Everything felt so fresh and new under the nearly cloudless sky. The apprehension that at first had accompanied Emma's news was gone and instead, Ari felt the anticipation of glorious new adventures. After all, she would be joining Mama in the women's hut this year, learning secrets that would bring her to the threshold of womanhood. And then, of course, there was Joey. Funny how different everything looked in the light of day.

Emma waited until breakfast to announce her intention to dance for Tommy. It just seemed fitting to tell the family when they had gathered once more under the old bhodi tree. Ari could barely contain the smiles and the restless shifting of her body in anticipation. When finally Emma clinked her juice glass with her fork to get everyone's attention, Ari held her breath and stared straight at Mama. "I've decided to ask the Elder's for permission to dance for Tommy Ahmanjaya," she said simply and then waited for what she knew would come next.

Mama screamed, sending a mouthful of coffee halfway across the table. Ari didn't know whether to laugh or join in the frenzy that ensued. Everyone started talking at once. Mem said how she had dreamed of the day she would serve Adi to Emma. It had been so many years since she had done so for Mama. And Mama said that this would be the best Celebration since the first time she danced for Papa because she would have both her daughters in the women's hut this year. Grandfather, of course, expounded at great length on the unfairness to the

287

other families that the three most beautiful women dancing this year would all be from the same family. Papa was obviously pleased for Emma, too. He kept using phrases like *fine boy* and *good family* and *perfect choice*, but Ari thought that something was distracting him from saying more. Maybe it was going to be hard for him after all, letting go of his Little Shadow.

It was nearly noon by the time Ari set out for Mem's house. She took the path to the Gathering Place and then followed the road as it wound around the north side of the school and out toward the valley floor. Along the way she passed through groves of King Palms and forests of New Zealand Fern Trees, bananas and mangoes, and brilliant frangipani. After a bit, she came to the fork in the road. The right led to the valley and the farming fields, whose terraces marked the western boundary of the valley and the beginning of the trail up to Pashmari Falls. Ari took the left, which meandered past two houses, one of which happened to be the Ahmanjayas. The road dead-ended at a high plastered wall with a carved teakwood gate set squarely in its middle. This was the entrance to Grandfather and Mem's.

There was a little wooden bench just to the right of the gate and on it, neatly placed, were a pair of canvas sandals and a woven reed sun hat. Together they announced Mem's presence in the house. It was just like her to know how to say things without words. Ari removed her own sandals and lined them up next to Mem's. Then she passed through the gate and into the front courtyard calling to her. There was no reply. Perhaps she was in her studio.

"Mem . . ." she called again. This time she was answered by the fluttering of feathers coming from the bird bath that stood at the far end of the courtyard. A single Ragianna was splashing about in its cool waters. How extraordinary, Ari thought. That was twice she had spotted the rare bird down from the Rain Forests. But perhaps it wasn't extraordinary at all. Everyone was drawn to this house. This ancient, peaceful, happy house.

This was *Surihana*, House of Paradise, a heavenly name for a heavenly place. Like the Great House, it was a collection of pavilions, built around courtyards and constructed of the most exquisite elements of Nature. There was sunshine everywhere, alluring scents of polished woods and fragrant flowers, and the artifacts of what Grandfather called lives well-lived. Occupying the center of the front courtyard was a large glassy turquoise pool. It was surrounded on three sides by broad terraced steps, cushioned for seating in several places, and leading to three pavilions—the dining pavilion to the left, the offices to the right, and the peak-roofed gathering room at the far end. Beyond the gathering room was a second courtyard, surrounded by the sleeping quarters—a place of quiet meditation.

Ari walked to the edge of the pool and dipped her foot in. The water felt cool and soothing. She wondered if Mem might like to join her later for a swim. "Why wait?" came Mem's voice across the courtyard. Ari hadn't seen her come in, and the suddenness of her appearance startled her, nearly tumbling her into the water. "Careful!" Mem cautioned.

Ari righted herself and looked up. Mem was coming toward her from the direction of the bird bath. The Ragianna had disappeared. "Why wait for what?" Ari asked her.

"For a swim. Weren't you going to ask me to join you later?"

Before Ari could respond, Mem had discarded her sarong and had dived into the water, leaving a flotilla of ripples behind her. In a flash, Ari was submerged. "Oh, that feels so good!" she exclaimed when she resurfaced next to Mem on the opposite side of the pool.

"It does, doesn't it," Mem smiled.

"Where did you come from? I didn't see you when I came into the courtyard."

"Oh, I was nearby. I answered you when you called, but I guess you didn't hear my voice."

A sudden breeze blew through the dining pavilion and into the courtyard, sending the wind chimes that hung from the porch rafters into song. Ari glanced in their direction and noticed for the first time that Mem's banquet table was set for company—a lot of company. "I thought you were coming to our house for dinner tonight, Mem," she said. "The Ahmanjayas are coming over."

Mem, who was treading water, grabbed onto the side of the pool. "Plans have changed. Emma and Tommy are going to the Elders this afternoon. As Emma's Adi, it is my responsibility to bring the families together afterwards."

"There are an awful lot of places set. Who's coming?"

"Well, there are the seven of us, Tommy, Joey, Kemala and Tao, Herry and Paku and their wives and, of course, Batara and Maru. That's seventeen of us. And I asked Ghidra to join us. She has known you children since you were babies."

"That's a lot of people to feed. What can I do to help?"

"Nothing, really. Everyone's bringing something. And, of course, we have three boxes of pork buns you brought back. But maybe you could help me serve and stay until it's all put away after. I don't want Emma lifting a finger tonight. This is her night. Hers and Tommy's."

Ari smiled. Somehow, she didn't feel like Emma was leaving her behind anymore. More like she was opening a door, and she'd be just on the other side when Ari decided to step through. That's how it had always been between them whenever changes were in the air

After a leisurely float around the pool, Ari and Mem retrieved their sarongs from where they had fallen on one of the blue and white striped cushions that dotted the varnished teakwood steps. Then they went to the office where Mem rummaged around for the list of paintings to be delivered to the Fujiri. Ari didn't know how she could find anything in there; it was so jammed-packed. It wasn't messy. It was just a study in organized clutter. There was a big old partners desk occupying the center of the room with a pair of high-backed chairs on either side. Over the years they had created matching fade marks on the smooth plank floor. Mem searched through the files and piles and, not finding what she was looking for, turned to the bookshelves, which ran the length of the outer wall under hinged wooden windows. They too were crammed full of textbooks and National Geographic magazines. "Ah, here it is!" Mem exclaimed, pulling a piece of lined notepad paper from the middle pages of an old *Look* magazine.

"How did it get there?" Ari laughed.

"Your Grandfather. He's always picking up whatever's handy to mark passages."

"I'm surprised you found it."

"Oh, I've lived with that old man for so long now that I've learned to think like him. It happens that way."

Ari followed Mem out of the office, through the gathering room and down the long-covered walkway to the left that separated the cooking pavilion from the rest of the house. There was a plate of lemon squares on the island, and they both grabbed one on their way out to the studio.

The studio sat a fair distance from the house, across the back gardens, and down by the stream. It was just a simple building—a pagoda roof over a wooden platform connected by retractable glass panels—but it was their special place, hers and Mem's. They had been coming here together ever since Ari was five. Surrounded by her paint pots and brushes and basking in the painter's light that came pouring through the abundant glass from the distant northern mountains, she got her first glimpse of the world that Mem saw through her soulful green eyes. "I love it here," she murmured.

Ari entered the studio, stood dead center under the roof peak and slowly turned in a circle, surveying each of the canvases Mem had lined up against the octagonal walls. They were all portraits of the Island, but they were more than just botanical studies of palm trees and rare orchids. So very much more.

"I wish I had seen these before," she told Mem. "It would have made things so much easier when I tried to do my own painting of the Island."

"Then you like them?"

"Oh, Mem, I think they're your best work ever." She walked toward a large painting on the north wall and stood in front of it. It was a painting of Herry on the beach at South Bay. He was squatting down in front of his canoe, carving out a delicate swoosh with his bone-handled knife. There was a group of young children sitting in a semi-circle on the opposite end of the boat, and their eyes were riveted to Herry's knife. As always, the corners of Herry's mouth pointed upwards in that contented, happy expression he wore whether he was talking or working or just thinking. "How perfectly Herry," Ari smiled and continued on around the room.

Painting after painting, the lush, vibrant foliage and jagged peaks and forests of king palms and sparkling waters all served as backdrops to the lives of the Islanders whose happiness Mem had captured perfectly with brush and paint. Ari continued down the paintings. "This captures Grandfather perfectly." Mem had painted a portrait of him sitting on the porch of the school, animated and gesturing, holding open a heavy leather-bound book with gilt-edged pages. He was surrounded by First-formers whose dark eyes and chubby-cheeked faces stared up at him with obvious reverence. A little boy was straining forward and reaching up to feel the thick paper pages, and his wide-eyed expression was priceless. Ari knew that this, too, was painted from memory.

"The showing would have been incomplete without a painting of your Grandfather pontificating!" Mem laughed.

Not all the paintings had people in them. There was a collection of small canvases devoted to some of the really rare orchids that grew up in the rain forest. And, of course, a larger one of a magnificent Bird of Paradise. And one of a stunning orange-plumed Raggiana. Then there was a particularly beautiful canvas of the old banyan tree under an orange sunset sky. Except that on second look Ari discovered two little girls peeking out from behind the tendrils that poured down from the canopy

Ari came to a particularly large canvas that must have measured at least six feet across depicting Celebration Night. There were Batara and Maru holding court and a ring of Islanders looking on at a gathering of dancers whose passionate expressions were reflected in the torchlight. On the far right, down toward the banyan tree, a couple was slipping away from the others. His arm was around her shoulders, and hers was around his waist, and they were wearing the family's Bird of Paradise signature silk. "So, Mem, who are they, you and Grandfather or Mama and Papa?"

Mem stared deeply into her eyes and smiled. "What makes you think they're any of us?"

"But ..." Ari began, but Mem had already walked on.

The last painting was also a large canvas, not as large as

Celebration Night, but certainly large enough to draw instant attention when patrons entered the Fujiri. Ari read the nameplate at the bottom of the simple wooden frame: *Morning in Paradise.* "Oh, Mem," she sighed. "I *love* this one!"

"Why is that?"

"I don't know exactly." She thought for a minute, all the time staring at the painting. "Maybe . . . maybe because every time I'm far away and wishing we were back home with you and Grandfather, this is the first picture that comes into my head. Funny, isn't it? I hadn't realized how much I had come to love our mornings here."

Ari turned toward Mem and saw her moist eyes. "I knew you would see," she whispered.

The painting depicted the Dolphin Lagoon at first light. The sky was a hazy orange, and the outcroppings of the verdant landscape were just awakening into full brilliance, but the rising sun had already toasted the sands to a golden brown. Mama, Papa, and Grandfather and Mem were walking out of the water toward the beach. Each man held an arm around his wife as they walked. Emma was just turning toward the palm grove and the roof peaks of the Great House that peered out from beyond. She was carrying tatami mats under her left arm and a half-filled glass coffee mug in her right hand, her long chestnut curls were barely aloft in the morning breeze. Ari stood a short distance from her. She was bent forward slightly, her outstretched arms and smiling face were waiting to receive the bundle of energy that was running toward her on pudgy little legs. James had that determined look on his face, the one with his eyes staring forward and the tip of his tongue poking out of the side of his mouth, and his disheveled hair was flying off in all directions, as usual, whenever he was in motion. Tippy was running about five paces behind him, and his tongue was hanging out in similar fashion.

"Oh, Mem, don't sell this one. Please!" Ari blurted out surprising herself with the force of her words.

Mem began to laugh. "It's every artist's dream to evoke an emotional response from their work, but that was almost primal!"

"I'm sorry, Mem."

"Don't be, child. I painted this one for you."

Ari stared at her, wide-eyed, lips parted, about to speak. She was going to ask Mem how she knew that this was the painting she would cherish above all the others. But then she thought better of it. She already knew the answer.

33

IT WAS A ceremonial evening, festive and convivial, one requiring the wearing of the family silks. Ari didn't want to go all the way back home again, so she showered at Mem's and put on one of her sarongs. Then she sat at Mem's dressing table and watched her deftly working honey and hibiscus extracts down the long strands of her freshly washed hair, one handful at a time. "Thanks, Mem, for doing this."

"Your grandfather loves the scent of hibiscus in my hair. I'm thinking it will please young Joseph as well," she replied. She flashed that devilish expression—the one she had handed down to Mama.

Grandfather was sitting in the gathering room when Ari came in. He had nestled himself comfortably into one of the deep-cushioned chairs that dotted the expansive room, and there was a tell-tale haze swirling just above his head, though any sign of his ancient Meerschaum had disappeared. "Oh, Grandfather, Mem's not going to approve of that!" Ari cautioned, pointing to the smoke.

"Your grandmother is so happy, I don't think she'll be too mad," he replied jovially. "Besides, the breezes are fresh tonight, and the scents from the gardens will soon overtake the last of the smoke."

"Well, it sounds like you've thought this out."

He didn't reply. He just sat there, his new National Geographic on his lap, looking rather pleased with himself.

Ari glanced around the gathering pavilion, a last check to make sure that everything was in its proper place before the guests arrived. It was a wonderful room, filled with ancient woods, teak and mahogany and rosewood, and hand-tooled furnishings from countries that no longer existed on political maps. Richly colored fabrics and intricately designed ceramic pots all sat amidst a collection of ferns and palms and exotic orchids. And, of course, one exquisite Bird of Paradise that was always in flower. When the four walls were completely opened, as they were tonight, what lay just beyond became part of the furnishings, too—the Japanese Maple in the back courtyard, the cascade and pond with its little humped bridge that occupied the side yard, and the smattering of bird houses and Buddhas, all of which, when uplit at night, gave the gathering pavilion a celestial glow.

This was where Grandfather and Mem spent their evenings when the family was off-Island. They lay together in the double Javanese lounger that curved in and out with the contours of their bodies, while they listened to music and read books or talked about their day. Sometimes they just sat quietly glancing around the room at the paintings and photographs and mementoes that reflected the richness of their lives. The octagonal pedestal table next to the lounger was reserved for their most important treasures. Ari was glad to see the montage of photos in the antique picture frame sitting among them. It had, indeed, been the perfect Christmas gift.

"What are you thinking, child?" Grandfather asked. She looked over at him and saw that he was staring at her from somewhere behind those deep green eyes.

"I was just thinking how much I love this house and everything in it. Especially at night, I think. It's almost magical, isn't it?"

"Well, your grandmother would be pleased to hear you say that. She and Ghidra worked tirelessly on the design of the lighting to get it just right. Sometimes I would come home and find that they had spent a whole day moving a couple of lights just a few inches."

"That sounds like them," Ari smiled.

"Yes, and I would try to get them to take a more scientific approach to the project to speed things up, but Mem would chastise me and tell me that if I was an artist, I wouldn't say such things."

"She's right you know, Grandfather. It took an artist's eye, I think, to create all this." She traced a wide arc with her arm as she said this.

"Perhaps," Grandfather retorted, "but it took science to create the lights and electricity and construction materials and engineering principles."

"But that's all just technology, Grandfather. It has nothing to do with creativity."

"Really, child!" he responded with flair. "Do you think the scientist creates technology in a vacuum? No! He...or she...creates with purpose and context, picturing first, for example, how illumination might make our world more useful, more beautiful, and only then does he or she create the means to illuminate. You must ask yourself, Arianna, what would art be without science?"

Ari thought about this for a moment. "About the same as science would be without art," she replied.

Grandfather got an expansive smile on his face. "That's right, Ari. Now you know what few, beyond Leonardo Da Vinci, have ever known."

At that moment, Mem walked up trailing the hors d'oeuvre cart behind her. The cart was laden with what Mem called nibbles. Fruits and vegetables with dipping sauces, little crab-filled dumplings that she had prepared some days ago and frozen in case the family decided to entertain. There was mango chutney and Twiller's Toast, and several varieties of Sushi that Mrs. Yamaguchi had prepared last-minute in her Mainland kitchen and had sent over on the evening launch. Ari couldn't begin to imagine how Mem had pulled everything together. She only heard the news about Emma this morning. "Ari," she said, "would you help me, please, to place these around the room. That way people can wander and eat and sit as they please."

"Sure, Mem," she smiled and moved about the room placing trays and plates on end tables, coffee tables, and down the length of the alter table that sat behind the large rattan sofa near the Bird of Paradise.

The families started arriving just after sunset. First Mama and Papa came in with Emma and James. Mama went straight away to the cooking pavilion carrying a large platter of Emma's favorite curried lamb and saffron rice, and James trailed after her clutching a covered bowl of fresh berries, which he stared at all the way down the walkway, willing it not to spill along the way. Papa slipped a pouch of his special blend into Grandfather's hand before carrying the pork buns and dipping sauces into the kitchen, and Emma stayed behind to receive guests. She looked particularly beautiful tonight. Amethyst earrings carved in the shape of faceted teardrops adorned her ears, and a single amethyst hung from her neck. Together with her deep purple silk shell, the amethysts were lively accompaniments to the purples and oranges and greens and whites of the family silk.

Kemala and Tao came next carrying fresh-baked breads and brandy and mints for later. Tao was grinning from ear to ear and Kemala couldn't keep the tears from her eyes when she hugged Emma. Tommy and Joey came striding in a few moments later looking like a matched pair of splendid carriage horses in their red and yellow and carrying chilled lobster salad and enough mango pie to feed an army. Emma grabbed the trays from Joey and led Tommy to the cooking pavilion. Joey went straight to Ari who was laying out the last of the hors d'oeuvres at the seating area overlooking the pond.

Without saying a word, Joey grabbed her arm and led her out the side yard to the little humped bridge over the pond. It was dark except for the uplights on the cascade and the torches at either end of the bridge. To anyone inside the house, they'd be little more than silhouettes. At the top of the bridge, he stopped abruptly, turned Ari until her back was against the bridge railing and pressed the full length of himself against her. He said nothing. He just put his hands on her cheeks, lifted her face toward his and kissed her. His kiss was passionate, almost desperate, and she could feel the stirrings in his body. When she opened her eyes, the look of longing on his face sent a pleasant wave of heat up and down the length of her body.

"I've been wanting to do that all day," he said breathlessly. "In fact, it's all I thought about last night. Ever since Tommy told me what he and Emma were planning. I just wish . . . I just wish you were old enough. Would you, Ari? Would you dance for me if you were old enough?"

She hesitated before answering. He knew what she was going to say even before she said it. "Joey," she purred, "isn't it enough for now to know that I can't ever imagine dancing for anyone but you?" He was looking down, and she gently lifted his chin until he was looking at her. She smiled at him until he smiled back.

"Okay," he said, slipping his arms around her waist. "It's enough for now." He kissed her, affectionately this time.

They returned to the house, hand-in-hand, to find that everyone had arrived. Batara and Maru were standing with Papa and Grandfather, Tao joining them. They were wearing their ceremonial jade over their white on white floral-etched family silk, and they were smiling so wide that their fleshy cheeks almost eclipsed their eyes. Tommy and Emma were deep in conversation with Mem and Gidhra, Herry and Paku and their wives were just returning from the cooking pavilion, and Herry was asking what he had to do to get a glass of Grandfather's special wine. Mama was standing at the side entrance with Kemala, sipping wine with one hand and stroking James's head with the other. The mothers smiled at Ari and Joey as they re-entered the room. "Perhaps we should put the leftovers in the freezer. Could be another party soon."

Dinner couldn't have been more perfect. There was an abundance of delicious dishes—special occasion dishes that weren't made for just any gathering. The conversation flowed with the wine, never interrupted by awkward silences, and laughter punctuated nearly every sentence. It had only been a few hours since Mama and Papa and Kemala and Tao had accompanied their eldest to the Council, and Kemala and Mama were still all a-twitter, as Papa called it, over their girlhood fantasies coming true. Mama assured everyone that Papa was doing a fair amount of twittering himself. In actuality, everyone was excited about the joining of the two families.

Ari spent most of the evening eating left-handed. Her right hand was occupied in affectionately holding Joey's hand, or lightly rubbing his thigh or gently squeezing his left shoulder.

It hadn't occurred to her before Joey's kiss on the bridge, but he probably felt just like she did sometimes; like Tommy, his best friend, was leaving him behind. But it must have occurred to Tommy. Whenever the conversation turned to the special significance of this year's Celebration, Tommy would say something like won't be long before we're saying that to you, little brother. And Emma would join in with references to Ari. Then Mama and Kemala would twitter again, and Papa and Tao would slap each other on the back and grin so wide that their smiles would practically extend beyond their faces.

It was close to midnight when they heard the first distant strains of a rhythmic melody flowing in on the breeze. They were still seated around Mem's big banquet table, enjoying the brandy and mints that Tao and Kemala had brought with them, all except James who had fallen asleep in the big Javanese lounger some time earlier. They stopped all conversation and just listened to the melody growing closer. Before long, a torchlight procession of Islanders crowded into the gardens outside the dining pavilion and, for several minutes, serenaded Tommy and Emma with ancient blessings for a long and happy life together. This was a rarely performed custom nowadays. For modern couples, dancing at Celebration was no longer a guarantee that the couple would marry. But it was apparent to everyone who had seen Tommy and Emma together that the bond between them was eternal. It's true, Ari thought. Seeing her sister now, sitting at the head of the table next to Tommy, there was a look on her face that, until now, she had only seen on Mama and Mem. And Tommy looked at Emma like he could just melt right into her. Maybe it was true what Mama had said. Two spirits could find each other again. It was just so romantic.

Ari turned to Joey and found him gazing at her. He looked so happy. "You are worth waiting for, Ari. For as long as it takes," he said tenderly. He slid his arm around her shoulder and kissed her cheek. Then he leaned back, blissful and contented, and basked in the torchlight and the melodies and the romance of the evening. This time it was Ari who smiled so wide that her smile practically extended beyond her face.

Joey stayed after the others had gone to help Ari clear away the rest of the party. There was surprisingly little to do for a crowd of seventeen. Most of the food platters went home with the people who had brought them, and as everyone arose from the table for the evening, they had carried their own place settings to the cooking pavilion.

"Thank you, children, for staying," Mem said, handing Joey the last wet goblet to dry. "It will be nice to wake up tomorrow to a clean house."

"Thank you for hosting the party for Tommy and Emma," Joey said sincerely. "I know it meant a lot to my brother."

"You are good boys, Joey, from good people. It was my pleasure to do it for the son of Tao and Kemala. And my hope is that I will have the pleasure of doing it again one day soon."

He smiled. "I hope so, too," he replied as he looked longingly at Ari before giving Mem a kiss on the cheek.

When they were done cleaning, Joey walked Ari back to the Great House. Along the way they stopped to dip their feet in the calm moonlit waters at South Bay. "We have a lot to talk about, don't we," Joey said as they waded ankle-deep in the gentle surf. "You'll be flying back home after the holidays, and I'll be going back to university. We'll be so far away from each other."

"I know. I hate thinking about that, Joey. I mean, it won't be that long until summer, and we're going to spend most of it here on the Island and all, but after that . . . it just gets hard to imagine. I don't suppose you could transfer to Berkeley?"

"I don't think so," he chuckled. "But maybe you and Emma could come here. The university is really good here and then all four of us could be together. Think about it, Ari. Wouldn't it be fun, the four of us at college together?"

"It would be great, Joey. Except that Mama and Papa and James would be all the way back in San Francisco."

"Not forever," Joey replied. "Your parents want to move to the Island when your dad retires. I heard him telling my dad that."

"I know, Joey, but not for a long time, I think. Papa just made a deal with the company to take a posting he doesn't even want in exchange for being posted permanently to San

Francisco afterwards. He did all that to keep the family together while Emma and I are in college. How could I tell him that I've decided to transfer to Mainland University instead? Besides, I don't even know if Emma wants to transfer. She loves Berkeley and she had to work awfully hard to get in there. We both did."

"But she does want to transfer, Ari. Tommy told me so."

"What! Emma never told me that." Ari felt a sinking feeling take hold of her stomach.

"Maybe she hasn't had a chance. Things have been moving pretty fast, and I think she and Tommy only talked about it this afternoon after going to the Council."

"I wonder if Mama and Papa know."

Joey put his hands on Ari's shoulders and squeezed. "Don't you want to be with me, Ari?" He was smiling at her and even in the moonlight she could see those dimples.

"You know I do. I just never thought about coming here now. I've spent such a long time trying to get into Berkeley. I never really thought about going anywhere else."

She suddenly grew silent, and a deep furrow overtook her forehead a frown replaced her smile. "What is it, Ari?" Joey asked, gently cradling her inside his powerful arms.

She looked up at him, trying to find the words before she spoke. "My family. I can't imagine being that far away from Mama and Papa and James. Not yet."

The sadness in her voice touched him. "Maybe they'd love an excuse to move to the Island earlier than they'd planned. Maybe your father only made that deal with the company because he thought you and Emma would be at Berkeley. Maybe he really wishes you were going to be here so that he could be here too."

Ari's face brightened a little and Joey knew he had successfully planted the seeds of an idea. She would do the rest. She would water those seeds and nurture them until she had grown them into a full-blown plan of action. That's how she had always done things. Even when they were kids. He would make some casual remark about how much he loved the mountain lagoon on hot humid days, and the next thing he'd know, she'd have organized all their friends into a day at the lagoon with cold drinks, baskets full of food, and beach towels for laying in the sun on the big flat rocks that faced the waterfall. She had even thought to bring a camera for taking pictures of the kids as they came hurtling over the falls into the water.

"Maybe you're right, Joey. It would be just like Papa to put off doing something he really wanted to do because of us." She took in a great gulp of air and blew it out slowly.

Ari looked up at him. The moon had lowered in the late-night sky and was striking him at an angle that accentuated the chiseling of his face and the definition of his muscular body. Maybe you won't have to wait so long after all, Ari thought. Then she took his hand and led him out of the surf toward home.

34

THE HOUSE WAS dark when Ari got home, except for the subdued glow that radiated out to the side garden from Emma's quarters. She knew her sister would still be up, and that she would be waiting for her return. "Emma," she called softly into the room.

"Ari, get in here! I've been waiting forever!"

Ari stretched out on the end of the bed. "So, when were you going to tell me that you want to transfer to Mainland University?" she asked, taking care to keep any trace of hurt out of her voice.

"How did you know? I was waiting up to talk to you about it now. I hadn't even thought about it until Tommy and I talked about it this afternoon."

"Joey told me."

"I'm sorry, Ari. I wanted to talk to you about it first. I haven't made up my mind about anything. I really want to be with Tommy, but the idea of leaving Berkeley, and the family and . . . and you . . . and we had such plans!"

"I wonder if this is what it was like for Mama. You know, leaving Grandfather and Mem when she married Papa."

"I don't know. She had already been away at college for a few years."

"Funny, isn't it, how hard changes can be even when it's the best change in the whole world. Although I don't guess it would be this hard if we weren't all scattered to the four corners of the earth."

"Ari, it's hard enough to think of being thousands of miles away from Mama and Papa and James, but being that far from you . . . I guess I always knew the day might come when we'd be worlds apart, but I wasn't ready for it to be this soon. I always kind of fantasized that I would end up back on the Island, teaching at the school, and you would live here too and be a world-famous artist, and Mama and Papa and James would come back and . . . oh, it would be so perfect, wouldn't it!"

"Paradise," Ari sighed. "Pure Paradise." She sat up and leaned in toward Emma. "Joey asked me if I would transfer with you."

"Oh, Ari. Would you? I was afraid to even ask you because I knew you had your heart set on Berkeley."

"I had my heart set on being at a really good university with you. And being close enough to the rest of the family where we could still see each other. It doesn't *have* to be Berkeley, I guess."

"Mainland University is one of the best in this part of the world. I heard Grandfather say so a whole bunch of times."

"I wonder if they have a good art department . . . and humanities. I want to double major if I can."

"We could find out. I already know I could get my teacher training here, and I could student teach with Grandfather and Mem, which would be perfect."

"I'd have to know. I mean, I would love to go to school with you and Joey and Tommy. Just thinking of the four of us being together like that, it would be so much fun. But I've always thought that girls who applied to colleges just to be with their boyfriends were really stupid. Isn't this the same thing? For me, I mean. Not for you and Tommy. You're older and your relationship is a *lot* further along."

"Well, giving up Berkeley is huge. There's no denying that. And I don't know anything about the Art Department here, but I did hear Mem say that the Cultural Studies Department, which I think is their Humanities, is one of the best anywhere. And as far as the rest goes, keeping the two of us together is not like some silly girl following her high school boyfriend around."

"I guess you're right, Emma. It is different for us. And I do think that we could probably make the school part work. But . . ."

"There's still Mama and Papa and James?"

"Yes. And Papa's taking that awful posting just so we can keep the family together in San Francisco while we're in college.

And James, what about James if we suddenly abandon him? The thought of telling him that I am going away and won't be seeing him very much anymore, well, I just don't know if I can do it to him. I mean, where's he going to go in a thunderstorm?"

"I don't have an answer for any of that," Emma admitted sadly. "I feel like I'm having to make a choice between the people I love most in the world. I hate that."

"Me too. But, you know, Joey said something."

"Said what?"

"He said that maybe Papa made his deal with the company because he thought it was what we wanted. Maybe if he knew we wanted to come here, he could get a posting close by. I heard Mama tell Mem that getting a permanent posting in the San Francisco office was considered a plum assignment. If Papa could get that I bet he could get something here. Don't you think?"

"I don't know. It might be too late for all that. But I think I'll be able to see things a lot clearer in the morning. Right now, it's enough just to take in everything that's happened to me since I got up. I need some sleep."

"Agreed," Ari yawned. Of course, both girls knew there'd be very little sleep for either of them that night.

35

IT WAS JAMES who awoke Ari from a fitful sleep next morning. He didn't come barreling into the room as usual. Nor did he yell or shake her or try to drag her from her bed. Instead, he came in quietly from the open garden entrance, tiptoed across the room, lifted the lightweight silky sheet that draped over her and slid silently into bed, nuzzling himself down into her outstretched arm and pulling it around him into an embrace. He lay there for what seemed like an eternity to a five-year-old, but he didn't mind. He was with his Ari, and for some reason that's all he wanted right now.

Ari awoke about a half hour later. "What a treat, seeing you first thing when I open my eyes," she said to her big guy, sliding her other arm around him in a bear hug. "How long have you been here?"

"Forever and ever," he smiled. "You wanna go swimming now, Ari?"

"Oh, James, that would be the best!"

She didn't have to ask if he was already in his bathing suit. But when he climbed off the bed and ran over to the tall yellow armoire where she kept her bathing suits, his orange covered bottom confirmed it. "Bring me the turquoise suit please, James."

"The one with the big purple flowers?"

"Yes, please. That's the one."

James rummaged around in Ari's bottom drawer until he found the top and the bottom of the bikini. "Here it is. Put it on, Ari. Put it on and let's go swimming!"

When James and Ari arrived at the Dolphin Lagoon, only Grandfather and Mem were there to greet them. "James!" Grandfather called from out on the reef. "I've been waiting and waiting forever. Swim to me, child." James dropped his *tommy* mats in a heap on the sand and went shrieking across the beach and splashed into the water, wading out until he was deep enough to go horizontal. Ari watched with a great deal of amusement and affection. Then she carefully unfurled enough mats for the whole family, placed a fresh beach towel on top of each one, and headed for the water herself.

"Good morning, Ari," Mem said, as Ari swam up beside her. Mem was floating on her back in the shallow morning waters inside the reef. She rose up and planted her feet in the sand as Ari did the same. "Did you have a restful night?"

"You already know I didn't, Mem," she laughed.

"There's a lot to think about, I know. For you, and I think perhaps a little for Emma herself. I don't think she was prepared for the speed at which events overtook her this past week."

"But you were prepared, weren't you?"

Mem laughed. "Of course, child. We've been watching those two since they were babies together. We knew this day would come."

"We?"

Mem didn't hear the question, or maybe she just ignored it. "I remember the impatience of youth," she said. "It must be so hard for Tommy and Emma to think about the miles and the years that separate them from their future together."

"It is, Mem. They don't want to be apart all that time."

"And you and Joey?"

"We don't want to either, but it's a little different for us, I think. I mean, I'm younger. It's not our time yet."

"You are very wise, Ari," Mem said with obvious pride.

"If I was all that wise, I wouldn't feel so confused all the time. I just wish I knew how to be in two places at once."

"Things have a way of working themselves out. It will come to you, child. Trust yourself." With that she swam off toward Grandfather and the ever-giggling James out on the reef, leaving Ari to float and think and float some more.

Mama and Papa and Emma finally straggled out to the beach about an hour later. They were carrying two big picnic baskets and a large beach blanket, and they were laying them all out when Ari came back from the reef where she and James had been watching the fish taking their early morning meal. "Hello," Papa called when he saw Ari approaching. "It's a beautiful morning, isn't it?"

"Yes, Papa, it sure is."

"We've brought juice and coffee and fresh fruit and pastries and some breakfast meats," said Mama. "We thought everyone might want to have breakfast on the beach today. There's not a breath of wind to blow sand in our food."

"Sounds delicious. Any lemon Danish?"

"Of course," Mama smiled. She dug deep into the white wicker basket and pulled out a braided and frosted five-inch circle of perfectly baked dough with a glossy yellow glob in the middle. "Here you go, Ari. Special delivery just for you!"

Ari grabbed one of the plates Emma had laid out on the blanket and put her Danish on it. Then she grabbed a napkin and a fresh cup of steamy coffee and headed for the furthest mat down the row. By the time she got herself situated, Emma had joined her. "You haven't said anything have you . . . to Mama and Papa?" Ari whispered.

"No. Of course not."

"Oh, Emma, I'm so glad to hear you say that. I thought about it half the night. We just can't break up the family like this. Not now. Not after everything Papa's done for us."

"I know, Ari. I . . ." She stopped abruptly when she saw Mama and Papa coming their way with James in tow and quickly pulled towels from mats so they could sit down.

"Thanks, Emma," Papa said, as he carefully lowered himself and his breakfast to the mat across from hers.

"You're welcome, Papa."

Mama settled James down next to Papa and laid out his breakfast before him. "So," she began when he was well into his banana, "I guess we have a lot of plans to make."

A look passed between Ari and Emma that she did not miss. "Emma, you and Mem will need to make time for each other. Perhaps, after the Fujiri show tomorrow. You have many things to do before Celebration Saturday night."

"I know, Mama. Mem and I talked a little about it last

night, and we're meeting on Friday. We're going to spend the whole day together."

"Good," she smiled. "You'll enjoy that, Emma. Mem is a good Adi. I remember when she taught me before my first Celebration." She stole a look at Papa, and they shared a brief memory together.

"Mama," Ari interjected, "how will I know what to do as your Adi?"

"Well, if you could spare a day away from Joey, we could spend Friday together too."

"I'd really like that. Joey promised his Uncle Herry a day to help him put the last layer of varnish on his canoe. Maybe he can do it then."

Grandfather and Mem had joined the family circle and were happily nibbling on some fresh pineapple spears. "Isn't this going to be fun," Mem said. "The whole family involved in Celebration this year."

"Can I come? Can I?" James asked through a mouthful of banana, a blob of which flew out of his open mouth and landed on Ari's mat, sending her into uncontrollable laughter.

Grandfather put his arm around James. "Well, James, I was just going to ask you if you could help with something really special."

"What? What?"

"While the women are busy doing whatever they do that day, the men have to work really hard setting up the Gathering Place. Do you think you could help your Papa light the torches at sunset?" Grandfather winked at Papa and then looked back down at James whose eyes had grown twice their normal size.

"Really, Grandfather! Really, I get to do the fire?"

Papa chimed in. "We need a really big boy to do that job, and all the men picked you!"

James shot a look across to Ari. "They picked me, Ari! They picked me!"

She looked back at him, sitting there between Grandfather and Papa, his little body quivering with excitement about being included in the festivities and talking a mile a minute about men's business to the two other men in the family. Mama and

Mem were, well, twittering about women things, and Emma was just leaning back with that dreamy look on her face that Ari knew meant she was picturing how it was going to be with Tommy come Celebration Night.

How could she and Emma tear all this apart? Was she ready? It was too soon, just too soon. What was she going to tell Joey?

36

IT WAS ALMOST ten o'clock by the time everyone left the beach. Grandfather and Mem were taking the midday launch to the Mainland to oversee preparations for the Fujiri opening, and Mama was on her way to Kemala's to spend the day twittering. Papa was going to make a few phone calls before joining Mama at the Ahmanjaya's when Tao returned from a morning call on the Tejara twins. James was, of course, spending the day in the water with the other children. And Ari and Emma were on their way to South Bay to meet Joey and Tommy.

Tommy sat opposite Emma and was holding both her hands in his. He spoke first. "Emma, I know you want to be with me, and I know you want to be with your family. And I don't want to pressure you into doing anything that would make you unhappy."

Emma smiled. "Thank you," she replied. It sounded a little silly, but she didn't know what else to say.

Now it was his turn to smile. "Joey and I have been talking. We don't think you and Ari can transfer here for another year."

"What?" Ari exclaimed. She hoped no one heard the relief in her voice.

Tommy continued. "I have a friend at the Business School who says his brother wanted to transfer here but was told it was already past the deadline."

"Oh, I didn't even think of that." Emma said.

"I don't think the four of us have thought this out at all. We just know we want to be together."

"So, what should we do?" Emma asked.

"Maybe we should use the next year to start preparing for

you two to move here—you know, you could make application to the university so that's done. And we could check into housing and tuition and all that. I think with a house on the Island you would get local tuition. The cost is pretty steep if you're a foreign student."

"Oh, Emma," Ari chimed in, "I don't think we should do all that without talking to Mama and Papa first. Any way you look at it we'll still be breaking up the family, even if it is not for another year. And besides, I'd feel like I was sneaking around behind their backs or something." She didn't care if she sounded like a baby saying that. It's just how she felt.

"Ari's right," Emma agreed. "But maybe we could start by talking to Mama about it when we get back to San Francisco. You know, kind of feel her out on the idea. She'll understand, and she might even have an idea on how we could make it all work."

"She'd know if it was even possible for Papa to get a different posting," Ari added.

Joey spoke for the first time. "So, what if Tommy and I get all the information about Mainland University—transfer deadlines, what classes you can carry over, how much it will cost, all of that . . ."

"And I need to know what programs are available in Humanities and if there's a good art department," Ari added. Would she be okay with giving up everything she had worked so hard for? If she were being honest with herself, she really didn't know.

"Does Mainland University have a study abroad program?" Ari asked, her eyes shining bright as she formulated a possible solution. "If so, maybe we could come here for a year and you could come to Berkeley for a year and then we'd have the best of both worlds!"

Joey hesitated. "I don't know. We could ask," he said half-heartedly, and Ari could tell he didn't really like the idea. "But what if after all that, your family still has to stay put in San Francisco? What then?" Joey wanted to know.

"I don't know." Ari had hoped for more from him. Some sign that Joey thought the idea might work. Being separated from the family for just one year didn't seem *that* bad to her, especially with all the holidays they'd be spending together. And there'd be a whole year for everyone to get used to the idea. Well, for her to get used to the idea anyway. But there was no use getting ahead of herself. There might not even be any study abroad programs. Still, it would have been nice to hear Joey say he'd be willing to meet her halfway.

They stayed at the beach another hour, talking about what it would be like at the university if the girls did come, and the friends the boys knew there, and the places they could go together. There was a little club a few blocks off campus where the food was plentiful and the beer and wine were inexpensive and you could sit outside in the courtyard on warm evenings under the Japanese lanterns and listen to folksingers and local bands, some of which were really pretty good. Joey said that the place was always packed on Friday and Saturday nights with college students and a few younger ones who tried to pass for eighteen, the legal drinking age there. It was a great date place.

Finally, it was Emma who ended the conversation with a suggestion that they spend the rest of the day up at the mountain lagoon with a picnic. Ari was relieved. It had been a long time since the four of them had climbed the eastern headlands to the lagoon. There was an escarpment there, some twenty feet high, whose deep stone face had been worn smooth by centuries of water pouring over its edge. Soon they would climb to the top and sit together in the water, she in front and Joey wrapped around her from behind, Tommy and Emma likewise beside them. And they would dig their heels into the stone, and inch forward on their bottoms until the force of the falls propelled them down the slide, through the air and into the crystal waters below. They would do that again and again and again until they had just strength enough left to make the descent back down the mountainside. Of course, it would probably be a little different today—more time in the grass and less time flying through the air but exhilarating none the less.

"Why are you smiling, Ari?" Emma asked, as they rounded the banyan tree on the way back home to gather provisions.

"I was just remembering the first time Mama ever let us go

to the mountain lagoon with the other kids—you know, without adult supervision. I felt so grown up and so carefree."

"I know. I want to feel like that right now. I don't want to have to think about anything else for a while. I'm beginning to feel kind of . . ."

"Panicked?"

"No. Not panicked exactly. But kind of stressed. It all happened so quickly, and I haven't even taken care of the whole Roger thing yet."

"Oh, I forgot about that," Ari said. "But really, Emma, I don't think that's going to be as bad as you might think. I really don't."

Emma didn't reply. At the front gate she suddenly stopped. "Ari," she began tentatively, "may I ask you something?"

"Sure, anything."

"Have you thought about what you're going to do this summer?"

"What do you mean, Emma?"

"You turn eighteen just before we return to the Island. That means you'll be old enough to dance at the next Celebration . . . if you want to, that is. And I get the feeling Joey's kind of expecting you to."

Now it was Ari's turn to panic.

37

FRIDAY ARRIVED WITH lightning speed. Ari knew it would. That's why she and Joey and Emma and Tommy were cramming as much into each of their days together as they could. They spent one glorious day up in the canopy beyond the Pashmari, traveling from tree-top to tree-top on the ancient system of ropes and pulleys that the Islanders had constructed decades earlier. It wasn't a mode of travel for the faint-hearted. In some places the lines were over one hundred feet above ground. But the four had been coming there since childhood and were adept at running the lines. That didn't stop Mama from breathing a sigh of relief when her girls returned home safely.

Another day, they borrowed Gidhra's sailboat and sailed around the Island, stopping midday at a beach up on the north side accessible only by water. It had been years since Ari had seen the beautiful crescent beach with the gentle river that flowed across its western end to the sea. It was called Jackdaw Bay after a scurvy eighteenth century pirate who was rumored to have buried a great treasure there and then died before he could come back and reclaim it. Of course, it was Grandfather who had told the story one day when the family accompanied the Ahmanjayas on a picnic there, and Ari long since suspected that he made it all up to occupy the four children with pails and shovels while the grown-ups relaxed over a glass or two of Grandfather's special wine.

Whatever the plans for the day, mornings at the Dolphin Lagoon were still reserved for the family. It was a sacred time, and Joey and Tommy understood that and never intruded. But dinners around the old stone table had grown each evening to include them and their parents. Sometimes they didn't get up from the table until well on to midnight. Except the night of the Fujiri opening, of course. That day the family grabbed a light meal of cold salads and cheesy bread and headed for the Mainland early. Mem was always nervous before an opening although Ari couldn't imagine why. Her shows were always well attended by Islanders and Mainlanders and even a good number of tourists from the yacht harbor. This show was no exception. By the end of the evening, over half the paintings had been sold, including the large canvas of Celebration Night, which Willie and Mallory's friends, the Torrences', bought to hang over the sofa of their Florida home.

Friday morning after breakfast, Ari showered and plaited her hair in one long braid and put on a pair of shorts and a tee top over a bikini and a comfortable pair of Keds. She wasn't sure where Mama was taking her, and she wanted to be prepared. When she got to Mama's quarters, the doors were open so she entered without knocking and walked down the wide hallway, stopping along the way to glance at some of the photographs of the family's life on the Island displayed the length of both walls. Even though it was an interior hallway, the pictures didn't require any lighting by day because the peaked roof overhead was comprised entirely of glass panels running down either side of a long wooden beam, an ingenious idea of Gidhra's to satisfy Mama's love of open spaces.

The hallway ended at a wide rectangular landing that ran perpendicular and was watched over by a tall jade quan yin with a smiling face standing in a recessed alcove in the far wall. To the left and down three steps was the bedroom constructed with polished woods and retractable glass walls like the rest of the house. To the right of the landing was a similar room, smaller than the bedroom and on the same level as the hallway. This was where Papa had his office.

Ari heard Papa's voice on the telephone there. He was telling someone named Mathews not to worry about something. That he thought he might have a solution to his problem, but when he spotted Ari standing at the threshold, he abruptly stopped in mid-sentence. "Mama's in there," he said looking through to the bedroom from his desk.

"Thanks, Papa," she smiled. As she turned to go, she heard him resume his conversation, in a lowered voice this time.

Mama's bedroom was larger than Ari's. There was one dramatic angular wall at the corner from which her four poster platform bed extended out several feet. A large portion of the wall was taken up with a family portrait in oils, done by Mem when James was just a year old. In the painting, Mama was sitting in the big rataan fan chair that sat in the corner of the gathering room next to the Bird of Paradise. She sat very tall, looking almost regal, her legs crossed at the ankles, her hands in her lap, her long blue-black hair hanging in lustrous sheets down her back and over her right shoulder. Papa was standing next to her, opposite the Bird of Paradise, with his hand resting on her other shoulder. Ari and Emma stood on either side of Mama, a little to the foreground, and James sat at her feet, bent forward in a little chubby ball. They were all dressed in their family silk sarongs, except for James who wore a little shirt of the same fabric.

From the bed the room swept around to the left along the back gardens to a comfortable sitting area where two over-sized soft-cushioned chairs and ottomans looked out toward the pond. A lamp table between the chairs, nightstands, two massive antique wardrobes and a magnificent ebony secretary with a village scene and raised soapstone figures completed the furnishings. There were touches of Mama's favorite clarets and soft golds everywhere—in the patterned sisal carpets and cushions and bedcovers and in the long vertical silk wall panels that were inset between carved mahogany stiles. There were yards and yards of gauzy fabrics, which fluttered in the breeze and, of course, several exquisite Chinese pots that were home to a variety of trees and wild orchids, many of which grew only on the Island. Like the other rooms in the house, this one was bathed in sunlight, not the kind that overheated and beat you down, but the kind that lifted you up.

"Mama," Ari called into the bathroom. "Are you almost ready?"

"Be right there," she called back. She emerged a few moments later with a towel wrapped around her hair. Her cheeks were still rosy and moist from a morning shower in her walled garden.

"Where's James?" Ari asked.

"Emma dropped him at South Bay on the way to Mem's. Herry and Paku are overseeing the water babies today."

"Oh, James ought to come home all giggles tonight. Those two know how to get the joint jumping."

"You're right there, Ari. I think it's virtually impossible to be in a bad mood in their presence."

Ari nodded. "So, what are we going to do today, Mama?"

Mama finished tucking her coral cotton camp shirt into her khaki shorts before answering. "Today, Ari, I'm going to share with you the secrets of the Island women." She smiled when she said this. "I've been waiting a long time for this day. I thought I'd be spending it with you and Emma, but now that Emma's decided to dance, it's the responsibility of Mem to pre-pare her for Celebration."

"I hope you're not too disappointed, Mama."

"Oh, of course not, Ari," she replied emphatically. "In fact, I'm kind of glad it turned out this way. Emma and I will have our own private time in the Women's Hut tomorrow night. I'm glad to get this time just for the two of us."

"You're not just saying that, Mama?"

"Arianna, you are my Island Child. You always have been. Emma's connection to the Island is every bit as strong as yours, but it comes from a different place. This Island is a part of you. It's in your soul. You can be thousands of miles away and still you can reach out and touch it. At least, that's how it feels to you."

"How did you know that, Mama?"

"Because that's how it feels to me when I'm thousands of miles away," she said.

Mama put her arms around Ari and held her there for longer than a hug. Then they headed for the courtyard, stopping first at the office to wave goodbye to Papa. He was hunched over his desk, furiously scribbling figures on a big yellow notepad and thumping buttons on his portable adding machine, a large pile of crumpled yellow paper on the floor at his feet. "What's Papa doing in there?" Ari whispered.

"Just trying to make two plus two add up to four," she replied cryptically. Ari knew better than to ask again.

Once outside the front gate, they turned right and headed up the service road a short distance to where it turned back toward the School. There they took the narrow road that branched off to the north and wound through an enclave of about a dozen neat little bungalows, dubbed the *Neighborhood* by its inhabitants. The houses were all sprinkled among the trees and perfectly sited to capture just enough sun and shade and cooling breezes to stay comfortable year-round. And each house bore the distinct signature of its occupants.

It wasn't far to a place where the path swept around to the east, widening at the turn just enough to let the sunlight beam down rather than filter in. There was a pair of torches stuck in the ground there just to the right, with three large polished stones at their base holding up a small pennant made from the family silk.

Ari followed Mama into the dense growth behind the torches, bending under branches here and there and following what was less a path and more a repeated trampling of the undergrowth over the years. About twenty yards ahead the path opened up into a secluded clearing, and when Ari emerged into the full sunlight and looked around, what she saw took her breath away.

Ari had heard Mama describe this place many times before, but she could never have envisioned this. It was like the Garden of Eden, secreted away on the earth, but not really part of this world. She was standing on a little grassy embankment, green and cool, which abutted an azure pool so pure that she could see clear to the bottom even where it was in shadow. It was large and free-form, and it zigged in and out of the palms and fern trees and verdant foliage that surrounded it. And everywhere there were little bursts of color made by wild hibiscus and red-hot ginger and varieties of orchids in colors so rich, she didn't even know how to recreate them on her paint palette.

At the opposite end of the pool there was an escarpment, not as tall as the one at the mountain lagoon, over which twin waterfalls spilled so gently that they barely made a splash when they hit the water below. Delicate ferns grew wild from its crevices and a carpet of fragrant jasmine spilled over its rocky ledges. Reigning over the peaceful sanctuary from its highest outcropping was a magnificent Bird of Paradise whose long pink beaks and brilliant orange and purple plumage thrust a good eight feet toward the sky and under its umbrella of broad green leaves grew even more, each only distinguishable from its neighbor by its crowning flower.

"I've never seen them grow like that," Ari said as she tried to count how many there were. Mama stood by her side.

"I know," Mama said. "It's a very special place."

"It must be overwhelmingly beautiful here at night," she murmured, "with the stars overhead and the night birds singing." She dropped to her knees and fell silent. There were just no adequate words for this.

Mama knelt beside her and waited. This was not a time for hurrying. At last, Ari spoke. "How ever did you find this place, Mama? It's not like it's right out in the open or anything."

"When I was a girl, I used to love to go exploring around the Island. Mem worried about me sometimes that maybe I was spending too much time alone, but Grandfather said that I was plenty social and that I would stop my wanderings when I found what I was looking for."

"What were you looking for, Mama?"

"Well, nothing really. I don't know. I just wanted to know what was out here. And then one day I came upon this place, and I knew instantly that I wanted it for Celebration Night. It's like it spoke to me. Do you ever feel like that Ari?"

"All the time when I'm on the Island."

"What about when you're off the Island?"

"No, I don't think it's ever happened" Ari answered. "How old were you when you first came here," she asked.

"I was fifteen, and I remember running home straight away to tell Mem because I was so afraid that someone else would find this place and snatch it up. After all, I wasn't even of age, and as it turned out, I was twenty-one by the time your Papa and I finally came here together."

"So how did you end up with this place, Mama?"

"Mem came with me to see it that very afternoon. And if you believe what she said to me then you'll know why no one else ever claimed it."

"What did she say, Mama?"

"She said, 'This place has been waiting for you, Mary. The Gods will speak to you and your lover here and to no one else.' She said that was the reason why no one had ever found this place before."

"Do you believe her, Mama?"

"Mem's never given me cause to doubt her. Has she ever given you any?"

"No. Never."

"Well, then."

They spent the rest of the morning there in the grass, talking about Celebration, and how tomorrow afternoon they would go together to the Women's Hut. Mama would bathe and prepare her body, and together they would listen to the stories of past Celebrations and hear once again of the passion Mrs. Padua shared all those years with Mr. Padua. She would say how it wasn't just woodcarving that he was good at with his hands, and everyone would laugh as they always did. As the afternoon wore on and the stories got grander, they would long for that moment when they would dance out into the Gathering Place and get their first glimpses of their men.

Mama shared with Ari stories of her own, things she had never told her before. About her first Celebration and how much she wanted to please Papa, and how she knew from the way he looked at her when she came dancing into the Gathering Place that night that anything she did would please him. And how their lovemaking never grew old or tired over the years because they never took the passion or each other for granted.

"Can I ask you something, Mama?" Ari asked with a mouth full of fruit.

"Of course, Ari."

Ari's cheeks turned a deep shade of red. "Was Papa your first?"

Mama smiled, her head tilting to the left as was her custom

when working out what to say. "Yes, but things were much different back then."

"Were you scared your first time?"

Mama's brow furrowed. "Ari, is there something you're not telling me? You know you can talk to me about anything?"

"No, it's nothing like that, Mama. It's just, well, with Emma and Tommy and everything it just got me thinking."

Mama smiled and Ari could see the look of relief that momentarily crossed her face. "I wouldn't say scared," Mama continued, "nervous might be more appropriate." She paused, a mischievous smile crossing her face. "Besides, your Papa and I well . . . I said I was a virgin, not a nun."

"Oh Mama!" Ari broke out in a fit of laughter and was soon joined by her giggles.

"Seriously though, Ari," Mama said after their giggles subsided, "when the time is right, and the man is right, you won't question it. That's how you'll know. I may have been nervous. That's a natural response. But I was never scared. I knew I was safe with Papa."

"Papa didn't mind that you were...?"

"If he had, we wouldn't be having this conversation. Any man who has a problem with it, isn't the kind of man you want to be with."

They talked well into the afternoon. About when Mama first met Papa, and how her heart used to jump every time the phone rang, and about the first time she brought him home to the Island to meet Grandfather and Mem. She talked about what it meant to her when Papa said that he felt like he had a real family for the first time in his life. And she reminded Ari how important it was to bring a complete woman to a relationship, and then find a man who nurtured the best in her, as Papa had done. Then they talked about other things, intimate things, and Ari began to understand the ways of women and how everything she ever needed to know about lovemaking, she would learn *with* her lover, if she had chosen wisely, and not *from* him. Because the art of lovemaking was not learned from more experienced partners or from books or bragging in boys' locker rooms or with giggly adolescent imaginings given voice at slumber parties. It developed over time in the physical explorations, the sharing of intimacies, the unexpected discoveries, and even in the joys and the tears of lives lived together. "It is a journey, Arianna, with no destination."

"But, Mama, how will I know when I'm . . . I'm . . ."

"On the right path?"

"I guess."

"When your joy is as great when giving pleasure as it is when receiving it, then you will know."

Ari thought about this. "So, Mama, are you saying that the Sexual Revolution is all wrong. That we're all supposed to wait until we meet the man we're going to marry?"

"Of course not. Not unless it's what's right for you. Ari, I'm glad there are more sexual freedoms in the West than there used to be. And I hope one day that women will be fully shed of that ridiculous "stud/slut" double standard. Women should be free to enjoy sexual pleasure the same as a man without condemnation. But "free love" is not about love at all; it's about sex, and the two should never be confused. Do you understand?"

"Not completely. How do you tell the difference between love and just, well you know?"

"I can't tell you that, Ari. It's different for everyone. You'll know when your time comes. When I met your father, I didn't have to ask. I just knew," Mama said as she put her arm around Ari and gave her a reassuring squeeze.

The rest of the day was spent with Mama explaining to Ari what her responsibilities would be as her Adi, and how she would need to gather Mama's provisions for the evening and arrange for someone to deliver them before sunset. Kemala's niece, Tia, and her brother had brought the hamper and linens last year and had placed them next to the three stones at the foot of the path. Perhaps, they would be willing to do the same this time.

Then she went over the list of things she would be wanting for the evening—two bottles of Grandfather's wine, and the pair of cut crystal goblets with the emerald stems that Mem had given her on her wedding day, and strawberries and confectioner's sugar and sweet grapes, tangy mango slices and a loaf of cranberry raisin bread. There was also a list of linens and mild soaps for washing and aromatic body oils and extra sarongs to come home in next morning should theirs get mussed. "Oh, and I'll need the sparker for lighting the torches and, let me see—oh, yes, I'll need Mrs. Kanjeera's package," she said, finishing the list.

"What's in the package, Mama?"

"You'll see when you unwrap it."

"I hope I remember everything."

"Don't worry, Ari. I'll write it all down for you."

"Good, because I feel nervous enough that you'd think *I* was dancing tomorrow," she laughed.

In time they headed for the Womens' Hut. Mama wanted to be alone with Ari when she entered the hut for the first time, as she had been with Mem all those years ago. The hut was actually the fourth side of a beautiful walled garden. Its outer wall was solid, for privacy, with only clerestory windows way up high just below the roof line. The inner wall was all glass and fully retractable and was always opened wide at Celebration. It looked out over the peaceful garden and its beautiful plantings and graceful willows, spring-fed pools for bathing and little benches for sitting and contemplating the evening ahead.

At the entrance, Ari waited as Mama pushed open the heavy plank gates and passed under the pagoda roof. She followed her inside and joined her on the little humped bridge that led to the garden center, taking care to first close the gates against those who weren't meant to be there yet.

Mama and Ari strolled the gardens together. The sun was warm, but the weeping willows provided enough shade for comfort, and the sea breezes, which were coming in from the west today, kept everything fresh.

Suddenly, they were interrupted by voices coming from the other side of the gates. "It might be Mrs. Kanjeera and her great granddaughter. I understand she is dancing this year."

"With an Island boy?" Ari wanted to know.

"I don't think so. I believe he's a very nice young man from the Mainland. She met him at the university. I understand he's going to be an engineer. Batara told me he's very smart. He even has some ideas about engineering a water system here on the Island that will save us a lot of wasted resources."

It was Emma and Mem who came through the gates when they opened. They were carrying a small basket and a picnic blanket and came straight to where Mama and Ari stood in the shaded grass beyond the bathing pool. "We thought we might find you here," Mem called across the bridge. "We've brought refreshments."

The basket was filled with a variety of breads and chilled fruits and a bottle of wine with four glasses. Mem handed the glasses around. They were her special cobalt blue glasses, the ones usually reserved for the Sunset Bench. Seeing them now was confirmation of what Ari had already come to realize—that this was a special day, a benchmark day, after which nothing would ever be the same between the four of them again.

Ari looked around the blanket at the women who had most influenced her life. They were smiling and relaxed and animated in their conversation, even Emma who should have been nervous, but didn't seem to be. She just looked, well, older somehow. But then, Ari felt older too. It wasn't until she had entered the Women's Hut that the feeling came over her completely— a feeling of having traversed a chasm between childhood and womanhood. But there it was, and she had proof of it. She knew now, with absolute certainty, that she wasn't ready to dance for Joey—not now and not even this summer. She needed time in the world first. And knowing this didn't make her feel like a baby being left behind by those who were older. Not anymore. It made her feel strong. It made her feel confident. It made her feel like a woman.

38

IT WAS IN the air when Ari awoke—an excitement, a buzz, like that moment of awakening on Christmas morning when consciousness overtakes the mind, and children suddenly remember that this is the day for opening all those fancy-wrapped packages under the tree that have been taunting them for weeks. Ari darted out of bed and grabbed a suit. In no time she was on the veranda outside Emma's quarters peering in at her empty bed. It wasn't surprising that Emma couldn't sleep the night before her first Celebration; just surprising that Ari hadn't awakened with her.

The Island had served up a perfect day. The sky overhead was a brilliant blue, the landscape was resplendent with flowers that had magically bloomed overnight, and the air was filled with the music of birds who on this day chose to sing arias, not songs. Grandfather said that he couldn't remember a Celebration that had gotten rained out or that was even gray or dismal. But Ari thought that today was especially beautiful. Maybe because, in a way, this was going to be her first Celebration. Not to dance, of course. Still, she was going to be Mama's Adi, and that came with its own importance.

Papa was chasing Mama into the water when Ari arrived at the Lagoon. He was in a playful mood, and from the way Mama taunted and teased him, it was obvious that she had every intention of taking advantage of it. "Good morning," he called without breaking stride.

"Good morning, Papa," she called back. In no time she was out on the reef where she joined James in chasing a school of yellow tang through the coral canyons and back to the shallows again. He certainly spent enough time in the water. At any given hour of the day you could hear his spontaneous laughter echo off the granite cliffs whenever he surfaced from the depths. He was such a happy little guy it was impossible not to be happy around him, and Ari loved him all the more for that.

It was still early when the family gathered together for a light breakfast on the beach. There'd be no lazing around the stone table today. There was much to do this morning. Mama and Papa were headed up to the Sunset Bench with Grandfather and Mem for a brief visit. They wouldn't be able to go later that day. And Ari had all her preparations for Mama to complete. "How will you be spending your morning, Emma," Mem wanted to know.

"Well, if Ari doesn't mind, I think I'll tag along with her. Is that all right?" she asked, turning to her sister.

"It would be great," Ari replied. "I'd love the company."

Back at the Great House, Ari got James washed and dressed and ready for Paku's eldest son to pick him up for the day. The teenagers on the Island, those who were sixteen or younger, took turns throughout the day and evening baby-sitting the little ones. It was their responsibility to come up with the activities, organize the work shifts, and arrange to put everything back in order by the next morning. Each Celebration they came together the week before, made their plans for keeping the little ones occupied and happy, and then submitted their plans for Maru's approval. Of course, the days were always spent at South Bay where they'd swim and have races and scavenger hunts and all sorts of contests for prizes. One year they even had a hunt for buried pirate's treasure with clues they could follow to a real-looking pirate chest that had been filled with gold-wrapped candy coins and little inexpensive party favors. Nights were spent in the western pavilion at the school, the one furthest from the Gathering Place. It was already stocked with games and equipment, art supplies, and a stack of cartoons and kids' movies borrowed from the lending library on the Mainland. There was a quiet room set up with mats and pillows and blankets for when it got really late. Some of the children slept there for the whole night, but most were picked up and carried back to their own beds in the wee hours.

James was standing next to Ari at his bedside, stuffing his blankie into his duffle bag. "Careful, James. You don't want your special blankie to get caught in the zipper," she cautioned.

He patted down the blankie until the last corner was safely tucked away. Then he zipped up the bag and handed it to Ari. "I don't wanna go to the school tonight, Ari. I wanna go with you," he said in a plaintive voice.

She bent down on one knee and put her hands gently on his shoulders. "You can't come tonight, James. I couldn't come when I was your age either. But you get to be there today. Nobody ever let me do that!"

"Really? You couldn't help the big people?"

"No, James. You're really special. Papa's going to come get you at the beach today just as soon as he gets back."

He thought about this for a moment. "I still don't wanna go to the school tonight."

"It'll be all right, James. You'll have fun there."

"Are you going to take care of me?"

"Not this year. Mama needs me to help her." His face looked so sad when she said this. "What if I come check on you during the night? Would you like that?"

"Would you come a whole bunch?"

"As often as I can. Okay?"

"But I don't wanna sleep at the school, Ari."

"Oh, James. Did you think that's why we were packing your blankie?"

"Yes."

"No, big guy. That's only if you get tired before I come get you. I promise. You're going home with me tonight. In fact, I was going to ask you if you would sleep in my quarters with me. Nobody else is going to be home. Just you and me and Tippy. We could have a slumber party."

"Just us, Ari?"

"Just us!"

"Oh boy!" he squealed, and Ari broke out laughing.

When James had been safely delivered into the keeping of Paku's son, Ari headed to Mama's quarters to start gathering her provisions. Emma was already there, rummaging through one of the closets. "Do you know where Mama keeps her silk-topped comforter—the one she uses for Celebration?" she asked Ari when she heard her approach. "Mama said I could use it tonight."

Ari pointed to the top shelf. "I was wondering why Mama didn't have it on her list. I wonder what she's— oh, Mrs. Kanjeera's package. Of course!"

"What?"

"That's what must be in the package Mama had me get from Mrs. Kanjeera the other day when Joey and I went into town. It's a new comforter for Celebration Night." Ari ran over to the bed where Mama had said she would leave the package. There it was, still neatly wrapped in brown paper and tied in string. She carefully pulled the string from the parcel and folded back the paper, revealing a beautiful, hand-stitched comforter, black canvas backed with a crème silk top. Mrs. Kanjeera had appliquéd a chain of interlocking emerald leaves all around the border, and in the center, she had placed a large medallion, encircled by a smaller version of the border, with a beautiful cluster of Bird of Paradise blossoms stitched in different textures of purple, pink, and orange dupioni.

"It's exquisite!" Emma sighed.

"I think it's the most beautiful thing I've ever seen. And feel how soft it is against your skin," Ari said, lifting a corner of it and brushing it across her cheek. Emma didn't say anything. She just stared at the quilt. "Emma? Are you all right?"

"Yes. I'm fine," she murmured.

Ari smiled. "Getting a little nervous?"

"No! Well . . . maybe just a little."

"You know, Emma, no one would fault you if you decided you weren't ready for this," Ari offered.

"Oh, Ari, I'm ready. I'm ready for tonight and tomorrow night and for the rest of my life." Emma sounded so sure, so confident.

"How do you know?"

"Because from the minute I saw Tommy on the beach that first night, it was like some powerful force drew us together. I can't explain it, Ari. It just happened.

By the time, Mama and Papa returned to the house, everything had been readied. Ari had assembled and packed all the provisions, taking care to place the food items in insulated chillers. And she and Emma had carried the large basket out to the service road where Jack Sarkua, one of Mr. Gupta's farm hands, picked it up in his truck and drove it out to the jungle entrance where Tia and her brother would only have a short distance to carry it.

Then she returned to her own quarters and bathed and oiled her body and took an especially long time working the fragrant conditioners through her long hair all the way to the ends. When she was done, she wrapped herself in her signature sarong and a green silk tube top and went out into the garden to pick a single fragrant gardenia to stick behind her right ear. Before leaving to join the others, she took one last look at herself in the full-length mirror. The reflection made the gardenia appear as if it were behind her left ear, the custom of women who had taken a lover, or were about to. She studied the woman in the mirror for a really long time, and then she spoke to her. "Soon enough!" she said and headed for the door.

39

FINALLY, IT WAS time to go. Ari went to Mama's quarters to tell her that everyone was waiting for her. She found her standing at the large antique secretary taking something from the little secret spring-loaded drawer where she kept her special treasures. It was a Chinese silk envelope, peacock blue and very old and stitched all over with delicate vines and flowers. Mama stood there for a long moment just smiling at the article in her hands. Suddenly Ari felt like she was intruding on a private moment. She retreated into the hallway where she cleared her throat loudly and announced it was time to go.

They all walked together as far as the banyan tree. Papa set down the tray of crab puffs Mama had prepared and slid his arms around her waist and gazed at her for a very long time. "I love you, Mary," he said at last, "in ways I couldn't even imagine when we were new." Then he kissed her on the lips, turned and headed for the Gathering Place where Grandfather, Tao, Tommy, and Joey and all the other men of the village and the woman who would not be dancing or serving Adi were assembling to set up for the festivities. Ari and Emma looked at each other and smiled.

There were flagpoles to erect and silks to raise so that the families would know where to sit, and the ceremonial chairs to bring out from storage for Batara and Maru, and the long drum (which Ari thought looked like a giant banana) that would be played by five drummers to be dragged out and set up at the east end of the green. There were tables to set up, coolers to fill, the fire pit to be tended, and the pig to be sliced, and the food to be carried in waves from the school kitchens. There were torches to be lit and the wine to be drunk. And, of course, someone needed to make sure that the area under the banyan tree was raked smooth and readied for whichever young onlookers decided to hide there from the unsuspecting adults.

Mem was waiting at the gates of the Women's Hut when Mary and the girls arrived. "Hello," she called exuberantly. "Have you ever seen a more perfect day?"

They entered the gates to find the gardens already filled with scores of women who had come together for one purpose. There were four generations of Padua women gathered near the bathing pool where Lucinda, Mrs. Padua's great-granddaughter, was just emerging into a big bath towel. Maru was holding court on the front steps of the hut and her jovial laughter and rosy cheeks indicated that she was not drinking from her first glass of wine. Kemala and her sisters-in-law were sitting in the shade of a willow tree sorting flowers for stringing into leis, and everywhere women were milling and reclining and nibbling and sipping and conversing in a restrained excitement that was kept in check only by the serenity of their surroundings.

Over the course of the afternoon, all the dancers took their turns at the bathing pool. Their Adis were there to assist them in all that they required. Ari was there with towels for Mama when she came out of the pool, and she massaged her with jasmine oils and conditioned her hair to a high shine. And she brought Mama sliced fruits and breads and filled her glass with wine when she required it. She strung flower leis together to cover her bare torso when she danced and sat with her and Emma and Mem and all the other women when Maru and Mrs. Padua began the stories of past Celebrations.

When they heard the first beating of the drums, they knew it was time. Ari and the other Adis retrieved the signature silk sarongs from where they had hung them in the fresh breezes and sunshine when they first arrived. She wrapped Mama's around her, and she draped flower leis on her, and she placed Mama's silver filigree Bird of Paradise clip snuggly just behind her left ear. She hugged Mama one last time. Mama didn't let go. She held Ari close and whispered in her ear. "Thank you, Arianna, for making this the happiest Celebration I have ever known."

When she reached the top of the little humped bridge, Ari stopped and turned back around to take one last look at the gardens. She wanted every detail of this place . . . no, of this day embedded in her memory. Mem and Gidhra were sitting together on the steps talking and laughing with that relaxed air of two old friends who had come here many times before. Mama and Emma were sitting together some ways off in a secluded spot under the cascading branches of a large willow. They were leaning in toward one another. Mama was talking, and Emma was silent and, from the expression on Emma's face, Ari knew that they were sharing some great secret. And then she saw Mama hand something to Emma. It was the Chinese silk envelope, peacock blue and very old, that she had seen Mama retrieve from her secret drawer. She watched Emma unwind the cord from the old horn button and raise the flap and remove a folded piece of thick parchment. Emma opened it and she read what was contained inside. Ari desperately wanted to know what was written on that parchment, but she knew it wasn't her time yet. For now, it was just her time to go.

The Gathering Place was significantly more raucous than the Women's Hut had been. Except, of course, for that part of the afternoon when the stories had been shared of skillful lovers and the women who made them that way. Ari arrived just in time to see the confusion of bare feet and brightly patterned sarongs rapidly dispersing toward the edge of the green where they organized themselves into family clusters under their signature flags. She could hear James's voice above the din. "This way, Papa. We have to light this one." She spotted him across the green. He was flying around the perimeter on Papa's shoulders, a sparker in his hand, leaving a trail of torch flames in his wake. And with each new flame, there was an outburst of his unmistakable laughter.

She watched Papa and James until they had galloped up the School steps and out of sight and then searched the green until she found the red and yellow silk flying at the far end of the green right next to her own. Joey and Tommy were already there, and Tao and Herry and Paku were just joining them. From the clumsy way they flopped to the ground, Ari guessed that the wine had been flowing for some time already. Grandfather sat a few feet to Joey's left and Ari headed for the empty space between them.

Joey jumped to his feet when he saw her approach. "You look beautiful," he said. He was bare-chested and his bronze skin was glistening from hours in the sun. Ari began to rethink her stance on whether or not she would be ready to dance this summer.

"I've missed you today," she returned, with a little more sass in her voice than either of them was used to. She kissed him briefly on the lips and took a seat next to him.

Grandfather reached over and grabbed her hand and gave it a little squeeze. "Happy?" he asked exuberantly. He, too, was bare-chested, and the only allusion to his age was the slight salting of the little tufts of chest hair that peeked out from behind his ti-leaf lei.

"Ecstatic!" she cried, squeezing his hand back.

Papa appeared a few moments later, flushed from his romp around the green with James or perhaps from the wine. He threw his arm around Ari. "I'll bet you're glad to be off the baby-sitting rotation this year."

"I am, Papa. It's like graduating to the big people's table at Thanksgiving."

Papa laughed just a little louder than usual. "Well, it doesn't get any better than this, does it, Arianna." He looked past her to Joey. "Okay. Maybe it does get better. Right, son?"

"Papa!" Ari squealed. She and Grandfather exchanged wide-eyed looks. "What's going on, Papa? You're up to something. I know that look!"

"Could be!" He grinned ear to ear. Ari was going to press him, but she knew it would do no good.

"What's with your dad?" Joey whispered in Ari's left ear.

"I don't know, Joey. Maybe . . ." She stopped short of saying anything out loud.

"Maybe what?"

"I don't know. Maybe it's just the day . . . or the wine." She willed her voice to sound calm but inside her heart was beating wildly. Ari did know that look. It always preceded something momentous for the family. She didn't dare hope what it might be. The Gods would think her greedy for wanting any more than this day had already brought her.

40

THE GODS HAD sent an artist's sun, big and orange and liquid. It was in its final descending arc over the western headlands now. When the Island was just a silhouetted image against a vibrant sky, the drums would begin again. Slowly at first, just a whisper to the women that their men were ready for them. Then as they emerged from the hut, the first timers in front and the experienced dancers following, the drums would oh so gradually increase in speed and volume, as would the heartbeats of everyone present. Ari looked skyward and waited. And all the families, who had come from near and far to share in this Celebration, looked skyward and waited, too.

The first beat of the drums and all eyes turned toward the east end of the Gathering Place. The women were coming now. Little bits of them could be spotted between the stands of palms that lined the path from the Women's Hut. Joey's grasp around Ari tightened. She turned her head and looked up at him. She could still see his face clearly in the diminishing light. He was smiling. Not the bemused smile of some adolescent frat boy. But a calm smile, an appreciative smile, a respectful smile. "I'm glad I'm here with you," she said, and nestled closer to him, before looking back toward where the women would enter. She didn't notice the heated, longing look Joey gave her.

Then she caught her first glimpse of Emma, leading the procession of dancers into the green. Ari didn't know why she had been chosen for this honor. Maybe because of the Islanders' happiness over the joining of the Heywoods and the Ahmanjayas after all these years or maybe out of respect for Grandfather and Mem or Tommy's great grandparents, Batara and Maru. Whatever the reason, Ari was glad for her and, judging from the look of pride on Papa's face and the single tear that glistened on his cheek, he was glad for his Little Shadow as well.

Emma never looked more beautiful. She had chosen to wear her short sarong, the one that hit a couple of inches above her knees, which exposed just enough of her legs to see the grace of her movements that her years in ballet had taught her. Her purple silk halter top was almost completely covered with the white orchid leis Mem had meticulously strung together for her, and there was a single white orchid behind her left ear. The only other embellishment was just a touch of soft pink lip gloss. Ari searched her face for some sign of the nervousness that had been there only that morning, but she could find none of it. Mem had prepared her well.

Ari didn't remember letting go of Joey and craning forward on her knees to catch every nuance of her sister's dance—how she inched closer to Tommy with each tiny fluid step, and how her hands reached out to him and her sensually swaying hips beckoned him, her deep blue eyes never leaving him no matter which way her body moved. How had Emma learned this dance? Ari wondered. Could Mem have taught her? Or was this dance inside every woman just waiting for the one who was worthy of it?

When Emma stood before Tommy, she bent forward and removed a single orchid lei from around her neck and placed it around his. Then, without a word between them, she took his hand and led him to the center of the green, but not before flashing Ari a smile that told her how glad she was that her sister was here to share this with her.

Next it was Mama and Mem's turn. They had been dancing all this time toward the eastern end of the green with the other experienced women, leaving center stage to the new dancers. Ari thought they resembled a chorus line, and when the principle dancers moved toward the ring of spectators to retrieve their partners, the chorus came forward to fill the empty space. But she knew they were more than that really. They had come to renew the vows they had made Celebrations ago, and this night was as sacred to them as it was to any first-time dancer.

Ari watched as Mem led Grandfather to the center of the dancers, not far from Emma and Tommy. And she watched as Mama and Papa followed after them and began their dance as the others had—not a breath of air between their bodies, not a word spoken. Ari remained on her knees, craned forward, mesmerized by the dances of the three women who had come before her and of the men who neither led nor followed them. There were three distinct dances. All were perfect, yet unrehearsed, learned instead from years of loving one another. Ari knew that she was witnessing the handing down of her own legacy, and it didn't frighten her or confuse her anymore.

All through the night, the drums kept beating and the dancers kept dancing and the spectators kept chanting and Ari kept remembering how in all the years she and Emma had talked about what it would be like to attend their first Celebration together—in whispered voices under the banyan tree and in high, soft beds with knees to chests and flannel nightgowns pulled around them, in Paris and London and Hong Kong and San Francisco—never had they once imagined that their first Celebration would be like this.

The festivities continued for several hours with the feasting and the talking, the laughing, and the endless supply of Mrs. Tanji's kiwi tarts. In time, everyone danced. Except Sita Gupta, of course, whose baby was sitting so low that everyone was sure it would arrive before morning. Earlier that day Kemala had handed her a walkie talkie and had assured her that she mustn't worry. Tao was just a beep away if she needed him. "Oh, I wouldn't dream of disturbing you on Celebration Night," Sita had said.

"Yes, but your baby might, and it wouldn't be the first."

It was nearly one in the morning when the festivities finally broke up. Ari had hugged Emma when she left for the night, and Mama and Papa and Grandfather and Mem a few minutes later. She and Joey had taken their places in line to thank Batara and Maru for this beautiful evening, and Batara and Maru said once more how blessed the Island had been at the joining of their two families, and perhaps soon it would be doubly blessed. Ari blushed.

They stayed for an hour more, helping with the clean-up,

and walking Mrs. Padua back to Joey's house where she would be spending the night. Then they strolled back up the road to the school where they hoped James would be fast asleep. The night was still warm, but the constant breeze off the Bay kept the air from going stale. Overhead, the sky was filled with constellations. "Isn't it amazing," she murmured, "to think of our ancestors finding their way here by reading those same stars?" They had stopped walking, and Ari was leaning back against Joey and looking up. She turned to face him. He was smiling that smile again—the one that sent butterflies fluttering around her stomach. "I wonder what the stars look like over Venice," she said.

"What made you say that?"

"I don't know. I've always dreamed of going to Venice. It was Mama and Papa's first posting, and the way they talk about it . . . I don't know, I just have to go there one day."

"I'll take you there, Ari. I'll take you anywhere you want to go. Just promise you'll always love me, Arianna, and I'll follow you anywhere." He leaned in toward her and kissed her. This time his hands traveled up her torso until they found her breasts. This time, she didn't push them away.

They found James sound asleep on one of the mats at the school. He was lying on his side in the fetal position, thumb in mouth, and well tangled up in his blankie. His cheeks were ruddy and he looked like he'd been crying. "He's been asking for you, Ari," Jesse Tanji whispered. He was Mrs. Tanji's fourteen-year-old. "He was fine all night until my mom came by to pick up Jake. Then he wanted to go home too."

"Oh, the poor little guy. I'll have to give him extra hugs tonight."

Joey bent down and picked up James and his blankie all in one bundle and positioned him until his head rested on his shoulder. James stirred a little but went right back to dreaming. "I'll carry him, Ari. No sense waking him up."

All the way back to the Great House, Joey gently rubbed James's shoulders. He was so tender with him, so sympathetic. "You're going to make a wonderful doctor, Joey."

"You think so?" He was obviously touched by Ari's comment.

"Of course I do. I think you'd be wonderful at anything you

decided to do," she replied softly.

Joey was still at the house when Mama and Papa came strolling in next morning. He was lying next to Ari in the double hammock on the back patio where they had spent the whole night talking under the stars. They had talked about everything. About their earliest memories of each other when their mothers used to take them to the beach and Ari, barely out of diapers and half naked, would chase after him with fistfuls of sand that she'd try to throw at him, but he would maneuver her so that the wind would blow the sand back at her, and she would fall for it every time. And they talked about the growing up years when he was her big brother, her protector, and they talked about the moment that all that changed. When their friendship had grown into so much more and how glad they were that it did but that they were so grateful for the friendship that started it all. They talked about Venice. It was so different talking about Venice with him. He promised to take her there one day soon, and she promised to wait until he could, and they both meant it.

Then they talked about what they were going to do when they parted tonight, the letters they'd write and the pictures they'd send. They talked about how they would survive if they had to spend four more years apart. "We'll just keep thinking about Venice," Joey said, and Ari loved him all the more for that.

When Mama ventured out on the patio with Papa and saw them there, she had to smile. How many nights had she and Ethan lain in that hammock, recounting the happiness of their lives together? He must have been thinking the same thing. His grasp around her waist tightened. "Did you two get any sleep?" she asked, as she tried unsuccessfully to stifle a yawn.

"No, Mama," Ari yawned in return. She suddenly realized how many hours had passed.

"Well, that'll be good practice for your first Celebration," Papa teased.

Ari got all red in the face. "Papa!" she exclaimed.

"Ethan!" Mama chastised.

But Joey just smiled.

41

THE DAY PROMISED to be a hot one. Emma and Ari were lying next to each other on their backs, soaking up the last suntan rays they'd be getting for a while. They each held at their sides a cool glass of iced green tea. Little droplets of condensation flowed and splashed onto their fingers. They spoke sporadically, but they didn't move except to occasionally lift their glasses to their lips. Somewhere out in the water, James was giving a swimming lesson to Tippy in his most authoritative voice. No one wanted to tell him that dogs could swim naturally. He was taking way too much pleasure in his accomplishments.

"I wish Tommy would hurry up and get here already," Emma murmured.

"You only left him an hour ago," Ari observed.

"I know. But there's so little time left. He's going back to school tonight, and we're leaving tomorrow and . . ." As soon as the words were out of her mouth, Emma was sorry. Ari had to say goodbye to Joey too. She didn't need reminding. "I'm sorry. It can't be easy for you either."

"That's okay," Ari sighed. "It must be especially hard for you. Going from Celebration one night to saying goodbye the next. It just doesn't seem fair."

"Fair or not, that's how it is."

Ari shifted her position a little until an uncomfortable lump of sand under her tatami dissolved away. She thought about rolling over on her stomach, but that required more energy than a lazy day at the Dolphin Lagoon provided. So she remained on her back, eyes closed behind dark glasses, knees up, feet buried in the warm sands just off the end of her mat, the fingers of her left hand lazily tracing figure eights at her side. She wanted to ask Emma about last night, but she knew that would be wrong, so she tried instead to think of something else to talk about, something that might distract her from her gnawing curiosity.

Fortunately, Emma jumped into the silence first. "So, you never said. How was your night with Joey?" she asked.

"Well, not like yours, but wonderful just the same."

"What did you do, after the Celebration I mean?"

"We picked up James at the school. Poor little guy had a rough time of it after his friends left. I think he was feeling pretty alone with all of us gone. Joey carried him all the way home. He was so sweet. And then we spent the rest of the night together in the double hammock. And we talked." Ari's voice grew soft as she faded back into the memory of last night.

"By the look on your face, you didn't spend the entire night just *talking*," Emma said with a bit of humor in her tone. Ari smiled at her sister. A smile that told Emma all she needed to know.

"I bet he is quite the kisser," Emma teased, "but how romantic!"

"In a way it was. Except, of course, that James spent most of the night in the hammock with us," Ari laughed.

"Maybe that was a blessing in disguise. I saw the way Joey looked at you last night."

"You're right. I don't know if it was the Island wine, or the Celebration, but . . ."

"But what?"

Ari glanced around to see if everyone was still in the water and then leaned in close to Emma's ear. "I know I would have been really, really sorry this morning if anything had happened. Still, I think if Joey had wanted to push it, I don't know for sure what I might have done. I'm just so unsure about everything."

Emma just smiled. She didn't say anything. The whole world looked different to her today. Mama had told her that it would be like that. "That's how you will know when you've chosen wisely," Mama had said.

"Ari?"

"Hmm?"

"Thanks for not asking me about last night."

"That's okay. Some things aren't meant to be shared. Not even between sisters."

42

PAPA WAS STANDING at a distance, chest-deep in water, when Ari came gliding up beside him. He looked very far away. "You look like you have something on your mind, Papa," she observed.

"Not at all," he lied. "I was just taking in a panoramic view." She followed his line of sight, from the Cliffside path that beckoned him each evening, across the gentle spray of breakwaters just outside the reef to the funny little cluster of palm trees that jutted out from the base of the verdant cliffs to the north, past turquoise waters shadowed by reefs, and lazy little ripples ambling into shore to the toasty golden sands where Emma lay sunbathing and daydreaming on her rolled-out mat. "I love starting out our days here together," he said. "There's something about having family rituals that makes life seem, I don't know, comfortable is not quite the right word."

Ari thought for a moment. "I'm not sure I know the right word either. I just know that having things you can count on—people you can count on—it just feels good."

Papa turned to look at Ari, steadying his feet in the shifting sands as he did. "I didn't know much about families until I met your Mama. But she taught me that all families have a unique rhythm of their own choosing. She calls it their comings and goings. And if they've chosen well, the family is happy and strong."

"We've chosen well, Papa. Don't you think?"

"I know we have, Ari, because I know how happy I am. Like how I feel coming out here each morning, or when I'm driving home from work and I can already see you and Emma and James there in the kitchen with your Mama. And I know that when I open the door I'll be greeted by laughter and great smells and James running toward me." Papa stopped. He obviously had a lot more on his mind, but it was going to stay there for now. "It's a gift having people you can count on. A gift on many levels. Especially, I think, when you live all over the world. Mama and I know how hard it can be when you live places just long enough to make good friends that you inevitably have to say goodbye to. That's why Mama works so hard to make every house a home with all her knick-knacks. And why we spend extended periods of time here. This Island is our real home. This is the safe harbor we always have to come back to."

"That's what makes the *going aways* possible, Papa. We can always count on what's waiting for us when we come back home again." As she said this, she looked across the lagoon at Mama, whose lithe body was just surfacing over the northern end of the reef. Emma was there waiting for her, having left her daydreaming for the companionship of the family. A moment later James appeared, followed by Grandfather and Mem and a whole lot of laughter. Papa knew it wasn't just the Island that Ari was talking about, and he was glad. It was going to make his news even that much sweeter.

43

IT WAS NEARLY noon when the family started heading toward the main beach. Uncle Tao and Kemala and the boys would arrive shortly, and there was just time enough to rinse off in the beachside shower and retrieve the smorgasbord of leftovers from the cooking pavilion. It wouldn't take long for Joey's family to close up their house for their return to the Mainland. It wasn't like closing up the Great House or anything. After all, Uncle Tao and Kemala spent every weekend on the Island, so they really only had a little tidying up to do.

Ari and Papa decided to take the long way back, veering off into one of the coral canyons that swept around a big outcropping of pastel yellow, pink and green, and lavender—the one that James said looked like a giant basket of Easter eggs.

When they reached the beach, Papa and Ari sprinted across the warm sands, water dripping from their hair and nose tips, just as Tommy and Joey appeared at the garden path carrying frosty pitchers of something lime green and one of Kemala's mango pies. "Mom and Dad are right behind us with the glasses," Joey called. His bare chest glistened from the humidity that coated his skin, and Ari noticed how it made the ins and outs of his muscles even more pronounced.

"I'll take that," she said, grabbing the pie from his left hand and setting it in the center of the blanket.

When she turned back toward him again, he grabbed her and hugged her affectionately. Her wet skin against his bare chest excited him, but he couldn't think about that now, not when everyone was around. "I've missed you this morning." he whispered in her ear.

A rustling from the garden path announced Kemala and Tao's arrival. "We're coming, we're coming!" Kemala sang as she bounced into sight waving glasses in both hands with Tao lumbering not far behind. They both had that day-after-Celebration look on their faces—energetic but a little sleepy around the eyes—and there was barely enough room on their faces for the big smiles they wore.

"This is as it should be," Grandfather said cheerfully when everyone had seated themselves around the blanket.

Kemala passed the glasses around. There was even a special one for James, with a thick heavy bottom that wouldn't tip over so easy. Mama poured something green into each one—even James's, though his came from the second pitcher. "What shall we drink to?" she asked when all drinks had been poured.

Kemala answered first. "How about to Celebrations, past and future," she said, pointing her glass toward Joey and Ari. They all raised their glasses and took a sip.

"I think we should drink to family. Old family and soon to be family," Mem said with a sweep of her glass toward the Ahmanjayas. "May we come together again like this, soon and often." Another sip taken.

"I've got the best one of all," Papa said. He raised up his glass and swept it around the blanket until he had passed it in front of everyone seated there. "To my new posting!"

Everyone just stared at him in silence. Ari waited for Mama to chastise him for bringing up Djakarta at a time like this, but she said nothing. She just sat there with an odd expression on her face. "Papa?" Ari ventured. "What's going on?"

"Yes, Papa, I don't get it," Emma added. "What are you up to?"

Mama giggled. "You better tell them, Ethan. They're all sitting down. They won't hurt themselves when they fall over."

"Tell us what?" several voices asked at once.

"That after Djakarta, I've decided to post myself right here."

"What!?" It was a communal shriek that could have been heard clear across the Island.

"What are you saying, old friend?" Tao wanted to know.

"I'm saying that after Djakarta, we're coming home for

good. No more globe-trotting." He wrapped his arm around Mary and waited for his news to sink in.

"But, Papa, what about San Francisco?" Ari asked. "You worked so hard to get that posting and now you're not even going to take it? I mean, how can you do that?"

"Oh, believe me, it's a lot easier to give away a coveted position than it is to get one."

"But what about Mr. Ramsey? You kind of created the San Francisco job. Isn't he going to be mad at you?"

"Well, Arthur is disappointed, of course, but not mad. The job was a good idea on its own merits, regardless of who fills it."

"Yes, but he can't be happy at losing you so suddenly."

"He's not losing me. Not just yet. I'm going to get Djakarta up and running for him just as I promised. And I won't leave until I have a replacement working at full speed. After that, I've promised him five years of making myself available periodically to train new management and set up the infrastructure for personnel who lack my experience and contacts. And I've already agreed to groom Matthews for my post in San Francisco."

"Wasn't he the man who took over for you when we left Hong Kong, Papa?" Emma asked.

"Yes. And in a way he started this whole thing. He called me just before we left for here to ask my advice. His wife has been terribly unhappy in Hong Kong. Her whole family lives in northern California, and she's been pressuring Mathews for some time now to ask for a reassignment to the States. Suddenly things just became so clear. I'd rather be in this part of the world. He'd rather be in that part of the world."

Ari still couldn't take it all in. "But, Papa," she said, "I thought you wanted the San Francisco posting so you could keep all of us together."

"I did. But that was before you and Emma decided you'd rather go to college here."

"What!"

"How . . . when . . . ?" That was all Emma could add.

Papa laughed. "Look, Mary, the Heywood girls are speechless! Hold the presses!"

"Papa," Emma tried again, "how did you know we were

looking to transfer here? I mean, we didn't know ourselves until a couple of days ago."

"To be honest, Emma, I had been thinking about this move for some time now. I thought I'd have to wait a few years before making it. You know, until you and Ari had graduated college. But when I saw you and Tommy at the beach party that first night, well, it occurred to me then that I might have to speed things up."

"But, Papa, I didn't even know then. You know, about wanting to transfer here or anything, really. How could you know?"

"For years, it's been my business to anticipate the needs of prospective clients before they even knew they had them. How hard could it be to anticipate the desires of my daughter? Besides, when I thought about it, what could be more practical? Why get your teaching degree halfway around the world from Tommy when you could get it right here, learning from the masters," he said with a sweeping gesture toward Grandfather and Mem. "And where you went, I knew Ari would want to go. So, I just watched and waited to see what would happen. And when you announced your intention to dance for Tommy that's when I put the wheels in motion. Not before talking it over with your mama, of course."

"You knew, Mama?" Ari asked.

"Not for sure. Not until last night."

"I wanted to tell Mama first, when we were alone."

Ari still couldn't take it all in. She looked up at Joey. He was staring back at her. His lips were slightly parted as if he were about to say something, but no sound came out. Ari never expected this and while it meant she could be with Joey much sooner than planned, it also meant giving up Berkeley and she just didn't know if she was ready to make that sacrifice so soon. Of course, she would follow her family back to the Island. That was a given, but she had hoped to be the one to make that decision herself. She needed more time to process Papa's announcement and figure it all out in her head.

44

IT WAS A tearful goodbye at the lagoon, but not a wholly sad one. Joey and Ari were spilling over with plans that now seemed not so far out of reach. One year. That's all they had to endure apart. Just Ari's freshman year at Berkeley. By summertime next year she would return for good. And there was still this summer together and Christmas and next Spring Break.

Most of the afternoon had been spent in deep discussion with Tommy and Emma. Plans made, tasks allocated, timetables set for Ari and Emma's transfer to Mainland University. They talked about sharing a house together just off campus. Tommy knew some boys who were graduating the Business School next year and would be vacating their bungalow on Grafton Square, a quiet park surrounded by historic houses. It was everyone's favorite address off-campus, and Tommy was first in line for the house. Of course, he'd have to tell a couple of his mates that they'd need to look for new housing, but he'd cross that bridge when he came to it.

When they weren't immersed in planning, they joined their families in an intergenerational feasting on food and drink and wild playfulness. There was a lot of chasing across the sand and playful tackling, diving with dolphins and wet bodies touching. The laughter was indistinguishable from that which echoed between the cliffs all those years ago when Mama and Kemala and Tao played here as children, and when they came here with their own children, watching them making tiny footprints in the sand. "It continues, doesn't it, Mem," Grandfather said, embracing her as he had since they, too, were very young.

"Yes," she smiled. "As it should."

Finally, it was time to say goodbye. Mama, Papa, Grandfather and Mem, and Tao and Kemala stood together some distance away, saying their own goodbyes and trying not to stare at the young couples. Of course, some tried harder than others. Ari and Joey had walked hand in hand down the beach to where a group of rocks would provide them some privacy to say goodbye.

"Are you sure you don't want me to come to the pier with you, Joey," Ari asked.

"That'll be too hard. I'd rather leave you here, Ari. At least that way I can pretend I'm just going back home to pick up a couple of things before coming back here again." She understood.

They wrapped themselves around each other and held on without speaking, he with his eyes open and memorizing every line of her body, and she with her eyes closed and doing the same. And then she watched him walk back down the garden path and disappear bits at a time beyond the layers of trees and shrubs and flowers that filled the back gardens. She had a vague sense of Emma somewhere to her right doing the same. She didn't need to see her to know she was there. She could feel her. That's how it had always been between them.

45

ARI ENTERED THE cooking pavilion just in time to see Mem closing the lid of the little woven reed basket, but she already knew what was inside. It was always the same when the four of them went up to the Sunset Bench. Mama carried the snacks, Grandfather the wine, Papa the flashlights for the return trip down the Cliffside path. And Mem, she carried her grandmother's basket containing four cobalt blue goblets—the ones she said took their color from the night sky over the Island. They were her favorite goblets, sparkling and flawless and very, very old. The only ones, she said, worthy of celebrating the sunset.

Mama appeared a few moments later wearing a fresh jade green sarong and creamy silk cropped shirt that made her eyes look even greener than normal. Her hair was wet and combed through with botanical oils and her Bird of Paradise comb was securely fastened behind her left ear. The glow on her skin and the subtle sweet fragrance that surrounded her reminded Ari that she needed to put an extra bottle of the jasmine-scented lotion into her own suitcase tonight. She no longer used the lotions made from the Tantu Orchid that grew in the shadows of the Pashmari Falls. They had been an adolescent attempt at establishing her own identity. It was Mama's jasmine that suited her best, and she was comfortable enough in her own skin now to imitate or diverge as personal style dictated.

"I looked for James in his quarters," Mama said, "but he wasn't there. Do you know where he's gotten to, Ari?"

"Yes, Mama," she replied. "He talked Emma into taking him to the lagoon for one last swim on the reef."

"I'm surprised he didn't get you to go," she smiled.

Ari returned her smile. "Well, I might join them. I don't know. Or maybe I'll just start packing or something." As she said this, her smile dissolved into an expression Mama knew well. A little sad, a little empty. It was the same expression she always wore when her time on the Island was coming to an end. Except that this time there was something more.

Mama came over to where Ari was standing and gently wrapped her arms around her. "You miss him already, don't you," she said. "But that's not all, is it?"

"I know I shouldn't feel this way . . .with Papa's news and all. I'm really excited, honest I am. Still . . . I feel like . . ."

"Never apologize for the way you feel, Ari. It's natural to have conflicting feelings, even if the change is a positive one that you want. It's not what you expected, and this is a totally normal reaction. No one ever knows what the future will hold. Life would be pretty boring if we did. I want you to know something though. If you want to go to Berkeley, Papa and I will fully support it. We'll miss you terribly, but we'd never be happy knowing you gave up something important to you."

"I don't want to be that far from you all, Mama. And I want to be with Joey. I guess I'm just surprised." Mama squeezed her hand, a look of understanding on her face.

"You've been gifted with the ability to choose your own path, Ari. This is one of those moments where opportunities are presented, but only you can choose how your story will be written. I wish I could tell you what to do, believe me it would make my job as your mama a lot easier. But only you can determine your path forward." She paused. "Why don't you go for a swim, Ari? The packing can wait," she suggested.

"I think I will," she said and headed off to the beach.

Ari had already been floating aimlessly in the lagoon for several minutes by the time her parents and grandparents appeared on the beach. She watched them from the water, as she often had, making their way across the sands in quiet procession—first Grandfather, then Mem, then Mama, and finally Papa. And she continued watching them, snaking in and out of view among the tall palms and wild impatiens that populated the craggy cliffs until she lost sight of them altogether. But this time she didn't close her eyes and continue floating in the cool, greeny-blue waters. Nor did she roll over and dive down to the peace and solitude of the coral jungle beneath her. Instead, she left the water and dashed across the sand to where she had dropped her towel and sarong. She didn't bother to dry off. She just grabbed the sarong, fitted it around her hips on the fly and headed for the path that would take her to the Bench. She didn't know why she did this any more than she knew why Grandfather and Mem and Mama and Papa went to the Bench every day. She only knew that something called them there—something primal, powerful, and impossible to ignore. And now, it seemed, it was calling her too.

"Where are you going, Ari?" Emma called from somewhere behind her.

Ari stopped abruptly and whirled around. How strange, she thought. She had forgotten that Emma and James were there. "I'm going up to the Bench," she called back.

Emma came out of the water from where she and James had been belly-crawling after little wiggly creatures in the shallows and ran over to where Ari stood. "You're going to the Bench?" she repeated. "How come?"

"I don't know," Ari answered honestly. "I just want to go."

Emma grabbed a long, sea-soaked lock of hair that had fallen across her face and tossed it back over her shoulder, sending a cool spray over Ari as she did so. "Sorry," she said, and added, "Do you mind if I come, too?"

"Of course not, but what about James?" She pointed at him trudging across the sand to see what he was missing.

"Oh!"

"Where ya goin? I wanna go, too!" he shouted, his little legs churning through the sand as fast as he could move them. Ari and Emma looked at each other and waited for James's breathless arrival.

"James," Ari began, "I'm going up to the Sunset Bench. It's an awfully hard climb, even for a big boy like you."

"I can do it, Ari. Honest I can. Please! Please!" It was almost a plaintive cry. Maybe, in his own way, James was being called by the Bench, too. And Emma. Maybe they were all meant to be at the Bench together today.

Ari didn't know what to do. It was selfish to leave Emma and James behind, but she was so anxious to be on her way. Emma understood and rescued her. "Why don't you go on ahead, Ari, and James and I will follow you up. We need to put Tippy in James's quarters before we go." They all glanced over at the puppy who was sniffing behind a baby sea turtle on its way back to the water.

Ari would always remember how they looked that day when she arrived at the Bench, as she stepped through the grove of broad-leafed banana trees that grew to the north and a little forward of the Bench. It was a memory she knew even then that would surface and resurface at random times in her life, but most definitely it would be there on the last day of her life. She didn't know how she knew this, and she didn't care. She was just glad that the memory would stay with her forever.

The eastern sky was already graying behind them, but the sepia light radiating out from the setting sun illuminated their faces and bathed them all in a warm golden mist. She raised her hand in front of her face and saw that the mist surrounded her too. She wasn't surprised. She had felt it the instant she came on to the plateau. And now she knew why they came to this hallowed place every night. Just as surely as she knew that, from this day forward, she would come here each evening she was on the Island.

Ari smiled remembering all the wild goings-on she had conjured up in her imagination when she was young. How disappointed she would have been then to find them like this—arranged in familiar poses, just quietly sharing a moment in time with no apparent purpose.

"Ari," Mama called to her, "I've been waiting for you." There was no surprise in her tone. But Ari was a little surprised when Mama pulled a fifth goblet from the little basket, filled it half-full with wine, topped it off with ice cubes and extended it toward her.

"How did you know I'd be coming?" she asked.

"It was your time," Mama replied, and Mem added, "I think

you better set aside a few of those cheesy puffs. I don't imagine Emma and James will be far behind."

Mem was right. About twenty minutes later James burst through the banana trees and tumbled onto the grassy opening in front of the Bench, and he continued to tumble and roll and turn half summersaults all the way to where Ari sat in the deep grass at Papa's feet. Then he crawled up Ari's outstretched legs and onto her lap and, drawing her arms around him in a comforting embrace, announced, "Cheesy puffs, please!" Everyone laughed.

It was a particularly magnificent sunset, one of those where the little fluffs of clouds were perfectly placed to create a whole palette of warm colors. Ari stared at it for a while, saying nothing, periodically lifting to her lips the goblet whose wine had turned to a pale pink from the numerous ice cubes that clinked against the glass. She waited until a question had fully formed itself inside her head, and then she asked. "Grandfather, how did you and Mem know to come here for the sunsets? I mean, there are so many other places you could have gone. What made you climb up here the first time?" She couldn't see his face from where she sat without turning around, but she knew he was smiling. He had just been invited to expound.

"We come here, child, because this place is sacred to us. It is the exact spot our people first set foot on this Island."

Ari began to giggle. "What did we do, Grandfather, drop out of the sky or something?"

"Something like that," he replied. He wasn't laughing. "This is where Jhoti and Saramem, the Father and Mother of our people, first stood and looked out over the mountains and valleys and oceans, and where they watched their first sunset. The Gods brought them here in hopes that they would see the promise of this place and want to live here."

Ari didn't want this night to end. No one did. Not even James who had settled peacefully onto her lap and was content to remain there for as long as she could bear the weight of him. When the last of the sun had disappeared behind the horizon, Papa lit the torches that were scattered about the plateau, and the whole family joined Ari and Emma and James in the grass. They talked for hours about the weeks they had just spent together, and how it seemed like just yesterday that Mem came running down the pier to greet Uncle Tao's boat, and how romantic the beach party had been for everyone (except James who wanted to know what *Roman tics* were). Ari and Emma talked about Mr. Gupta's prize Arabians, and Mama said how much she and Papa had enjoyed riding them that day they slipped away to the Pashmari Falls. Ari and Emma exchanged knowing glances but didn't say anything. And, of course, they spoke about Celebration and how everything had changed for all of them that night. But it had changed especially for Emma and even for Ari. They were no longer the same girls who had kicked off their shoes and stepped barefoot onto the Island only two weeks ago.

They talked about Papa's news, and how wonderful it was going to be to come home for good, to raise James in the bosom of his people, and for Emma and Ari to be so close by. Mem began to cry a little and Grandfather called her a silly old woman, but when his face briefly turned toward one of the nearby torches, Ari saw the moistness in his eyes as well.

Mama turned toward Papa to say something, but when she did, Ari knew that she was really speaking to everyone. "I'm not sorry, Ethan, for all the years and all the distant postings. How could I be? It would have meant no bottles on the mantelpiece or Christmas Carols in all those languages."

"Or Bellinis after midnight," he offered.

"That too," she purred, and then continued. "Or rickety old trains to Khatmandu or little attic bedrooms in London townhouses or polished marble floors in Paris apartments where our girls played Ice Capades in their stocking feet. Remember?" She paused to brush his cheek with her fingertips. "And James never would have seen the big ships steaming into Hong Kong harbor from the house on the hill." She turned toward Ari. "Remember how he used to make you pick him up and hold him in front of the telescope on the portico?"

"And he kept closing the wrong eye all the time and thought the telescope was broken," Ari laughed.

The talking and the laughing and the remembering went

on like that until no one could hold off tomorrow any longer. As they were gathering themselves together for the return trip down the Cliffside path, Ari took one last look at the breathtaking view that stretched out before her. Moonbeams on the rippling waters, silhouettes of jagged mountains against star-filled skies and little twinkling lights that peeked out from the houses hidden among the palm groves where she knew that other families had gathered together to share the stories of their own days. Mama came and stood beside her and together they took in the view. Mama sighed. "It is Paradise, isn't it, Arianna."

Ari turned and looked toward the family who were already heading in the direction of the banana trees—and James's sweet, innocent face resting on Papa's broad shoulder, Grandfather and Mem nattering away about the family's return this summer, and Emma, her sister, her friend, her opposite end of the same circle, who would always be there for all the important moments in her life. And then she looked back at Mama, the one who had opened the door to the world of women and let her peek in.

"I love you, Mama."

"I love you too, Arianna." And with one last look at the view, both Heywood women walked back, hand-in-hand, to the Great House to begin readying themselves to rejoin the hustle and bustle of the real world.

Part Three

Djakarta

46

ARI FELT IT the moment she entered the terminal building. There was something, something not quite right. Like a movie director had tried to create an airport scene but had gotten the elements wrong. There were too many people for the size of the building but too little sound for the number of people. There were none of the usual background noises. No conversations overlapping one another. No laughter or calling after children. And there were no smiles even when families and friends reunited. There was just a crush of people in constant motion, eyes averted, trying to escape a public place as quickly as possible before someone noticed them.

At least that's how it seemed to Ari as she stood in the middle of the Customs Hall, scanning the perimeter for the one face that would make her feel better. But then she remembered what Mama had said when they were packing up to come to Djakarta. *We must make the best of things for Papa's sake. He's already got enough on his mind.*

Well, maybe she was making more of things than were really there. After all, it wasn't like there was anything really horrible going on. In fact, the airport was rather orderly—peaceful even. Just the way Papa had described things in his letters and phone calls. And even Mrs. Dhani, the high school librarian, had said that the troubles of 1965 were long over. And she should know; she was born in Indonesia and still had family there.

She glanced down at James who was standing close beside her, clutching her hand so tightly that his fingertips had turned deep purple. He looked so tiny and vulnerable down there. The Djakarta airport was intimidating enough at eye-level, but at knee-level it had to be frightening. "Would you like me to hold you, James?"

He let go of Ari's hand and raised both arms toward her in silent reply. She handed her duffel bag to Emma and swooped him up. "I won't let anything bad happen to you, James," she said, holding him especially close to her.

"Promise, Ari?"

"I promise," she replied. And she meant it. She really did.

Papa appeared shortly looking like a familiar, cherished landmark on alien terrain. He stood tall among the crowds of travelers scurrying for the exits and incongruously relaxed. He was dressed in a pair of pleated linen trousers, which were a shade darker than the light khaki linen shirt he wore open at the throat, and Ari was sure that meant he had no intention of going to the office today. She was glad for that. This separation had set the whole family adrift in uncharted waters, and she wasn't going to feel comfortable again until they had re-established the natural rhythms of their comings and goings in their new home.

"Ethan!" Mama called exuberantly across the space that still separated them. A nearby soldier looked in her direction but made no move to leave the wall he was leaning against.

"Mary!" he called out and waved back.

In seconds they were all huddled together, hugging one another, and exchanging greetings. When it was Ari's turn to hug Papa, she closed her eyes and caught the faintest whiff of his scent—bay rum and cognac-scented tobacco—and she felt the apprehension that had surrounded her for several weeks now just melt away.

"So, college girl," he said to her, "how does it feel to be all grown up?"

"I just graduated Thursday, Papa," she laughed. "I haven't exactly had a chance to feel anything yet."

"Well, you better get with it, Ari, because in exactly twenty days and," he said, looking at his watch and calculating, "five and a half hours you will officially be eighteen!"

"Well, Ethan," Mama chimed in, "we better get home so we can start on the party plans. You know how Ari likes to drag out her birthday over several days!"

The ride from the airport to the Menteng District where their house was located took them through urban scenery that was surprisingly familiar—a hodgepodge of European colonial architecture with ancient Asian detail, some ancient Asian architecture with European colonial detail, and a smattering of gray, nondescript contemporary public structures—hotels and offices and government buildings mostly—which were large and out of scale with their predecessors and which were meant as proof somehow that the country had entered into the twentieth century. Of course, there was a strong Dutch influence from centuries of colonization (or imperialism, depending upon the point of view) when Djakarta was known to the rest of the world as Batavia.

On the way, they sped past a district of fetid canals and shanty houses built of whatever scraps and refuse the rest of society had discarded. There were women there, kneeling in the mud, some with babies tied to their backs, trying to wash the dirt from their family's meager clothing, children chasing barefoot with sticks and balls, and teenaged boys standing around with apparently nothing more to do than contemplate the fact that, just like their houses, they too were considered the scraps and refuse of Djakartan society. "I guess for some people it just doesn't matter whose government is in power," Ari murmured, her face pressed against the window glass.

Mama was sitting next to her on the big back seat of the company limo. She had been noticeably quiet until now. "We are very lucky, Ari. We have so many opportunities to be happy," she observed. "This would be a good time to remember that."

The Menteng District was just as Papa had described it—an exclusive enclave of Indo-European bungalows with manicured lawns and exquisite gardens. The district had been built by the Dutch Colonial Government in the 1920's and then, as now, it was the preferred address of bureaucrats, diplomats, and the "cream" of Djakartan society. There were parks for the children to play in and avenues of towering, ancient shade trees, and private clubs, trendy cafes, and street vendors on nearly every corner selling Nasi Gila, the traditional fried rice dish of chicken, sausage, and eggs. Ari guessed that not much had changed in this neighborhood since the glory days of the Dutch East India Company. Apparently, changes in government affected the very rich about as much as they affected the very poor. It wasn't fair really, and that made Ari feel a little guilty, especially at how relieved she felt to be entering the Menteng and leaving the shanty town far behind.

Somewhere well inside the confines of the district, the car turned down a particularly beautiful avenue, quiet and sun-dappled under a canopy of giant acacia trees. It was lined on either side by long, winding driveways leading to large houses, pieces of which were visible over walls and through gates and beyond lush gardens constantly tended by an army of native workmen.

"Here we are," Papa said, as the driver pulled through the gates and up the fourth driveway on the left. Ari quickly rolled down the window and craned her neck sideways and watched the house come into view.

It was a beautiful house, long and single-storied, gleaming white in the sunshine, and looking especially clean and bright against the brilliant greens of the surrounding trees and sloping, manicured lawns. It was built of brick and rich clay tiles instead of the native woods of traditional Javanese architecture but with the Indonesian signature of a joglo roof—the high, flat-topped double roof, which sloped down and extended far past the outer walls to create deep, covered columned verandas encircling the house. Walls of mahogany French doors warmed the masonry and caught the cross breezes, which was fortunate because Ari doubted that ceiling fans alone could keep the house cool in the Djakarta climate, which would be humid even now in the dry season. And everywhere there was porcelain and tile—tributes to the history of Dutch rule in the region. Inlaid tile verandas, and intricately painted pots under palms, and a large plaque next to the double entry doors that held a hand-painted welcome repeated in three languages. Ari suspected that they were only a preview of the blue and white Delft tiled walls she was likely to find inside in the kitchen and baths.

A staff of servants came with the house. Mama wasn't particularly pleased about that. Not that she didn't need people to care for the house if she was going to spend time with the children and get her writing done and do the kind of entertaining that would be expected of the wife of an important American businessman. But this was different than hiring Mrs. Nari who ran her own cleaning business from the Island. These people weren't thought of as providing a service. They were servants. That never sat well with Mama or any of the family really. But it was a concession she'd have to live with. In the current business climate in Djakarta, the appearance of wealth and power had to be maintained to open the necessary doors. "Besides," Papa had said to her, "if we don't hire them, they'll be even worse off than they are now. But I've already told Arthur that we'll be paying them an American wage, just as we've done before."

"You're a good man, Ethan," Mama had said, knowing where the American wage really came from. "And maybe, at least for the nine months you'll be here, the staff will have the chance to be treated with the respect they deserve. But I can't promise I won't do a little clandestine dusting when the neighbors aren't watching!"

Ari knew the minute she entered the house that it had originally been built for a diplomat of some sort. The size of the reception hall gave it away. It was no mere foyer, but a large room tailor-made for receiving lines and a discreet group of white-gloved servants waiting to take coats and offer champagne from perfectly polished silver trays. For now, though, there was a line of just six people waiting to welcome Mr. Heywood's family home, and they were all hoping that they would be as kind and gracious as the master of the house.

"Everyone," Papa began, "this is my family." He put his arm gently around Mary's shoulders. "This is my wife, Mrs. Heywood."

"How do you do?" she smiled.

"And these are my children," Papa continued. Pointing to each one in turn he said, "This is my oldest daughter, Emma. And this is my youngest, Arianna. And that rumpled bundle in her arms is my son, James."

"How do you do?" the girls repeated Mama's courtesy.

Then Papa introduced the staff to the family, and they

shook hands one by one. Mama smiled and made eye contact with each one—something invisible people in a society are not always used to, and they responded warmly, as people always did to Mama. There were the two young women in their early twenties, Arina and Suti. They were the housekeepers. And then there was Mrs. Rukmana. She was the cook and wife of Mr. Rukmana, Papa's driver. They were an older couple, with grown children living in Singapore. They lived in an apartment over the garage. The last two men were brothers, Tono and Parjo (Joe for short), and they kept the grounds and did light repair work and maintenance on the house. Ari guessed that they were in their mid-thirties. Both wore wedding bands, as did Arina but not Suti, and both were short and stocky and strongly built.

When the introductions were completed, Papa thanked everyone and they dispersed, all except Mr. Rukmana who waited discreetly a few steps behind him. Ari gave James to Papa and bent down to retrieve her suitcase, but Mr. Rukmana stepped in. "I take that for you, Miss," he said softly, with a voice that was only slightly admonishing.

"Thank you," Ari smiled. It was going to take some getting used to again—the rules of class etiquette.

While Mr. Rukmana dispatched all the suitcases to their proper quarters, Papa took the family on a brief tour of the house. It was surprisingly light and bright, and every room opened out onto the gardens. Off the reception hall to the left was a huge company dining room meant more for holding court than just lingering over a meal. To the right was a typically furnished parlor with a grouping of sofas in soft shades of salmon and pillows that matched the chintz-covered chairs, all surrounding the ever-present fireplace, which natives in this part of the world found so amusing. Off to one end was a magnificent grand piano, which immediately caught Emma's eye, and to the other a bridge table around which Ari was sure that some double-chinned, bejeweled matrons had often sat, bidding four spades much to the dismay of their partners. As with the rest of the house, the walls and ceilings were china white and heavily molded, the floors were highly polished mahogany, and the outer walls were almost exclusively made up of an endless series of French doors. And, of course, there were turkish rugs and potted palms and gilt-framed oil paintings, mostly Dutch, scattered throughout the room.

On past the doors of a paneled office, they came to a long room that ran perpendicular along the back of the house. It was sparsely furnished and was obviously meant to serve as a ballroom. Down a hall to the left was a writing room meant for ladies and their endless stream of correspondences. Next was the morning room that looked out over a pond in the back garden and was where the family would take most of their meals. And that led to the kitchens where Ari just caught a glimpse of the Delft tiled wall through the crack in the door Papa held open.

On the other side of the ballroom was the bedroom wing. A pair of heavy carved doors separated it from the rest of the house. They were open now, but Ari noticed that they were equipped with dead bolts, the vestiges of more violent times. Down a short hallway, past two ample guest bedrooms and baths, was a second set of carved doors (also with deadbolts) leading to a perpendicular hallway and six more bedrooms. A turn to the right led to the nursery and the connecting bedrooms and baths that traditionally housed the younger children and their nanny. To the left were two large bedrooms and adjoining baths with identical décor and, beyond them, the master suite. Mama was amused to see that the master suite contained two bedrooms on either side of an adjoining door, a concession to an antiquated notion of civility, which made it all right for a husband and wife to have sex as long as they pretended not to. She wasn't as amused by the wrought iron gates bordering every pair of French doors in the bedroom wing to be closed and locked tight each night to keep out any predators who might be lurking in the darkness.

Ethan knew what Mary was thinking. He always knew. "It will be all right, Mary."

She looked up at him and smiled. "You promise?" she asked.

"I promise," he replied. Papa meant it when he said it. He really did.

47

"SO, WHAT'S ON everyone's agenda today?" Papa asked one morning as the family sat around the table in the morning room taking breakfast.

Mama answered first. "Arina very kindly offered to bring her little boy to work with her today so that James would have someone to play with and that means I can accompany the girls to the Club for a swim." Mama had wanted to bring the boys to the Club, too, but Arina had made some excuse about Beni just having recovered from an ear infection. Perhaps it was too much to expect that the mostly-expatriate Club members would accept the housekeeper's son in their pool. Not all that long ago they wouldn't have accepted Mama either. Or maybe Arina just didn't want to expose her son to a life he could never have. Mama didn't know, but it was obvious from the outset that Arina was uncomfortable with the idea of Beni going anywhere near the Club so Mama settled for what she hoped would be just the first of a continuous series of play dates behind garden walls.

"May I be excused, Mama?" James asked, using the manners he had been practicing for weeks before coming to Djakarta. He wasn't looking at Mama when he said this though. His eyes were firmly fixed on the matching red bikes that had magically appeared on the back veranda overnight.

"Yes, James. Take your dishes to the kitchen on your way please."

"Okay," he answered and hurried away carrying his breakfast dishes.

Mama and Arina shot a quick glance toward one another and shared a brief *Mommy moment* before returning to their assigned roles. "I take good care of them, ma'am," the house-keeper assured her.

"Thank you, Arina. I'm so looking forward to this afternoon."

Papa turned to the girls. "Will the Pembrokes be there today?" he asked.

"*William* will be there!" Emma exclaimed in an exaggerated voice.

Ari ignored her. "William called and said that he and Martin will be there with their mom by lunchtime." William was the younger of the two Pembroke brothers by three years. He was two years younger than Ari and had a huge crush on her. He was always trying to show off for her in the pool, which was kind of comical considering his pale English skin and still gawky physique. But he was awfully nice, and Ari didn't want to hurt his feelings. So when he asked her to go with him to a Club dance, she told him that she wasn't free to accept because she had a boyfriend, but that they could meet up there and she would be sure to save him some dances, especially the last one. That seemed to satisfy him.

"You've been seeing a lot of Miles' boys. I'm glad," Papa said. "It's nice to see familiar faces, isn't it?" Ari wasn't sure if Papa was talking about William and Martin or Mr. and Mrs. Pembroke. She imagined it could get pretty lonely for him too if there were no old friends in new postings.

The Club was quintessential European Colonial. Heavy white columns surrounding "miles and miles" of covered veran-das, polished wood, potted palms, and a lot of smartly uniformed natives serving a lot of gin and limes to mostly pale-skinned for-eigners with a handful of Indonesian elite sprinkled throughout. It could have been the stage set for a movie. "I half expect to see Sean Connery sitting by the pool, ordering a martini—shaken, not stirred," Emma had joked the first time they entered.

"Well, I guess I'm showing my age," Mama had replied. "I was expecting Ronald Coleman!"

The Club was not far from the house. It sat just inside the perimeter of the Menteng. Certainly, if they were in America, Mama and the girls would have walked. But Mr. Rukmana had insisted on driving them. Ari didn't know if it was for their safety or if he considered it inappropriate for ladies of his household to be seen unattended by servants, but they agreed to the ride, and Mr. Rukmana seemed relieved.

It was almost eleven thirty by the time Mama and the girls reached the Club, and the day was already sticky. Two uniformed doormen in red caps and a lot of shiny brass buttons quickly ushered them inside. "Thank you, Ali. Thank you, Hari," they all said, and their smiles were warmly received. They continued down a wide central hall whose walls were lined with black and white photographs of past members and trophy-toting polo players and bare-legged tennis champions. There was a bar on the right and a genteel looking salon on the left and Ari was sure that, unlike today, the former had originally been designated *men only*.

At the far end of the hall were two large glass doors through which the pool, lawns, and dozens of bright blue, white, and yellow striped umbrellas were easily visible. Sophie Pembroke was already waiting on the other side. "Hello," she called from underneath a large umbrella and an equally large straw hat. She was waving discreetly with one hand, like Queen Elizabeth, just quarter turns of the wrist, and holding a tall gin and lime with the other. Unlike most Brits, she took ice in her drink, at least when her husband was posted to the tropics.

There was something really attractive about Sophie Pembroke even though she wasn't particularly beautiful. She had pale skin, slightly freckled from the tropical sun, and hazel eyes that were soft and welcoming. She had a short, soft figure that was just a few pounds overweight in some places. Her chestnut hair was wavy to the nape of her neck, and it always looked as if she had just stepped out of the beauty parlor. Ari suspected that even today, if she suddenly untied the apricot chiffon streamers that held her hat to her head and tossed it away, she still wouldn't have a hair out of place. With her matching apricot suit and ribbon-trimmed terry robe and freshly manicured toes and fingers, Mrs. Pembroke looked exactly as Mama always described her—a perfectly turned-out English gentlewoman. But that description belied the woman who hid beneath the years of proper upbringing. Sophie Pembroke knew how to have fun!

No sooner had Mama and the girls sat down than a man with graying hair and dark skin arrived to take their drink order. "How kind you are, Mr. Jata, to take such good care of us," Mama greeted him. "And does this day find your wife and children well?" This last courtesy she spoke in his native Bahasa.

He answered her in English. "Very well, ma'am. Thank you for asking."

Ari watched him walk away. He neither hurried nor dawdled. His walk was upright and dignified and not even that snob, Mrs. Wilmead, who represented everything native Indonesians hated about westerners, would patronize him.

Sophie's voice returned Ari's attention to the table. "So, have you heard?" she began in a lowered tone. "That pompous ass, Wilmead, has been sent down."

"What!" Ari exclaimed with Mama.

"Oh, sorry," Ari said. "It's just that I was thinking about Mrs. Wilmead when you said that. You must have been reading my mind."

"I've been dying to tell someone," Sophie continued with an air of enjoyment.

"Sent down," Mama repeated. "You make it sound like he's been expelled from school."

"To an Englishman of his class, it's just as bad," she laughed. Ari loved that laugh. It wasn't forced or contained. It just seemed to flow out of her like a melody.

"What happened?" Mama wanted to know.

"No one is saying. There's just a collective sigh of relief at the company. Wilmead was senior, you know. As far as Djakarta was concerned, he represented us all, didn't he?"

"Will this mean a promotion for Miles?"

"We're hoping. Though that would mean a longer stay here, and I don't know how I feel about that. There's something that's just not quite right about this place."

Ari and Emma had been sitting quietly, listening to the conversation while they applied Coppertone to their skin. They had taken off the cotton kaftans they wore as cover-ups, exposing their one-piece Oleg Cassini bathing suits, pink for Ari and a soft shade of turquoise for Emma. Mama's was black. The suits were identical, except for the color—scoop-necked and low-backed with just enough coverage to be considered proper. There would be no bikinis here, not in this heavily religious country. Not even for the privacy of sunbathing behind garden walls. When Ari heard Mrs. Pembroke's comment, she leaned over toward Emma and whispered. "See, it's not just me who feels like that." Emma simply nodded in reply.

Ever since that first day in the airport, Ari had had this vague feeling that something here was, well, like Mrs. Pembroke said, *not quite right*. Everything seemed peaceful and polite on the surface, but she had this feeling that everyone was just playing the roles that were expected of them. Like when Mrs. Wilmead suddenly tried to befriend Mama at the Club last week, rudely turning her back on Mrs. Pembroke, the wife of a subordinate, when she asked Mama to tea. Obviously, Papa's position in the business community here was important enough even to elevate Mama to the A-list, at least temporarily. Mama had politely answered that she would check her social calendar and ring her in the morning. She wanted to check with Papa first to see if she had to go.

And then there were the odd looks that sometimes greeted the simplest courtesies. They were hard to describe. They were so subtle and fleeting, lurking just behind the eyes, a mixture of surprise and appreciation, of mistrust, and even resentment sometimes. But that last was only a couple of times and only from strangers they met in shops or restaurants who didn't know them. She knew that Mrs. Rukmana had come to genuinely like the family. And Arina and Suti too. She didn't know about the men yet. They were more guarded.

It's not like she hadn't seen those looks before in other countries where East and West came together. But this wasn't just about East vs. West. Within the East itself there were so many factions that didn't seem to respect each other. There were Communists (who were less visible for now) and Christians and Buddhists and Muslims and Hindus and all those sub-cultures from the different islands. Then there were the competing political factions and the foreign nations who manipulated from the shadows to put their favorites in power. And periodically they all crashed into one another and violence erupted like it did in 1965. It was all so confusing and uncertain. Maybe that was it. Maybe she was just afraid that some little thing might ignite the violence again.

Ari wasn't hearing the conversation around the table anymore. Mama and Emma were intently listening to Mrs. Pembroke's good-natured stream of local gossip, and Mama was teasing her about being able to take the English girl out of the village but not the village gossip out of the English girl. Ari was just staring through the forest of umbrellas, past the sparkling blue-tiled pool to a path on the other side that led from the back door of the kitchens to a small gate in the exterior wall. She was watching an employee walk down the path pushing a large refuse bin on wheels. When he got to the gate, he opened it and went on through to the alley, turned left and disappeared. The gate remained open until he returned.

Ari couldn't take her eyes from that dirty, dank foreign world that lurked just beyond the luxurious confines of the Club. It wasn't the dilapidated building with the piles of old rusty corrugated tin piled high behind it that captured her attention. It was the children who gathered there, waiting for a Club employee to appear so they could follow him down the alley to the refuse bins and go through the garbage for whatever meager leftovers might serve as a feast at their tables. And suddenly Ari understood what really had been bothering her all this time. It was the almost brazen display of poverty in Djakarta within inches of the wealthy who didn't seem to even notice, much less care.

She remembered that first day driving in from the airport. How from one single viewpoint she could see fancy cars and modern hotel buildings and horrific slums all at the same time without even having to turn her head. It was just like now, looking past the gin and limes and half-eaten fancy sandwiches, past sunbathers and swimmers and the four elderly ladies who played bridge in the shade of the big tamarind tree every day, past the manicured people and equally manicured gardens to those hungry and tattered children who were just trying to survive. It was more than the poor being invisible to the rich. It was almost like the rich were flaunting their wealth to the poor as a continual reminder of their own superiority.

Ari wondered if the poor people here were thinking the same thing she was. It would have to make them awfully angry if they did. In America poor people were kept kind of hidden away for the most part, in segregated neighborhoods or isolated sharecroppers' shacks in the rural south. Americans could pretend that everyone had an equal opportunity to succeed given the *proper attitude*. But here it was like the wealthy openly disregarded the poor. Ari wasn't sure which was worse.

48

IT WAS WILLIAM Pembroke who brought Ari out of her thoughts. He and his brother returned to the table from the pool dripping wet. Standing just behind her, William proceeded to shake himself out like an old shaggy dog that had just had a bath, splattering Ari's bare back where her single braid failed to cover. "William!" she squealed, louder than she had wished. "That's cold!"

"Oh, sorry," he lied and slumped down into the empty chair next to her.

Mr. Jata arrived just then with the drink order and a plate of assorted sandwiches. He set the plate in the center of the table and deftly twirled it until the *special* sandwiches, the ones that still had their crusts on, were facing Ari.

Mama took one of the quarter-cut sandwiches and slowly bit into it and waited for Sophie to resume gossiping (or *sharing vital information*, as she preferred to call it), but her friend changed course. "You must tell me what you've been up to the last couple of days, Mary. We haven't seen you and the children here since Monday."

"I know, Sophie. I should have phoned, but it was all so sudden. Ethan was called into meetings of some sort. So, he told Mr. Rukmana that he wouldn't be needing him during the day, and Mr. Rukmana offered to take the family around Djakarta to see the sites. He's taken us to some wonderful places."

"Where did you go, Ari?" William asked.

"Oh, we've been all sorts of places. Mr. Rukmana took us through the Kota, Old Batavi, and—"

"Did you see Sunda Kelapa?" he interrupted enthusiastically. "That's my favorite." Sunda Kelapa was the port where dozens of

377

tall-masted wooden schooners arrived each day to deposit trade goods from the outer islands and refill their holds with Javanese goods. William had a model of one of them among his collection of sailing ships in his room. "I don't know how those men run up and down those skinny, wobbly boards all day without falling in the water," he said. "Especially balancing all that heavy stuff they carry."

"It really is like watching a circus tightrope act, isn't it?" Mrs. Pembroke added.

"It is, Mrs. Pembroke," Ari replied. "Maybe that's why James liked it so much there. That plus he's always been fascinated by big ships, especially the old-fashioned kind like those."

"Oh, James went with you on your excursions, Mary?"

"He did, and he was really quite well-behaved. He so wanted to come with us wherever we went. I think he's missing his puppy terribly. We had to drop Tippy off at the Island on the way here. No sense trying to bring a dog here for only three weeks."

"Well, it was a good choice going to Sunda Kelapa. Those big ships, all stacked up there the way they are, they're pretty awe-inspiring even for an adult."

"I think that was Mr. Rukmana's intention in taking us there. He knew it would keep James's attention. In fact, when we got there, he offered to hold James's hand and walk with him up and down the pier to give the girls and me a chance to spend a little uninterrupted time together. He was so sweet. I watched the two of them strolling together, stopping every once in a while to talk to one of the sailors. I think maybe Mr. Rukmana used to take his own son there on outings when he was a little boy. He seemed to be enjoying himself as much as James was."

"And where is our little cyclone today?"

"He's playing at home with the son of one of our housemaids. When we left them, they were racing their bikes around the perimeter garden path like they were in the Monte Carlo. I expect to come home to numerous skinned knees and elbows."

Martin laughed, "I don't think William or I spent a day of our childhoods without bandages on. Mother says they were part of our wardrobe."

The afternoon continued on like that. Laughing and joking and gossiping as privileged families had done under the striped umbrellas for decades. Periodically they all took laps in the pool to wash off the heat, and when even the shade of the umbrella got too close, Ari and Emma moved to the shallow end of the pool and stood in the water and hung their elbows over the sides, waiting for William and Martin's inevitable sneak attack at their ankles. Ari and Emma liked being with William and Martin. They were proper English boys with enough Carnaby Street thrown in to be fun. And there were no romantic complications, not even from William, to make things awkward. They were just four friends, familiar faces from London where they had known each other as children, all card-carrying members of the gypsy life—something no outsiders would ever understand. Even though they hadn't seen each other for almost six years (except for that one week a few years back when the Pembrokes breezed into Hong Kong), that gypsy life bonded them to one another and made coming to Djakarta far better than it might have been.

After a while Ari forgot about the ugly world that sat just beyond the gate in the back wall. And she forgot about the children whose days were spent combing the garbage for their survival. She made plans with the others to go to the next dance together and to spend the afternoon tomorrow listening to albums on the boys' portable record player. When William and Martin said they would come over to Ari and Emma's after lunch, she quickly suggested that they go to the boys' house instead. It was just two blocks away and well inside the Menteng and the only place that even Mr. Rukmana said was okay for the girls to walk to by themselves. It was nice to have at least one thing about Djakarta that was just simple and comfortable.

49

PAPA WAS ALREADY home when Mama and the girls returned from the Club. He had obviously been home for some while. He was sitting on the back veranda in one of the big rattan loungers just outside the morning room. There was a platter of sliced mangoes on the wrought iron side table next to him and a half-drunk gin and tonic next to that, and an alabaster ashtray containing his favorite pipe, from which a cloud of smoke curled upwards and dissolved into the air moved by the palm-bladed ceiling fans overhead. He was wearing his Djakarta casuals, as he called them, a short-sleeved yellow linen shirt hanging loosely over white pleated linen trousers. He wore topsiders on his feet with no socks. When he saw Mama and the girls enter, he quickly put down his newspaper on top of a stack of mail and jumped up to greet them.

Before anyone could say a word, James and Beni came shrieking by on the stone path that separated the veranda from a particularly beautiful little lily pond. "Mama! Watch me, watch me!" James yelled as he blew past her and out of sight around a Royal Poinciana tree whose ancient limbs spread out in all directions providing a lovely bit of shade over the well-manicured lawns.

"I guess they've been at it all day," Papa said as he hugged Mama hello.

"I hope they haven't been too much trouble for Arina."

"I don't think so. I think Arina is pleased to have her boy with her."

"Well, yes and no," Mama remarked as shrieks echoed from some distant place.

Just then Mrs. Rukmana appeared at the kitchen door

with a tray of cool drinks and biscuits. She set them on the long glass table in the middle of the loungers. She looked the same as always—dark hair pulled straight back into a tight chignon, gray streak perfectly placed two inches from center, starched and pressed high-collared tunic under a freshly laundered apron, and that eternally calm expression, which diverted attention from the dark eyes under heavy lids that never stopped recording every detail of her surroundings and the people who filled them. "Perhaps the boys would stop for a sweet," she suggested. "Surely they must be tired by now." There was just a hint of exhaustion in her voice.

"I have a feeling we might have to hold the biscuits out and let them grab one on their way by—like brass rings on a carousel," Mama smiled. She instantly realized that her carousel reference was meaningless to Mrs. Rukmana, but the older woman smiled anyway. Then she pivoted around and returned to her duties in the kitchen. She wasn't one to waste time.

Ari fell back into one of the deep loungers and waited for James and Beni to make their next pass on their shiny red bikes. It would take a minute or two. The grounds were large and the path wound all the way around the perimeter, serpentine-like through trees and flower beds, across the back lawns, past a screened summerhouse that overlooked a second, larger pond, through the rose gardens and back to the veranda again. She could hear the clatter of wheels on the stones growing fainter and then louder each time they disappeared into the trees and came out into the open again.

Papa had reseated himself in his chair. He eyed the kitchen door and then leaned in toward the others who, by now, had all seated themselves, kicked off their shoes, and taken their first long, refreshing sip of today's fruity concoction. "Mrs. Rukmana mentioned to me that Arina comes a long distance across the city to get here," he said. "By the time she gets home at night, she has very little time with her son. I think she fears for him when she's not there. She doesn't exactly live in the Menteng from what I understand."

"Oh, Ethan, she doesn't live in that dreadful place down by the canal, does she?"

"No. She has full-time employment. She and Beni live with her mother and several other family members in a small house on the outskirts of the city."

"Where's her husband?"

"Apparently he disappeared in '65."

"How awful! Was he a Communist?"

"I'm told not, but that didn't much matter back then. A lot of innocent people, including innocent communists, got swept away in the violence."

"Careful, Papa, the ghost of Joe McCarthy may come swooping down out of the sky in a fighter plane," Emma said with obvious disdain.

"I'd be worried if McCarthy had even half the military record he claimed to have. But then most bullies are also liars." There was a hint of anger in his eyes as he remembered the *dark days*, as he often referred to the early fifties. It quickly passed.

"How do you know all this about Arina, Papa?" Ari asked in a lowered voice.

"I made inquiries about all the staff members before I came in March. I wanted to know who would be in the house with my wife and children."

Mama smiled at him. "Who takes care of Beni when Arina is here?" she asked.

"Her mother and one of the aunties."

"Then why does she worry about him? It sounds like he's getting good care from people who love him."

"You would think," Papa replied, "but there's something going on there that makes Arina very uncomfortable any-time the subject of her family arises. When I first interviewed her, I asked questions about her family—just casual questions intended to put her at ease. It had the opposite effect."

Just then James and Beni came whizzing by again. Their laughter was so infectious that the whole family broke into giggles. Ari turned to see Arina standing at the kitchen door, watching her Beni at play with the foreigner's son. He was so happy that she had to smile. She didn't do that very often. When Mama saw her standing there, she called her over. "I sorry, Mrs. Heywood. I go back to work now," she said in a timid voice.

"Arina, you work very hard," Mama assured her. "You deserve a break. I just wanted to thank you for taking care of James this afternoon. I hope he wasn't too much trouble."

"Oh no, Mrs. Heywood! Beni and James just laugh and play all day. It is good to hear children laughing."

"Then you wouldn't mind bringing Beni here again? It's so good for James to have a friend to play with."

Arina's long, oval face broadened into a heart-shape as her smile spread. "Oh, Mrs. Heywood, he can come how you say. He is so happy here."

"Well, we shall have to talk to Mrs. Rukmana, of course. And Suti. But I don't think there'll be any problem."

"I promise. I do all my work, and I make the boys be good! They not trouble for you or Mrs. Rukmana."

It was Papa who spoke next, and when he did his voice was especially gentle and kind. "Arina, you mustn't worry that we will send Beni away if he isn't good all the time. *All* little boys get into trouble sometimes. Even good boys. We are so happy to have Beni here. In fact, I must remember to add something to your pay each week. If you are going to add baby-sitting to your housekeeping duties, you must be paid for that."

Arina stared back at him in disbelief. It was that same look that James had on his face the first time he saw his brand-new puppy on Christmas morning. That joyous disbelief that comes after months of not daring to hope that something will come true, and then finding out that it did. *Life couldn't really be this good. Could it?* Arina mumbled thank you and then kept repeating it all the way back to the kitchen where she burst through the doors before anyone could see her tears. Ari watched her go. That's when she spotted Mrs. Rukmana standing just inside the doorway. She was staring back at Ari, motionless and without expression, as if she had been inadvertently suspended in time. And then the corners of her mouth turned upward, so slightly that it might have been missed by anyone who didn't know the habitually somber woman. Mrs. Rukmana approved of these foreigners.

"So how was your day, Ethan?" Mama asked when the family was alone on the veranda again.

"It went well," he replied. "I should have agreements in place before you and the children return to the Island."

"Really! You are a genius, aren't you," she said affectionately.

"I am, rather," he replied. Papa drained the last of his gin and tonic and set the glass on the side table. "Actually, I'm thinking that if nothing happens in the interim, I might be able to break free for a week or so and fly back to the Island with you and the children." He waited for his words to sink in before the inevitable eruption.

"Really, Papa?"

"Oh, Papa, that would be just too perfect!"

"Ethan!" Mama's outburst was followed by a leap into Papa's lap where she wrapped her arms around him and then settled back comfortably in the crook of his arm.

"Now, I don't want you to get your hopes too high. Business is pretty volatile here. You never can be certain that the government will hold to its word. But I've got everything in place, and it's as much to their advantage that things go forward as it is to ours. So that's generally a formula for success even in situations like this one here."

"Oh, Ethan, I know you'll make it. Won't that be wonderful, girls! All of us together again on the Island."

"Speaking of the Island . . ." Papa shifted Mama a little forward on his lap until he was able to reach the pile of mail that had been hiding under the newspaper. "It looks like somebody's got mail!" He pulled two identical square envelopes from the pile with the familiar green postmarks of the Mainland Postal Service.

Emma and Ari jumped up from their loungers simultaneously and lunged at the letters, nearly toppling Mama to the floor. "Girls, a little decorum," Mama said, but she was laughing at their eagerness.

It seemed like forever since Ari and Emma had heard from the boys. Not since those first letters that were waiting for them when they arrived in Djakarta. Mail in this part of the world could be so slow. But now they were holding the letters in their hands. Nice big fat letters! They left the veranda and went to Ari's room where they sat cross-legged on her bed, facing each other. A soft breeze was flowing in from the open veranda doors, and it caused a rhythmic fluttering in the mosquito netting over their heads."

They opened their letters and read silently.

Dear Ari,

I can't believe you're almost here. We have so much to talk about. So much planning to do. Tommy and I went to the university admissions office before we left campus for the summer and asked them to send all the transfer information and applications. They arrived in the mail pouch on yesterday's launch. Along with our final grades. I did well except for trig. Why I even have to take that stuff is beyond me. Like I'm really going to use it when I'm a doctor. I don't ever remember seeing my dad doing trig. Not in the office or around the dinner table or anywhere. And I'm sure Dr. Greenhood never even heard of trigonometry.

Oh well, we have better things to talk about. Your Grandfather told me that you'll be arriving on June 30th. I know that's two days after your birthday, but I want to celebrate it with you anyway. Just the two of us. I thought maybe we could sail over to the Blue Lagoon Resort and have dinner at their floating restaurant. Dinner by torchlight under the stars. That's when I'm going to give you your birthday present. I'm not going to tell you what it is, but I'll give you a hint. It's small and shiny and almost as beautiful as you are.

If you're thinking that I'm going to try and seduce you, you're right, Ari. From the very first minute you get here! I'll have plenty of chances you know. We'll be together for two whole months. I'll have to be working some of the time. It's not like it used to be when I was a kid and could just take the whole summer off to play. Funny, isn't it? You spend your whole childhood wishing you could be treated like a grown-up, and then when you are, you wish you could be treated like a kid again. Except now that I have you, I'm glad to be grown up.

Have you thought at all about this summer and about Celebration? I think about it all the time. How much I want to make love to you. You're the first girl I ever thought was worth waiting for and I'll wait for as long as it takes. Honest! Don't think I won't try, though, to make the wait as short as possible!

I probably won't have time to write again before you get here. So, I'm going to spend the time just thinking about all the things we're going to do together this summer. How we'll begin every day at the Dolphin Lagoon and end every night with a walk along the Bay. How when Celebration night comes, it will be perfect no matter what we do because I'll be doing it with you. I better go now before this letter gets so mushy I sound like a girl—no offence.

Joey

Ari put her letter down and glanced up at Emma who was still reading Tommy's letter. Her spray of pale freckles, newly-acquired at the Club pool, graced her checks above her constant smile as her blue eyes slowly tracked across each line. Ari knew that if both her hands weren't busy holding the note paper, one of them would have been twirling a strand of hair around her finger. When Emma finished, she carefully refolded the letter on its original creases and slid it back into its envelope. "I can't wait to see Tommy," she sighed. "I've been trying not to get too excited. But now that we're almost home, oh, Ari, I love him so much. I just can't stand being away from him."

"I know," Ari replied. But even as she was saying it, she knew it wasn't the same for her as it was for Emma. Tommy and Emma had made love to each other. Ari hadn't even experienced a single day of college yet.

She reached over and opened the top drawer of the nightstand and pulled out a packet of letters tied in a green ribbon. She slid Joey's latest letter on top of the others and returned them to the drawer.

"He must really love you, Ari. Boys don't write letters to girls very often. What did he say?" Emma asked with the smallest hint of concern in her voice. Emma knew her so well.

"Well, everything is fine, but he brought up the whole thing about Celebration again. He says that if I'm not ready, he'll wait. For as long as it takes."

"So, what's the problem then?"

"I don't know. Maybe I just feel like I'm always running to catch up with the three of you. I've never been to college. Never lived out of the house on my own. Suddenly I'm supposed to skip over all that and go right to . . . well, you know."

"Ari, if you can't even say it out loud, you're definitely not ready to do it," Emma said with a laugh.

Ari fell silent for a moment. She was trying to figure out just how to ask Emma something, but she just didn't know how to say it. Emma pre-empted her. "You want to ask me if I was really ready when Tommy and I made love."

"Were you?"

"Yes. I was. But that's not to say that I wasn't nervous about it. Everyone's nervous their first time."

"But you had no doubts?"

"None."

"But how did you know?"

"I don't know, I just did. I don't think there are any rules for knowing when you're ready. It's not like it used to be in the West where women were never supposed to make love until their wedding night. I think Berkeley has just about obliterated that idea, don't you?" she laughed.

"In some ways I think it was easier in the old days when the choices weren't really ours."

"Easier but not better."

Ari didn't respond. She just sat staring at her lap with that tell-tale furrow in the middle of her forehead and her eyes squinting almost to slits.

Emma waited, before saying "I can tell you this, Ari, I was not ready a year ago."

Ari looked up, her expression slowly dissolving into calmness. "Really?" she asked.

"Really, Ari. I can't tell you how different things are from the first day you go to college and start living on your own. I never would have been ready for anything like this when I was still in high school. You'll see. So, don't feel like you have to catch up to the rest of us. That will happen fast enough next fall. Besides, wanting to fit in is never a reason for making love. That's probably why they're so strict about that with high school kids on the Island. Being in high school is all about fitting in."

"Thanks, Emma. What would I do without you? You've just gotten so old and wise since you *did it* with Tommy!"

Emma grabbed a pillow and swatted it at Ari, but that didn't stop her from laughing.

They stayed there talking in Ari's room until Mrs. Rukmana's chimes called them to dinner. Periodically, they stopped to listen to the voices coming through the pairs of French doors that opened out to the back veranda. To James and Beni whizzing by on their marathon bike race, and Mama and Papa whose relaxed conversation and occasional laughter made even this place feel familiar. And they talked about their impending reunion with Tommy and Joey and how they would spend their days together. And their nights. They talked about the house on Grafton Square and Papa's retirement from the Company and how their lives had changed so fast that sometimes it just took their breath away.

"I think it happens like that sometimes, you know," Emma observed. "Your life seems to just chug along at the same speed year after year and then suddenly WHAM! I'm glad things worked out with Roger the way they did though. I don't think I could be quite this happy if I knew I had hurt him."

"You were so nervous about telling him when we got back from Spring Break. Remember? Turns out he was more nervous than you. What was that girl's name again? Debbie something."

"Debbie McGowan. To think he had been trying to find a way to break up with me since January. I don't know how I would have felt then if Roger had broken up with me for her, but I sure wish he had. As wonderful as my time with Tommy was, I still couldn't get rid of that guilty feeling that I was cheating on Roger. All seems kind of silly now."

"Well, it's past, and we've got the best summer of our lives to look forward to, don't we?"

"Ten more days, Ari. Just ten more days!"

50

SATURDAY ARRIVED AND with it a surprise from Papa. "You've got me for the whole weekend," he announced as the family sat around the morning room table taking breakfast. Sunlight was sneaking in through the French doors in diffused rays, and it caught Mama's lustrous hair as she whirled her head around, sending little sparkles outward in a sweeping arc.

"Really, Ethan? No meetings?"

He smiled back at her. Even after all these years she was still so beautiful to him. The way she looked. The melody in her voice. The familiar jasmine-scented smell of her that sometimes reached into his dreams in the middle of the night and caused him to awake with a smile on his face. "I know I've been busy since you all got here," he admitted. "I can usually control the clock better than this, but here it's harder."

Mary reached over and cupped her delicate hand over his. It felt cool and soft, but there was nothing weak in it. "Ethan," she sighed, "I know that here you have to take your meetings when you can get them. It's all right. Besides, the sooner you get your business done in Djakarta, the sooner we can retire to the Island permanently. We're almost there. It's really just a matter of months now."

Ari had finished her breakfast and was helping James scoop his muffin crumbs into her napkin. "Arina isn't here today, James. We must clean up after ourselves, so Mrs. Rukmana doesn't get too tired."

"I can carry my plate, Ari. And I can carry yours, too."

"Thank you, James. One at a time."

"Okay," he agreed and headed for the kitchen carefully

balancing the first plate on the palms of both hands.

James was so cheerful today. Ari thought he might still be a little moody after finding out that Beni wasn't coming this weekend. She had found him yesterday, sitting on the wooden bench near the front door, swinging his little legs back and forth above the veranda floor, silently watching the taxi Papa had ordered moving slowly down the drive, taking Arina and Beni home. He didn't say anything to Ari when she sat down next to him. He just grabbed her arm and wrapped it around his neck and sank into her. "You know, James," she had said, "I've really missed you the last couple of days. I'm glad you have a new friend to play with, but I'm even gladder that I get you all to myself this weekend."

James didn't respond right away. Finally, "Ya' wanna maybe go swimming with me, Ari?" His voice was thin and just a little sorrowful.

"Sure, big guy. We could have races across the pool and everything."

That seemed to mollify him. Still, Ari was surprised at just how cheerful he was this morning. "Papa," he called as he hurtled through the door from the kitchen, "can we go swimming now? Please, Papa. Ari and me are going to race and everything."

Papa grabbed James up in his lap and sat him down with a ceremonious thump. "I think that's a great way to spend the day. In fact, I could use a swim myself. But we'll have to come home a little early because I have another surprise for you."

"A surprise for me?"

"Well, James, it's actually a surprise for everyone. We're going to the puppet theatre tonight."

"The Wayang, Ethan? How wonderful!" Mama exclaimed.

"I was hoping we could see the Wayang before we left Djakarta," Emma added. "William and Martin went a few weeks ago. I don't think William liked it much, but Martin did."

"They do the whole show with shadows, don't they?" Ari asked.

"I believe so. But Mrs. Rukmana can tell you more than I. Her uncle is the Dalang—the Puppet Master. In Indonesian society, that's a very great honor, you know. It's much like being a priest."

"Will she and Mr. Rukmana be coming with us?"

"I asked them and, of course, at first they declined. The whole caste thing, you know. But then I told them how much it would mean to us to meet the Dalang and that we would need a personal introduction, and Mrs. Rukmana arranged everything. We're going early to the theatre to meet her uncle and learn about the Wayang firsthand."

They arrived at the theatre that evening well rested from their day at the Club, which was mostly spent swimming and sunbathing and eating and spending time together again. Just before lunch, Papa had organized a mini-Olympics racing meet down the length of the pool, which James won by just beating out Ari at the last stroke. And Papa pulled him out of the pool and stuck him on his shoulders and did a spirited, yet appropriate, victory lap around the pool. Mr. Jata congratulated James and brought him a special iced treat in celebration and said how he had never seen a boy of James's years swim the whole length of the pool, let alone so fast. William and Martin, who were there with their parents, made a big fuss over James. He didn't mind in the slightest being the recipient of so much attention. And for just a few hours it felt to Ari as if they hadn't really moved to Djakarta at all.

The Dalang was just as Ari had pictured him. Ancient, wise, and serene but with the robust movements of a much younger man, which probably accounted for the glossy sheen of his skin and the high color in his cheeks. He was compact under his colorful flowing robes, and his long, pure-white hair and narrow flowing beard, which cascaded down his chest from the point of his chin, held not a single streak of gray. When Mrs. Rukmana ushered the family into the small room off the darkened hallway, he rose from where he was kneeling in front of a long wooden chest and greeted each of them by name. Ari was surprised to hear the perfect English, British-accented even, and he must have caught the slight widening of her eyes because when he greeted her, he explained. "I am blessed with an ear for language and music. Now you hear the years I spent in England as a young student. Later you will hear my native tongue."

When they were seated in the theatre, Ari turned to Emma who was sitting on her left just past the unusually quiet James. "Why didn't you say anything in there?" she whispered to her sister over James's head.

"I was afraid I'd say something stupid in front of the Dalang," she whispered back.

"Oh, how could you be frightened of that sweet old man?"

"I wasn't frightened of him. It's Mrs. Rukmana who'll be staring down at me at breakfast tomorrow."

Ari looked over at where Mrs. Rukmana sat with her husband at a discreet distance from the family. "I see your point!"

The theatre was exactly how the Dalang had described it—small and intimate with patrons sitting in ascending rows of padded benches, which swept from one side of the stage to the other in a broad arc. Across the stage was a large screen, probably twenty feet long and five feet high, which stretched over trunks of banana trees whose soft bark held the puppets erect when the Dalang's assistant placed them there. There was a long wooden box called a Kotak at the front of the stage. It held all the puppets, and when it was emptied, the Dalang would tap it with tiny tongs held between the fingers of his left hand and toes of his right foot to punctuate speech or actions at the appropriate time. There were strategically placed lanterns for making shadows and, there was a gamelon orchestra with thirteen instrumentalists playing a variety of gongs and bronze bars, drums and genders, which were a kind of xylophone with fourteen keys, each over their own resonating tube. All of the instruments were set into extraordinarily carved wooden boxes or platforms or animal shapes, any one of which would have made a beautiful objet d'art in the finest homes.

"I can't even imagine what it must take to coordinate the actions of over a hundred puppets and thirteen musicians and assistants, and tell the stories let alone move the puppets, sing the songs and recite the poems."

"And to present it all in shadowplay. It's almost more than you can take in at one time, isn't it?" Papa observed.

He was right. Watching the Dalang during the performance that evening, and the extraordinary precision of his actions, and his almost imperceptible cues that made the music play and the puppets come and go and the scenes transition from sadness to celebration, from love to war, from solemn to comical without a pause or misstep, all executed with the grace of a ballet dancer and the power of a Majapahit warrior. It was almost incomprehensible how one man could successfully orchestrate it all.

51

PAPA WAS IN the office when he heard Ari call him. "Papa! Papa!" There was anxiety in her voice and urgency in her footsteps. His thoughts flew to James.

"What is it, Ari?" he called as he ran to meet her. "Is everyone all right?"

They nearly collided at the ballroom entrance. Ari was out of breath and took a moment to compose herself. "We're all fine, Papa. It's Arina and Beni. You need to come see them. Someone has beaten them."

"What! Are you sure?"

"She says they just had an accident, but I can tell that's not true. She's very frightened. Mama's with her."

He followed Ari through to the kitchen to where Mama and Arina sat in two of the ladderback chairs that surrounded a big plank table. Beni was cradled in Arina's arms and she was gently caressing his cheek. When she saw Papa coming, she lowered her head and waited. "Arina," he began as he lowered himself into an adjacent chair. "Please, look at me."

She hesitated and then slowly lifted her face toward him. "My god!" he exclaimed. "Who did this to you?" There were bruises on her cheeks, and one eye was blackened shut. Beni had a dark purple splotch on his arm where someone obviously had grabbed him. His hair was disheveled, and his cheeks were tear stained, and his thumb had uncharacteristically found his mouth.

"I have accident, Mr. Heywood. Please, I just have accident."

"No you didn't, Arina. Someone has done this to you. Please don't be frightened. You're safe here and I'm going to help you."

"You cannot help me, Mr. Heywood."

"Of course I can. But first you must tell me everything. Does your family know about this?"

She looked at him, obviously still undecided as to what she would tell him. Then, "They do this, Mr. Heywood. My family. They do this." Her voice was barely a whisper.

"What!" Mama gasped. "Who? Why?"

"My uncle," she sputtered. "He say I bring trouble to family. We lose business, we lose house, people die. My fault he say."

Papa glanced over at Mama and then back at Arina again. When he resumed, his voice was even and unemotional. "I know there was trouble for your family a couple of years ago, Arina. That's when your husband disappeared during the violence. But how could that be your fault?"

"My uncle say I marry PKI. I bring soldiers to house. He tell me not to marry. But Jaya not PKI. He not!" she proclaimed with finality.

"Jaya was your husband?" Mama inquired.

"Yes, ma'am. And he was good man. Not like my uncle say. My uncle never like Jaya."

"Why not?"

"He want me marry someone else. Old man with big store. But I marry Jaya."

Ari had been standing behind Papa this whole time listening to Arina's story. It was like she was watching a movie or something. Not that she didn't know that things like this went on in the world. Women being invisible until someone decides to beat them for an infraction of rules that would never apply to her own life. It's just so different seeing things first-hand. She wanted to do something, anything, but all she could do was stand there with her hands resting on Papa's shoulders like a child in a tag game, safe as long as she was touching home base.

She listened as Arina recounted the whole story. How two years ago the soldiers came to take her husband away. He had never done anything, but still they came. And when her uncle's first son tried to stop them, he was taken, too. Her uncle screamed and screamed that his son was innocent, but they would not listen. Before the soldiers left, they set fire to the house and to the adjoining family business where they made furniture for the big houses. All the money that her uncle kept hidden under the floor (he did not trust banks) was burned up, too. The family had to go live in a little two-room house on the outskirts of the city. Everyone had to take jobs where they could find them and bring the money home to her uncle. He divided it up as he saw fit. There was never much left for Arina or Beni, even now with Papa's generous salary.

"I still don't understand why your uncle blamed you, Arina," Mama remarked.

"I think I do," Papa said, but offered no explanation. "What I don't understand is why, after all this time, your uncle got angry enough at you all over again to hurt you like this."

Arina gathered herself for what was obviously a great effort to speak. "A man come last night. He tell my uncle his son never come home."

"Your uncle still hoped that his son was alive?"

"Yes. As I hope same for Jaya. Some come back. Some find families again. But now we know they never come back. This man saw Jaya die. He die with my uncle's son and many other men."

"And your uncle got mad at you all over again?"

"He drink all night. He get crazy. He take Beni from me. He say if he cannot have his son, I cannot have mine." She pointed to her blackened eye. "He do this when I try get Beni back."

"Oh, you poor thing," Mama murmured. "How did you finally get away?"

"I hit him with chair. Then I take Beni, and I run."

"But, Arina, that's miles from here. How did you get here this morning?"

"I walk all night."

Papa rose from his chair. He turned to Mrs. Rukmana who had been standing quietly in the background waiting for the instructions she knew would come. "Would you please get some cold cloths and the first-aid supplies and see what you can do? Don't hesitate to call my doctor if you feel he is needed."

"I will take care of everything, sir."

"I leave Arina and Beni in your capable hands then," he smiled. Then, to Ari, "Find Emma and James. I think they're playing soldiers in the nursery. Keep James there until we get things sorted out."

"Right, Papa," she replied and wheeled out of the room.

"Come with me, Mary." Mama followed him out of the kitchen to the privacy of the office. When they were behind closed doors, he suddenly grabbed her and held on. He didn't speak at first. He just held her, and Mama could feel the trembling in his body, and she didn't know if it was fear or anger. He tightened his embrace and said, "If anyone ever did that to you or to our children, I don't know what I'd do, Mary. I don't know what I'd do."

When he had regained his composure, Papa stood back and took a deep breath. Then he led Mama to the large leather sofa. "Arina cannot go back to that house," he proclaimed. "She's lucky that evil old man didn't kill her and Beni."

"Oh, Ethan, I can't believe it would have come to that. He was crazy and grief-stricken, but I can't believe he'd deliberately kill them. Do you really think he is capable of that?"

"Why not? He had Jaya killed!"

"What!" Mama gasped. "Why do you say that, Ethan?"

"Because his actions aren't those of a grief-stricken man. He's feeling guilty for the death of his son, and he's got to find someone else to blame it on or he'll go mad. I'd bet my pension that he was the one who denounced Jaya as PKI. He was the one who brought the soldiers to his own home. He never counted on his son standing up for Jaya."

"Oh, Ethan," she looked up at him and said what she knew they were both thinking at that moment. "I wish we could just pack our bags right now and go home for good."

"Soon, Mary. Very soon. But for now, we need to focus on the problem at hand. Arina and Beni cannot go back to that house. They're coming to live here with us. We'll fix up the apartment behind the kitchen for them."

Mama's face brightened. "I'll bet Arina has never had a bedroom of her own, much less Beni. We could fix it up so nice for them, Ethan. There's that sweet little parlor, and the verandah, and that great big claw foot tub. And that little Pullman kitchen has everything they need."

On her way back to the kitchen to tell Arina the good news, Mama stopped by the nursery to fill the children in and to prepare James for what he would encounter so that he wouldn't be frightened. "Arina and Beni had a little accident, James. Like when you fell off your bike that time and got your knee all bloody. Remember? It looked horrible, but it mended really fast. Arina and Beni will mend fast too. Especially now that they're going to live here with us."

"They are, Mama? Really? Beni's going to live here? Oh boy!"

Mama smiled down at her precious little boy. Life, for him, was so simple. And she would keep it that way for just as long as she possibly could.

52

"*HAPPY BIRFDAY TO you. Happy birfday to you. Happy birfday, Dear Ariiiiiii. Happy birfday to you.*" Ari burst into giggles at James's operatic rendition before she was even fully awake. When she finally did open her eyes, she found James, still in his jammies and bare feet, straddling her ribcage and Mama and Papa and Emma standing at the foot of the bed.

"Happy birthday!" they all shouted and threw paper streamers up into the air and watched them float down, covering the white eyelet duvet and a good bit of James with a rainbow of colors. This was the traditional birthday awakening ceremony in the Heywood household.

"We await your orders, young woman," Papa said, poising a pencil above a paper notepad. It was also tradition that the birthday person got to lay out the schedule for the whole day—anything they wanted to do, and everyone else went along with it. They got to choose the menu for each meal, and where they'd eat them, and even how the birthday table would be decorated. And, of course, they got to choose the flavor of the birthday cake.

Ari pulled James to her side with some difficulty and sat upright. "Well," she began, "for breakfast I'd like chilled fruit and—"

"Please! No more rice!" Emma begged. "I think I'll always remember Djakarta for the way people here eat rice for breakfast, lunch and dinner."

"How about chilled fruit and pancakes with some of that maple syrup Mama's been hiding in the pantry on the third shelf up."

"You saw that?" Mama laughed.

"Yes, I did. You didn't by chance bring it along just in case I wanted it for my birthday, did you?"

"Perhaps."

"Okay then. That's what we'll have for breakfast."

Papa wrote *fruit and pancakes with maple syrup*. "Next?" he asked, pencil poised in the air again.

"Well, if you don't think it would be too much trouble—"

"There's no such thing as *too much trouble* for a birthday request," Mama assured her.

"Then I kind of don't feel like doing a lot of running around Djakarta today. I was thinking that maybe we could drive up to the Puncak Highlands for a picnic. It's supposed to be so beautiful up there in the mountains. It would almost be like being back home on the Island. At least it's the closest we could come to it here. What do you all think?"

Ari watched as smiles spread across everyone's faces simultaneously like water colors on rice paper. "What a brilliant idea!" Mama exclaimed.

"That only leaves dinner. Let me guess," Mama said, "peanut chicken and doughy rolls to sop up the sauce and white cake with butter cream frosting."

53

ARI WATCHED OUT the window as the car sped south along the Bogor road toward the Puncak Highland and the cool, misty morning that awaited her there. She was glad to be leaving the heat and congestion of the city behind. But mostly, she was glad to be leaving behind that almost imperceptible anxiety that first surrounded her that day in the Djakarta airport. She hadn't felt it in a while, but then the morning she walked into the kitchen and found Arina and Beni there, bruised and beaten and sobbing uncontrollably, the feeling returned and hadn't left again until just now.

Ari had to admit that she had actually come to like Djakarta much more than she had intended, until then anyway. The parks and the museums, the shops and restaurants (especially that beautiful little café in Old Batavia where they served home-grown Arabica coffee and European-style pastries to foreigners who couldn't look at another dish of rice), and the rich art and culture and history. It was kind of seductive in a way. Even the people turned out to be far nicer than she thought they would be, if sometimes a little guarded around foreigners. But then foreigners had given them cause to feel that way, hadn't they?

Mama had been watching her from the front seat. Eighteen years old, she thought. Where have the years gone, my precious baby girl? She didn't lament their passing, not too much anyway. After all, there were such glorious years yet to experience. Retirement to the Island. It had come sooner than she had expected. But she shouldn't think about that now. First, there was the memory of this day to make. And then, day after tomorrow they'd all be flying away home together, like a flock of Canadian geese at the end of a cold winter. She'd feel that little pang in her stomach when the wheels touched down on the tarmac, and she'd stand at the open door of the cabin and breathe in the air of home. And even though Ethan could only stay for a week, she wouldn't think about that for a single second that they were together. She would stay in the present and live it for all it was worth.

She hadn't felt the smile creeping across her face. Not when she imagined Ethan standing there naked before her, the light of the torches silhouetting his body and the sound of falling water muffling the thumping of her heart. Nor did she hear the audible giggle that escaped her when she silently chided herself for not staying in the present now. This was Ari's eighteenth birthday. One glorious memory at a time, she thought.

"Mama what are you laughing about?" Ari asked, having finally returned from her own thoughts.

"I'm just so happy to be here together," she replied. "What a lovely way to spend your birthday, Ari. I'm so glad you thought of this."

Mama turned round and scooted over toward Papa on the bench seat. His right arm raised up automatically to receive her and, when she was in position, lowered down again and wrapped around her shoulder. They looked like a couple of teenagers on their way to Mel's Drive-in on a Friday night. When the transmission suddenly shifted to a lower gear signifying the ascent of the road, Papa removed his arm and prepared to negotiate the curves in the road up to the mountains.

The drive took them through forests and up mountainsides and past vistas that extended for miles and miles over lush green terraced tea fields and rooftops of distant plantation houses. Along the way they encountered roadside vendors and big bungalows residing next door to single-room, tin-roofed shacks with the proverbial goat tied up outside, and one beautifully grizzled old man, white-haired and bony-kneed, walking down the side of the road with a pipe in his mouth and a red conical hat on his head. By the time Papa turned the car onto a dirt track that meandered through a centuries-old forest before opening up onto a sun-drenched plateau, all the windows were rolled down and the car was filled with cool mountain air, wind-blown hair, and five Heywoods, renewed and refreshed and ready to celebrate.

"Oh, Papa!" Ari exclaimed, standing at the edge of the plateau and looking out over the valley flowing away from her in ripple after ripple of emerald splendor. "This is *gorgeous!*"

Papa stood next to her, his hand resting gently on her back. He wasn't smiling as much as grinning. "It is spectacular, isn't it?" They were looking out over the terraced tea fields of a particularly lovely plantation whose house and gardens sat on a little precipice across the valley. On three sides were sculpted mountains, heavily vegetated, from which a symphony of birds and monkeys periodically interrupted the silence. Because of the unique contours and elevations of the surrounding land, the owners were able to sit on their terrace and look out across everything they owned without having to get up from the cushions of their loungers except to refill their gin and limes.

The mists never gathered over the valley that day to obscure the view. It never rained or thundered as was the custom in that region. They wouldn't have cared if it had. They'd just have moved their lying about and nibbling on Mrs. Rukmana's surprises inside the car until it became dry enough to go out again. But today, the Gods had decreed a perfect day for celebrating Ari's eighteenth birthday. Just enough clouds floating by, one or two at a time, to make interesting shadows over the fields and brilliant contrasts with the blue of the sky. They sent sunshine to warm them and fresh breezes to cool them and nothing more than that to distract them from the single most important occupation of the day—just being together.

They were all lying about the perimeter of the picnic blanket in various lazy poses. Papa was lying on his back, hands behind his head, with one knee up and the other leg crossing it. His shoes were off, and the bottom of his feet looked like they belonged to one of the field hands who stooped over the tea plants way down below. Mama was lying perpendicular to him and had her head resting on his stomach. James was sound asleep in a little ball where their bodies made a ninety-degree angle. Ari and Emma were both lying on their backs looking straight up while feeling for and picking at the opposite sides of a giant biscuit. "I was sure," Emma said between bites, "that you were going to choose Borobudur for your birthday celebration, Ari. I thought for sure you'd never leave Java without seeing one of the Ancient Wonders of the World. I even bet Papa on it," she added.

"I'm sorry I lost the bet for you, Emma."

"I didn't lose, actually. Papa thought you'd want to go to the Bogor Gardens. They're spectacular and a lot closer."

"Well, they were both high up on my list. And I'd love to see them some day."

"Borobudur is supposed to be even ghostlier than Angkor Wat," Mama declared. Just imagine, a Buddhist monument, eleven centuries old, rising up from Central Java.

"I understand it's built in platforms," Papa added, "a little bit like steps of a pyramid. Nine of them, if I'm not mistaken. And they're covered in over twenty-six hundred relief panels and over five hundred Buddhas and parapets and domes."

"Sounds like you've been doing your homework, Papa," Ari interrupted.

"Well, after Emma mentioned Borobudur, I thought I'd be prepared, just in case."

"I might have gone there if it was closer, but, I don't know, for some reason I just didn't feel like doing anything today that would kind of take over my birthday. I wanted us to be the center of things, not Buddha. I don't know why, really. But suddenly my birthday got personal, private. Oh, I don't know how to explain it."

Mama rolled over and sat up until she was facing Ari. "You don't have to explain. I guessed that this was how you'd want to spend the day."

"You two really are joined at the hip, aren't you, Mary."

"Maybe. But if that's so, James is tied to Ari's other hip. He didn't put up a fuss about not being able to play with Beni today, and he didn't even ask if Beni could come with us. Obviously, this was the day he chose as well."

Ari smiled over at the little bundle who was still sleeping soundly next to his Papa. "Of course, that's only because

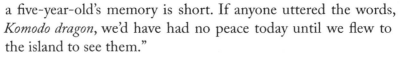

a five-year-old's memory is short. If anyone uttered the words, *Komodo dragon*, we'd have had no peace today until we flew to the island to see them."

"You're probably right, Ari," Mama agreed. "We will have to get him there before Christmas, I'm afraid, Ethan," she reminded him. "We did promise."

Talk of Christmas sent everyone's thoughts to the Island, and until it was time to pack up the picnic basket and return to the city, they sat around the blanket sharing their excitement over their impending return home. Ari and Emma already had their suitcases out and opened on their matching chaise lounges, and they had been filling them for the last couple of days with things they knew they wouldn't use again before boarding the plane day after tomorrow. Mama had been doing the same for herself and James. Papa's she would leave until tomorrow. She was superstitious about some things. She didn't want any last-minute emergencies at work cropping up to make her unpack his bag. Besides, she could have him ready to leave on thirty minutes notice. How long did it take to pack a sarong, bathing trunks, underwear, and a couple of Island casual outfits? She could do it in her sleep.

"So," Papa began after a little gust of wind blew through the plateau and left again, "what's the first thing everyone's going to do when we get back home?"

"I know the first thing *Emma's* going to do," Ari teased.

"I know the first thing Joey's going to expect *you* to do!" she shot back.

"Emma!" Ari exclaimed with a large amount of embarrassment on her face.

Papa glanced at Mama and then over at Ari. "You're not feeling pressured, are you? Just because you're eighteen? That's the age of consent not obligation."

"Joey would never pressure me, Papa. Even if he wanted to, he couldn't get away with it. The whole Island would know, and Batara and Maru would never bless us."

"You're right there."

"So, what has everyone got planned for the Island? Anything in particular?" Mama asked again.

"I plan to do absolutely nothing but wake up in the morning, stumble down to the lagoon for a wake-up swim, and then do whatever the spirit moves me to do at the moment," Papa announced. "There will be no clocks, no phones, no meetings, no memoranda, and no one who's ever even heard of Indonesia getting anywhere near my day or my night for one whole week. Except the family, of course. That leaves me with a lot of hours to fill, Mary!" Papa winked at her, a large smile growing on his face.

The conversation continued on like that all afternoon. A communal daydream about going home again. And Ari said how she and Joey were sailing to the floating restaurant to celebrate her birthday, and Emma said how Tommy had planned a day for the four of them to go down to the university and look around and go see the house on Grafton Square where they'd all be living together in the not-too-distant future. Mama said how, of course, James would spend the whole summer in his bathing trunks, and show off for his Papa every chance he got, and Papa said he thought there'd be a lot of chances because things really were falling into place rather nicely at work. He had every reason to believe that come August, he'd have almost the whole month at home with the family.

When the family returned home late that afternoon, they found the table already set. Arina had strung colorful paper flowers across the doorways to make the room more festive. Mrs. Rukmana had finished the cake, which she had asked Mama if she could bake personally for Miss Ari, as she wouldn't be making dinner that evening.

After all the talk up on the Highland about going home, Ari showed up to dinner wearing her emerald green cap-sleeved blouse and the family's signature sarong. It was her eighteenth birthday, and if she couldn't celebrate it on the Island, she'd bring as much of the Island to the party as she could. Everyone else must have been thinking the same thing because when she arrived in the morning room (which she preferred to the ceremonial dining room), she found the whole family dressed in their signature sarongs, even little James who, with his short squat little body, looked a bit more like an enchilada than a native. "Oh, how perfect!" Ari cried. And it was. It truly was.

Before the cake came out, Ari opened her presents. "Open mine first, Ari. Please!" James pleaded. He was sitting on her left, and as he spoke, he popped up suddenly on his knees and lunged toward her, nearly spilling his juice.

"You bet I will, big guy," she said, grabbing the juice just in time to avert an accident.

James grabbed a little fabric pouch from the pile of presents on the table and handed it to her. It had been made from a scrap of yellow and green rice patterned fabric, which Ari recognized from the fabric used to make Arina's curtains and duvet. The pouch was puckered in places and the stitches were big and uneven. "Did you make this all by yourself, James?" she asked in surprise.

"Arina helped me. She told me where to put the needle in, but I did it all by myself!" he proudly announced.

"Well I can't wait to see what's inside." She carefully untied the ribbon that held the pouch closed and opened it wide enough to look inside. "Oh, James," she sighed.

"I made it for you, Ari. Mama took me to the bead store, and I picked out all the beads, and I put them on the wire. See. They're really, really pretty."

Ari pulled a strand of delicate jade beads carved to look like rosebuds from the bag. After every tenth bead, there was a larger white bead with the same carving. At the bottom of the strand were three of the large beads all in a row. "James worked a long, long time on those, Ari. Just for you," Mama informed her. "Didn't he do a beautiful job?"

"It's just about the most beautiful necklace I've ever seen, James. Thank you," she said, putting it on.

"Mama showed me how. I had to count to ten and put a white one on and count to ten again. See?"

"Come here, James," she said and picked him up and put him on her lap. She wrapped her arms around him and gave him a big squeeze. "I will love this forever and ever and ever!"

"Then how come you're crying, Ari?"

A single tear was making its way down her cheek, and James stopped it with his finger. "Because you make me so happy to be your big sister," she replied.

Next Ari opened Emma's gift. It was a beautiful diary, obviously hand-made, covered in a piece of the family's signature silk and embroidered with Ari's initials. It closed with silk ties on the side. When Ari opened it and saw the watermark on the paper, she knew what Emma had done. "This is from that shop in Paris where they sell all that beautiful stationary, isn't it?"

Emma smiled. "I wanted to give you something special to remember your eighteenth birthday. You're officially a woman now, and you're in love, and you're about to have the best summer of your whole life. I just thought you should have a really special place to record every last memory of it."

"Emma, thank you. You're going to make me cry all over again."

There was still one more present to open. Whatever it was, was hidden away inside a large wooden box about three feet long and fairly flat. The box itself was mahogany and there was an emblem of some sort inlaid in teakwood in the center of the top. Ari didn't know what it meant. It was obviously Indonesian, but she thought it looked familiar. "What a beautiful box," she said. "It's a gift all by itself."

"Well, then, your father and I will keep what's inside for ourselves."

"Oh, no you don't," Ari replied.

She opened the card that came with it and read it aloud. *This is to remind you that you can always find beauty even where you least expect it. Love always, Mama and Papa*

Ari slid back the clasp and raised the top of the box, hiding its contents from the others momentarily. She gasped loud enough to bring Mrs. Rukmana into the room from where she had been standing discreetly in the kitchen doorway. "I think that means we've chosen wisely, Mrs. Rukmana. We can't thank you enough for your assistance," Papa said.

"What's in the box?" Emma asked, still unable to see its contents.

Ari lifted James from her lap and stood up. Carefully she reached into the box with both hands and slowly pulled out a Wayang Kulit puppet, made of genuine water buffalo, bone-handled and hand-painted. It was Shrikandi, and somehow Ari

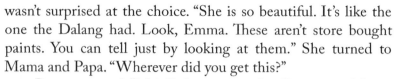

wasn't surprised at the choice. "She is so beautiful. It's like the one the Dalang had. Look, Emma. These aren't store bought paints. You can tell just by looking at them." She turned to Mama and Papa. "Wherever did you get this?"

Papa answered. "Mrs. Rukmana very kindly arranged for us to meet one of the Dalang's students. He's been studying with him since he was a small child. And he has learned to make the puppets using the same methods the Dalang's grandfather used. This is one of his. Mrs. Rukmana tells us that this student will be very famous one day."

Ari turned and looked at the usually stern-faced woman who was standing just behind her. She was almost smiling. "Thank you so much, Mrs. Rukmana. I don't even know what to say. This is so special. It will always remind me of the Dalang and of you."

"Me?"

"Of course. You've made my stay here in Djakarta very special. I won't forget you."

"I won't forget you either, Miss Ari. I won't forget any of you," she said in an uncharacteristically unguarded moment. Then she wheeled around and returned to the kitchen mumbling something about coffee getting cold, leaving the family to stare silently at one another in disbelief.

They stayed long around the table that evening talking about their time together in Djakarta, and how glad they were to see Papa that first day in the airport, and how when they first drove up the drive of the Menteng house Ari thought she'd never leave the grounds again until it was time to fly home. Emma said how she didn't want to admit it but that she had felt the same way. They talked about how much more pleasant things had turned out (due mostly to Papa's preparations), and how much they enjoyed their days at the Club with the Pembrokes, and the museums and Old Batavia and Sunda Kelapa and their meeting with the Dalang. And they talked about how much fun the afternoon had been, just lazing around together. How Highlands were even more beautiful than they had expected. Emma said she wondered if the plantation owners ever climbed up to the plateau in the evenings like their family went to the

Bench and Papa said that he didn't imagine they ever found the need to stray too far from their verandah. They could see everything they wanted to from there.

That brought the conversation back to the Island again. They talked on and on about all that this summer would bring them, and how after that there'd be so little time until Christmas when their lives would set a new course, and how happy Grandfather and Mem were at the prospect of the whole family coming back home to stay. They spoke once more of morning swims, evening strolls, and dinner under the stars around the old stone table.

It was late when they all went to bed. Ari peeked in on the others to tell them again how much their presents had meant to her, and how wonderful this birthday had been. Emma was already in bed re-reading Tommy's letters when she entered her room. She hadn't braided her hair as she usually did before going to bed. Her hair spread on her pillow in silky ribbons, and in the light of the bed table lamp, it resembled a halo. They exchanged a few words, promised each other to be up early next morning to finish packing, and then Ari headed for the door. "I'm glad you're my big sister, Emma," she said and disappeared into the hallway.

James had crawled into bed with Mama and Papa. He was curled up in a little ball between them, not quite asleep yet. Mama had changed into a sleeveless white cotton gown, the one that covered her to her ankles, but still let a hint of her silhouette through. Papa was bare-chested, wearing just a pair of matching draw-string pajama bottoms, one leg of which was visible where it stuck out from under the covers. They were both sitting upright against propped-up pillows and looked as if they had been waiting for her.

James stirred. "Are you still wearing my beads, Ari?" he asked through a yawn.

"I sure am. See?" she replied leaning over Papa to receive a hug from his outstretched arms. When she had nestled him back down again, she sat on the edge of the bed. "Who's the *bestest* brother in the whole wide world?" she asked him.

James grinned from ear to ear. "I am, Ari. I'm the *bestest!*" he declared, stifling another yawn.

Papa grabbed a lock of Ari's hair, twirled it around his finger and gave it a playful tug. "I'm glad you came in to say goodnight before going to bed," he told her.

"Oh, I'm not ready for this birthday to end just yet," she replied. "I think I'll go out and sit in the summer house for a while. It's so peaceful out in the gardens tonight."

"You're never ready for your birthday to be over. It's usually dragged out to a multi-week event," he laughed.

"Well, this time I'll have help. I know Grandfather and Mem are planning something. I just don't know what."

She had hoped to get some hint from Papa's expression, but he gave none. He just smiled at her, that warm, familiar smile that had always been there for her, no matter his mood or the demands of his day. "I'm so proud of the woman you've become," he said, and bent forward and kissed her forehead.

"That means a lot to me, you know."

She rose and walked to the other side of the bed. Mama rose and met her halfway, walking her to the door. "So, Arianna," she said, "are you ready to go home?"

"You know I am, Mama. I miss it. And, don't laugh when I tell you this, but I think the Island misses me too."

"Of course it does. That's why when you're far, far away, you can hear the Island calling your name."

"What?"

Mama didn't reply. She just put her arms around her and hugged her a little longer than usual. And Ari felt the softness of her cheek next to hers and the silkiness of her hair on her arm as she hugged her back. She breathed in the familiar jasmine scent of her that from her earliest memory had made her feel safe and happy. "Sweet dreams, my Island child," Mama whispered, and returned to her bed. Ari watched her go with that beautiful, fluid glide she hoped would be hers one day. She watched her slip between the sheets and slide toward the middle and roll over on her side until she was facing Papa. She rested her head on her pillow only inches from his face, and she reached for his hand and held it over James. Together they stayed like that, a sheltering cocoon around their baby boy.

Ari was half-way down the garden path when she stopped

and turned back toward the house once more. She had been trying to figure out how Mama knew. Ari never told anyone about hearing her name, not even Emma. She thought she'd be locked up in the booby-hatch. Not that she heard voices all the time or anything. It only happened in her dreams sometimes or in that place just between wake and sleep. But she knew now that there was more to it than that because there was only one way Mama could have known that the Island had been calling her. "It calls you too. Doesn't it, Mama?"

54

ARI WAS SURPRISED to find herself still in the summerhouse when she awoke. She was lying on one of the striped chaises with a view of the lily pond through the floor-to-ceiling screens. Joey's letters were still neatly stacked on the rattan side table in two piles—*read* and *unread*. She had paused between letters to look out over the gardens and back toward the rooftop of the main house, which was only visible in bits and pieces through the trees. The last thing she remembered was staring at the light of the flickering garden torches and thinking, I'll just close my eyes for a minute.

She didn't know how much time had passed. The sky was still dark and the torches were still flickering. But there seemed to be too much light coming from them now. Slowly, she lifted herself onto her elbows and shook her head to remove the fog that still remained there. Then she glanced back toward the house again where she imagined Mama and Papa and Emma and James were all peacefully sleeping and dreaming of their imminent return home. That's when she knew.

Ari bolted from the summerhouse, toppling the side table and spilling Joey's letters across the floor. She didn't care. "Mama! Papa!" she screamed and kept on running. Through the rose garden and back down the stone path to the house where her family slept. Her heart was beating in her ears and stones were cutting the bottoms of her bare feet. She didn't care. "Mama! Papa! Where are you?"

She could see the house now and the flames that engulfed the bedroom wing. They lit the gardens, revealing Mrs. Rukmana standing some distance from the verandah in her nightgown and robe. Arina and Beni were in the grass at her feet. "Mrs.

Rukmana, where are they? Where's my family?" Ari shrieked over the rumbling and the cracking and creaking.

Mrs. Rukmana stared straight ahead and pointed.

"But they had to have gotten out. Please, Mrs. Rukmana! Where are they?"

Mr. Rukmana suddenly appeared from around the far side of the house. His movements were frantic, and his face was purple and glistening. Ari ran to meet him. "Mr. Rukmana!" she called out. "Did you see them out front? Are they there, Mr. Rukmana? Please tell me they're all right!" she pleaded.

He said nothing. He just put his hands on her shoulders in an uncharacteristically familiar way and mournfully shook his head from side to side. Ari's mind began to race through a jumble of disjointed thoughts and images. *This can't be happening. This only happens to other people. Why them? Why me?* She stared into the flames, which were now leaping skyward from the top of the joglo roof, and she saw them all, running across the sands under the early morning sky, and trotting up the Cliffside path at sunset, and sitting under the stars around the old stone table with nothing more on the agenda than just being together. *It's true*, she thought. *Your life does flash before your eyes.*

That was the last thing she'd remember about that night for a very long time. The rest would remain hidden in the horror of the moment. Later, they would tell her how she had squirmed free from Mr. Rukmana's hold on her and how she had run toward the house and disappeared into the smoke that billowed out from it. They would tell her how Mr. Rukmana went in after her and only found her in the darkness by crawling toward the screams that emanated from somewhere on the floor. And how she also would have died that night if Mr. Rukmana hadn't crawled back out of the house, dragging her then unconscious body behind him. There were many things she would come to learn about that night, but there was one thing that no one would ever be able to tell her. How could she possibly go on without them?

"Mama! Papa! Emma! James!"

Part Four

The Island

55

"ARIANNA, ARIANNA," MEM'S voice was gentle and soothing. Still, Ari wished she'd go away. She didn't want to wake up just yet. She especially didn't want to open her eyes. She didn't want to see Mem standing there at the veranda entrance to her guest quarters. She didn't want to see the bathing suit and sarong she wore to the lagoon for her morning swim or the droplets of sea water that were surely falling from the end of her braid, or the rose in her cheeks or anything else that might remind her. *Morning swims and evening strolls and dinner under the stars around the old stone table.*

She hadn't been to the Great House since returning to the Island, preferring to stay with Grandfather and Mem at *Surihana*. She couldn't bring herself to even glance up the hill at the house. The house that held so many happy memories that could never be again. Ari pulled herself up on her elbows and slowly opened her eyes.

"Good morning, Mem," she said without emotion.

"Good morning, Arianna," Mem replied. "Breakfast in ten minutes on the back terrace. And don't say you're not hungry."

"Thank you, Mem. I'll be there."

That's how every morning began now. Polite exchanges. That's the least she could do. Be polite. She never intended to feel happy again. In fact, she never intended to feel *anything* again. That would take practice and discipline, she knew. But she was almost there. Eight months, fifteen days and a few odd hours and not a tear shed. Not a single one.

Ari had little recollection of the fire. Just a murky impression of shock that quickly turned to horror that touched on madness. A week later she woke up in a Djakarta hospital to find Grandfather and Mem sitting by her bedside. They had looked to her like a matching pair of porcelain bookends, upright and stoic, hands folded in laps, both wearing crisp white cotton tunics over matching trousers, with no ornamentation other than the plain leather ties that held their hair in place at the nape of their necks. At first, when she saw their ghostly gray pallor, she thought that maybe they were dead. Maybe they were all dead. But then she couldn't imagine that their next lives would have begun in that sterile, institutional green and white hospital room.

Next came months of bed rest at *Surihana*. Islanders came and went, and they brought her flowers and words of condolence, which floated around her like butterflies on a breeze that never landed. Sometimes they cried when they spoke to her. Especially Tao and Kemala who broke down when they saw her for the first time. But she never spoke to any of them. Not a single word. She just remained inside the confines of her own body, hiding from the realities that surely would still be there whenever she ventured out. She regretted the anguish this caused Grandfather and Mem, but she couldn't help it. It was all she could do to just go on breathing.

Joey came. Every day at first. His voice was reassuring and just a bit more cheerful than he meant it to be. And he told her over and over how he would always take care of her and never let anything bad happen to her ever again. If only she would come back to him. When Tommy came, he didn't say anything. He just sat next to her on the bed and held her hand. She was grateful to him for understanding. There simply was nothing to say that could possibly make any difference now.

Eventually, Joey and Tommy returned to school and the steady stream of well-wishers became a steady trickle, and Ari settled into the monotonous routine of merely existing until her life ended of its own accord. Her birthday passed without celebration, despite how hard Mem and Grandfather tried. One year. *So, this is how it's going to be,* she whispered. *Each day indistinguishable from the last. Each night never-ending.* And that's how it was. Until the night when Mama came to visit.

Ari had been deep into another dreamless sleep when

something awakened her. The scent of jasmine? She didn't know. But when she opened her eyes Mama was there, looking just as she had always looked in the best of times. Hair flowing freely down her back, feet bare, wearing a silk sarong and cropped cotton shirt that exposed her slender waist. She was standing beside her bed, looking down on her and smiling the same smile that had always greeted her when she and Mama had been separated for even the shortest time. Mama's voice, when she spoke, held no hint of sadness or despair.

You are my Island Child, Arianna. My only legacy now. I need you to continue. Papa and Emma and James need you to continue. Then she was gone, and Ari shivered, pulling the blanket up over her shoulders. Ari was alone again and for the first time, she let herself cry.

56

MEM WAS STANDING at the island in the cooking pavilion, arranging fresh pineapple spears on a Koa wood platter that already contained kiwi and mango and purple berries, the perfect complement to Ari's favorite breakfast muffins. "It's beautiful, Mem," Grandfather observed, with a sweeping gesture toward the platter. "Even your breakfasts are a work of art."

She smiled thinly at the praise. "I'm glad you think so. I don't think it will make much difference to Ari though," she said sadly. "Still, an effort must be made, I suppose."

"You sound discouraged, Mem."

"I am."

"Has something happened?"

"No. That's just it, Joseph. Nothing's happened. It's been a year since the fire, and Ari's not getting any better."

Joseph heard the weariness in her voice and saw the dullness in her once-lively eyes and his heart ached for her. "I know it must seem like that sometimes," he said, "but we must be patient. Healing comes in small steps."

"Not this small!" she replied emphatically, pounding her fist on the butcher block in exasperation. "Don't you see it, Joseph? Ari never talks about them. She never says their names out loud. And we're afraid to speak their names for fear we might upset her. It's as if Mary and Ethan and Emma and that sweet baby, James, never even existed!" She grabbed the edge of the island, steadying herself, closing her eyes as she did so. When she opened them again, she was calm. "Remember, Joseph, how their voices used to float through *Surihana* when they were here. And how often their names were spoken when they were not.

422

Joseph rushed around the island and wrapped himself around her, stroking her as she began to cry. "I miss that, too," he said in a barely audible whisper.

They stood together for some time, suspended between their concern for Ari and their own profound grief. At last, Joseph spoke. "Do you remember how happy we were that night Ari finally spoke to us?"

"I thought that was the beginning of the healing," Mem sighed.

"It was," he assured her.

"But, Joseph, Ari really isn't any further along now than she was then. I was just in to wake her, and . . ."

"What happened, Mem?" he asked, gently. "Was she uncivil to you?"

"Of course not," Mem replied, just managing a hint of a smile. "Quite the opposite, really. She was so completely *polite*!"

"You make that sound like a bad thing, Mem."

"It is when it's the politeness of strangers." Mem's lips started to quiver, and words became difficult. "Oh, Joseph, Arianna is all we have left. But it's as if she died that night too."

The last word escaped Mem as a great wail. Her shoulders slumped and her knees buckled, and she collapsed into Grandfather's arms, tears pouring uncontrollably down her cheeks.

Ari had been standing in the shadows at the entrance to the cooking pavilion, listening to the conversation. She had done a lot of hiding in shadows since leaving her bed. No one to engage there or make her talk or, even worse, make her think. But now she propelled herself toward Mem on a wave of emotion. Mem was sobbing, and it broke Ari's heart to see and to know that she was the cause. "Oh, Mem, I'm so sorry! I'm so sorry!" she cried through the deluge of her own tears.

Grandfather watched her approaching. He wasn't sorry for Ari's distress. He had waited for this moment for a very long time.

"I'm so sorry," Ari said for the hundredth time over breakfast. "I know I've been selfish. I was just so confused. Waking up in the hospital. I didn't even know where I was. Or if I was just in the middle of some horrible nightmare, and Mama was going to come wake me up any minute. And when I knew that it was all real, I didn't know what to do."

"Arianna, don't be so hard on yourself," Grandfather said. "Grief is a difficult process to go through under normal circumstances. But this, coming so suddenly and so violently and so very early in your life."

"I guess," she sighed, wiping a stray tear from her cheek. "But I'm scared, Grandfather."

"Of what, child?"

"Pretty much everything, I guess."

"That's natural, Ari. When you've lost as much as you have, it's tempting to just give up on life. If you don't have anything— or anyone—then you have nothing to lose."

"But you and Mem haven't given up."

"We still have you, child."

She looked at him when he said this and traced with her eyes the little lines that had appeared on his face since Djakarta. And then at Mem and the single white streak that now ran from her left temple all the way to the bottom of her braid. For the first time she saw how precariously their strength floated upon the surface above a torrent of pain they had been unable to release. Because of her.

"So, how do we begin?" she asked.

Grandfather reached over and gently squeezed her hand. "We begin together."

First, they mourned. Just talking about Mama and Papa and Emma and James, Just hearing their names out loud produced rivers of tears from all of them. Even Tippy, who had taken to following Ari everywhere she went, cried a low, despondent howl at the mere mention of James. Ari was consumed by what she had lost. She wasn't ready for fond memories, and she especially wasn't ready to return to the places of those memories. So, she never went to the Dolphin Lagoon or the Sunset Bench, and she still hadn't laid eyes on the Great House since returning from Djakarta. Pretty much, she just stayed inside the walls of *Surihana*. It was enough to deal with all the pictures that Grandfather and Mem kept about the place.

Particularly those on the octagonal table. She just wasn't ready to deal with ghosts.

"I don't know how you do it, Mem," she said to her one day over lunch by the pool. They had made a pitcher of iced green tea and fresh mint and prepared hummus and cucumber sandwiches and had set them on the little rattan table outside the office, waiting for Grandfather's return from a meeting with Batara. "You and Grandfather still go everywhere we used to spend time together. How can you stand it? Seeing Paradise ruined, I mean. It's not like you've had any more experience with this kind of thing than I have."

"Don't be so sure, Ari. *Paradise* isn't a place where nothing bad ever happens."

"But—" Ari was interrupted by the squeak of the front gate hinges and Grandfather's sudden appearance striding toward them.

"You didn't need to wait on lunch for me," he said.

"But you're glad we did, aren't you, old man?" Mem smiled, reaching up and squeezing his hand as he bent down to kiss her. Little bits of playfulness between them had recently reappeared, and it felt warm and familiar. Ari let out a little laugh before quickly reining it back in.

Grandfather regarded her for a moment. "You needn't be afraid to be happy, child."

No matter how often it happened, it still startled her every time Grandfather knew what she was thinking even before she did. "I know," she answered. Ari sat quietly looking at Grandfather and Mem. Looking at what was left of the family she had once known.

Grandfather spoke for her. "You want to ask us about the fire, don't you, Ari?"

"Yes."

"How much do you want to know?"

"I don't *want* to know anything, but I have to know or I won't ever be able to get past that night."

"Are you sure you're ready?"

"No, but I have to know."

57

ARINA'S UNCLE HAD set the fire. But not before he killed Emma where she slept and then Papa and Mama and James. He would have killed Ari too but in his drunkenness, he accidentally spilled petrol on his own clothing while dousing beds and drapes and doorways. He died in the fire with the others that night before he had a chance to exact his full revenge against all those he blamed for his own pitiful circumstances. Only Beni was meant to live. The boy was to be payment for the loss of his own son.

The flames were still contained pretty much in the bedroom wing when Ari ran into the house, so she sustained no visible burns, but the smoke was everywhere, thick and black. She had inhaled quite a bit of it before Mr. Rukmana could pull her out. She didn't really feel any lasting effects from it. But then she hadn't exactly been exerting herself.

As Ari listened to Grandfather recounting the details of that night, she could feel the emotions stirring—the sadness, the fear. But it was the anger that troubled her. Mama had been right about Djakarta and the dangers that lurked just behind the welcome signs. And, for just an instant, Ari was mad at Papa all over again for bringing them there. But at least she knew she shouldn't be, and that would have to be good enough for now.

"Mr. Rukmana must think I'm horrible," she said when Grandfather had finished. "Not a word from me since the fire. Not even a *thank you*."

"We've remained in contact with the Rukmanas," he replied. "They understand. But perhaps, if you're ready now, you might want to write them yourself."

"I'll do it today. I owe them that."

"You'll need their new address. By the time the fire was put out there wasn't much left of the house. I understand the owner is going to rebuild eventually, but the Rukmanas needed employment in the meantime."

"You know where they're working?"

"Yes. They went to work for your friends over there. The Pembrokes."

"Really?" Ari exclaimed. She didn't know why exactly, but that pleased her that they were all there in Djakarta together.

"And Arina and Beni? Did they go to the Pembrokes, too?"

"I'm afraid they've disappeared," Grandfather told her.

"What! What do you mean?"

"Mr. Rukmana thinks that she might have been frightened that the authorities would blame her. Or maybe she just blamed herself, but by the time Mrs. Rukmana went to find them to tell them that the fire was out, she and Beni were gone."

Ari stared at Grandfather, brow furrowed, saying nothing. He and Mem waited. "I know where they've gone," she said at last. "That horrible place down by the canal. The people there are invisible. We've got to find them, Grandfather. Please! We've got to find them and bring them here."

A smile began to slowly spreading itself across Grandfather's face. He didn't have to look at Mem to know that she wore one, too. "Then, Arianna," he said softly, "that's exactly what *we* shall do."

58

THAT WAS THE second time Ari thought about that horrible night in Djakarta and how it affected the lives of someone other than herself. Small steps, maybe. But they were steps, nonetheless, and Grandfather and Mem knew their significance. Ari had traveled from within herself, from the shadows to the outer boundaries of *Surihana*. The arrival of Arina and Beni would draw her out of her walled sanctuary and back into the Island community where her extended family had been anxiously waiting to receive her all these months. Small steps or a million miles. "That all depends upon your perspective," Grandfather told Mem, that evening at the Bench.

"You do know, Joseph, that if we can find Arina and Beni and bring them here, Ari will throw herself into their lives, but that won't be the same as getting on with her own life."

"Of course not. But it will be a dress rehearsal. Patience, Mem."

Finding Arina and Beni was not difficult. They were living where Ari said they would be. Well, not living exactly. Barely surviving by the look of them when Grandfather was finally able to bring them to the Island. It took some convincing to persuade Arina to attempt the journey. She had resigned herself to living and dying down by the canal, and she had already seen where every attempt in her life to be happy had gotten her. But then there was her Beni and, in the end, her mother's heart and Grandfather's persistence gave her the courage she needed to try one last time.

Ari and Mem were waiting at the beach when Uncle Tao's boat pulled into South Bay bringing Grandfather and Arina and Beni to the Island. It was Ari's first time venturing out from *Surihana*, and it was easier than she thought it would be. Of course, the path from the house to the beach took her through the west end of the Gathering Place, near the school. The Great House and the Dolphin Lagoon and the Sunset Bench and even the big rocks over the Bay where she and Joey used to talk for hours were all at the eastern end.

She tried to keep the horror off her face when she first saw Arina and Beni. They had had a chance to bathe, and Grandfather had obviously bought them new clothes for the journey, but their clothes billowed off their emaciated bodies and couldn't hide the starvation and deprivation that had been their circumstances since Arina's uncle set the fire. The last time Ari had spoken to Arina, she was so full of hope and enthusiasm for what lay ahead for her and Beni. Now, there was nothing in her eyes or her expression to tell you she was actually alive, except maybe for the slight fear Ari thought she saw there. Fear maybe at seeing her again, the daughter of the family her uncle had murdered.

Ari let go of Mem's hand and ran toward Arina and embraced her warmly. "Welcome home," she said.

"Thank you, Miss Ari. Thank you for letting my Beni come to this beautiful place."

"Arina, I'm so sorry I didn't think to bring you here when I first came home. Can you ever forgive me?"

Ari didn't wait for an answer. She quickly knelt down until she was eye-level with Beni. "Welcome home, Beni," she smiled. He just stared past her with dark eyes that looked like two huge black holes that had been carved out of his bony face. It worried her, his silence, until she realized what he was staring at. "Oh, Tippy! Come, boy! Come meet a new friend!"

Tippy came bounding up and jumped up on Beni and started licking his face all over. Ari corralled him and told him to sit, which he did. When Beni caught his breath, he looked at Ari, and then back at Tippy, and the littlest hint of a smile briefly flashed across his face. "Tippy!" he repeated. "He James's dog."

Ari remembered how James used to go on and on to Beni about Tippy, the *Wonder Dog*. And the more he prattled, the bigger and braver and more wondrous Tippy became. *"And Tippy and me go swimming like the big boys. And we find snakes and monkeys. And Tippy and me climb up big, big, big rocks, this big."* He'd reach his arms way up into the air when he said this and stand on his tippy toes.

Ari laughed out loud at the thought of her baby brother's antics. And it suddenly occurred to her that this was the first time she had thought about him without crying. Grandfather and Mem had been trying to assure her that one day she would find a way to make the leap from mourning to remembering, but she hadn't been able to even imagine it. Who would have thought that this emaciated little waif would be the one to show her the way. "Yes, Beni, he was James's dog. And now James wants us to take care of him. Can you do that?"

"Yes, ma'am," the little boy answered with a serious look on his thin face.

Ari did throw herself into Arina and Beni's lives. She nursed them, and she found Arina work with Mrs. Nari, and she brought Beni to school and stayed with him each day until he was able to come all by himself like a big boy. Every single night Beni came to her quarters from across the courtyard where he and Arina slept with his little book bag over his shoulder, and Ari tutored him until he began catching up with his classmates.

In April, Old Batara and Maru suggested that the bungalow that had belonged to Ghidra's great aunt who had just passed this winter be fixed up as a permanent home for Arina and Beni. When Arina heard this, she dissolved into tears. She had never had a home of her own. And to think that these people would be the ones to give it to her after what her family had taken from them.

It was a beautiful little bungalow. Sunny and bright with fresh breezes flowing through every room. Ghidra's great aunt had an eye for color, being one of the Island's most accomplished fabric designers, and from the little parlor to the kitchen to the two bedrooms and covered porch that wrapped itself all the way round the exterior, the pastels and warm woods and potted plants and hand-dyed fabrics all conspired to make this home a cheerful, happy place to live. But best of all, it was located in the Neighborhood, just three doors down from the Tejaras, a family neighborhood filled with the sounds of children playing and laughing, innocent and untouched by the evils that befell children elsewhere. How different a sound it was than those made by the children along the canal, when indeed they had the strength to make a sound. It gave Arina hope, if not for herself, at least for Beni that he had a chance in this life to be happy.

59

SUMMER ARRIVED WITH the usual fanfare—students, laden down with the products of their labors, screaming across the gathering place toward three whole months of no shoes, no homework, and no responsibilities of any kind beyond their normal chores. Ari stood on the steps with Grandfather and Mem and watched them go. Some of the older students, the ones who were graduating this year, headed straight for the beach. It was a kind of ritual. They came to the last day of school with bathing suits under their clothes. At final bell, they went to the beach, put their papers under a coconut, discarded their clothes and splashed into South Bay. There would already be a lot of Islanders waiting there to watch them and hand them tall drinks and dry towels when they finally emerged from the water. Ari would head there soon. But, for now, she was content to watch Beni skipping across the lawn to where Arina waited with Mrs. Tejara. He was holding up the reading medal he earned for having learned the most in the shortest time, and their delighted expressions displayed just the right amount of appreciation.

"Our little Beni is doing wonderfully, isn't he?" Mem observed.

"He's not the only one, if my spies are accurate," Grandfather added with a playful note.

"What are you talking about, old man?"

He just stood there, rocking back and forth, doing his wide-eyed Charlie Chaplin impersonation.

"Come on, Grandfather, give!" Ari urged.

"Well, I have it on good authority that Arina has been seen strolling on the beach in the evenings in the company of Kenji Gupta's youngest brother."

"Ravi? How do you know?"

"Your Uncle Tao told me. He heard it from Herry who got it from Paku who said he's seen them on several occasions."

Mem chuckled. "Well, you old gossip!"

"We're going to have to build a beauty parlor on the Island so you bunch of roosters will have a place to *cluck*," Ari teased.

Ghidra and Kemala had been standing a short distance away listening to the laughter emanating from their friends. It was a song that hadn't been heard on the Island for a long time. "They're coming back to us, aren't they?" Ghidra observed.

"Yes, I think maybe they are," Kemala replied. "But it won't ever really be quite the same, will it?"

"No. Not for them. Or for you either. You lost your best friend when Mary died, and we've all been so concerned about Joseph and Mem and Ari, I don't think we thought enough about you and Tao."

"I think it was especially hard for Tao," Kemala said. "He and Mary were friends since they were in diapers together. Just last night he was saying how he still half expects to see her and Ethan coming down the path from the Great House on their way to a stroll on the beach."

"It's been forever since the Great House was open. I miss it," Ghidra said a bit sadly.

"We had high hopes that maybe Joey and Ari would be the ones to reopen it. But it looks like a joining of the Heywoods and Ahmanjayas just isn't in the cards."

"Does Ari know yet?"

"About Joey and Lili Yao? I don't think Mem has told her."

"Well, maybe she'll be all right with it," Ghidra offered. "She was the one who rejected him."

"But that was so soon after the fire. Maybe she regrets that now."

"Or maybe I'm the one who's regretting it," Kemala smiled. "You know, the idea of Mary and Ethan and Tao and me continuing on through our children or something. Anyway, no use speculating. We'll know tomorrow."

"How's that?" Ghidra asked.

"Joey's coming home for the summer."

60

ARI WAS SITTING on the little bench under the Japanese Maple when Grandfather and Mem returned from their morning swim at the lagoon. She had already prepared breakfast and was awaiting their arrival before pushing down the plunger on the coffee carafe and setting out the food. "Good swim?" she inquired cheerfully.

"Quite good!" Grandfather assured her.

"Then I'll just go and set out the breakfast on the back terrace."

She got up to go and Mem stopped her. "Ari, wait a moment, would you? There's something I—we've been meaning to speak to you about."

Ari turned back to face them. "Oh, you mean about Joey and Lili Yao?" she smiled.

"Arianna Elizabeth Heywood! How long have you known?"

"About a month, I guess. I overheard a couple of the teaching assistants talking about it one morning when I brought Beni to school."

"Are you all right, child?" Grandfather wanted to know.

"I am now. At first it was a bit of a shock. You know, hearing that he was seeing someone else. Not that he didn't have every right to. I was the one who rejected him. Still, even if we don't belong together like that, I think I'm always going to be just a little jealous of any woman he falls in love with."

"He's coming in on the evening launch," Grandfather said as he gently laid a hand on her shoulder.

That startled Ari into silence. When she spoke again her voice was surprisingly spirited. "I'm glad he's coming home," she exclaimed. "We have a lot to say to each other." When neither

Mem nor Grandfather replied, she continued. "I've been thinking a lot about this lately. I used to think I turned Joey away
because I just wasn't going to love anyone again. I was determined not to feel anything again. But it was more than that."
She paused to organize her thoughts.

"What do you think it was?" Mem asked.

"We had such plans, Mem. Tommy and Emma and Joey
and me. We were going to go to college together, and share
a house, and double-date and...and...just do everything
together. But when Emma died, being with Joey didn't feel the
same anymore. And I got to thinking that if that were so, maybe
Joey and I weren't meant to love each other that way after all.
Maybe we just got swept up in Tommy and Emma's happiness
and for me, maybe just a little, it was the idea of not being the
little baby left behind by the other three. I don't know how to
say it exactly, but maybe I wasn't as grown up as I liked to think
I was, and I was really in love with the idea of being in love.
Does any of this make sense?"

Grandfather and Mem smiled at one another and then at
Ari. "It does," Mem assured her. But Mem knew Ari was afraid
to feel again, even if she refused to admit it to herself, and she
worried about it day and night.

61

WHEN GRANDFATHER AND Mem returned from the Bench that night and found Ari's note they weren't surprised. *Gone to the Rock* is all it said.

Ari knew Joey would come when the torches were lit and the moon was on its ascending arc. There he was, loping up the beach toward her, in a pair of soft, bleached-out denims and no shirt or shoes. His hair was longer than the last time she had seen him, and it moved up and down in perfect time to each one of his long, vigorous strides. When he got within range, he saw that she was smiling and waving wildly, and he was relieved to see a bit of his old Ari back again. But it also unsettled him. The sight of her standing up there, tall and statuesque, feet spread and planted firmly on the rock, hair swirling out in all directions, rekindled a momentary stirring in him that he thought had died when he fell in love with Lili.

They embraced as if nothing had ever changed between them. But it had changed, Ari knew, and it needed talking about straight away. No avoidance. No awkward small talk. "I know about Lili," she announced before he had a chance to speak.

He backed away, and she could see the startled look on his face. "You never were one to beat around the bush," he laughed. He grabbed her hand and dropped down onto the rock, pulling her with him, until they were sitting opposite each other, cross-legged, elbows on knees and leaning in.

"It's all right, Joey. Really. You deserve to be happy."

"You don't hate me too much?"

"That's funny," she smiled up at him. "I was going to ask you the same thing."

"How could I ever hate you, Ari?

"Oh, Joey, I was just horrible to you when I came back from Djakarta. I didn't mean to be. I just couldn't help it."

"No one could blame you for that. But I sure got an earful from my parents when I told them about Lili. I felt like I'd not only betrayed you but the whole Island."

"I'm sorry, Joey. It's not fair to you or to her. Speaking of which, how did you two end up together anyway? I mean, I knew she had her sights on you way back when we went to lunch there the last time. I just didn't know you'd fall so easy," she teased.

"What are you talking about?"

"Never mind. Just tell me about her."

"We met at school. She's really smart, Ari. She skipped a grade. That's why she started at the university when she was only seventeen. She's eighteen now."

"Oh, the age of consent," Ari smiled.

"Never mind about that," he retorted. "Besides, it's not the age of consent in her family. Anyway, if I may continue without interruption," he said, putting his hand over her mouth. "We met at school. She's in pre-med too, taking eighteen units a semester and going to summer session. She plans to finish her undergrad work in three years."

Ari listened as Joey went on to tell her everything about Lili. About the day they met, and their first date, and how worried he was at first that she was too young, but how she's so much more sophisticated than her years, wiser and more worldly than you'd expect from one so gentle and unassuming. She could hear the love in his voice and the happiness that Lili had brought him. And she was glad for him. She truly was. Even if she was just the tiniest bit jealous, not necessarily of Lili, but more because she knew she'd never have that kind of love for someone herself.

"Was Mrs. Yao okay with you two? I mean, with the cultural difference and all?" Ari asked. "I like her a lot, but I wouldn't want her mad at me."

"I thought it was going to be an issue. Lili did too. But Mrs. Yao has great respect for our people. You know your Grandfather and Mem were very helpful to her many years ago when her husband died. She says she's never forgotten that."

"This all sounds pretty serious."

"Well, we've been together since last fall. It's too soon to tell about the future, but I know I'll never be sorry that I loved her. Just like I'll never be sorry for loving you, Ari. You do know that I still love you, don't you? I always will." Ari smiled but didn't reply.

They stayed on the rock late into the night, talking about everything. How she wasn't sure she could ever leave *Surihana* or be anything or do anything beyond just trying to be helpful around the house and maybe the Island and with the school children, of course. And they talked about Emma and Tommy and how devastated he was and still is and probably always would be. Ari said how she understood because she had lost her sister and her best friend and the person who was always there whenever she imagined the happiness she would know in her life.

Then she told him about Djakarta and everything she could remember about the fire, which was more now than it once had been. And what it was like running into the house. The searing heat. The smoke that blanketed her and blinded her eyes and filled her nose and lungs. The terror. The desperation. The despair. The surrender. The last thing she remembered was begging the Gods to not let her family suffer. She had no way of knowing that they were already dead.

Joey held back the tears that threaten to form and grabbed both of Ari's hands and didn't let go. "I can't even imagine how terrifying that night must have been for you. I'm so sorry. I'm so sorry."

The rest of the night they spent conjuring up old times. They started slowly at first, just feeling their way through the multitude of fond memories from which they could choose.

"My dad says you haven't been back to the Great House since you came home."

"I haven't been anywhere our family used to spend time together. Except *Surihana*, of course."

"Let me take you, Ari. We'll start slow, and I won't force you to do anything you don't think you're ready to do. I promise. You can trust me."

She thought for a moment before answering. Then with one deep breathe in said, "I can't, Joey. I'm just not ready," she exhaled. "I'm just not ready. I'm sorry."

"Don't be sorry, Ari. It's okay," Joey said, comforting her in his arms. They sat in silence for a few minutes before she heard his voice again.

"Someday you'll have to go back, you know that right." He wasn't asking her a question. "You can't live in the past forever. You'll have to let them go." Ari knew that Joey was only doing what he thought was best for her, but she couldn't help her rising anger and her next words were sharper than she intended.

"Why does everyone keep telling me that? No one understands. Not you, not Mem, not Grandfather. No one gets it."

"I'm sure Grandfather and Mem understand, they suffered a loss too."

"It's not the same, Joey." Ari sniffled and wiped a tear away with the back of her hand. "They still have each other. I have no one. No one!" she emphasized. Joey reached over to hug her. It was a friendly hug, but nothing more.

"I'm sorry, Joey. I didn't mean—" her voice trailed off.

"I know, Ari. It's okay."

Mem heard Ari return in the night. And she waited for nearly an hour before making her nightly check on her. As always, she stood on the veranda outside Ari's quarters and listened for her breathing and squinted until she could just make out her figure and then she heard the sound of quiet weeping. It had been nearly two years, but Ari still cried herself to sleep every night. Mem pursed her lips and shook her head, not in anger, but in frustration. Frustration that she was unable to help Ari leave her past behind. It's not that she wanted her to forget them, how could she? But Mem knew it was time for her to look back on the happy times and look forward to her future. It's what Ethan and Mary would have wanted. She'd tried to help, but Ari was still stuck in Djakarta and she didn't know what to do. As Mem turned away, she heard Ari whisper "I love you. I'm so sorry for everything. Please forgive me. Forgive me that I couldn't save you." A tear ran down Mem's check.

The next morning was full of sunshine and blue skies and fresh breezes. Even one of the wild peacocks that inhabited the grove of tall trees that ran down to the stream behind the house had decided to strut around the courtyard today, fanning his tail and parading his elegance.

"Good morning!" she called across the courtyard when Grandfather and Mem appeared. Mem noticed the tired look in Ari's eyes, but was encouraged by her chipper greeting.

"Well, good morning back!" Grandfather replied. "What are you doing up so early?"

"I thought maybe I would join you at the Lagoon for a morning swim."

Grandfather and Mem exchanged glances and squeezed the hands they were already clasping. "We'd be honored," he said with a slight bow.

They went to the cooking pavilion and prepared a basket of fruits and breads and sliced ham from last night's dinner and a thermos of chilled guava juice.

They grabbed towels, beach mats, and the blanket that always awaited the spontaneous picnic on the seat of the fan chair that sat poolside in the front courtyard. And like a little brigade of soldiers they marched down the road toward the Dolphin Lagoon.

It was the first of many such mornings that summer and Mem hoped that maybe Ari was finally starting to move forward. But each night Mem heard Ari cry and send up her whispered apology to the heavens.

Tommy didn't return to the Island that summer, but Lili came over to visit Joey. Ari welcomed her into the group like any *sister* would. She watched Lili and Joey together. Like any good friend, she was glad for them both, but she had to admit it hurt watching them so happy together, and she knew that while she and Joey would always be friends, it would never be the same. But nothing would really ever be the same, would it?

62

TIME SEEMED TO pass quickly, and the next several years came and went uneventfully. Ari immersed herself in the Island community, ready to take part in any activity or celebration where work needed doing or committees needed organizing. And she was happy to stand up for Arina on her wedding day and so proud of Beni who stood with Ravi, his adopted daddy. She even served Adi to Lili at her first Celebration when finally Mrs. Yao gave permission to the engaged couple to dance.

But when Grandfather and Mem suggested that maybe she should enroll at the university, that it was never too late to get a good education, she declined. "Seeing all those students blithely going along, living the life that was supposed to be mine, I know it's wrong, but I think I would begin to resent them. I hate to admit it, but there's still a little residual *why me* floating around in my brain."

"But you know how important education has always been to our family. We hate to see you give that up, Arianna," Grandfather lamented.

"But why should I have to give it up," she replied, with the wily grin she sometimes borrowed from him. "The two best teachers on the face of the earth live right here on the Island."

"I'm guessing, child, you already have a plan?"

"I was thinking that we could get the Student Handbook from Mainland University and chart a course of Independent Study. We could get the reading lists and we could discuss the books and argue and debate and maybe I might even win a point or two along the way."

"Have you thought at all about what you would like to focus on?" Mem wanted to know.

"Well, literature, of course, and classical archaeology."

"Archaeology?"

"Yes. I guess I've always been fascinated with ancient things like statues and frescoes and buildings and, well, everything. They say so much about who a people were. They speak to you, you know, long after the people who made them have left this life."

"Where did all that come from?"

"I think it started when I was really little. I wasn't even James's age the first time I remember standing in front of the two stone statues near the gathering pavilion at the Great House. You know the ones that I always thought looked like you and Grandfather."

"Yes, those," Mem smiled.

"Something about them. I don't know. I could almost hear voices if I stared at them long enough."

"Okay then," Grandfather said. "Anything else?"

"Literature. All kinds. Classical. Modern. Ethnic. But it has to include Dickens. Anything British."

And so Ari did complete her university education. It was by no means easy. Grandfather and Mem saw to that, along with their old friend, Malcolm Bostwick, Department Chair for the School of Cultural Studies. Of course, Old Willie was enlisted as Ari's mentor in cultural anthropology. Who better? His coursework was rigorous and class hours long. Night classes were conducted around the dinner table at *Surihana*—few lectures and much discourse—with Grandfather and Mem as active participants. But by day Ari could be spotted almost anywhere, usually in the company of one of her teachers, strolling together across the Gathering Place and down the beach or through the central valley and up the terraced hillsides or sailing out beyond the headlands in Old Willie's little fishing boat, always deep in animated conversation, and always accompanied by a rucksack full of books and a Kodak camera. It felt good to let her intellect run wild. She hadn't let anything run wild in a very long time. And if she was to spend the rest of her life keeping her emotions in check, at least she had her intellect to ignite a little passion.

In the fall of her senior year, Ari disappeared into Mem's studio behind *Surihana* and remained there from morning until near sunset for weeks at a time. The Islanders were glad that Ari was painting again, but no one more so than Mem who often joined her there. Ari wouldn't tell the Islanders what she was painting beyond telling them that she was working on her senior thesis, and that it was probably the first one ever written in oils.

In early June there was a showing of Ari's paintings at the Fujiri Gallery on the Mainland. Everyone came, including a large gathering of Mainlanders who had known Ari since she was very little. Professor Bostwick came and the entire panel to whom Ari had already presented her senior thesis. The panel's chairman gave the opening remarks. She said that it was most unusual to see a senior thesis hanging on the walls of an art gallery, but most thrilling for an art lover like herself. Then Grandfather spoke. He shared a few anecdotes of long hours spent discussing and debating and planning and proceeding. Of arguments over the commonly accepted versus the courage of conviction. And when Mem ceremoniously cleared her throat, signaling him that he had digressed too far, he gave over the stage to Professor Bostwick, if somewhat reluctantly.

When the professor stepped forward, he peered out at his audience through his bottle-thick horned-rimmed glasses with an expression that gently chastised whisperers into silence. He really was almost a caricature of himself, Ari thought, as she stared back at him. His clothes were clean, but a bit rumpled, especially around the elbows of his favorite Khaki green cardigan, and his hair was disheveled and obviously hadn't been barber-cut in a very long time. But the voice that projected out from him to the back of the room was polished, precise, and very, very British.

"The French called it *Paradis*," he began, "which they borrowed from the Latin, *Paradises*, which was taken from the

Greek, *Paradeiso*, which came from an Eastern Old Iranian word for *walled enclosure—Pairidaeza*. We can find its name written in Akkadian and Arabic and Aramaic and Hebrew and still know that we have not yet found all traces of it. And what does this tell us? That from the beginning of time humankind, in all its cultural manifestations and despite all its conflicts and confrontations, has joined together in the quest to find that most elusive of all places—*Paradise*. Sadly, most have failed in the attempt and they have rationalized their failure by conjuring up images of *Paradise* where only the immortals could live. Sacred gardens, hallowed halls, eternal life."

He paused, smiling broadly, and began slowly to sweep his hand around in a wide arc, his index finger extended toward the audience. "However, those of you here tonight who are Islanders and those of us who have been privileged to be invited into your homes, we know that there is a paradise right here on earth where the most common among us may walk with the immortals with equal stature. It is a paradise that requires of its inhabitants neither great wealth nor power nor even perfect goodness. And it requires no great expedition to the ends of the earth to find it. Just a short sail from the end of the Mainland pier."

The professor turned to look at Ari who stood nearby with Grandfather and Mem and Batara and Maru. And from his expression Ari guessed that he was trying to work out what he would say next, which seemed odd to her since his remarks thus far were obviously so familiar to him. "I have a confession to make," he said at last, turning back to the audience. "For many years now I have felt—dare I say it? A bit, well, envious, yes, envious," he repeated almost to himself. "If not for an accident of birth, I thought, I should have lived on the Island, shouldn't I? It never occurred to me, until that splendid day Miss Heywood walked into the conference room at McFaddon Hall and presented to our panel her senior thesis, that my attitude was no different than that of all those before me who had sought *Paradise* and failed. But that day, Miss Heywood presented to us something rarely found in the cultural artifacts of humankind's existence—a promise of Paradise, which is both tangible and attainable to anyone who seeks it. It is a paradise whose secret lies not in some exotic location but in one simple truth. That truth, well, perhaps I may convey it best by paraphrasing an ancient wisdom from Buddhist teachings. *There is no path to Paradise. Paradise is the path.*"

He paused briefly to let his last remark settle in and to scrutinize the faces of his audience, as was his habit in class, for signs of confusion or enlightenment. Then he shifted his champagne glass to his right hand and motioned Ari to come forward with his left. "On behalf of all of us here today, I want to thank you, Miss Heywood, for this breathtakingly beautiful, and deeply thought-provoking exhibit. And on behalf of myself, Arianna, I want to thank you for informing my thinking and illuminating my way."

"Here here!" the audience answered and dispersed around the gallery in search of their own illumination or reaffirmation depending upon their circumstance.

63

"THIS MUST BE what it's like to wait for reviews after the opening of a Broadway Show in New York," Ari observed in a whispered remark to Mem. "How do you do this all the time?"

"It was hard at first," she admitted. "But for an artist, once you find your voice, it's really only important that *you* like what you have to say. Of course, I was too young to know that then, but, in time, my art became widely appreciated, and I was glad I didn't change my voice to please someone else."

"I don't know, Mem. I don't think I'll ever be as wise or self-assured as you."

They remained there at the edges of the exhibit until Ari had scrutinized enough smiling faces to feel confident in going forth and mingling among them. It wasn't that she was afraid of their criticism. After all, the only ones there who would be critical of her were Professor Bostwick and the panel, and they'd already shown their approval of her work with their compliments and their A grade. But she didn't want to disappoint anyone, especially the Islanders. If the voice in her paintings *lied*, they'd be the ones to know it.

She took a slow, circuitous route around the gallery, always staying to the backs of patrons who were examining her work, listening for their comments. Mem watched her do this from the shelter of a giant areca palm, one of several that had been brought in to stage the exhibit. It was strange to be the one standing in the shadows, observing from a distance, but for now that's where she needed to remain. Ari had spent long enough on the periphery of her own life. It was time for her to take center stage. In more ways than just this one.

But Mem already knew what Ari was just now beginning to glean from the bits of conversation she overheard. Her paintings were brilliant. She had captured the very essence of Island life and with that, the very essence of Paradise itself. The moment he laid eyes on Ari's paintings, Malcolm Bostwick understood the anthropological, the cultural, no, the *spiritual* significance of Ari's work. The enormity of it. All those millennia spent in the futile search for *Paradise,* only to have its secrets revealed in the paintings of a young woman. Mem smiled. She knew Mary and Ethen would be proud of the woman their little girl was becoming. Still Mem worried. She knew Ari was looking from the outside in and that her newfound confidence was as fragile as the bright corals of the lagoon during a raging storm.

Ari meandered over to where Kemala and Tao stood in front of a large canvas she called *Coming Home.* In it she had painted the coming together of friends and family at the end of another day. The evening launch was tied up at the end of the pier, and there was a scattering of people on the beach and, of course, children splashing in the water, and there was a kaleidoscope of sarongs and business suits inter-mingling just beyond the gang plank. She had watched this scene unfold a thousand times, sitting with Grandfather and Mem on the Sunset Bench, and it had always captivated her long before she really knew why. It was the incongruity of the clothes, which if you knew the Islanders who wore them, wasn't incongruous at all.

Painting after painting, the lush, vibrant foliage and jagged peaks and forests of coconut palms and sparkling waters all served as backdrops to the lives of the Islanders whose happiness she had captured perfectly with brush and paint. On one canvas she had painted Batara and Maru, steadfast and sturdy and constant as the tides, welcoming Joey and Lili's newborn daughter into the Island community at her Naming Ceremony. This painting held a special place in Ari's heart. Joey and Lili had asked Ari to serve as Godmother to their little girl. On another, old Mr. Padua was standing in front of a beautiful mahogany screen. His face was as intricately carved as his work, and his eyes were so clear and intensely dark that, placed on that ancient face, they seemed almost incongruous.

Not all the paintings had people in them. There was a collection of small canvases devoted to some of the rare flowers that called the Island home. And the collection would not have been complete without the larger piece of a magnificent Bird of Paradise that stood near the gallery entrance. This was the last of her paintings and held special meaning to Ari. Mama had cared for and carried her Bird of Paradise from posting to posting and back to the Island again over and over and over as if it was her fourth child. Papa could never quite understand why and often grumbled about having to make special arrangements to bring the plant in and out of different countries, although he always smiled, shook his head and kissed Mama on the forehead before making the necessary preparations. *"For you, my Bird of Paradise, I will do anything."* Ari smiled remembering how Papa had often called Mama his *Bird of Paradise.* Then there was a particularly beautiful canvas of the old banyan tree under an orange sunset sky, which, if examined closely, revealed two little girls peeking out from behind the tendrils that poured down from the canopy. Ari and Mem stopped to examine each one of them, but they stood the longest in front of the painting of the old stone table under the bhodi tree. The candles were lit, as were the torches, but neither was as luminous as the star-studded sky. Ari couldn't bring herself to paint the family in this one. It took everything she had to paint them in another. So, she set the table with seven places and left it at that.

There were three mural-sized canvases that drew large crowds, particularly among the Mainlanders. The first depicted Maru and Mem on the steps of the women's hut, regaling soon-to-be dancers with stories of past Celebrations. In the background were several pairs of women, first-time dancers and their Adis, among them a beautiful dark-haired woman and a chestnut-haired girl. The woman was handing something to the girl. It was peacock blue and looked to be very, very old.

The next canvas was of Celebration Night. In it Batara and Maru were holding court with a ring of Islanders in signature silks looking on and a gathering of dancers whose passionate expressions were reflected in the torchlight. On the far right, down toward the banyan tree, a couple was slipping away from the others. His arm was around her shoulder, and hers was around his waist, and they were wearing the family's Bird of Paradise signature silk. "So, Ari, who are they, Grandfather and me or Mama and Papa?"

"Both. Or neither. I'm not sure," she said and walked on.

The last painting was also a large canvas, not as large as *Celebration Night*, but certainly large enough to draw instant attention. The nameplate at the bottom of the simple wooden frame read: *Morning in Paradise*. It depicted the Dolphin Lagoon at first light. The sky was a hazy orange, and the outcroppings of the verdant landscape were just awakening into full brilliance, but the rising sun had already toasted the sands to a golden brown. Mama and Papa and Grandfather and Mem were walking out of the water toward the beach. Each man held an arm around his wife as they walked. Emma was just turning toward the palm grove and the roof peaks of the Great House that peered out from beyond. She was carrying tatami mats under her left arm and a half-filled glass coffee mug in her right hand, and her long chestnut curls were barely aloft in the morning breeze. James was a bundle of energy running toward the water on pudgy legs. Tippy was running about five paces behind him. Ari was inconspicuously absent from the painting.

Grandfather and Mem and Ari remained at the gallery long after the others had left. They wanted to walk through one last time, just the three of them. When they came to the room where *Celebration Night* hung, they saw a lone figure standing there, staring up at the painting. He was motionless, and even though his back was to them, they knew who he was. Ari hadn't seen him come in. Maybe he had waited until the others had left. Grandfather and Mem retreated to another room, and Ari approached the man and quietly slipped her hand into his. "I'm glad you've come, Tommy." That was all that passed between them.

64

THEY WERE A little late getting to the Bench that night, but they knew that the Gods wouldn't mind.

They had to stop by Kemala and Tao's to tell them about Tommy. He rarely came to the Island any more, and even though Ari sent him an invitation to the exhibit and wrote a special note telling him how much it would mean to her if he came, she was certain that he wouldn't. It had been a wonderful surprise to find him there, and they knew it would ease his parents' worries if they knew.

But it wasn't Tommy who occupied their conversation at the Bench that night. It was Ari. "I'm so proud of you, child," Grandfather said lovingly. "I saw Maru wiping tears from her eyes and heard Batara saying, *she is Mem's granddaughter, you know.*"

Ari smiled at hearing that. Well, at least she thought she smiled. Her mouth had been turned upward pretty much for the last two hours straight. "It did go very well, didn't it?"

"Yes," he agreed. With a glance past her to Mem, "So where do you go next?"

"What do you mean *next*? Haven't I arrived yet?" she laughed. She waited for a response but got none, so she looked from Mem to Grandfather and asked, "What are you trying to say?"

"Nothing so bad to have caused that frown on your face," Grandfather answered lightly. "It's just that you've come so far, Arianna, since . . . since Djakarta. You only need to think of poor Tommy to know that."

"We must do something for him," Ari said sadly.

"Yes, we must. And we will, in time. But now we're talking about you." Grandfather wouldn't be diverted.

"But I've made a very nice life for myself here, with the help

450

of you and Mem, of course. Besides, Professor Bostwick and a whole panel of really smart people say that I've—how did he put it again?" she asked with just a touch of playful arrogance in her voice. "Oh, yes—I've *unlocked the door to Paradise*. What else do I need to do?"

"Walk through it, Ari."

She stared at Grandfather, trying to discern from his expression what he was getting at, but she saw nothing there. "I don't understand," she said at last. "I thought I already had."

"No, Ari. You stand at the portal and look through at the rest of us living our lives here, but you haven't chosen to make a life for yourself. Not yet, that is."

Ari didn't respond. She just sat looking perplexed. Mem tried another tack. "Think of it this way, Ari. As an artist, you could fill the de Young Museum with paintings of your life before Djakarta. But what would you paint of your life since?"

"I'm here at the Bench, aren't I? And I go to the lagoon with you in the morning. And I've been to all the Celebrations, and never miss a party, and I even served Adi to Lili."

"Yes, Ari, you've kept yourself very busy in the lives of others. But what would you paint of *your* life since Djakarta?"

"Oh," she murmured. She had been sitting on one end of the Bench, facing Grandfather and Mem, casually leaning back against the smooth curve of the arm. She shifted her feet to sit upright. "I think about that sometimes. You know, if it's enough to just be content with your life. Never excited by it."

"We mustn't underrate contentment," Grandfather offered.

"No, Grandfather, we mustn't. But is it enough? When I started painting again, I began to wonder about that. Especially when I painted *Morning in Paradise*."

"Why that one in particular?" Mem asked.

"Because it wasn't just old memories that came back to me then. It was old feelings. They came in little bursts. And I had worked so hard for so long to keep my emotions within certain boundaries that I had almost forgotten what it was like to feel." She suddenly bolted up from her seat and turned to face them. "I want to feel like that again. I really do. But I don't even know how to begin."

Mem reached for Ari's hands and gently pulled her down to sit in the space she and Grandfather made between them. "What's the last thing you remember ever dreaming of that was just for you? Whether it included anyone else or not, you just knew you were going to make it happen."

It startled Ari how quickly the answer came to her mind and spilled out her mouth. "Venice. I've always dreamed of going to Venice."

"Funny," Grandfather replied to no one in particular. "That's where your parents started their lives together. It's a place of new beginnings."

"I truly have always dreamed of going to Venice," she repeated as if she hadn't heard him. "I would rent a villa in the Dorsoduro near the Campo Santa Marguerita. Tuscan gold and forest green and shades of burnt sienna."

It was very late when they all retired to bed that night. Ari turned out her bedside light and slipped under the silken sheets in her bedroom at *Surihana* and lay her head on her pillow and closed her eyes. *I'm going to Venice.* That's what she had said, and she couldn't take it back now. She was going to Venice, all by herself, and there she would begin again. There she would walk through the portal. Or at least try.

Ari had easily drifted into sleep that night. One minute she was thinking about Venice and the next minute she was dreaming about it. Mama and Papa were there in her dream, looking not as they did in the little family album, but exactly as they had the last time they all sat together around the old stone table under the giant bhodi tree. Ari awoke next morning to a calmness she hadn't felt in a very long time. It didn't surprise her though. Neither did the faint whiff of jasmine that hovered over her head. Or the cognac-scented haze from Papa's Special Blend.

A few weeks later Ari found herself on the dock saying goodbye to Grandfather and Mem. Her excitement at finally going to Venice was boiling over, but at the same time Ari had to admit that there was a little bit of nervousness growing in her stomach. She knew that this was her chance to begin again, to find her own path, but she had no idea how to do that or what awaited her when she arrived, and the unknown is always a scary thing to face.

Part Five

Venice

65

"WHEN YOU GO to Venice for the very first time, Arianna, arrive at sunset."

"Why, Mama? Why sunset?"

"Because the colors are their most breathtaking then."

"Is that when you first saw Venice?"

"Yes."

"Tell me, Mama. Tell me again what it was like the first time you saw Venice."

This was how she remembered the conversation going while she was sitting down in front of the big mirror, watching Mama, who stood behind her, brushing away the day's tangles from her long, ebony hair.

"We stood on the open deck of the vaporetto, your Papa and I. It wasn't one of those speedy water taxis. Our boat stopped at every landing on its way down the Canalazza."

"And what did you see, Mama, from the deck of the vaporetto?" Ari had asked.

"We saw the last of the sunlight reflecting off the window glass of the great palazzos. We saw the rich mustard golds and earthy terra cottas and soft celadon greens of ancient plastered walls. And giant silk banners fluttering in the wind, scarlet red geraniums cascading out of window boxes, brightly striped barber poles jutting out of the water, and gilt-edged gondolas that almost paled next to the color-ful men who piloted them. The lights looked like a thousand fireflies converging on Venice. They just started popping on everywhere—in homes and restaurants and in little antiquated streetlamps. The lights were soft and golden and just a little misty looking, like they were coming on in a London fog. Except that there was no fog."

This was when Mama had stopped brushing Ari's hair and

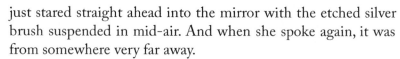

just stared straight ahead into the mirror with the etched silver brush suspended in mid-air. And when she spoke again, it was from somewhere very far away.

"I saw something. Something so beautiful . . . so magical that at first I wasn't sure it was real."

"What did you see, Mama?"

"The colors, Arianna, all the colors of the city began to vanish before our very eyes. Slowly, slowly fading away until there was nothing left but the black silhouette of Venice against an imperial purple sky. It was like watching velvet wrap the city."

66

"*I'M HERE, MAMA,*" Ari whispered. Ari stood on the deck of the vaporetto as it glided under the Rialto Bridge. Her voice echoed off the arched masonry overhead, and it startled her a bit how loud her words came back to her.

"*Scuzzi, Senorina?*" a silver-haired gentleman asked. He had been standing next to her since he boarded the vaporetto in the Canneregio. Ari had noticed him instantly because he carried a bouquet of freshly cut dahlias in his right hand and wore a gold wedding band, worn and scratched from years of wearing, on his left.

"Oh, I'm sorry," she replied. She could feel her embarrassment in the warming of her cheeks. "I was just remembering something my mother used to say about the first time she saw Venice."

The man smiled broadly, revealing a perfect row of gleaming white teeth. "It is quite surprising, is it not? The purple sky. I have lived in Venice for many years now, and it still astonishes me." The man spoke English with an odd blend of Italian staccato and British refinement.

"Cambridge or Oxford?" Ari asked with a smile.

"Cambridge. Class of '24," he replied. "I would have graduated sooner but for the war."

Ari mentally calculated his age to be early seventies. "Have you always lived here? Except for college, I mean."

"No. I was born and raised in London. Hampstead Heath actually. My father was English, but my mother was native-born Venetian. I was raised on stories of the beauty, the magic of this city."

"So after you completed your education, you just had to experience it for yourself?"

"Quite so. Although we never really complete our education, do we?"

Ari laughed. "You sound just like my grandfather." In fact, the man resembled Grandfather a little. He had the same upright bearing, the same tranquility of expression, and his jacket and trousers were exquisitely tailored and held just a hint of scented pipe tobacco. Then there were the flowers, which Ari was sure were destined for a beautiful Murano vase on a linen-topped table set for two.

"I am sure I would like your grandfather," the man replied with a smile that was oddly familiar. Passengers began repositioning themselves, signaling the imminent arrival at the next vaporetto stop. "Ca' Rezzonico," the man pointed to the illuminated sign. "Will you be getting off here?"

"No. I get off at the next Dorsoduro stop, the Academia."

"Ahhh, then we shall be neighbors of sorts. That is my stop also."

They continued conversing until it was their turn to disembark. Ari got in line behind the old gentleman and followed him as he stepped onto the dock with an agility that belied his age.

"It's been a pleasure meeting you," Ari said, extending her hand. The man clasped her hand.

"Perhaps we shall meet again," the old gentleman replied. He reached into his inside jacket pocket, pulled out a small leather wallet and extracted a business card. Handing it to her, he said, "Should you need anything while you are here, please do not hesitate to call."

"*Mille grazie.*" She said and slid the card into the zipper compartment of her knapsack.

She was halfway across the Campo di Carita when she stopped suddenly to retrieve from her pocket the crumpled scrap of paper containing Grandfather's directions to the little villa that waited for her in the maze of streets and bridges and quiet tree-lined canals secreted away somewhere between the Academia and the Salute. She must have been squinting at the paper for some time, the light of the streetlamps being rather dim there, because she heard an old gentleman call out to her. "*Scuse, Signorina.* Are you lost?"

Ari smiled back at him, and then glanced past him to the black silhouette of Venice against the imperial purple sky. "Actually, *Signore,* I think I've just been found."

67

THROUGH AN OLD friend, Grandfather had helped Ari secure a place to call home while in Venice. She had no trouble finding Professor Pezzolo's villa. Grandfather's directions had taken her straight there. Well, not straight exactly. All of Venice meandered. But after a succession of turning up alleys, going over pontes, and down canals, she made her way to the Casa di Hippocampus, *House of the Seahorse*, so named for the golden ornaments found on the gondolas, which generations of the professor's ancestors had lovingly produced.

The villa was bordered on one side by a small canal. Another slightly larger one ran behind. The villa fronted a pretty little residential square whose centerpiece was a large tree, which by daylight Ari was sure provided shade for the park benches that surrounded its broad, gnarled trunk. The square was empty now, but there were lights on in the surrounding villas, and the spicy aromas that wafted out through their open windows carried with them the multi-generational voices of families who were just now gathering around heavy plank tables in ancient tiled kitchens.

The professor's villa was a two-story building, modern by Venetian standards, having been built in the late eighteenth century. It had none of the palatial ornamentation of the Byzantine and Renaissance houses along the Grand Canal. But Ari found its simplicity warm and inviting. Ochre colored plaster walls. Hunter green shutters and window boxes filled with vibrant geraniums and rustic wooden columns and porch railings just slightly off kilter with age. It had once been a single residence but, at some point, had been divided into three flats, two of which faced an interior courtyard that was just visible through a tall wrought iron gate, accessible from the square. The third flat, the only one that was two stories was accessed by a separate gate at the end of a narrow passageway on the side of the building. This led to the professor's private garden and front door.

Ari peeked through the gate into the courtyard momentarily and mentally noted the ten brass seahorse finials atop the gate posts, which Mem had said would identify the villa. Then she continued on before turning to the right, down the narrow passageway, using the faint yellow glow of a pair of iron coach lights at the far end to guide her way. From the well-worn look of the cobbled path and dark stains on the stucco wall, Ari was certain that the waters of the canal frequently washed over the walkway during heavy rain and the annual floods and she was grateful that Mem had insisted she pack her rubber Dickersons at the last minute.

Finally, Ari arrived at the wrought iron gate that led into the professor's private garden. The gate unlocked with a clanking sound and opened with a low squeal, revealing a beautiful little garden that Ari immediately recognized as the source of the painting that sat above the john in the guest bathroom at *Surihana*. The garden was softly lit and lushly planted. It was too dark now to see it clearly, but on first impression it looked exactly as she had imagined it from Mem's description. She glanced toward her left to the far end of the garden and could just make out a gate that Mem said led to a small terrace of grass overlooking the back canal. Then, locking the gate behind her, she headed for the large beveled glass door that stood in the center of an entire wall of glass tucked under the second story balcony.

She would have rung the large brass bell that hung from an ornamental hook, again fashioned into a seahorse, but the professor was away in Herculaneum in search of old bones, and the housekeeper, who came once a week to tidy up, didn't come until tomorrow. But she had left the key exactly where Mem said it would be—under the potted palm in the majolica urn to the right of the door.

Most of the lower level was occupied by a large great room,

with high plastered ceilings imbedded with rustically hewn beams and giant arched windows on either end to bring in the sunlight. An open gourmet kitchen ran along the wall opposite the front door and was separated from the dining and living areas by a long, tiled island and a series of identical little drop lights whose soft green glass shades had obviously been produced on nearby Murano. To the left was a large trestle dining table, very old, around which Mem had said the professor regularly entertained his many friends, and there was a comfortable looking group of overstuffed chairs and a companionable sofa surrounding a beautifully tiled fireplace whose mantle was laden with photographs and artifacts of the professor's life. All together the ancient wood and plaster and tile work, the Italian landscapes in layered oils and heavy frames, the collections of majolica pitchers and plates and the sprinkling of art glass and Venetian masks and a pair of black iron chandeliers gave the home exquisite charm and warmth and welcome.

The two doors flanking the kitchen led to an office and guest room, each with their own bath. Ari decided to look at those tomorrow in the daylight. The professor had insisted that she take the master suite during her stay, which occupied the whole of the upstairs. He said that stumbling out of bed, blurry-eyed and barefoot, and standing on the balcony to gaze out at the view at first light was an experience not to be missed. She had asked Mem to describe what she would see, but Mem had declined. "I don't want to ruin the moment," she had explained. "Let what you see wash over you in waves. Feel it. Breathe it in."

"I will, Mem," Ari murmured as if her grandmother was in the room with her.

There was a large envelope that had Ari's name printed on it in big red letters propped up against a rooster pitcher on the island. In it she found a note from the professor and a typed out set of instructions for the villa—how the electricity worked, where the water shut-off was, and when the best time to get a hot shower or bath was. There was information about the comings and goings of Brunna, the housekeeper, and the gardener, and when the utility bills were due. Ari had insisted on paying those since she'd be staying in the professor's home for an extended time and he had refused to accept any rent from her. There were lists of favorite restaurants, cafés, and shops and business hours for the produce and fish markets. There was also a set of telephone numbers for emergencies and for friends of the professor who might be of assistance in his absence. Obviously, a great deal of trouble had been taken in compiling this list— too much trouble for a single houseguest and Ari surmised that the professor's little villa always had someone in residence when he went away. The professor's note confirmed as much.

> *Dear Ari,*
>
> *My Roseanna and I have lived in this house fifty-three years. She is a happy house. When we are away from her, it comforts us to know that she is not dark and lonely. We have been blessed by many friends who have cared for her in our absence. Thank you for being one of them.*
>
> *Anthony Pezzolo*
>
> *P.S. Brunna will have left you a cold supper in the ice box. So, you must eat and then you must rest. Venice waits to welcome you in the morning.*

Ari folded the letter and slid it back into the envelope. She didn't know whether to smile or cry. The professor's letter was so sweet, but it was so sad too. His Rosanna had died last year, but he wrote as if she was still here with him. Looking around now at the home that had witnessed so many of their happy memories, Ari could almost feel her presence. "I'm going to be happy here too," she said out loud to the photograph on the mantle of the professor and his wife on their wedding day. Then she went to the ice box, grabbed the plate of bread and cheeses and meats, and headed for the stairs and the deep feather bed that she knew was waiting to cradle her to sleep. First, of course, she would place a trunk call to her grandparents to let them know she had arrived safely, but the suitcases, which Grandfather had thankfully sent ahead of her, could wait one more day to be unpacked.

68

ARI OPENED HER eyes and stared up at the ceiling until she remembered why it was pale ocher and heavily timbered instead of peaked and polished like the ceilings of *Surihana*. Once again, she had dreamed that she still lived happily with Mama and Papa and Emma and James. It was her recurring dream, and most often she awoke from it feeling a little sad but resigned to making the best of whatever happened next. So, she was wholly unprepared for the feeling of anticipation that had somehow overtaken her in the night.

She sat up, drawing her knees to her chest, and looked around the large room from the deeply feathered iron bed that occupied the wall opposite the balcony. The bed was pale green and very old—the perfect backdrop for its crisp, white European bed linens, and it creaked softly when she moved, which made her smile a little. The rest of the room was furnished in heavily carved woods that were a perfect accompaniment to the rustic architecture—a tall wardrobe, which stood angled in one corner mirroring the tiled fireplace in the other, a long mirrored dresser, a glass-front secretary where Ari was sure Roseanna had written her multi-page letters to Mem, a small curio filled with delicate treasures, and two deep-cushioned chairs facing the fireplace, hunter green and slightly misshapen from years of bottoms shifting lazily in front of the fire. As with the downstairs, the floors were planked and sloping, adding to the heaviness of the architecture, which might have felt oppressive if not for the high ceilings and the beautiful windows through which the morning light was already streaming. Ari stretched once more before getting out of bed and heading toward the balcony hidden from view by yards and yards of sheer, gathered curtains.

An audible gasp escaped her as her eyes adjusted to the light and her senses took in the view. She was glad Mem hadn't spoiled the moment by revealing too much. Beyond the small garden with its varieties of lush green foliage and flowering shrubs and a small but very green bit of lawn, flowed a canal—uncharacteristically wide and sunny and glassy smooth running between tree-lined neighborhoods of unconnected villas, whose equally uncharacteristic gardens contributed to the impression that the Venetians had dedicated this part of their city to Mother Nature. And standing proud and steadfast over the tallest tree branches and tiled roofs of this exquisite sanctuary were the domes and buttresses of the Santa Maria della Salute, the famous Baroque church erected to celebrate the end of the plague in the seventeenth century.

A rush of morning air blew in as Ari opened the glass-paneled doors, rustling her thin cotton nightgown and tousling the hair she had been too tired to braid last night. Moving quickly toward the balcony railing, she planted her forearms there, leaning over to stare at the view. She wasn't looking for anything in particular. She just wanted to breathe it all in. So, she didn't immediately notice the black lacquered gondola with the red velvet seats slowly gliding past the garden's stone railing. Nor did she immediately notice the man lounging comfortably aft—the double-breasted jacket of his three-piece suit lying on the seat next to him over a leather briefcase, the top button of his pale blue shirt unfastened and his wide silk tie loosely knotted around his neck.

69

EVERYTHING HAD ALWAYS come easily to Michael Alexander McGregor. Women liked him. Universities liked him. His students liked him. Men wanted to be like him. He pretty much had always gotten whatever he wanted. Knowing that had never given him a swelled head. He had just taken it in stride, not thinking much about it really. His life was just the way it was, like a river whose current was steadily taking him around the next bend and the next and the next.

Until he saw her on the balcony—the statuesque woman in the thin cotton gown that gave just the faintest hint of the seductive body that hid beneath it. He was mesmerized by her. Not by her beauty alone (he had known many beautiful women) but by something else. Something he couldn't name. In a way, she seemed familiar to him, but he knew there was no way he would ever forget meeting someone as breathtaking. His heart skipped when he saw her eyes turn toward him, lingering longer than just a casual glance. He watched her as long as he could, until the gondola was well past the idyllic little villa. And for the first time in his thirty-four years, he realized that his easy self-confidence, which he had always enjoyed, was no more a product of his creation than most things in his life. He couldn't take his eyes from her and inexplicably, he knew that of all the days of his life, he would remember this one most especially and that seemed to haunt him.

70

ARI STOOD IN the middle of the large tiled bath-room, toweling off after a lukewarm shower. She was late bathing that morning and most of the hot water had already been used by the other residents of the villa. She had remained on the balcony for some time after the man in the gondola was well out of sight. Maybe she was hoping he would circle around again. That would have been a very *Italian* thing to do. But then all Italian men flirt, and she couldn't have taken that very seriously, could she? She laughed at herself. But he had looked at her (or at least she thought he had) and it was what she had seen in his eyes that struck her as most extraordinary.

"...I was the sun that filled his skies in the morning and the stars that filled his skies at night and that every breath he took was just so he could spend one more moment on this earth with me."

"Is this what it felt like, Mama?" Ari said aloud, bemused. "When you first saw Papa?" Perhaps she had just imagined the whole thing, the splendor of Venice clouding her mind with romantic ideas.

Like the rest of the house, the bathroom was charming. It was brightly tiled in thick, hand-made vanilla-colored field tiles across the floor and three-quarters of the way up the walls to the light blue plaster, interspersed with patterned tiles in vivid jewel tones depicting flowers and vines and birds. Collections of porcelain encircled the room on a plate rail that divided the plaster work from the tiles. Two white pedestal sinks on either side of a rustic country armoire, a footed tub and a mirrored dressing table between two large windows completed the room.

Ari unpacked her suitcases and slid them under the bed out of sight. She had brought an assortment of clothes, from western chic to eastern simplicity, with a liberal supply of tunics and trousers for comfortably lounging around the house. She put on a pair of blue jeans and a blouse that had amazingly escaped wrinkling and, glancing at her sandals that still sat next to the bed where she had kicked them off the night before, headed downstairs to begin her day.

Predictably, there was a Bialetti Moka Coffee Maker sitting on the back of the big industrial stove. Bialtetti had been making them in Italy since 1933 and almost every home had one. Ari unscrewed the chambers, filled the bottom one with water, set the filter in and filled it with some aromatic dark roast Italian coffee, reconnected the chambers and set the pot on the stove.

While the coffee brewed and the rolls warmed in the oven, Ari went out to take a closer look at the garden. It was wider than it was deep, running the full length of the villa and probably thirty feet toward the canal. The space had been perfectly laid out to provide interest without losing serenity to too much fuss. Right outside the doors was a lovely stone loggia furnished in deep cushioned settees and a large square wooden table and chairs for outdoor dining. The stone path ambled past planting beds, and ornamental trees and ended at two tiled stairs that led to the small patch of grass and stone railing that butted up against the canal several feet below. There was a smattering of garden art and architectural bric-a-brac that had been skillfully transformed into flower pots.

Ari went back into the house and poured coffee into a large glass mug, grabbed a warm roll, and headed for the teak chairs at the water's edge. She set her mug on the wide, flat arm of one of the chairs and lowered herself carefully into it. Stretching out her legs in front of her, she sank back, lifted the mug to her lips, and breathed in her first sip of morning coffee in Venice.

She sat there for an hour or two, glad to be stationary after such a long journey to get there and enjoying the quiet act of watching Venice go by. It was a perfect place to people watch— peaceful and private, without the bustle of the Grand Canal, but populated enough to provide an interesting array of humanity going by.

It was a residential neighborhood with few tourists save those trying to get between tourist attractions. And it was particularly lovely with all the space between homes, much of it filled with gardens and trees and plenty of sunshine that rarely found its way to the narrow, twisting streets and canals of some of the more densely built and populated sestieres.

Ari was deep in thought when a clanking sound followed by a low squeal turned her attention to the garden gate behind her and the short, round woman who came through it. She was dressed simply in a long-gathered skirt and over-blouse and her salt and pepper hair was pulled back off her face in a tight bun. Her eyes were dark and her cheeks splotchy purple and her smile upon seeing Ari instantly welcoming. "Ahh, Signorina Heywood?"

"Yes, and you must be Brunna," she replied, coming forward to greet the housekeeper. "Please call me Ari."

"You find everything okay?"

"Yes, thank you. And thank you especially for dinner last night. I am very grateful to you."

They continued to talk for a half hour more over a cup of coffee, and Ari learned all about Brunna and her many children and even more grandchildren, and the years she had worked for the Professor and his dear wife, Roseanna. Ari shared with her a little of her life, the good parts mostly, and explained how she had come to live in the Professor's house, and said how she couldn't wait to grab her tour book and head out around Venice.

"No, no, Signorina Ari. No books today. Books are for later. Today you walk and you find Venice. *Capice?*"

"Yes, Brunna, I understand. It will be like a treasure hunt" she replied, adding *"caccia al tesoro,"* seeing Brunna's puzzled expression.

"Si, si, un caccia al tesoro!"

A few minutes later she said goodbye to Brunna who had already retrieved her bucket, mop, and duster from the cleaning closet and was busily exiling the week's dusty residue from the villa. Her plan was to wander around each of the six sestieres, one at a time, jotting down in a small spiral notebook places to which she'd like to return and spend more time. She already knew some of the places she'd go—the Salute, the Doges Palace, places like that—but it was the yet to be discovered places that excited her most. After all, she hadn't come here to tour Venice, but to live here. She wanted to go where the locals went and become one of them. She wanted to know by name the woman with the flour-covered fingers who would serve her at her favorite pasticciera, and the man with the wine-stained apron who would greet her at her favorite trattoria. She especially wanted to know the name of the dark-haired man in the black lacquered gondola. If only he would sail by again.

71

MICHAEL WAS AN art historian who had quickly gained a reputation as a well-respected expert in his field. Having committed himself fully to his career, he had enjoyed great success and acclaim for his published works and lectures, both of which had taken him around the world. He currently held the title of Reader at his university in England. But right now, his mind was far from his work. He couldn't stop thinking about her, which was most unusual given that he was in Venice for purely professional reasons. Not through his morning meetings with the European distributors for his latest publication. Not even when they lunched together for the afternoon at Do Forni, a restaurant near Piazza San Marco, which was chosen specifically to impress him with its celebrated restaurateur and his equally celebrated clientele. The food and wine were excellent, as promised, but he'd have been just as happy lunching at the little family-run trattoria near the Zattere where he took most of his evening meals. In fact, throughout the meal he found himself drifting there and imagining late night suppers with the beautiful woman from the balcony, sharing bottles of wine from Signore Vincelli's vineyard. When he failed to respond to a question for a second time, one of his companions joked, "*Devi essere innamorato* " You must be in love.

Michael shook his head and smiled. "When would I ever find time for such a thing?" He finished the last sip of wine in his glass before reaching for the bottle to pour another.

After lunch, he headed back to his hotel on foot. He usually traveled that way in Venice. This morning had been an exception. He had been taking breakfast in the tiny garden of his hotel, when Signora Antonelli, the proprietor's wife, brought her eldest son to his table to introduce him to the *Signore Inglese*. *"E gondolier!"* she had informed him as she brought him another of his favorite breakfast rolls. He couldn't refuse her obvious desire to drum up business for her son. So he rode round-about through the canals on his way to his business meeting, listening to Maximo's practiced discourse on the beauty of Venice, until he spotted the woman peering down from the balcony, her long black hair fanning out in the breeze, capturing the illumination of the morning sun on each lustrous strand. And suddenly he was suspended in silence, Maximo's voice having faded away, along with the sound of the oar inside the rowlock and the rippling of the water and the little girl across the canal whose lyrical voice had so enchanted him just a moment ago calling her puppy back into the house. They were all gone and only the woman remained.

Michael looked up to see the Academia Bridge just ahead. A fifteen-minute walk beyond the bridge and he'd be back at his hotel. If he hurried, he could catch Maximo before he left for his evening shift.

72

BRUNNA WAS GONE by the time Ari returned to the villa, but there was a salad in the refrigerator and a fresh Italian loaf and a small lasagna still warm from the oven waiting for her. Ari made a mental note to be sure and make a nice lunch for Brunna next week to show her appreciation.

She searched the kitchen drawers until she found the utensils, which in Italy were sure to include a corkscrew or two. Then she opened the bottle of Prosecco Frizzante she had bought from the little wine shop near the square. The proprietor, a frail-looking elderly man with a surprisingly resonant voice, had suggested the chilled, lightly sparkling white wine as the perfect antidote for a hot day and tired feet. "They use also for Bellinis," said the proprietor.

"My mother and father used to drink Bellinis when they lived here in Venice."

"Ah, yes, it is the drink of lovers," he smiled.

"Well, then, I hope to return for another bottle of Prosecco very soon," she replied, thinking of the man in the black lacquered gondola.

"I am sure of it, Signorina. Venice would not permit a beautiful woman to be...how you say...donna sola?" *A lonely woman*, Ari thought and sighed.

Sitting in her chair at the end of the garden overlooking the canal, freshly bathed, barefoot and comfortably clothed in a long white cotton skirt and sleeveless lace-up blouse, she opened the little notebook she had carried with her through the Dorsoduro today and read the list of places she planned to revisit. Then she set the open notebook on her lap and lifted her wine glass to the waning sun and watched its light dance off the bubbles that were slowly floating to the top. She lowered the glass to her lips and took a long slow sip of her first Venice wine. It wasn't until she settled back into her chair and gazed out over the tranquil canal that she saw the telltale ripples of an approaching gondola and then she saw the dark-haired man, gliding toward her, looking somewhat more rumpled but still strikingly handsome. She was close enough now to see his face clearly. But it was when he removed his sunglasses to get a better look at her that she knew she hadn't come all the way to Venice solely to find herself. It was his eyes that told her so—his emerald green eyes that, until now, she had only known three other people, besides her, to possess—Mama, Grandfather, and Mem. His look captured every nerve in her mind. He sailed by without stopping, but she didn't worry. Something told her she would see him again.

73

ARI ROSE EARLY the next morning, showered (in hot water this time), dressed in comfortable trousers and a red, white, and black stripped sleeveless sweater, and ran downstairs to get a cup of coffee, a pear from the big wooden bowl on the kitchen island and, hopefully, her morning glimpse of him as he floated by in the gondola. She wasn't disappointed. Like clockwork he was there, more casually dressed today in jeans and an oxford shirt. His briefcase, Ari noticed, was conspicuously absent.

The man smiled at her as he sailed by, and she heard the gondolier call out to him, "*perché non parli con la bella signora, Inglese?*" Why don't you talk to the beautiful lady, Englishman?

"He's English," Ari said out loud. "I'd never have guessed." She rolled this new idea of him over and over in her mind. *I could have sworn he was Italian. Except for his eyes. Their color belongs to the Island. I wonder what he's doing here.* For a moment it crossed her mind that the Gods had sent him to her, but that was way more than she wanted to get her mind around on a beautiful sunny day in Venice, so she headed out, notebook in hand to explore the city.

It took two more days of meandering around to cover all six sestieres. When she was done, she had a formidable list of places to visit. There were the usual tourist sights on one list—the Piazza San Marco with its famous campanile and the even more famous St. Mark's Basilica and, of course, the Ponte di Rialto upon which you could watch the tourists of Venice float by on the shiny black gondolas expertly guided by the quintessential gondolier in his red and white striped shirt. But then there were also the hidden places. Those workshops cosseted behind partially open doors in back alley walls where Ari caught glimpses of families tooling leather or binding books or marbleizing paper or taking from the ovens the sweet Venetian pastries that were colorfully displayed in *pasticceria* windows all over the city. And then there were the storefront windows themselves. Venice was famous for them. *Each a work of art, carefully drawn and exquisitely colored.* At least, that's how one travel writer described them. It almost reminded her of the Christmas windows in San Francisco. How each told a story and she smiled at the memory of her last Christmas in the city. And each day began and ended as the one before it—with the Englishman sailing by. Except that now he smiled at her and waved.

74

ARI AWOKE WITH a start. She didn't need a clock to tell her she had overslept. Unable to sleep last night, she had arisen shortly before two and had sat at Signora Pezzolo's secretary writing Grandfather and Mem a nice long letter. Then she had fallen back in bed and slept until the little dog across the canal awoke her with his bark.

She ran out onto the balcony and stood for several minutes hoping to see her Englishman go by, but she knew she had missed him. She could only hope that he would come back again at five. If he did, she would call out to him this time.

Over a late breakfast, she pulled out her notebook and began reading through it, trying to determine where she should begin her sightseeing, but it was hard to choose. There were so many wonderful places to go. She decided to clean out her knapsack knowing that ideas sometimes appeared in the midst of the most mundane tasks. She threw out an old Kleenex, an empty water bottle and a couple of empty Kodak boxes. Then she felt in the bottom of the main compartment for spent rolls of film. She found two and put them in the nightstand drawer with the others. She slipped her hand into the zipper pocket and pulled out a small, rectangular piece of stiff paper. "I forgot all about this," she smiled, recognizing the business card of the old gentleman she had met on the vaporetto her first night in Venice. She turned the card over and read it.

Dr. William Thatcher
Art Restoration
Gallerie dell'Academia
Venice, Italy

"He restores art at the Academia. How wonderful!" Ari exclaimed. She had her starting place. She thought of calling the number on the bottom right of the card but decided against it. He might feel obligated to take time from his work. "I'll just say hello while I'm there and be off."

After showering, Ari stood in front of the antique armoire that once belonged to the Professor's wife, contemplating what to wear. She sighed and bit her lip. Her eyes finally came to rest on a red and white knit wrap dress. *Perfect!* she thought. They were all the rage these days, thanks to Diane Von Furstenberg. Downstairs, she checked the contents of her knapsack one last time to ensure she wasn't forgetting anything and then headed out the door.

While the canals gave Venice its charm, they also proved to be a bit of an impediment to her forward progress and not knowing exactly where she was going, coupled with the fact that she had a terrible sense of direction, Ari often found herself at a dead end with no bridge in sight. But eventually, she found herself standing in front of the *Gallerie dell'Academia,* which overlooked the Grand Canal. The building itself was a work of art and Ari spent several minutes taking in every detail of its white marble façade and its intricately carved moldings and Corinthian columns. Many of the artists, such as Carpaccio and Bellini, whose work hung on the museum walls, had influenced the whole history of European art, and Ari couldn't wait to explore it herself.

A young woman sitting behind a desk with a sign that read *Informazioni* smiled at Ari as she made her way through the heavy wooden doors. "*Posso aiutarla?*" May I help you? Ari was told that Dr. Thatcher was scheduled to give a public lecture at 4:00 p.m. and that she would be more than welcome to attend. Taking a museum map from the pile that sat ready for visitors on the desk, Ari began planning the next two hours. To Ari, art was not meant to be viewed but felt, so she knew that it would be impossible to see the entire museum and all its precious art in one day, but she could take note of where to return the next time.

The two hours passed quickly, and soon she arrived in "Hall 4" just as the silver-haired man was approaching the lectern to peer out upon the congregation of academics and art lovers and unsuspecting tourists who sat with rapt anticipation. At first it appeared that every seat was occupied. But she finally found a place to sit near the middle of the room. She placed her knapsack under her seat and settled in just as Dottore Thatcher's discussion of "Modern Restoration Techniques" began.

Ari noticed a man sitting several rows in front of her. She was immediately struck by his raven hair and the gentle rise and fall of his broad shoulders. She felt a small flutter of anticipation at the idea. *It couldn't possibly be him, could it?* Still she spent the rest of the time watching him, willing him to turn around, and wondering if she would be met with his most extraordinary eyes.

When the lecture ended, Ari bent to retrieve her knapsack from under her seat and upon standing, was startled to find a pair of emerald green eyes staring back at her in surprise. She'd known he was handsome; some might describe him as classically beautiful, but stunning seemed more appropriate. She guessed he stood over 6 feet. Taller than she expected. His bronzed skin glistened in the sharp lights of the lecture hall setting off his eyes, which were a deeper green than the densest rainforest on the Island. The gentle curve of his lip and the slightest dimple on his chin softened his high cheekbones and aquiline nose that invoked the idealized marble statues housed within the museum's wall. He was impeccably tailored in an expensive navy suit that hugged his broad shoulders, hinting at the power that lay beneath. A perfectly starched cream-colored shirt, coupled with a burgundy tie, gave him the appearance of having just stepped off the cover of an Italian fashion magazine.

"Hello," he said, his voice deep and smooth. "At last we meet."

"Hi," Ari said with a slight wobble in her voice. They stood in silence, staring at each other as the crowd around them thinned to a small trickle.

"Will you join me for dinner?" Michael asked. Ari felt light-headed, although whether that was from a lack of food since she'd skipped lunch lost in the beauty of the museum's treasures, or his presence she couldn't quite tell. "Okay," she said taking his outstretched hand for balance as she shuffled her way between the narrow row of seats.

They began walking toward the Ponte dell'Accademia, which arched gracefully over the busy waterway providing safe passage to the other side of the canal. Suddenly Michael stopped and turned toward her. "So 'girl from the balcony' what should I call you?"

"My name is Arianna," she said. "But everyone calls me Ari."

"Arianna," he repeated. "That's a beautiful name. I'm Michael."

As they walked and made small talk, Ari wondered if Michael noticed the women (and men) who stopped to stare as he walked by. She found it hard not to stare herself and nearly ran into a group of tourists gawking at the gondolas navigating the narrow waterway.

"Watch out," Michael said and laughed as he pulled her toward him to avoid a collision. He held her against his side slightly longer than was necessary before releasing her and continuing on.

"Do you live in Venice?" Ari asked, brushing her hair out of her eyes in an attempt to collect herself.

"No, I'm here on business." Michael stopped and pointed to a building overlooking the Grand Canal. "Here we are," he said opening the small iron gate to the restaurant's patio. Wooden tables sat perfectly arranged under a white and yellow striped awning, providing its occupants with an unobstructed view of the waterway and the marble dome of the church sitting on the opposite side. As Michael led her to the far end of the café, she breathed in the trail of his scent—worn leather and spice. She closed her eyes and inhaled again letting the smell etch deep into her memory.

"And you? Are you just visiting?" Michael asked seating her, before shrugging off his suit jacket and draping it over the back of his chair. His vest hugged his broad chest and accentuated his long torso and slim waistline. Michael loosened his tie and opened the top button of his shirt with a content sigh.

"Signore McGregor! Buona sera," a short silver-haired man yelled exuberantly as he quickly navigated his way through the tables. "So good to see you again," he said and then spotting Ari, he smiled. "Welcome, Signorina."

"Ciao, Signore Vincelli," Michael said, greeting him with a warm handshake and smile.

"Perhaps a glass of wine to toast this most beautiful evening of romance?" Signore Vincelli asked in a thick Italian accent as he dramatically swept his arm toward the canal. Michael looked at Ari with raised eyebrows and she nodded her head.

"*Possiamo avere una bottiglia del vostro vino della casa…rosso, per favore?*" The British lilt of Michael's accent disappeared as fluid Italian rolled off his tongue.

Signore Vincelli returned in short order and poured a small amount into Michael's glass. Ari watched as he slowly swirled the ruby red liquid before holding it to the candlelight and she held her breath as she watched his lips settle on the glass before taking a small sip. "*Perfetto.*" Signore Vincelli smiled and poured two glasses, setting the bottle on the table before turning his attention elsewhere.

Michael held up his glass. "To unexpected encounters."

"Salute," Ari raised her glass and took her first sip. Her mouth instantly filled with vibrant flavors, a tang of a full bodied Dolcetto balanced by the soft sweetness of Zinfandel. "Mmm," she said swallowing, "this is delicious."

He smiled. "I'll tell you a little secret about Italian wines." He paused for effect and leaned closer. "The house wine is always the best." Ari smiled.

"So," he said setting down his wine glass, leaning back casually. "What brings you to Venice?"

"Well," she began, unsure of how to answer without giving away secrets that she was not prepared to invite to the table. "I've always dreamed of coming here and one day, I finally decided to do it." Settling back into her chair, Ari gazed across the water. The view was spectacular with the sun barely visible above the church's giant dome, the oranges and reds reminding Ari of a painting she had once seen, Monet's *San Giorgio Maggiore*.

"I don't think I'll ever tire of all of this," she said as she watched the Venetian sky begin its nightly kaleidoscope of color.

The faded violets and deep purples would soon follow before the twinkling lights of the stars would make their grand entrance. "It's like an artist has taken a paintbrush to the sky and captured perfection. I'd love to paint this someday although I don't think I could ever do it justice."

"You're an artist?" Michael asked.

"Not really," Ari answered. "I had some pieces shown in a gallery once, but nothing professional. I love painting though. It's an escape from reality." Michael noticed a dark shadow briefly wash over her beautiful face, but as quickly as it came, it was gone. Ari cleared her throat. "You said you were here for business? What do you do? No wait, let me guess," Ari said with a teasing smile in her eyes spurred by the wine. "If I had to guess, I would say you're...a spy...like James Bond."

Michael laughed. "No. Unfortunately my life isn't quite that glamorous. I'm an academic."

Ari's eyebrows rose in surprise and she laughed.

"Really? You don't look like any professor I've ever met." Ari's face instantly grew hot. "*Oh god! Did I really just say that out loud?*" she thought.

The corner of his mouth twitched. "Why thank you. I'm going to take that as a compliment." Michael took a small sip of his wine. "I'm actually quite boring though."

"I wouldn't say that at all. Do you specialize in any particular area?"

"Art history," he responded.

"Really?" Ari said with enthusiasm, her eyes lighting up in the candlelight. "Do you focus on a particular period?"

"Mostly the late Roman Empire, although I'm interested in all types of art really," he said, catching the eye of a passing waiter to order a second bottle of wine. "I'm currently researching the Byzantine Era."

It was rare that he had the chance to talk about his work to anyone outside of the academic world and her interest invigorated him. Most of the women he had taken to dinner, and there had been many, had smiled and said, "*oh, that's nice*" before shifting the conversation back to a more superficial topic of their own choosing. Michael had devoted most of his adult life to his studies and it felt good to be able to share his enthusiasm with someone.

"So, what about you?" he asked.

"The whole university thing didn't go as planned for me." Michael saw the same dark shadow spread across her face. "I ended up doing my studies long distance. Classical archeology and literature."

"That's an interesting combination." He leaned forward to pour more wine into her empty glass.

"I know, right?" Ari laughed, the wine helping to loosen her nerves. "It's just that I've always believed the past speaks to you if you take the time to listen," Ari said. "There's so much you can learn about people from the things they leave behind. But you already know that." She laughed. "I'd give anything to see Pompeii while I'm here."

The rest of the evening passed with sharing stories and generally getting to know one another. Ari told Michael about her adventures in Paris and San Francisco and London and all the other exotic places she had lived, except for Djakarta of course, and he reciprocated in kind. Michael couldn't take his eyes from her and soon his mind began to wonder to places it shouldn't, and he discreetly shifted in his chair before pouring the remaining wine of their second bottle (or maybe it was their third—he might have lost count) equally into their glasses. Ari yawned and looking around, realized they were the only ones left on the patio.

"Where are you staying? I'll walk to you to your hotel." Michael said taking her hand.

"It's not necessary," Ari replied.

"A gentleman always walks his date to the front door," he said and with a smile he took her arm in his.

When they arrived at the old rusted gate leading into the private garden, Ari stopped and turned toward Michael. "Thank you for dinner," she said. "I had a really nice time."

"Me too," he replied and paused, as if wanting to say more. He ran his fingers through his hair, brushing back the gentle waves that had begun to form in the late hours. "Goodnight, Ari."

"Goodnight, Michael," she said and turned to open the lock.

"Ari?" Michael's voice was barely above a whisper. The carriage lights did little to illuminate the passageway, but she could clearly see the look in his eyes. She stood motionless in front of him, her breath shallow and frequent. Finally, Michael reached out his hand, tentatively at first, running his fingers up the side of her neck. Ari responded in kind, tracing the clean lines of his cheekbone and the rough shadow of the early morning upon his face.

Michael's hand found its way to the small of her back and he gently pulled her to him. He bent to kiss her and without meaning to, she rose to meet him halfway. He tasted of wine. Ari ran her hands inside his jacket, feeling the sharp outline of his collarbone, and then the curve of his shoulders before entwining her fingers in his thick, black hair.

Suddenly he let her go and Ari shivered as the heat of his body gave way to the nighttime chill. "I'm sorry," he said breathing heavily.

"Sorry for what?"

"I shouldn't have kissed you like that," Michael said shaking his head. "At least not without asking first."

"I wouldn't have let you if I didn't want you to," she whispered. His shoulders visibly relaxed, and he reached out to her once more.

"Can I see you again?" Michael asked.

"Yes, I'd like that." Ari replied.

Once inside the professor's villa she leaned against the door and, dropping her knapsack at her feet, closed her eyes and slid to the ground, the taste of his mouth still lingering on her lips.

75

ARI SPENT THE entirety of the next day at the villa painting and lost in her work, she didn't realize how quickly time had passed until she noticed the light on her canvas begin to change. After taking a shower and towel drying her hair, Ari began the ritual of finding something to wear and by the time she had decided, her entire wardrobe sat in piles and heaps on the iron bed. In the end, not surprisingly, she picked the first thing she had put on. The vibrant oranges and purples and greens of the dress's abstract designs reminded Ari of Mama's Bird of Paradise. She had just finished applying lip gloss when she heard the iron-gate creak outside, followed a few seconds later by a knock on the front door.

Michael had discarded the formality of his three-piece suit for the more casual look of a navy blue oxford and faded jeans, which she noticed left little to the imagination. A beige merino wool sweater hung from his shoulders.

"I thought we could sit by the canal and have a picnic," Michael said as he began to unpack the bags he'd been carrying. "I stopped to grab a few things on my way over, but if you'd rather go out that's fine too."

"I love picnics," Ari said, as she opened the drawer to find the bottle opener and take two wine glasses from the drying rack. "We used to picnic by the lagoon and the waterfalls on the Island and on my birthday once we…" Her voice trailed off. Ari forced a smile to her lips and grabbed the wool blanket draped over the back of one of the fireside chairs, motioning for Michael to follow her through the garden and down to the small lawn overlooking the still waters of the canal.

Once they were settled, Michael opened the bottle of wine,

while Ari laid out the food. After filling themselves with anti-pasti and Italian bread, they laid side by side, wine glasses in hand. Their conversation from the previous night continued with ease, like old friends getting to know each other once again.

"So, how did you decide on art history?" Ari asked, sipping her wine.

"It was kind of an accident," Michael said. "My family has a long history of barristers and MPs, and my two brothers and I were expected to follow that tradition without question," Michael said and then rolled his eyes. "My brothers fell in line, but I'm the black sheep in the family, I guess." He laughed. "It's pretty embarrassing but at the time it seemed like a good idea," he paused to take a sip of wine. "At uni there was a girl I thought was really cute, and she was enrolled in an art history course. I needed to fill a few more course hours, so it was like killing two birds with one stone."

Ari giggled. "And did it work?"

"Yeah, but surprisingly in the end, art history held my attention longer than she did."

"It's funny," Ari said with a thoughtful look in her eye as she glanced at the gondola gliding passed. "The smallest, seemingly inconsequential decision can completely alter the course of your entire life." Ari broke off another piece of bread and dipped it in olive oil.

Michael sat upright and faced her; cross legged. "How so?"

"Well, just what you said. In the bigger picture, taking a course to meet some girl isn't that significant. But as a result, you set in motion an entirely new future that you wouldn't have had otherwise."

"True," Michael said reaching to fill her wine glass. "Sounds like you speak from experience?"

She took two large swallows of wine and a deep breath. "Yes, I do. I fell asleep outside." And then she told Michael all about the posting in Djakarta and how it was supposed to be the last and how the entire family was looking forward to returning to the Island permanently.

"It was my eighteenth birthday." Her voice shook as the events of that night flooded her mind. "I fell asleep in the garden.

That's why I wasn't inside when it happened," she paused and took another sip of wine. "I ran into the house. I tried to find them, but the smoke was so thick I couldn't breathe and that's the last thing I remember until I work up in the hospital days later." Ari fell silent.

"Oh, Ari," Michael said. "I'm so sorry."

"It's all right. I just haven't talked about it to anyone in a while. It's funny, at first I didn't feel anything. It was like there was nothing inside." Ari paused. "I think I believed that if I didn't talk about it, then it didn't really happen."

"You don't have to talk about it now if you don't want to."

Ari turned her head toward the waterway. "The worst part of the whole thing is the guilt," she continued as if not hearing him. "After they were gone, I couldn't stop thinking back to all the times we fought or disagreed or times that I wasn't a good daughter or sister. I'd take it all back now if I could. I just hope they know how much I loved them."

"Ari," Michael said sadly. "Don't do that to yourself. I'm sure your family knows how much you loved them. It's a common response to the sudden loss of loved-ones to feel guilty about all the things we might have done or said if only we'd known what was coming, but you can't carry that with you forever."

"I know," she admitted. "And I've tried hard not to, but sometimes it's just impossible not to feel it."

A warm breeze stirred Ari's hair and Michael reached over slowly to tuck an unruly piece of it behind her ear. His fingers lightly brushed her neck and in doing so caused gooseflesh to prickle on her skin. Michael pulled her closer, and she leaned against him with a sigh. He kissed the crown of her head and together they silently watched the changing colors of the sky.

"Tell me more about your Island?" he asked eventually.

As Ari described her Island, the waters of the canal in front of him transformed into the sparkling azure blues of her Island lagoon. The grass of the professor's lawn, to the warm glowing sun-toasted sands of the beaches. Michael felt the sweetly scented tropical breeze kiss his face, and as if by metamorphous, the dome of the Santa Della Maria became a towering lush mountain rainforest and the hum of a boat motoring up the canal into the bubble and splash of a nearby waterfall. And as she continued, his world became colored with vermillion and violet and emerald greens and deep cerulean blues.

"It's a very special place. Many of the families have been there on and off for generations, passing down traditions to the younger Islanders to carry with them and continue their legacy." And then she told him all about *it*, hopeful that he would understand and not change his mind about wanting to be there.

76

SITTING ON THE blanket beside her, Michael imagined what it would be like to see her dance at the Celebration she spoke of—her hips swaying to the beat of the drums and the torch light reflecting off her soft skin. He envisioned what it would be like taking her in his arms afterward and what she would feel like as she trembled beneath him. He hoped she didn't notice the effect her words were having on him.

She felt his fingers, which had been rhythmically brushing up and down her bare arm, suddenly still. "Have you ever danced for anyone?" Michael asked, knowing he had no right but wanting to know anyway.

"No. It's never been my time, I guess. I haven't really ever thought about it, at least not for a long time." A sense of relief coursed through Michael's body.

They remained on the blanket, overlooking the canal until long after the purple skies of Venice turned black.

"Do you have plans tomorrow?" Ari asked as they stepped into the warmth of the professor's living room long after the moon had made her appearance. "I'd like to explore. Maybe head out to the country and take some pictures The Professor has left me the use of his Fiat."

Michael didn't answer. Instead he pulled Ari to him before closing his mouth over hers, his body pressing her against the stucco wall of the professor's living room. He tasted of wine mixed with the sweetness of Amaretto from the biscotti they had shared earlier in the evening, and the smell of leather and spice mingled with the jasmine she had dabbed on her neck earlier was intoxicating.

In the past, Michael would never have hesitated to take a woman to bed, but something was different about Ari. Sex was always an ending for him, not a beginning, and he wasn't ready for whatever this was to end. "I'll see you tomorrow," he whispered breathlessly before opening the door and stepping out into the fog that had enveloped the sleeping city in the early morning hours.

77

SURELY MICHAEL DIDN'T believe in love at first sight. He was much too logical and practical. His romantic dalliances, if you could call them that, existed primarily in the physical sense where he maintained command and power. He wasn't cold hearted about it, but he just hadn't carved out a place in his life for someone else and didn't think it fair to make it seem otherwise. He rarely questioned this. It wasn't that he didn't want Ari. God, it was all he thought about since seeing her on the villa balcony the very first time, and he had a feeling that she'd accept him if he asked, but something told him it wasn't their time yet, which is why he now found himself walking back to an empty hotel room alone.

Ari lay in bed unable to quiet her mind. Late at night on the Island, after everyone had retired to their sleeping quarters, she had often lain awake wondering what it would be like when she met him. At first, her imaginings were those of a young teenager, flirty and innocent. But as she grew older, they became more sensual in nature and once in a while, the images her mind created would be so detailed and vivid, she would unconsciously respond in an excitement of heat and she remembered the first night she had ever explored her own body and how her touch unexpectedly unleashed an intense wave that brought her crashing ashore wrapped in a euphoric relaxation. She had yet to experience the full intimacy shared by a man and woman. This night, right before falling asleep, she began to image what it would be like with Michael.

78

"MORNING," MICHAEL SAID when Ari opened the door. He looked especially handsome to her today in a navy blue shirt, jeans, and grey blazer. He handed her a cup of coffee and gave her a brief kiss.

As Ari finished her coffee, Michael perused the photos and keepsakes cluttering nearly every flat surface in the professor's living room. By the looks of it, he'd led an adventurous life. One photo showed him on top of a camel with the Great Pyramids in the background. In another he was shrouded in the ghostly mists of Machu Piccho and in yet another, clad in the stereo-typical khakis and wide brimmed hat, he stood on the bow of a small boat as it traveled up a river surrounded by densely jungled forests. Ari wasn't sure, but guessed it was probably somewhere in the Amazon. But her favorite photos by far were the small black and white ones of the professor and his wife, Roseanna. They aged from photo to photo, but the passion visible in his eyes and the love with which he looked at her never faltered. It reminded Ari of what Mama said years ago:

"He looked at me like I was the sun that filled his skies in the morning and the stars that filled his skies at night and that every breath he took was just so he could spend one more moment on this earth with me."

"Hey, look at this," Michael said picking up one of the framed photos sitting on the end table near the fireplace. She took the photo from his outstretched hand. It showed a much younger professor dressed in blazer and tie.

"That's a Harrow uniform," he smiled.

"Harrow?" Ari asked looking up from the photo. "Like the boarding school?"

"Yeah. My brothers and I went there. My sister went to Wycombe Abbey. I always felt a bit sorry for her. At least I had William and Anthony with me."

Michael's childhood couldn't have been more different from Ari's. His ancestral home outside of York had been in the family since the reign of Henry VII, when his many times great grandfather had been gifted the estate as reward for his loyalty to the House of Lancaster during the struggles of the fifteenth century. Michael's father spent much of his time in London, accompanied by his mother, leaving Michael and his siblings in the care of Ms. Roland, the governess.

Ari never understood why parents sent their children away to school, but she knew plenty who did. Many of Papa's colleagues, for instance, sent their children away instead of moving them from posting to posting and Ari remembered how horrified she had been when she overheard the terrible Mrs. Wilmead tell Mama she should consider it for her girls, and she remembered running to Mama in tears, begging not to be sent away to school and the relief she had felt when Mama had unequivocally stated, *"over my dead body."*

"I better finish getting ready," Ari said, and she quickly disappeared upstairs. Ari had risen early to lay out her outfit for the day—hip hugging jeans and a pink plaid button up which she knotted just above her waistline. She smiled as she looked in the mirror, a noticeable and rather unexpected confidence radiating from her reflection.

"We'll have to take the vaporetto to the mainland," Ari said as she read the handwritten directions the professor left her. "It looks like his car is parked not too far from the dock, so it should be easy to find."

It turned out it wasn't all that easy. Together, they walked in circles before finally figuring out that the professor's directions lacked a few key details. Nevertheless, they finally found the little Fiat parked at the far end of what loosely passed for a parking lot. The car had a slightly musty smell, like the stale air of an old home and the seats, worn and cracked, no longer had the soft leather feel they once did. When Michael turned the key, the engine sputtered to life, coughing out a puff of dark, acrid smoke. "Where to?" he asked, putting the car into gear.

Ari pulled a map from her knapsack. There were few people on the road, which was good considering that the tiny car couldn't sustain the brisk pace of the posted speed limit. As they continued to drive, the flats of the Venetian plain slowly began to give way to the wave-like undulations of the Dolamite foothills. The misty buttercream sky artfully complemented the jewel-like hues of the green hills, and where the sun peeked through, the land was touched by gold and amber hues. It was as if the entire landscape were alive and breathing, stretching with each movement of the light. Ari knew that beauty like this would only last a minute or two.

"Stop here for a second, Michael." Ari jumped out of the car before it came to a full stop. Mem and Grandfather had given her a Leica camera as a bon voyage present, and she knew this exact moment and place would be an inspiration for a future painting.

Back in the car, Ari unfolded the map once more and spread it across her legs. She had no destination in mind for that was when the most amazing discoveries were made, but her growling stomach seemed to have other plans.

Michael laughed. "Guessing you're hungry?"

"What gave it away," Ari smiled.

On the lookout for a village that might hold the promise of lunch, they continued driving, and soon the once faint outline of the mountains outside the cracked and dirty windshield grew in detail, as if the Gods had applied another layer of paint to the world they constantly created. Ari could see each distinct peak take shape as it rose high above the hills of evergreens— courtesans at the foot of their kings. Icy blue glaciers reflected the sun like diamonds hidden among the craggy rocks and the thin ribbons of shimmering silver cascading down the sheer rock face provided the only indication that they had once been completely covered in winter's white snow.

"Over there," Michal said pointing. Ari followed the direction of his outstretched arm and saw the outline of a campanile just visible in the distance.

Time had long ago faded the brilliantly colored stucco

buildings, but here and there patches of pale color hinted at their once glorious past. The narrow streets were barely wide enough to accommodate a car, but Ari guessed that most of the village's residents never travelled far enough to need one. The two- and three-story buildings rising on either side cast much of the street in shadow, their arched entranceways flush with the cobblestones. Peeking inside, Ari could see that many of them led into private courtyards and lush gardens. The monotony of the aged brown stone was broken by the bright reds and pinks of window boxed geraniums and the bright greens of creeping ivy.

Most Italian villages lacked the familiar grid like street pattern of modern cities and after many twists, turns and dead ends, they eventually made their way to the central piazza. The heartbeat of village life, the large open square was surrounded by store fronts and fruit and vegetable stands and the scent of freshly baked bread. Residents greeted each other with a flourish of arms and smiles as they went about their day and in the center stood a large lion, intricately carved from marble, its flowing mane blowing in an ancient wind and its soulful eyes giving the impression that life lay just below the hard-stone surface. *Aslan*, Ari thought and smiled.

At the far corner of the square, Ari spotted a little café and caught the smell of freshly baked bread. Small wrought iron tables and chairs were intimately arranged under the green awning that extended from the pale pink façade of the stucco building just above its first-floor windows. The building itself rose another two stories and probably served as home to the café's owner and family. Michael followed Ari as she snaked her way through the tables, before settling on one at the far end of the patio.

Not long after, a rotund woman with grey hair and a welcoming smile made her way toward them, stopping to amicably greet each patron with an exuberant "*ciao*" on her way.

After a lunch of Spaghetti Bolognese, Ari leaned back in her chair completely content. Taking a sip of wine, she smiled. "I don't think I've been this happy in a long time." An answering grin broke out wide on Michael's face.

"Excuse me, ma'am," Ari was startled by the sound of a woman's voice with the soft, sweet southern drawl of what Papa had often referred to as coming from a *Georgia Peach*. "Would y'all mind takin' a picture of us?" Ari turned and smiled.

"Sure," she said, taking the camera from the woman's hand. When she looked through the view finder, she couldn't help but notice the way the woman briefly looked down at the shiny ring on her left hand as she snuggled close to the young man sitting by her side. She snapped several pictures and handed the camera back with a smile.

"Would you mind taking one of us as well?" Michael asked as he removed Ari's camera from its bag. Michael scooted his chair closer to Ari and pulled her into his side. Ari couldn't see the look on Michael's face as the shutter snapped. Not until she returned to the Island and had the images developed would she see it.

"He looked at me like I was the sun that filled his skies in the morning and the stars that filled his skies at night and that every breath he took was just so he could spend one more moment on this earth with me."

79

"WOULD YOU LIKE to come in?" Ari asked when they returned to the villa.

Ari dumped her knapsack on the chair and slipped out of her shoes. The cold floor felt good on her bare feet, and she sighed in relief. She was tired, but she wasn't ready for the day to end just yet.

"Would you like a glass of wine?" Ari asked. Michael followed her into the kitchen.

"Salute," Ari said lifting her glass. The savory taste filled her mouth followed by the sweeter taste of strawberries as each layer of the grape revealed itself. She closed her eyes, letting it wash over her.

Michael set his glass on the counter and turned toward her. Her eyes remained closed as his fingers traced the curve of her neck. Ari shivered. He loved the way she reacted to his touch. Michael took the glass from her hand and placed it next to his before lifting her effortlessly onto the counter. The cool tile provided a startling juxtaposition to the heat radiating from her body and she trembled. She arched her neck as his lips nibbled at her skin making his way down to the curve of her shoulder before his fingers slowly found the knot at her waist.

The ancient wood floor creaked as he carried her up the stairs and laid her gently on the iron bed. Michael stood and pulled his t-shirt over his head before carelessly discarding it over the back of the writing desk chair. Even in the dim light, Ari could see his lean muscle and strongly sculpted features, but his movements were graceful and fluid. *The Gods crafted a masterpiece when they made him,* she thought.

Michael ran his hand down Ari's exposed skin, eliciting a

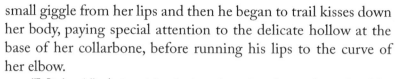

small giggle from her lips and then he began to trail kisses down her body, paying special attention to the delicate hollow at the base of her collarbone, before running his lips to the curve of her elbow.

"Michael," Ari said placing her hand on his shoulder, drawing his eyes to her. "I don't . . . I mean I've never . . .," Ari stammered feeling the heat rise on her checks.

He stopped and sat back on his heels. "I know," he said, taking her hand. "It's okay." He leaned forward to tuck a piece of hair behind her ear and then kissed her gently on the lips. "We don't have to."

"You're okay?" she asked embarrassed. "It doesn't bother you?"

Michael lay beside her and shook his head. "I'm here with you, aren't I?" A smile tugged at the corner of his mouth, and he kissed her again before wrapping Ari securely in his arms. She didn't know how long it took to fall asleep. Not long, she guessed, as the next thing she remembered was hearing Michael whisper her name. When she sleepily opened her eyes, the light from the window promised the arrival of the sun.

"Arianna?"

"Hmm?" She stretched and snuggled deeper under the fluffy comforter.

"Will you dance for me someday?" Ari's eyes flew open.

"You mean at Celebration?"

Michael breathed in the faint scent of jasmine as her movement stirred the air. Jasmine had always been a favorite of his, but he had no memory of why. "If you'll have me that is."

The following day Michael had meetings and then a luncheon with Dr. Thatcher. He'd invited her to join them, but she politely declined in order to return to L'Accademia alone, this time dedicating the hours necessary to truly live the artwork within. But that night saw them together again under the yellow and white stripped awning of the little trattoria.

The sound of knocking woke Ari early the next morning. She sleepily made her way downstairs, tying her emerald green silk robe around her waist before opening the door.

"Good morning," Michael said, placing a kiss on her cheek

before handing her a cup of coffee.

"What time is it?" Ari asked her voice rough with sleep.

"It's early but we need to get going," Michael replied.

"Where are we going?" she asked, shuffling toward the kitchen. He leaned to give her a proper good morning kiss, but she turned her head.

"I haven't brushed my teeth yet." He laughed and shook his head. "Go pack an overnight bag and some comfortable shoes," he said, patting her playfully on the backside.

"Where are we going?" she asked again, the sleep lifting from her eyes with each sip of hot coffee.

"Pompeii," he answered with a grin. "You said you've always wanted to go, so let's go."

80

ARI JUMPED OUT of bed and ran to the window to catch her first glimpse of the bustling waterfront and the famous mountain that overlooked the Bay of Naples. She wanted to throw her clothes on and rush out the door right away, but Michael was still sleeping. Ari watched as he smiled and turned on his side. It wasn't like Pompeii was going anywhere anytime soon, but as she glanced back at the lush green slope of the huge mountain rising before her, she wasn't entirely sure that was true.

The deep blue waters of the bay shimmered before her as the light from the morning sun danced across its smooth surface and the Neapolitans began their day. Fishermen were readying their boats and shops were opening their doors and children were running and laughing free from care. People greeted each other and cars and Vespas raced by at an alarming speed given how narrow the streets were. She laughed as a Vespa driven by a young boy with a grandfatherly old man clinging to his waist swept by.

She heard Michael stir behind her. "I can't believe I'm really here," she said. Michael gave her a sleepy smile. "Come on. Let's go," Ari urged. "I don't want to waste another second."

Ari had never fully embraced the changing fashion of the 1970s, what with its polyester hot pants and palazzos that were wider at the bottom than the waist upon which they sat. But one trend she did like was the one-piece jumpsuit, which by its very nature cut the time needed to get ready by half. Michael softly kissed the exposed skin of her shoulder as she adjusted the halter top of her denim one-piece to ensure everything was adequately tucked in place and secure. Ari ran her fingers through

502

her loose hair before grabbing her sunglasses from the table.

"You're beautiful, you know that," Michael said. Ari smiled, a blush spreading across her tanned skin.

After a quick breakfast of baked rolls, the hollow ones that Ari loved to slather with ample amounts of Nutella, they boarded the train to take them to Pompeii Scavia. There they mixed and mingled with the tourists emerging from buses aligned outside the entrance gate. It made Ari sad to see how many people were crowded into the ruined city, and it angered her to see parents ignoring their kids as they ran up and down the sidewalks yelling and screaming and disregarding the posted *"Non Toccare"* and *"Non Entrare,"* signs. Pompeii wasn't just another tourist site; it was the final resting place of the people who perished when the volcano erupted in 79 AD and deserved more respect than many of its visitors were showing.

Once inside, the rolling and uneven stone streets and the deep grooves from the passage of chariots and carts of old were a careless walker's worst nightmare. Ari made sure to watch where she stepped to avoid stubbing a toe or twisting an ankle. She recognized many of the sites from photos and books she had studied over the years, but none of them compared to seeing the real thing. There were the elevated stepping stones that allowed for safe passage when water regularly cleansed the city streets, and the forum whose remaining columns hinted at what was once a grand two story colonnaded portico flanked by shops and stalls that had served the wealthy residents of the seaside town. As she took it all in, Ari heard ghostly voices of the shop owners and merchants hawking their wares and the hushed conversation of lovers hidden in dark corners and the lively laughter of children or the clip-clop of horse hoof on the stone streets as visitors descended on the giant open space to sell and trade their goods. Ari closed her eyes and let the feeling of the city wash over her. The air was heavy and still, and she knew that Mama had been right. There really was such a thing as spirit of place.

While the public forum and spaces were impressive, Ari knew the city's real treasures lay in the residential ruins. Very few privately owned homes had survived the centuries, but because of the circumstance surrounding Pompeii, many were preserved giving archeologists and historians an extraordinary opportunity to study everyday life in the ancient empire. Pompeii displayed a shocking example of the stark differences between the upper and lower classes in Roman society, and it reminded Ari a little of what she had seen in Djakarta. But today she had no place for those memories.

As they walked hand in hand through one of the larger villas on the outskirts of the city, Ari was amazed at the level of detail that had survived the centuries. Typical of villas of the time, each room surrounded a large colonnaded atrium, which once housed beautiful gardens. Although a little worse for wear, the walls were covered in brightly colored frescos and the floors with intricate mosaic scenes, from which many of the villas took their name. A small trench ran from room to room, which would have once flowed with wine, explaining the images of wild parties and orgies depicted on many of the painted walls.

"It's kind of ironic," Ari said.

"What is?" Michael replied as he looked closer at a particularly scandalous fresco.

"The very thing that destroyed the city was the one thing that saved it in the end."

81

WHEN THEY ARRIVED back at the hotel, Michael led Ari to the roof top terrace overlooking the bay.

"Close your eyes," he said before opening the door to the outside. "Absolutely no peeking," he ordered. He took Ari's hands to guide her through the double doors and into the open air. She shuffled forward with small, slow steps to avoid tripping.

"Okay," Michael said once they stopped. "You can open them now." It took her a moment to get her bearings, but when she did the scene unfolding before her took her breath away. The sun's evening rays painted the sky in shades of reds and bright oranges and turned the wispy clouds above into rivers of molten lava. As the sun drew closer to the watery line of the horizon, its flamboyant colors burned to embers before lavenders and dark purples began to cool the sky above. The pinks and peaches of the sun's final bow gave way to the soft yellows and creams of the full moon, which rose over the mountain, silhouetting it against the ever-darkening night sky. Soon everything was awash in moonglow, the reflection cutting a deep gash in the midnight black of the still waters below, and as families and friends came together around dinner tables throughout the city, twinkling lights began to fill the hillside, mirroring the shinning stars above.

"Let's sit," Michael said guiding her forward with a light touch of his hand. Ari sat silently, her eyes fixed on the moon.

"Have you ever experienced a moment so significant that you don't just remember it, but you live it over and over again?" Ari asked. "This will always be one of those moments for me."

"Signore, signora, buona sera." A young, handsome waiter

505

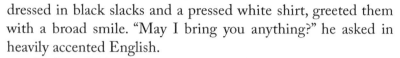

dressed in black slacks and a pressed white shirt, greeted them with a broad smile. "May I bring you anything?" he asked in heavily accented English.

"I think I'd like a Bellini. Grazie," Ari thanked him.

Michael brought Ari's hand to his lips. "I'll have the same," he said without taking his eyes from her.

When the waiter returned, Ari held the champagne glass toward the sky letting the moonlight shine through the amber liquid and the sparkling bubbles which danced around a single red raspberry. *To you, Mama,* she thought before turning her attention back to Michael.

"To a night to remember," he said raising his glass.

"Yes," she answered with a smile. "Definitely a night to remember."

82

NOT NEEDING TO return until the start of term, Michael extended his time in Italy and had happily accepted Ari's invitation to stay with her at the professor's villa. Their days started with coffee and ended with wine, and together they explored the region by car and the city by foot and each other by moonlight. But as fall grew ever closer, both knew that their time together was drawing to a close.

"I guess this is goodbye," Ari said, her throat thick with the tears she was fighting to keep from overflowing, as she stood on the wooden dock jutting out into the Grand Canal.

"Signore, the water taxi is leaving," said the little man attempting to corral the numerous tourists and their even more numerous bags into the little boat before departing for the mainland and the airport.

"Not goodbye," Michael said. "More of a see you soon." He pulled her to him. "Soon," he repeated as he stole one last kiss from her lips before turning to board. Ari stood on the dock as the water taxi grew smaller and smaller until she could no longer see him. Then she slowly walked back to the villa.

She trudged upstairs before falling into bed. She wasn't sure how long she cried or when she had finally fallen asleep, but when she woke the sky had already faded from purple to black.

Looking at her reflection in the mirror, Ari was greeted by a splotchy red face with tear stained cheeks and puffy eyes. "Get ahold of yourself, Ari," she scolded wiping away another tear. Sniffling, she noticed a folded paper on the writing desk, her name neatly written on the front.

Ari,

Before I knew you, I saw the world in black and white. Now, it's colored with the purples, oranges, reds and the greens of your Island. I'm not sure what this is between us, but whatever it is has not ended for me. Please wait for me, Ari. I'll be with you soon.
Missing you already,

Michael

A week later, Ari closed the door to the professor's villa for the final time and headed toward the dock that would begin her journey home. Dr. Thatcher had come to help her with her bags and to see her off, closing her journey full circle. Despite the fact that she had already shipped some of her belongings and art supplies to Mem, her bags were much heavier than she remembered them being when she first arrived, and she was slightly out of breath when she finally reached the dock. Ari hugged the Professor and thanked him for his help.

"It's been a real pleasure, Arianna Heywood," he smiled warmly.

"Likewise," Ari smiled back. "I will miss all this," she said as she swept her gaze across the cityscape.

"You cannot leave Venice sad, Ms. Heywood."

"I'm not sad," Ari sniffled. "It's just that Venice was so much more than I expected it to be, it's hard to say goodbye."

"Venice is special that way," he replied. "I met the love of my life here too." Ari looked at him surprised, but when he offered nothing more, she hugged him goodbye and thanked him once again.

"You're welcome, my dear." He kissed her cheek and helped her onto the waiting water taxi.

Appropriately, the purple skies of Venice were just beginning to darken as the little boat pulled away from the dock—a perfect bookend to her arrival.

Part Six

The Island

83

AS THE LAUNCH approached the shore, Ari could see the waving figures of Grandfather and Mem. The Island welcomed her back with open arms. When she stepped off the gently bobbing boat and felt the Island sands between her bare toes once again, she knew she was home.

"Mem! Grandfather!" Ari yelled as she threw her arms around them. "I've missed you."

"Welcome home," Mem smiled wrapping her arms around Ari. "Now, let me look at you." Standing at arm's length, Mem looked Ari up and down before a broad smile grew across her face.

"So," she said. "Who is he?" Mem's eyes gleamed in the waning sun.

"How did you know?" Ari asked surprised.

"Because I saw that same look on your mama's face once," Mem answered.

"Oh, Mem," Ari hugged her tight once again and as they walked back to *Surihana*, Ari told her everything. Almost everything anyway.

"I felt like I could tell him anything, Mem. We talked about Mama and Papa and the Island, and I told him what happened in Djakarta and shared things that I've never told anyone." Mem smiled. "He wants to come here, Mem. He wants me to dance for him." Mem stopped abruptly.

"Am I crazy, Mem?" Ari asked. "I mean, I barely know him, but I feel like I've known him my whole life."

"Perhaps you have," Mem answered as she continued toward *Surihana*. Before Ari could say more, their conversation was interrupted by enthusiastic barking.

"Tippy!" Ari embraced him, scratching his ears and nuzzling her nose into the soft fur of his neck. "I missed you so much." Tippy ran ahead, yipping with excitement as they made their way into the courtyard.

By the time Ari retired to her sleeping quarters later that night, she was too tired to unpack. She pulled a pair of pajamas from her carry on and with it a crisp white pillowcase that smelled of old English leather and spice. She hoped the Professor wouldn't notice it had gone missing.

84

HOME FOR SEVERAL weeks now, Ari awoke just as the sun was peeking over the jungled mountains. She knew that the Island would soon wake and with it the boisterous laughter of school children returning to their studies from summer break. If she wanted a few minutes of peace by the lagoon, she'd need to dress and go soon.

"Good morning, Mem," Ari said as she walked into *Surihana*'s cooking pavilion. "I was thinking about heading down to the lagoon for a swim. Would you like to join me?" Ari asked as she poured herself a cup of coffee and took a seat on one of the swivel stools.

Mem smiled. "I'll pack a breakfast."

Ari offered to help, but Mem waved her off, telling her to go and enjoy a quiet swim. After arranging her Tatami mat on the beach, Ari dove into the clear warm water of the lagoon. A large sea turtle gracefully glided nearby, and the fish darted in and out of the bright coral as their underwater world came to life.

Small ripples of water washed over her bare skin as she floated on her back, and she began to think. Prior to Venice, she simply existed, refusing to think about a future without her family in it. She lived half a life and was content to do so. But since returning to the Island, everything felt different, and Ari knew it was finally time to begin living again.

By the time Ari returned to her mat, Grandfather and Mem had joined her.

"Good swim, Ari?" Grandfather asked.

"I was just thinking," Ari said with a mouth full of juicy mango. "I'd like to open the Great House again." Ari had avoided her family home all together, afraid to return to where so many of her memories lived. Mem and Grandfather had seen to its upkeep over the years, but it remained otherwise untouched. Mem smiled and squeezed Ari's hand

"Would you like help?"

"No," Ari replied. "I think this is something I need to do by myself."

That afternoon she made her way up the jungle path toward the Great House. Ari was anxious. As she laid her hand upon the giant iron doorknob, she felt her heart beating wildly in her chest and, taking a deep breath, she slowly pushed open the ornately carved door and stepped over the threshold into her past.

The moveable walls remained shut, blocking out much of the natural light that Ari remembered. A sudden flood of emotion washed over her. As Ari's eyes adjusted to the dim light, she could see the shadow of Papa sitting in his leather chair by the fire, smoking his pipe and reading the evening news with James at his feet building his Lincoln Logs. And Emma lay reading one of her fashion magazines on the couch as Mama tended her Bird of Paradise. All at once, they looked at her. *"Welcome home,"* they said. *"We've been waiting for you."*

Ari spent the rest of the day simply walking from room to room, letting her emotions run free. She ran her fingertips over Papa's leather books in his study and spun the globe that still sat on the shelf behind his desk. She swung in the hammock that overlooked the lush garden and listened to the babbling waterfall as it cascaded down the black lava rocks into the pond below—one of the many sounds of her childhood she had tried hard to forget. Emma's Island clothes hung in garment bags in her closet and her favorite perfume sat on her dresser. A picture of Tommy was tucked in the mirror above. James's room bore the mark of a little boy. Mem had cleaned up his toys, but it remained otherwise untouched. A line of teddy bears sat upon his small bed. She reached for one, hugging it to her chest, inhaling the scent that still clung to its soft fur. She paused before opening the door to Mama and Papa's sleeping quarters. *"Another day,"* she thought.

It took weeks, but soon the house was fully open. Well, fully open except for Mama and Papa's room. Dust covers had been removed, exposing the unused furniture to the world once again. Ari rearranged family photos throughout the house, adding her own to the collection. She filled the vases with tropical flowers and moved Mama's Bird of Paradise to its place of honor above the fireplace once more and with each passing day, she felt more and more at home.

One afternoon, Mem and Grandfather joined her for lunch in the kitchen.

"You look happy child," Mem observed, and Ari smiled peacefully.

"What do you plan to do now?" Grandfather interjected.

"I need to finish going through Emma's closet and the cushions in the summer house still need to be cleaned." Ari answered.

"No, I meant long term," Grandfather said. "Have you thought about what you want to do, Ari? Who you want to be?" Ari's eyebrows furrowed deep in thought.

"I don't really know, Grandfather. I'd like to start painting again."

"Well, that's certainly a start," Mem said, before finishing her glass of wine and handing it to Grandfather to fill once more.

85

THE ISLAND'S SUMMER breezes gradually faded and soon the northernly winds came to visit and with them the building excitement of the holidays. Soon family and friends would return to the Island to celebrate. Ari had suggested hosting Christmas Eve dinner at the Great House and had invited all the Island families to celebrate. It would be the first gathering at the Great House since the Heywoods departed the island for Djakarta.

As Ari walked up the jungle path, her hair still wrapped in a towel from her early morning swim in the lagoon, she heard a distant ring. The phone on Papa's desk rarely rang, and it took her a second to realize exactly what the unfamiliar sound was. Michael's well-read letters, once neatly organized, went flying as she reached across the desk to pick up the phone before the caller hung up.

"Hello," she said, breathless from her sprint. All she could hear was the pop and crackle of static. "Hello?" she said again but received no answer. She was just about to replace the receiver when she heard a voice, far away fighting the bad connection and her heart fluttered.

"Ari?" his voice crackled. "Ari? Can you hear me?"

"Michael!" Ari replied loudly to be heard over the static. "Yes. I'm here."

"God, it's good to hear your voice," he said. "How are you?"

It wasn't a long conversation. After all, long distance calls to and from the Island did not come cheap.

"I miss you, Ari," Michael said after they had briefed each other on the latest goings on. "The picture you sent, the one from the little café, is on my desk. I look at it every day." Ari smiled knowing that the same picture sat framed on her bedside table.

"I miss you too," she replied.

The line crackled and popped, making it difficult to hear. "So," Michael's voice broke through the noise. "I'm going to have a bit of time off when term is over. I was thinking I could come see you. I mean if you still want me to." He sounded unsure.

Ari smiled. "Yes, I'd love that," she said and tried to keep her voice steady. "I've missed you so much, Michael."

"Me too. We'll talk soon, okay?"

"Okay," Ari replied. "Goodbye, Michael."

"Goodbye, Arianna."

Ari floated her way to the gently swaying hammock outside and fell lazily into its comforting folds and smiled. She closed her eyes and let the sounds of the Island carry her away.

86

ARI COUNTED DOWN the days until Christmas. All Michael's travel arrangements were made and soon he'd be here. She'd spent countless nights imagining what it would be like to see him again and often replayed the same scene over and over in her head with a few changes here and there as her mind shaped the perfect fantasy. He would step off the launch, the Island breeze rustling his perfect black hair, and then he would look up and see her standing there waiting. Their eyes would lock and then he'd smile, the one that was mischievous and scintillating, before striding toward her, taking her in his arms and bending to kiss her. It was all terribly romantic.

She sat in her studio at the Great House, looking around at her finished canvases with a feeling of pride. She couldn't wait to show them to Michael. It had taken her months, but she was almost finished. In one painting she had captured her first glimpse of Venice and the little dock with its gently bobbing black gondolas and stripped poles that began her journey. In the distance she painted the giant dome of the famous church and, above everything, the velvety purples of the Venetian sky. She titled it *Un Nuovo Inizio—A New Beginning*. In another, she painted the small wrought iron balcony, adorned with bright red and pink geraniums, overlooking the calm waters of a small canal. The bow of an approaching Gondola was just visible at the edge of the canvas. It was titled *Un Incontro Inaspettato—An Unexpected Encounter*. She painted the Professor's garden with its colorful flowers, winding paths, and an open gate that led to the lawn by the canal. If you looked closely, you could see the slightest hint of a shadow on the green grass where two lovers lay side by side. This one she titled *Un Nuovo Capitolo—A New Chapter.*

And of course, there were paintings of San Marco Square and the campanile, L'Accademia, and the Rialto Bridge and several unknown places she happened upon while walking. And finally, on her easel sat the beginnings of her last canvas. Still untitled, she had just finished outlining the shadow of the mountain.

Suddenly the phone in Papa's study began to ring. Ari set her pencil aside.

"Hello?" Ari said.

Even over the crackle of the international line, she could hear the resigned sadness in his voice. "Hi, Ari. It's Michael. We need to talk."

This time Ari didn't float to the hammock. She didn't float anywhere. Instead she trudged to the gathering pavilion and fell onto the couch with an audible *plop* and a sigh. One of Michael's colleagues at the university had suddenly resigned after it came out that he was on overly friendly terms with a female student, and Michael was asked to fill the vacancy until a more permanent solution could be found. It wouldn't have mattered had the university also not asked him to replace the troublesome professor in an upcoming lecture series scheduled to take place over the holiday break in Florence. Ari understood, but it didn't quell her disappointment any. *Maybe it's for the best*, she thought. As she sat on the couch, she tried to convince herself that long distance relationships never worked anyway. Something always came up, at no fault of either party. It was just the way things were. That night, all she saw in her mind was the black abyss of empty dreams.

87

THE TEA POT was beginning to whistle alerting her the water was ready for her coffee when Ari heard the phone ring, so she quickly removed it from the stove. As she made her way into the study, a small quiver of excitement took hold deep in her belly but was quickly extinguished when she heard the voice of Professor Bostwick, the head of the Department of Cultural Studies at Mainland University on the other end. He wanted to meet with her in person before the holidays to discuss a proposition that he thought she would find interesting. After arranging to meet the following day, Ari hung up the phone and returned to the cooking pavilion to pour herself a strong cup of coffee and anxiously wondered what he wanted to talk to her about.

The next morning, Ari boarded the launch bound for the mainland. Her red and white wrap dress was strikingly out of place on the sands of the Island and having gone barefoot much of the time, her red wedge sandals felt like a heavy, foreign burden on her feet.

When the launch reached its destination, Ari disembarked with the other passengers and made her way toward the main street. The waterfront was busier than usual today with last minute preparations for the coming holidays. Many of the shops would close tomorrow and not reopen until after the New Year.

It didn't take long to reach the east entrance to the university. The high arching entrance reminded Ari of the Sather Gate that welcomed students to the Berkeley campus on Telegraph Avenue. The white stone buildings that once housed colonial government offices dotted the perimeter of park like expanses of velvety green grass, providing a sharp juxtaposition to the deep emerald greens of the surrounding landscape.

McKay Hall housed the Department of Cultural Studies. It had been built in the late 1800s to serve as a clubhouse for the area's more well-to-do residents. The white stone of the two-story building stood out brilliantly in the sunlight and was dotted by tall rectangular windows flanked by cerulean blue shutters. The pediment atop the Doric columned portico showed the intricately carved logo of the former club depicting a gathering of the area's tropical flora atop the Union Jack. As Ari entered the building through the heavy, ornately designed wood door, she was met with a rush of cold air from within as she removed her sunglasses.

Very little of the building's interior design had changed over the years although several of the public rooms were repurposed to accommodate classrooms and small lecture halls. The black and white marble floor of the entryway was polished to a high sheen and a massive double staircase led to the second story balustrade where most of the private and administrative offices were located. Large crystal chandeliers hung from the coffered ceilings, radiating shimmering rainbows across the cream-colored walls as the bright mid-day sun filtered through the front windows. Ari's footsteps echoed loudly off the marble stairs as she made her way to the second floor before finding the door with Professor Bostwick's name etched into the frosted glass. She knocked quietly.

"It's open," he said.

"Hello, Professor," Ari said as she closed the door behind her. Decorated in the traditional English style, Professor Bostwick's office with its many leather-bound books and dimly lit banker's lamps would have met Papa's approval, and it was obvious from the sweet smell of tobacco that the Professor enjoyed a pipe or two during his office hours.

"Ms. Heywood," he greeted her as he rose from his chair. "Thank you for coming on such short notice. Please," he said, gesturing toward one of the two leather chairs sitting opposite his over-sized desk. Never one to waste time, he continued immediately.

"I visited Mem while you were in Venice. She showed me several of the works you shipped back. I'd like, with your permission naturally, to exhibit them at the Fujiri in May. We have an Italian installation we'll be exhibiting, and your work would complement it nicely."

"I'd be honored," Ari said smiling. "I've just finished several new pieces."

"Wonderful. Let's shore up the details after the holidays then." Ari smiled and rose to leave as the professor opened his desk drawer and removed a pouch of fresh tobacco.

"One more thing," he said, motioning for Ari to sit again. "Do you mind?" he asked before filling his pipe. Ari shook her head. The professor took several deep puffs and exhaled a cloud of smoke.

"Mainland University has received funding to expand our Art Department. We're working with several other universities world-wide to give students the opportunity to take their studies abroad. As you can imagine, we're overjoyed. As part of the program, we will be offering a four-year degree in the visual arts, which is what I want to talk to you about. We would like you to oversee it."

Wide-eyed, Ari didn't know quite what to say. It certainly never entered her mind as she boarded the launch earlier in the day that she'd be offered such an opportunity.

"It would be a lot of work, I know, so take some time to think about it," he said.

After promising to follow up after the holidays, Ari retraced her steps back to the waterfront and waited for the afternoon launch to arrive. She knew accepting the professor's offer meant rooting her life firmly to the Island and while it would always be her home, did it hold everything she wanted? Logically, she knew Michael had no place in her decision, or at least shouldn't, but the illogical side of her couldn't help it. Her eyes searched the empty horizon. *What should I do, Mama*? She waited for a sign, but none came.

As they prepared dinner later that evening, Ari told Mem what had transpired in the professor's office earlier that day and quickly realized that it wasn't news to her.

"Why didn't you say anything?" Ari asked, but before Mem could answer Grandfather appeared with an armful of packages newly arrived from the Mainland.

"Ari, there's something here for you," he said as he entered the cooking pavilion slightly out of breath from the climb up to the Great House. Ari quickly washed and dried her hands before hugging him. She sat at the counter and carefully slid a knife across the brown paper. Inside, she found an envelope and a velvet box.

"Well, what is it?" asked Grandfather, who was chewing on a piece of mango ignoring the reproachful look on Mem's face.

"It's beautiful," Ari said as she held up an ivory and jade hair comb in the shape of a Bird of Paradise.

"Oh, Ari," Mem said setting down her knife. "It's just like—"

"I know," Ari said. One of Mama's most prized possessions—the platinum and emerald hair combs Papa had given her for her fortieth birthday, and which she had lent to Ari all those years ago on New Year's Eve. Ari remembered watching Mama pin them into her hair the night of Papa's welcome reception in Djakarta. She carefully laid the comb back atop the silk fold of the velvet box, before reaching for the envelope. She read his note silently and exhaled audibly as she put it back into its envelope. His note held no promises.

> *I saw this in a little shop in Florence, and it made me think of you. Merry Christmas, Arianna.*
>
> *Michael*

"You know, Ari," Mem said with a gentle squeeze on her shoulder, "things have an amazing way of working themselves out, but if you lose hope too soon, you'll never know."

88

IT WAS THE first Christmas back in the Great House, and Ari wanted to make sure it was extra special. She decided to borrow one of Mama's silk sarongs reserved only for the most celebratory of occasions and used one of her jade pins to fasten the delicate emerald green silk over her left shoulder. Ari sat on the little bench at Mama's dressing table, her hands twisting her hair into a casual updo before she pinned it with Michael's gift.

The evening started out with eggnog and Old-Fashions on the garden patio and sparkling cider for those not yet old enough to partake in too much holiday cheer. As Ari sipped from Papa's favorite highball glass, the fiery tang of whiskey tempered by the sweetness of the muddled bitters and sugar cube warmed her like a small potbellied stove on a cold snowy evening, and for the first time all day, she felt her shoulders unwind into complete relaxation.

The stone table was festively decorated and set with Mama's special occasion china—the delicate Noritaki with yellow and cream and hand painted gold lace. Mem had spent hours carving delicate apple birds and grapefruit roses to accompany the palm fronds and hibiscus flowers woven between Mama's silver candle sticks. Ari had tried to help, but her apple bird looked like something straight out of an LSD induced nightmare and both she and Mem agreed her efforts would be better suited elsewhere.

When Ari announced that dinner was ready to be served, everyone gathered around the stone table as bottles of Grandfather's special Island wine passed from hand to hand and soon the once empty glasses shimmered ruby red. Grandfather smiled at Ari as she set the last platter of food on the table.

"This is your home now, Ari," Grandfather said. "You should sit here." As he pulled out the chair that had belonged to Papa, the table grew silent.

"Thank you, Grandfather," she said with a smile and slowly took her seat. As the food was passed, Ari looked at the faces of all of those who had come to celebrate. Kemala and Tao and Joey and Lili and their little girl who Ari had been overjoyed to find out would soon be a big sister. To Joey's left sat Tommy and next to him, his fiancé, Julie.

Of course, Arina and Beni and Ravi were there too. Even Old Willie ventured away from the water long enough to celebrate. Old Batara and Maru, the Island elders, sat next to Grandfather and Mem. Ari looked out to the gathering pavilion, where she saw the ghosts of those no longer with her, but not gone, looking on with smiles, and she smiled back, raising her glass with a small nod.

The festivities lasted well into the night with the adults gathering around the stone table, drinking wine and reminiscing about the past. There were a lot of "*remember when*" memories shared, which usually resulted in an eruption of laughter and happy tears. There were many hearty congratulations, toasts, and well wishes for Ari when Mem broke the news that she would be joining Mainland University in the fall as the Director of the Visual Arts Program. Beni and the other children had fallen asleep on the couch. Ari sat back and watched, listening to the animated conversation, which grew and grew as more and more wine was poured.

The moon had long ago begun its journey home when Ari bid Mem and Grandfather goodnight and retired to bed. She carefully undressed and pulled the comb from her hair, placing it back in its velvet box. She ran the tip of her finger over the smooth jade stones. "Merry Christmas," she whispered and turned out the light.

89

"THAT'S ALL FOR today," Michael said as he gathered his papers from the lectern and followed the last of the students out of the hall. England wasn't particularly famous for its weather, or rather it was but not for the reason one would hope, and this winter had certainly lived up to expectations. Unfortunately, spring wasn't looking any more promising. Michael wrapped his wool scarf around his neck before shoving his hands in the pockets of his overcoat.

A constant spitting rain, the cold type that couldn't quite make up its mind if it wanted to freeze or not, tapped on the window, as Michael sat at his desk marking the latest round of exams. He put down his pencil and sat back in his chair which creaked with age, pinching the bridge of his nose in a vain attempt to quiet the pounding in his head. He picked up the framed photo sitting on his desk. He'd hoped as time moved on that his feelings for her would fade. It wasn't that he wanted them to necessarily, it was just that he knew logically it would be for the best. But if anything, the time away from her had done the exact opposite.

Whether on purpose or not, his life had been consumed by work. When he wasn't in the hall lecturing or meeting with students or grading exams and papers, he was at his desk writing his book or on the phone discussing upcoming guest lectures and events. His thoughts should be focused elsewhere and not on her.

A knock on the door interrupted his thoughts, irritating him more than it should. "Come in," he said gruffly. Professor Evans greeted him as he entered.

"How are you, Michael?"

"Fine thank you, sir" he replied to the department head. "I hope you are doing well."

"I am, thank you. I'd like to talk to you about your future here with the university."

"Certainly," Michael replied with a slight hesitation.

"You have represented this institution to the highest of standards. This coupled with the high level of international distinction your publications and lectures have garnered deserves to be acknowledged. The university is preparing to award you a Personal Chair. You'll receive a formal written notification, but I wanted the chance to speak with you myself. After all, you were one of my students once." Professor Evens smiled. "You do know I take full credit for your success, right?" He laughed.

Michael sat back and ran his fingers through his hair. There wasn't an academic Michael knew who wouldn't jump at the chance to receive such a position, so it surprised him when he didn't feel an immediate sense of joy. It was the culmination of everything he had done in his professional career, but it also meant a fixed residence away from her. Michael bit his lower lip and drummed his fingers on his desk as was his habit when deep in thought. There was only one logical decision to be made.

"It would be an honor, sir," he said.

"Splendid!"

After bidding the professor goodbye, he opened his desk drawer and took out a sheet of paper. An hour later, he quickly penned his name and folded the paper into an envelope, packed his briefcase, turned off his desk lamp and locked his office door. On his way out, he stopped by the faculty mailroom and slipped the letter into the outgoing mail slot, hoping it would be well received.

90

FINALLY, IT WAS the day of Ari's art show. Ironically, it was one year to the day since she'd left for Venice. She lay in her bed at the Great House, watching the darkness of night fade into the early morning light. Tippy was curled up in a little fur ball by her side and when she reached out a hand to scratch his head, he opened his sleepy eyes, yawned and stretched before jumping off of the bed to trot outside and relieve himself in his designated corner of the yard.

After enjoying a cup of coffee in the quiet setting of the veranda overlooking the gently sparkling waters of the lagoon, Ari busied herself around the Great House, putting all her nervous energy into cleaning and organizing. Around midday, she heard Mem calling to her.

"Have you eaten anything today, Ari?" Mem asked as she entered the gathering pavilion where Ari was busy arranging and rearranging the brightly colored throw pillows on the couch.

"I had some berries for breakfast," Ari replied.

"You need to eat, child," Mem admonished. "It won't do you any good to faint in front of everyone tonight. Besides, you get grumpy when you're hungry, just like your father." Ari smiled, remembering Mama repeatedly chastising Papa for not eating before she shoved a snack in his mouth.

Mem placed two large packages on the counter. "Let's sit and eat. I brought buns," Mem said with a smile. At the mention of Ms. Yao's steamed buns, Ari's stomach growled and after setting the table for two, she took her place beside Mem, who had just finished pouring wine.

"And this is for you," Mem said placing a large box in front of Ari. "Open it."

"Oh, Mem, it's beautiful!" Ari exclaimed as she held up a mint green chiffon evening gown and admired the delicate sleeves and detailed eggshell bead work that gathered the fabric in gentle folds at the base of a V-neck. The dress looked familiar, but she couldn't quite place it in her mind.

"It was your Mama's, Ari." That's when Ari remembered the photo of Mama and Papa at their first formal event together. Papa carried the photo with him everywhere, and it was the first thing that found a new home on his desk with each new posting.

Once Mem left, Ari drew herself a hot bath scenting the water with jasmine oil. As the warm water washed over her, her muscles relaxed, and the nerves she had felt all day began to dissipate with the steam. She closed her eyes and let her mind wander. At first, she thought about nothing at all, but soon the emptiness began to fill with images of Michael. There had been no more phone calls. In their letters, they had congratulated one another on their newly appointed positions, but no mention of seeing each other again had been made. And while Ari was sad, she would always be grateful that Michael had come into her life, however briefly.

She rose from the warm water and toweled off her wet skin before slipping into her silk robe and tying it around her waist. She brushed her hair until it shone like black diamonds before carefully placing Michael's comb. Mama's teardrop jade earrings perfectly complemented both the comb and her dress. Ari opened the inlaid wood jewelry box that sat on her dressing table and pulled out the necklace James had made for her eighteenth birthday. She brought it to her lips. "I miss you, big guy."

91

AT THE FUJIRI, Ari was just finishing a last inspection of her paintings when people began to arrive, and it wasn't long before the gallery was filled. She mingled with the crowd, answering questions and blushing with each compliment that was directed her way. Appropriately she had titled her show *Trovare L'Amore in Italia*— Finding Love in Italy. Ari heard the clink of metal on glass and turned her head toward the small stage that was set at one end of the gallery to see Professor Bostwick smiling at the crowd.

"Hello, everyone," he began in a booming voice that carried throughout the gallery. "I want to thank you all for coming tonight. Many of you attended Ms. Heywood's showing here before, and I think I can speak for everyone when I say to Ari, you have outdone yourself this time." Ari blushed a deep red as all eyes turned toward her and the crowd broke out in applause. Ari reluctantly took the microphone from the Professor's outstretched hand.

"Thank you, everyone," Ari said as she looked around the room, overwhelmed by the number of people who stood before her. Many she had known since childhood. She scanned the room looking for the one face she hoped to see, but the only emerald green eyes she saw staring back at her belong to Grandfather and Mem.

"You have no idea how much it means to me to have you all here." She laughed nervously. "I once asked Mem why she painted, and she told me it was '*because painting is a conversation that words fail to convey.*' I didn't quite understand her at the time, but for those of you who know her, you know her wisdom reaches far beyond the present." She saw many heads nod in agreement. "So," she continued. "I want to thank someone who is not here tonight. Someone who probably will never see any of this, but who influenced it all and will never know." She noticed Mem squeeze Grandfather's hand, smiling at him with that loving look they shared, the one that belied their years of marriage and age. Ari quickly handed the microphone back to the Professor as the gallery broke out in warm applause.

"Congratulations, Ari," Mem hugged her tight. "I am so proud of you. And not just for tonight, for everything you've done and everything you will do. You really have found your voice."

"It's funny, Mem. I can't explain it, but I feel like I've finally arrived at where I'm supposed to be. I feel comfortable, but not in the same way I did before. I guess it's more that I finally feel like I've found peace. I miss them terribly, but I'm not afraid to remember the happiness we shared. I realize now how grateful I am to have had what time I did with them. I was lucky to have a loving family when so many never have that chance." She thought of Arina and Beni and the life they had fled from. "I no longer feel the guilt of moving on without them."

"Yes," Mem gently squeezed Ari's hand. "But I think there is more yet to come." Mem smiled, her eyes holding that mysterious gleam that always seemed to appear when she knew more than she was willing to reveal.

As Mem joined Grandfather across the room, Ari stood in front of her favorite painting and studied the golden moon, rising over the dark shadow of the mountain, its light reflecting off still waters like the wake of a departing ship. On a table in the foreground, two champagne glasses stood side by side. She called it *Una Notte da Ricordare*—A Night to Remember.

"It was a night to remember, wasn't it?" She froze as the scent of leather and spice filled the air around her.

"Hello, Arianna," he whispered in her ear. She turned and opened her eyes, half expecting him to be gone, but this time it wasn't her mind, but her eyes, that saw two brilliant emeralds shining back.

"Michael?" Her voice caught heavy in her throat, and she blinked back the tears as a rush of uncontrolled emotion took hold of her. He wrapped her in his arms, and their bodies melted together like candlewax, the low hum of voices in the background fading to white noise and for a moment the world existed just for them.

"You're wearing it," Michael said as he ran his fingers over the comb in her hair.

"Always," she replied. And then shaking her head, "But how are you here? How did you know?" she stammered.

A faint smile lurked at the corner of his mouth. "I have my ways."

"You must be Michael," Mem said from behind.

"And you must be Mem!" Michael kissed both of her cheeks before gently placing one on the top of her hand. "It is so nice to finally meet you." Mem smiled back, a rosy glow showing on her tanned skin. Ari looked from Mem to Grandfather and then Michael before looking back again. All three shared the same guilty grin.

Yes, Mem thought, *some love stories are meant to last forever.* But every so often a bit of interference goes a long way, and she thanked the Gods above that the Elders had agreed to change the date of Celebration at her request.

92

GRANDFATHER AND MEM accompanied Michael and Ari back to the Great House later that night for a celebratory drink that would have turned into two or three had Mem not so subtly pulled Grandfather down the jungle path behind her. Ari waved goodbye and breathed a sigh of relief as she turned to walk inside. Finally, they were alone. She heard a rumble of distant thunder as she bent to remove her shoes, and with the rumble came the smell of the rains that would refresh the Island by morning.

"I still can't believe you're here," Ari said as she watched Michael loosen his tie. The light from torches in the garden bathed the room in a soft, flickering glow.

"I hope it's okay that I am," Michael said as he came closer. Ari closed her eyes and felt the whisper of his fingertips as they traced the outline of her cheek and softly brushed against her lower lip and with an intimate familiarity, he continued to draw down the slope of her neck and along her collarbone, past the gentle rise and fall of her breasts and then down the length of her arm before taking her hand and bringing it to his lips.

"Will you still dance for me?" he asked. Ari cupped a hand to his cheek, her fingers exploring the soft, silkiness of his freshly shaven skin as they locked eyes. Michael's jaw tensed under her touch and she rose on tiptoe to bring her lips to his. He was soft and warm and tasted of fresh mint and whiskey. It wasn't the sloppy, fast-paced movements of sexual desperation that so often followed a long separation. Instead it was the gentle, smooth touch of lovers, two bodies perfectly fitted together. She never answered him, but it didn't matter. They both knew.

That night, sleep didn't come to Michael immediately

despite the long hours of travel. Instead, he lay awake listening to the unfamiliar sounds of the Island as he watched Ari sleep beside him. He wondered nervously what tomorrow would bring, knowing that whatever it was would change him forever. He worried about what would happen when he had to leave again. He wouldn't be able to stay more than a week, maybe a few days longer at the most and there was no promise of what would come next. Before Ari, Michael had thrived in the certainty of control, but now he felt as if he was falling into an abyss with no idea of when or if he'd ever hit bottom, and for the first time in his life, he was scared. Ari sighed in her sleep and rolled toward him. He studied her, the little flutter of her eyes as she dreamed, the faint smile that appeared on her lips, and the way her body lay against his side. Then, he closed his eyes and let his own exhaustion overtake him.

93

"I'LL SEE YOU tonight, okay?" Michael whispered, before running down the beach to catch Grandfather, Joey, and the other Island men whose responsibility it was to prepare the bonfires for the evening's festivities.

"You know, Ari," Mem said as they stood side by side watching the rising piles of wood that would soon be lit into roaring mountains of light, "he wrote to us asking for our permission to come to the Island. Your Papa did the same thing years ago."

"Why didn't you tell me?" Ari asked.

"It wasn't for me to tell," Mem replied. "He's a good man, Ari. Your Mama and Papa would be proud."

Life on days like this was lived on many levels, much like a wedding day with the bride and groom looking forward, parents and grandparents remembering back, and all rejoicing in the present. In households throughout the Island, families were engaged in similar activities in preparation for the evening's events. The children, who would spend the evening in the upper school pavilion (the one facing the yard, not the village green), gathered together games and toys and other amusements to occupy themselves for the evening. The teenagers, not quite old enough to attend the Celebration, prepared projects and stories to occupy the children as they took turns watching them through the night until their parents picked up their sleepy little waifs and took them to their own beds.

While the men were busy setting up the gathering place and making trips to the mainland to pick up Islanders and their guests, the women and almost women who had not chosen to dance on this night busied themselves preparing the feast that

535

would nourish the revelers. There was all manner of island delicacies—salads and breads and fruits and rice dishes, all made
from the bounty of the Island and there was fish, whatever was
most eager to hop into Old Willie's fishing boat that morning.
As the morning hours gave way to noon, the aroma of curry and
ginger and saffron, lemon grass, nutmeg and cinnamon began
to intermingle with the fragrances from nature, creating a tropical symphony for the senses. Preparations gradually gave way to
convivial conversation, much of which was spurred on by wine.

As the day wore on, mothers and daughters began to break
away in pairs from the boisterous events taking place on the
beach. And as mothers spoke of the secrets of making love to a
man and as their daughters smiled timidly and blushed, Ari felt
a small pang of jealousy.

"Ari, what's wrong?" Mem asked, as she dangled her feet in
the cool blue waters of the lagoon next to her. Ari remembered
the vision of Emma and Mama on the bench in the garden
as both awaited the beating drums and how Mama had given
Emma a silk purse, and how Emma had cried when she read
the note inside. Ari would never have that chance to experience
such a moment and conflicting emotions of sadness and anger
washed over her before she felt Mem's arms embrace her in a
circle of warmth and comfort.

"She's here," Mem said. "Even if you can't see her."

"I know, Mem," Ari said as a tear trickled down her cheeks.

"Come," Mem said placing a reassuring squeeze on Ari's
knee. "We don't have much time."

Ari rose and brushed sand off the back of her shorts.
"Where are we going?"

"You'll see when we get there. I just need to make one stop
first." Mem hurried off, leaving Ari in her wake.

"Stay here, Ari. I'll just be a few minutes," Mem said when
they reached the front gate of *Surihana*. True to her word, Mem
returned trailing a small wagon filled with boxes and baskets
behind her. Ari followed her until they eventually turned down
a narrow road that led past a row of bungalows and it was then
that Ari knew where they were going.

Soon Ari saw the pair of torches stuck in the ground

marking its entrance. Much as she had done years before with Mama, Ari followed Mem up the path toward the clearing that she knew lay ahead. The path, if you could call it that, had long been overgrown with bright red bromeliads and lush green ferns, hibiscus bushes, and creeping jasmine. It wasn't easy to pull the small wagon through the dense vegetation, but when Ari emerged into the full sunlight, the scene took her breath away just as it had the first time.

The deep waters of the pool looked like a carpet of diamonds and sapphires as the sun's bright rays shown down through the overhanding palms. Ari closed her eyes, letting the sounds of the jungle and the splash of the waterfall as it poured and danced over the lava rock wash over her. The air was perfumed by the smell of gardenia and frangipani, and, of course, there was the jasmine. Always the jasmine. And just as regally as before, the giant Bird of Paradise stood resplendent in full bloom.

Mem followed Ari's gaze. "Ari, did anyone ever tell you why the Bird of Paradise is our family symbol?" Ari shook her head.

Mem spread out a blanket and beckoned for Ari to sit beside her. "Many generations ago on the eve of the first Celebration, our ancestors planted a Bird of Paradise to commemorate the night." She nodded her head toward the flower that stood atop the rocky escarpment. "It is said that so long as the flower blooms, their love story continues to be written and each time a new chapter is ready to begin, the original flower will drop a single seed. And the legend says that when it sprouts, they will find each other again."

Ari sat silently. "Do you really believe it's true, Mem? Can some love stories really last forever?"

Mem's gaze fell upon the clump of fresh green leaves, partially hidden by its larger siblings. It had yet to bloom for the first time, but Mem knew it was ready. "Absolutely," she said, retrieving a large basket from the wagon before kneeling to sit once again on the blanket. "But more importantly, do you?" Ari sat beside her, silently contemplating Mem's revelation. The basket was full of food—fresh fruits and nuts and Mrs. Yao's pork buns and dumplings. Mem poured two glasses of wine, and Ari arranged the food for them to share.

As she sipped on her wine, Mem began to unpack the remaining boxes and baskets from the wagon. She took the large flat one and placed it in front of Ari. Ari lifted the top and peeled back the layers of tissue paper to reveal its contents— Mama's emerald silk comforter. Hugging it to her chest, Ari let the soft fabric rub against her cheek.

"I gave that to your Mama on the eve of her first Celebration," Mem explained fingering the soft fabric in remembrance and Ari realized that today must be just as difficult for Mem as it was for her.

Ari spread the comforter flat on the cool grass by the sparkling pool. Mem placed another box, this one smaller, in front of Ari and waited for her to open it. Inside, were several glass bottles of clear liquid, a bowl, and a neatly folded towel. She took them out one by one.

"What's this for?" Ari asked.

"It is tradition," Mem answered and for the rest of the afternoon she divulged the secrets known only to the Island women.

94

THEY RETURNED TO the beach just as the fading sun was giving way to the vibrant oranges and vermillion and purple hues that were indicative of the Island sunsets.

"It's time, Ari," Mem said pulling her toward the Women's Hut. As Ari followed Mem up the path, she looked back at Michael and their eyes caught for the briefest of seconds. He smiled at her and then turned back to Tommy and Joey, who were overcome with the celebratory mood of the evening and were laughing and giggling like a group of high school girls. A light breeze tugged at Ari's hair and a faint smell of jasmine followed her into the Women's Hut.

"Hello, Mama," she whispered.

"Ari, I have something for you," Mem said as she beckoned her to follow. "On the day you were born, I gave this to your mama to give to you on the eve of your first Celebration." Ari took the package and begin to unwrap the brown paper. When the contents revealed themselves, Ari gasped. She lightly grazed her fingertips over the soft silkiness of the sarong that lay inside.

"Oh, Mem, it's beautiful!" she exclaimed as she stood up to wrap the silk around her. The deep emerald green background stood in contrast to the bright silks of the Bird of Paradise, which had been hand sewn with gold thread. Mem helped Ari out of her day clothes and into the bathing pool that awaited the dancers, both new and experienced, as they arrived.

After bathing, Mem helped Ari dry before massaging her with jasmine oil. As she sat with the other dancers under the willow tree, sipping on glasses of wine and waiting to hear the first of the drums beat, Ari felt Mama and Emma's presence all around her.

Mem wrapped the sarong around Ari's hips and then secured the ivory and jade Bird of Paradise comb in her hair, which she wore long and straight. She adorned Ari's slender neck with leis made of delicate purple orchids that rested lightly on her bare breasts before beckoning her to sit on one of the wooden benches scattered around the walled garden. Without saying a word, Mem placed a small silk purse in her hand and walked back to join the others.

Ari turned the purse over in her hand. It was the same one she'd seen on Mama's dressing table the last time they were together on the Island. She untied the silk string that bound the purse shut. She carefully unfolded its faded creases one by one.

Arianna,

Life is a journey with many twists and turns. Some will bring you joy, while others will bring you great sorrow. We cannot always choose what happens to us in life; we can only choose how we shall deal with it. Many opportunities will be presented to you along the way. You will be deserving of each one, so do not be afraid to accept them. They are not gifts, they are rewards. There will also be many obstacles. There will be times when you feel like giving up. Do not let the obstacles determine your path. Only you have the power to write your story.

I cannot wish for you intelligence of mind, compassion of heart, or a joyous spirit because, to my great happiness, you already possess these things. So, this is my dream for you now. May you find Sanctuary, that place where you know who you are and you like what you know, where dreams go beyond your wildest imaginings, where life is celebrated, not merely lived, and where love is only the beginning.

If I could give you a road map to Sanctuary, I would, but everyone's path is determined by the choices they make along the way. The only wisdom I can pass to you is this— dreams are the wishes we hope will come true; passions are the dreams worth fighting for. Passions are not something to be defined. They are something to be felt. Some are meant to be shared, while others are meant to be yours alone. Passions are the pillars upon which Sanctuary is built. Don't ever stop fighting for them. Tonight, you will share one of the greatest of all. Never let it fade.

Forever and beyond,
Mama

Ari traced her finger over the graceful curves of Mama's handwriting. She carefully folded the letter and placed it back in its pouch. *"Thank you, Mama."* Ari sat in silence until she heard the drums begin to beat. She turned her eyes toward the twinkling diamonds in the night sky. *"I love you."* Ari took a long breath before rising to join the other dancers who were gathering near the entrance of the Women's Hut.

Finally, it was time. It didn't take Ari long to find Michael. He sat cross legged in a traditional Island sarong, the glow of the Celebration fires lightly reflecting off his bronzed skin and his striking green eyes, which even in the darkness were vividly alive like a tiger stalking its prey in the darkness of night.

The drums and flames and movements surrounding him faded to nothingness when Michael saw Ari emerge from the hut. If it were just a physical attraction, he would have taken her in Venice the first night they met. But it was much more than her beauty that attracted him, although he had never seen anyone or anything as beautiful as she looked tonight. Ari began to dance in front of him, her hips gently swaying seductively in perfect rhythm with the beating drums. Later he would swear it had been the heat of the brightly burning fires, but if he were honest with himself, he'd admit that the realization of his feelings for her had brought tears to his eyes.

As couples began to leave the Gathering Place hand in hand, Ari knew that it was time. Neither spoke a word as they walked together passed the banyan tree and along the road that would lead them to the lit torches. Ari took Michael's hand as she led him through the mimosa grove. The earth was cool and damp and soft underfoot and was a welcome respite from the hot sands and heat of the bonfires on the beach. Only dappled light from the full moon managed to filter through the fern-like leaves. Another hundred feet and the path would come out into the light again and make its final turn toward a clearing.

As Ari set out the provisions Mem had prepared for the evening, Michael surveyed their loving place for the first time. His eyes moved first to the fern covered escarpment over which twin waterfalls splashed into the small blue pool below in perfect harmony, sending continuous ripples toward the edge. The ripples reflected the light from the torches that were dotted around the clearing, creating a sort of soothing, hypnotic monotony.

They were encircled in a forest of lush, tropical foliage in colors and textures made even richer by the ethereal glow of the moonlight. There were low growing flamboyants, reaching out their brilliant orange blossoms like an umbrella over the soft green grasses below. Standing in perfect contrast to the colorful blanket beneath were the dark forms of the tall, stately coconut palms.

Michael had always been in control, especially when he was about to make love to a woman. But now this evening—this place—was bewitching him with its sights, its sounds, and its sweet fragrances that hung in the warm, wet air. He didn't know if this was a good or a bad thing. It frightened him a little. He struggled to return to the script he had written for lovemaking. It had always served him well. The woman undressed first as he watched. That made her vulnerable in her nakedness and that's when he took command. He then would quickly remove his own clothes and take her to him. He gave only those pleasures that confirmed the stories of his sexual prowess and took only those that would not make him vulnerable to the woman. He liked being in control, or at least he thought he did; it was all he knew.

Ari's fingers moved to the flowers that covered his bare chest. She removed each strand with a deliberate slowness, never speaking, never taking her eyes from his. And then her fingers moved to the knot in his sarong until it too lay on the ground at her feet. Michael took a step forward and Ari held her breath.

"Arianna, you are so beautiful," he said, running his warm

palm up the bare flesh of her arm. His fingertips gently traced the line of her cheek bone. His eyes were partially hidden by his hair, curled in the island humidity, but Ari knew they were bright with lust. The torch light highlighted his sharp jaw line and the sculpted muscles of his chest, which rose and fell slowly with each breath.

"Arianna?"

"Yes?" she answered back.

"I love you." His voice was barely above a whisper. He had never said the words to anyone because he had never truly felt them before. But with Ari it was different. It had been different from the moment he first saw her on the balcony.

"I love you too," she said as she gazed up at him.

Michael gently pulled her lips to his. He didn't open his mouth or deepen his kiss. He just let his lips rest on hers. Ari pressed her body to his and tangled her fingers in the hair at the base of his neck. He tightened his arms around her waist.

One by one he began to remove the fragrant necklaces draped from her neck until at last, her full round breasts revealed themselves to him. As his hand gently caressed her exposed skin, he slowly fell to his knees in front of her. Ari trembled with anticipation and she gasped as Michael gently nipped at the exposed point of her breast. He continued until she could no longer distinguish between intense pleasure and pain. Michael lightly blew cool air on her wet skin, never taking his eyes from hers, before leisurely untying her sarong watching as the soft silk gently floated to the ground baring Ari to him completely.

Michael stared at her naked body. Her long, black hair that reflected even moonlight; those green eyes, not hazel eyes pretending to be green, but deep emerald eyes that hid no secrets; her long, graceful neck that led to her full breasts, which stood over the tapered waist that was so small he could nearly encircle it with his two hands to the rounded hips that led to the legs that never ended. He opened his mouth to speak, but only a whisper came out. "You take my breath away."

"Well then, that's only fair," she smiled back. She gently pulled on his hand, urging him toward the silk comforter.

"It's tradition," Ari began as she took one of the glass bottles and poured a small amount of the liquid into the Koa bowl. "It's to cleanse the spirit." Kneeling behind him, she gently began to wash his neck, moving down to his shoulders and then his back.

"Most people look at death as an ending," she continued. "But the Islanders look at it as a new beginning. It's like the next chapter in an infinite story and tonight is the celebration of its new beginning." Ari paused to dip the towel into the little bowl again before moving around to his front, where she sat and began to cleanse his face. "They say for some, it is their first meeting and for others, they have met many times before. The Islanders believe that some are destined to be together throughout all of time."

She didn't wait for him to respond, but continued to cleanse his torso, before gently pressing him back. First, she washed his inner thigh, which sent a pulse of lightening throughout his body and caused him to respond in kind to her touch. His hardness was amplified by her carefully taking him with her hand as she continued to cleanse him. There was no script for this.

She rose once more and removing the cork from one of the smaller glass bottles, held it under her nose and inhaled deeply. Michael propped himself on his elbows, watching her as she closed her eyes letting her head fall back.

"This is the oil of the Island flowers," Ari said, and she poured a small bit of it onto her hand and began to rub his skin.

Once she finished, it was his turn. He cleansed her body, revealing skin that glowed like diamond dust in the flickering firelight. He watched her respond to his oiled hands as he ran them up and down in small circles.

His hand gently cupped her bare breast and he trailed wet kisses down her neck before drawing her into his mouth. He flicked his eyes toward her, but they were closed, her head tilted back. The sounds escaping her lips gave him all the encouragement he needed.

"Will you tell me if I hurt you?" he asked and Ari nodded. Michael lay her back on the comforter, the silky strands of her hair framing her face. Were he an inexperienced lover, the whole thing would already be over. He stilled, waiting for her to relax around him. He wished he could stop time. He began to move within her in slow graceful motions. They moved together in a perfect rhythm, knowing how to respond to the movements of the other as if they had made love hundreds of times before. He felt her tighten around him and he started to move quicker. She whispered his name as she fell and Michael followed her; her name ripped from his lips. When their shared breath slowed, Michael withdrew and laid beside Ari, letting the silk of the comforter cool his heated skin. He took her hand in his and brought it to his lips, placing a soft kiss on her oiled skin.

They made love several times that night—sometimes slowly, other times with a heated desperate passion. In between, they rested in each other's arms or dipped into the cool waters of the natural pool, letting the waterfall wash over their naked bodies. They sipped wine and fed each other from the basket of food. They laughed and talked and as the sun was beginning to rise over the horizon, they fell asleep in each other's arms. By the time they awoke, the young Bird of Paradise had flowered.

95

THE EASTERN SKY was just beginning to wake with the rising sun, coloring the clouds above with a pinkish hue and casting a golden glow over the horizon. The lagoon was still dark with sleep, but soon the sun's light would turn its deep sapphire waters turquoise, ushering in a new day. Ari lay in bed, listening to the sounds of the Island come alive, her naked body glistening with the warmth of the air. She watched the rhythmic rise and fall of Michael's chest as he slumbered beside her, before lifting the white sheet that lay low on his hips exposing the chiseled V of his abdomen and then gently, so as not to wake him right away, she straddled his hips, eliciting a small groan from deep within his throat. The corner of his mouth quirked slightly before a lazy smile spread across his face and then he opened his eyes and watched as she silently moved above him.

Afterward, Ari rose from bed, picked up her silk robe that had been flung to the floor in a late-night moment of passion and made her way to the cooking pavilion. She filled the tea pot and set it on the stove to boil, then took down the blue and white porcelain canister in which she kept freshly roasted coffee beans. She ground them by hand in the antique iron grinder hanging on the wall next to the sink. Ari loved the smell of freshly ground beans, and she let it transport her back to San Francisco, when Papa would wake early and the earthly, rich smell of his coffee would find its way upstairs. She poured the steaming water over the grounds in the French Press, setting it aside to steep and turned her attention to the croissants that needed warming and the ripe fruit that needed cutting.

The rising sun vividly lit the swirling clouds above on fire, signaling that rain would visit the Island by nightfall. Ari took a seat at the table on the veranda overlooking the lush greenery of Mama's garden and was thankful for the quiet time she found to clear her head. Most of the last few days had been spent with Michael secreted away in the Great House or in the clearing next to the waterfall under the giant Bird of Paradise. Sometimes they made love hard and fast seeking nothing but the crashing waves of pleasure their coupling brought. Other times it was slow and deep, something that didn't exist on the earthly world, drawing breath from one another as their bodies moved together.

"Good morning," Michael said cheerfully as he stepped onto the stone patio and took a seat beside Ari. He poured a cup of coffee as Ari pushed a plate of hot croissants and fresh sliced mango and pineapple in his direction. "That was quite the wakeup call," Michael chuckled, as a mischievous grin spread across his face.

Michael's thumb lightly brushed her hand as they sat in silence sipping coffee, while the occasional bird song and the rustle of palm fronds as the breeze rose off the water below played in the background. With each rise and fall of the sun, their time together grew shorter and both knew that tonight would be their last. Their lives were a world apart—his in England and hers on the Island and despite how much Michael wanted to, he knew it was unfair to ask her to come with him. Setting down his mug, he turned to Ari and took her hand firmly in his.

"Ari, I need to talk to you about something."

"I know," Ari said, placing her half-eaten croissant on the table. "It's time."

"I don't want to go, Ari. You must know that." Michael watched as an array of emotions passed over her face and the silence grew heavy on his shoulders.

Ari swallowed painfully and tightly squeezed her eyes shut. "Please don't ask me to come with you." Her voice cracked under the strain of struggling to stop the tears from spilling down her cheeks.

"I won't," he replied, barely above a whisper. "I love you too much to ask that of you."

"But what now?" Ari dabbed at her eyes.

"Honestly? I don't know. But this isn't goodbye." He wiped another tear from her cheek. "Term is almost over. I can come back, and you can come visit. We'll make it work."

"But what about the fall? You'll have to leave again, and I'll be here working at the university and you know long distance relationships never really work, even if you think they will."

Michael exhaled and slumped back in his chair, knowing there was no more to be said.

That evening they lay side by side in the cool, damp grass of their loving spot. As if knowing it was their last night together, the Island rose to the occasion by displaying an artist's sunset with brilliant shades of topaz and ruby that slowly faded to a soft pink before being overtaken by the purples and blues of nighttime. Michael tucked a piece of wayward hair behind Ari's ear and softly stroked the outline of her face and as the stars began to dot the darkening sky, he made love to her, both knowing it would be for the last time.

96

FROM SOMEWHERE DOWN the mountain she heard two short blasts, signaling that the launch would be leaving for the mainland soon. They stood together in the garden, Ari's head resting on Michael's shoulder as he held her tightly to his chest. Eventually he released her and exhaled heavily, tenderly brushing the soft skin of Ari's cheek with his fingertip. He slung his leather bag over his shoulder. The warmth of his touch cooled as he began to slip away and soon the last bond between them was broken. She watched until he disappeared behind the dense curtain of greenery.

She stood motionless and let the numbness overtake her. "Where's my happy ending, Mama?" she asked the empty sky. But no answer came, not even in birdsong. Ari didn't feel like returning to the Great House just yet, so instead she turned toward the little path that led up the jungled hillside and to the hidden clearing overlooking the lagoon below.

She sat on the Sunset Bench, as she had so many times before, looking down past the craggy cliffs graying in the twilight; past coconut palms and wild impatiens; past viridian ferns that nestled in the shadows and viney bougainvillea that danced on the winds and crystalline waters that plunged and splashed and cascaded their way back home to the sea. There she paused, as always, to gaze at the tranquil lagoon and to listen to the laughter of the new water babies as it floated up from the beach on the warm, sweet air. It was not the carefully conceived laughter of adults, but the full-bellied laughter of the very young who know nothing of social graces or care. "Innocence," she whispered and wished she could remember what that felt like.

From the western edge of the lagoon, she heard the faint

murmurings of friends and family coming together again at the end of another day. The voices emanated from the old wooden dock where Islanders gathered to await the return of the evening launch from the Mainland. She watched as the last of them trickled out of the palm grove in two's and three's, strolled down the beach past neat rows of dugout canoes and headed out over the water between the gaily painted little fishing boats that bobbed up and down in perfect 4/4 time. The Islanders looked almost indistinguishable from their ancestors, milling about in their bare feet and richly patterned sarongs, but soon the illusion would end with the arrival of the launch and the impeccably tailored suits that nightly filed down her gangplank.

She had been coming to the bench for many years now, climbing the Cliffside path with flashlight in hand for the safe return home after sunset. Tonight, though she carried a bottle of Grandfather's wine and her favorite goblet, the cobalt blue one that Mem said took its color from the night sky over the Island. She held the goblet at arm's length and spun it gently by the stem until she was mesmerized by the kaleidoscopic patterns of light and shadow that danced on her arm. *This goblet should have been Mama's.*

She put the goblet to her lips and sipped long and slow and let the wine wash over her tongue before swallowing. By the time it had cooled her throat all the way down, she had turned her thoughts to a happier time—the day she first came to the bench, that glorious spring when the family returned to the Island from Papa's posting in San Francisco. She remembered that day clearly, how she left the cool, jade-blue waters of the lagoon behind and followed after Grandfather and Mem and Mama and Papa as they snaked in and out of view on their daily ascent to the bench. And she remembered the arduous climb and how hot and breathless she felt, and how, when she finally reached the shade of the plateau, the cool damp of the jungle floor on her bare feet renewed her. She could almost hear the bits of laughter and easy conversation that had reached her ears long before she was in sight of the bench and how, when she finally arrived there, she found the couples already lounging comfortably, sharing a bottle of Grandfather's chilled Island wine, red-cheeked and smiling and, as always, demonstrably affectionate.

She could hear them speaking, even now, about that day and many before it in no particular order, just a random collection of remembrances, which together fashioned a collage of their family history, or at least a small part of one. They were recalling some of the special places to which Papa's work had taken the family—the funny little attic bedroom in London, and the marble floors in the Paris apartment where she and Emma played Ice Capades in their stocking feet, and the big house that perched on the peak over Hong Kong where she held little James up to the telescope on the veranda so he could watch the ships come into port.

When Mama looked up and saw her approaching, she didn't seem surprised. She just smiled and said, "I've been waiting for you," and without further comment, handed her a half-filled goblet of wine, her first, which had been well diluted to a pale pink color by the numerous ice cubes that clinked against the glass.

She remembered exactly how everyone looked that day. Grandfather sitting at one end of the bench, his arms wrapped around Mem except when he was expounding with animated gestures on the great mysteries of life; Mem, whose gentle expression on her still beautiful face belied the depth of her wisdom—a wisdom that came from just living life, not over-thinking it; Mama, whose extraordinary elegance was evident even in bare feet and a sarong and hair still wet from her after-noon swim to the reef. And Papa, sprawling lazily next to Mama, smiling and relaxed, a million miles from the corporate world that loomed just off-shore. His sandy brown hair and blue eyes looked so incongruous next to the black hair and green almond eyes that filled the rest of the bench.

That was the day she began imagining the man with whom she would share her own sunsets, peering up at Mem and that expression she wore when she looked at Grandfather, as if she were seeing him for the very first time, and finding that same expression reinvented on Mama's face, like a fashion trend that was repeating itself with a slightly different twist. And as young women often do, she began molding the image of him in her mind and it acquired detail and depth until finally, one day, she imagined him into reality. The sunsets they shared were everything she knew they would be—wet, warm bodies and cool Island breezes, lusty red wine and Van Gogh skies. But even her wildest imaginings couldn't prepare her for the sunrises and how she would feel each time she awoke beside him, and listened for the changes in the pattern of his breathing, and watched the slight shifts of his body as he dreamed, waiting for that moment just before waking when he would stretch and roll and reach out for her. "Arianna," he would whisper and nothing more.

The sun was in its descending arc over the western headland now. It was an artist's sun, all big and orange, spreading its sepia light over the Island, transforming it from brilliant contrasts to silhouetted images against a vibrant sky. There was a light trail that extended across the lagoon and out to the open sea, a *golden touch* she had called it when she was very young. But first she needed to cry the tears she had been suppressing all that day. It wasn't a moment of weakness. She just needed to leave the tears behind. And when the last one had descended her cheek and dissolved into the fabric of her linen shirt, she knew she was ready. So, she resettled herself on the sleek wooden bench that Grandfather had lovingly crafted out of a single koa log all those years ago, and into which he and Mem had carved their names and Mama and Papa after them. Then she followed the light trail and searched the horizon until she found what she was looking for—the boat that was sailing away with everything she loved most in this world. She stared at it for a very long time, watching it grow smaller and smaller. Then she closed her eyes and tried to remember what her life had been like before Michael.

She didn't know how much time had passed when she finally opened them again. She looked at the blue goblet in her hand. It was empty. Ari wrapped the goblet in its soft cloth and bent to put it back in the basket. Suddenly, something caught her eye. Under the fold of a napkin, she found the green silk purse, the one Mem had given her on Celebration night. She must have put it there for safekeeping and didn't remember the next morning. She unwound the silk ties that were held in place by the Bird of Paradise clasp and carefully pulled out the folded letter. She looked at Mama's handwriting, perfectly formed across the paper in her graceful hand, and she read through the letter once and then once again, letting Mama's words rattle around in her head.

There will also be many obstacles. There will be times when you feel like giving up. Do not let the obstacles determine your path. Only you have the power to write your story.

"Oh, Mama," Ari whispered. "I wish you were here." Ari brought the letter to her lips and gently kissed the fading ink.

"But I am here, Ari. I always have been."

Ari sat motionless.

"Write your story, Arianna. It is time."

97

THE LAUNCH WAS gone, but she knew if she hurried Old Willie would take her to the mainland and maybe, just maybe she could catch him. She raced as fast as she could down the steep cliff side toward the jungle path that would lead her to the beach. She paused just long enough to slow her breathing before taking off again in the direction of the dock. She scanned the line of gently bobbing boats, looking for Old Willie but he was nowhere to be seen, so she stood on the beach watching as the last of the sun's light dipped below the horizon before walking back to the Great House—alone.

In its infancy, the moon provided very little light by which to find her way. Barefoot, she took her time to avoid stumbling over a rock or wayward tree root. She rounded the last curve in the path, where the dense greenery of the jungle gave way to the open space of the Great House garden.

He stood on the patio, his back to her, silhouetted in the light from within the gathering pavilion. She watched as the breeze played with the black curls of his hair and how his broad shoulders rose and fell with each breath he took and then she ran her eyes down the length of his body. When she looked up again, she found him staring back, his emerald eyes glowing brilliantly in the torch light. Ari watched as he strode across the lawn. Michael pulled her to him, bringing her lips forcefully to his. He moved against her with unrestrained urgency, and Ari hungrily pushed back, seeking the sweet warmth of his mouth.

"I couldn't leave," he said breathlessly against her. "Not when knowing it meant leaving behind what I want more than anything in the world."

"But what about the university?"

"Shh." He kissed the hollow of her temple. "Let me worry about that. What matters most right now is this," he took her hand and brought it to his chest, where his heart beat fast and strong. "When I die, I don't want to see images of a life spent alone. I want my life to mean something. I want to see us—our memories together." He tilted her head, seeking her eyes. "I think I loved you long before we met, Ari." He paused to kiss her again, this time slow and gentle. "I don't know how, but I've always known."

"What do we do now?" she asked.

A half-smile spread across his face. "Well that, Ms. Heywood, depends entirely upon your answer." And then she watched as Michael took both her hands in his and bent down on one knee.

Epilogue

HE SAT ON the Sunset Bench and closed his eyes and listened until he was lost in the music and the rhythm of his own breathing. He liked this part of his evening ritual best, even more than watching the sun drop into the ocean. But tonight, something was different. Tonight, memories came to him, one after another, like the constant waves that kissed the warm sands far below. The midnight black of his hair had long given way to the silvers and grays of age, and as he opened his emerald eyes, they flooded with tears.

It had been one year since she'd journeyed to find the family she lost. Even now he could feel the pain that ripped through him and twisted his heart as he saw her chest rise and fall and then still as he held her in his arms.

They had gone to the Sunset Bench every day, and he knew she would be pleased he had continued the custom after her passing. Once, long ago, he had asked her why she did this. *"I go to say goodnight to the Island, Michael, and to thank the Gods for one more day of happiness here,"* she had answered.

Michael sighed. The Sunset Bench had born witness to some of his happiest memories. This is where he had watched her walk toward him on a carpet of red hibiscus, her mother's wedding dress hanging delicately from her shoulders, the Bird of Paradise comb pinned in the silky strands of her hair, while the golden glow of the setting sun kissed the leaves above and washed his world in a warm amber glow.

He remembered the look on her face when she first glimpsed the four Birds of Paradise he had secretly planted earlier that day at the edge of the clearing and how her eyes shimmered with tears when she read the names on the stones

556

laid in front of each—her family. The emotions he had felt that evening when their lips met for the first time as husband and wife washed over him again, as they often did when he made his nightly visit to the Sunset Bench, and he brushed the back of his hand across his wet cheek.

The evening of their wedding, there had been a great celebration at the Gathering Place. The Islanders and their guests had come together to create a feast that rivaled the biggest Celebrations, and Grandfather had ensured everyone was more than merry with ample bottles of his special wine. The guests were still enjoying the festivities when he and Ari had walked hand in hand toward their loving place. He remembered what her soft skin felt like under his touch when he finally unbuttoned the last pearl holding her dress, how she smelled faintly of jasmine and how her hair had looked as it cascaded down her back when he released it from her comb. Their love making had always been exciting and new. But the emotion of making love to his wife for the first time had nearly shattered him.

A few weeks later, Ari had welcomed the first students to the Cultural Studies and Art Department at the university and as the newly appointed professor of Art History, he had proudly taken his place by her side. While Professor Evans had been disappointed in his resignation, he had offered him many opportunities to guest lecture throughout the years.

And, it was on the Sunset Bench a year later that Ari had guided his hand to her stomach and told him that he was going to be a father. Michael remembered how beautiful she looked as she grew with his child. And soon they welcomed James Ethan McGregor into their world. Emma Mary McGregor would complete their little family two years later.

He thought of Venice and of the memories they had shared. Every year they visited the place where they had found each other again. They stayed at the professor's villa on the canal, the one with the balcony and the little garden and the iron bed, and he remembered the day a package had arrived on the Island addressed to the McGregors. Inside lay an old, rusted iron key and a note that read: *I hope that you find as much love as my Roseanna and I did inside these walls.* That same day another letter arrived with the news that the professor's spirit had journeyed to find his beloved again.

The last ferry leaving for the mainland blasted its horn signaling its imminent departure. A warm breeze washed over him. Slowly, he slipped to his knees in front of the sleek wooden bench. He ran his hand over the names carved in the bench years ago. "I thought our names should be carved here too," he said, taking his Swiss Army knife from his pocket and inscribing the bench. Then he sat once more and with a sigh, lifted his eyes to the Van Gogh sky and followed the swirls of crimson and gold all the way to the horizon where his Arianna awaited him.

"Oh, Michael, I've been waiting and waiting forever."

A peaceful smile spread across his face. "I know, sweetheart, but I'll find you soon." Then surrendering, he closed his eyes and let their next chapter begin.

Some love stories truly are meant to last forever.

About the Authors

MARILYN ANNE HUGHES was born in Southern California but spent her formative years in the San Francisco Bay Area with her parents and older sister. She graduated from the University of California–Berkeley with a degree in Sociology and received an advanced degree in Elementary Education. After moving with her husband to Aspen, Colorado, Marilyn spent the next 20 years as a public school teacher and elementary education consultant and lecturer. She and her family moved to Pinehurst, North Carolina, in 1996 and shortly thereafter, she was diagnosed with breast and advanced ovarian cancer. She began writing Bird of Paradise as a life gift for her daughter, Emily. She passed away in 2012 leaving the novel unfinished—for Emily to complete.

EMILY HUGHES JOHNSON was born in Aspen, Colorado where she enjoyed skiing, dancing ballet and playing golf. At the age of 13, she and her family moved to Pinehurst, North Carolina. She attended University of North Carolina–Chapel Hill and graduated with a degree in Journalism and Mass Communication with a concentration in Public Relations, but her passion has always been creative writing. She currently resides in Raleigh, North Carolina, with her husband and son. Emily enjoys playing golf, running, kickboxing, reading, and spending time with her family. Finishing her mother's work has been one of the greatest honors of her life.